Transactions of the Royal Historical Society

SIXTH SERIES

XIX

CAMBRIDGE
UNIVERSITY PRESS

Published by the Press Syndicate of the University of Cambridge
The Edinburgh Building, Cambridge CB2 8RU, United Kingdom
32 Avenue of the Americas, New York, NY 10013–2473, USA
477 Williamstown Road, Port Melbourne, VIC 3207 Australia
Ruiz de Alarcón 13, 28014 Madrid, Spain

A catalogue record for this book is available from the British Library

First published 2009

ISBN 9780 521 194020 hardback

SUBSCRIPTIONS. The serial publications of the Royal Historical Society, *Royal Historical Society Transactions* (ISSN 0080–4401) and Camden Fifth Series (ISSN 0960–1163) volumes may be purchased together on annual subscription. The 2009 subscription price (which includes print and electronic access) is £109 (US$183 in the USA, Canada and Mexico) and includes Camden Fifth Series, volumes 34 and 35 (published in July and December) and Transactions Sixth Series, volume 19 (published in December). Japanese prices are available from Kinokuniya Company Ltd, PO Box 55, Chitose, Tokyo 156, Japan. EU subscribers (outside the UK) who are not registered for VAT should add VAT at their country's rate. VAT registered subscribers should provide their VAT registration number.

Subscription orders, which must be accompanied by payment, may be sent to a bookseller, subscription agent or direct to the publisher: Cambridge University Press, The Edinburgh Building, Shaftesbury Road, Cambridge CB2 8RU, UK; or in the USA, Canada and Mexico; Cambridge University Press, Journals Fulfillment Department, 100 Brook Hill Drive, West Nyack, New York 10994–2133, USA. Prices include delivery by air.

SINGLE VOLUMES AND BACK VOLUMES. A list of Royal Historical Society volumes available from Cambridge University Press may be obtained from the Humanities Marketing Department at the address above.

Printed and bound in the United Kingdom at the University Press, Cambridge

CONTENTS

PAGE

Presidential Address: Britain and Globalisation since 1850:
IV: The Creation of the Washington Consensus   1
Martin Daunton

Representation *c*. 800: Arab, Byzantine, Carolingian   37
Leslie Brubaker

Humanism and Reform in Pre-Reformation English Monasteries   57
James G. Clark

Lord Burghley and *il Cortegiano*: Civil and Martial Models of
Courtliness in Elizabethan England *(The Alexander Prize Essay)*   95
Mary Partridge

Communicating Empire: The Habsburgs and their Critics,
1700–1919 *(The Prothero Lecture)*   117
R. J. W. Evans

The Slave Trade, Abolition and Public Memory   139
James Walvin

Cultures of Exchange: Atlantic Africa in the Era of the Slave Trade   151
David Richardson

Slaves out of Context: Domestic Slavery and the Anglo-Indian
Family, *C*. 1780–1830   181
Margot Finn

Report of Council for 2008–2009   205

Transactions of the RHS 19 (2009), pp. 1–35 © Royal Historical Society 2009
doi:10.1017/S0080440109990028

TRANSACTIONS OF THE
ROYAL HISTORICAL SOCIETY

PRESIDENTIAL ADDRESS

By Martin Daunton

BRITAIN AND GLOBALISATION SINCE 1850: IV THE CREATION OF THE WASHINGTON CONSENSUS

READ 28 NOVEMBER 2008

ABSTRACT. In August 1971, President Nixon ended the convertibility of the dollar into gold, so precipitating a crisis in the Bretton Woods system which was not successfully resolved by the Smithsonian agreement in December 1971. The pound was soon free to float and the role of sterling as a reserve currency was seriously weakened. The members of the European Economic Community attempted to create stability between their own currencies, which left the British government in a dilemma about whether to join the European monetary experiment to complement membership of the Community. The address considers the tensions and difficulties facing the Conservative and Labour governments of the 1970s, and the response of the Thatcher government after 1979. The trade-off in the 'trilemma' between the three variables of exchange rates, capital movements and domestic monetary policy changed in a major way.

When the title for this final presidential address went to press in 2007, the imminent demise of the Washington consensus did not seem likely; when this volume of the *Transactions* is published in November 2009, it might well have been given a decent burial. But I will not hasten to change the title to 'the rise and demise of the Washington consensus': my concern today is with the emergence of a new set of assumptions about the proper management of the world economy and Britain's place within it, in response to the collapse of the Bretton Woods system of fixed exchange rates after Nixon's announcement of the suspension of the convertibility of the dollar into gold on 15 August 1971, and the subsequent failure of the Smithsonian agreement of December 1971 to reestablish pegged exchanges. The result was the emergence of greater capital mobility, floating exchanges and the creation of new financial instruments which were celebrated (until recently) by Alan Greenspan and Gordon Brown as the basis for economic prosperity. In today's lecture, I will consider how this new order came about, and how politicians and officials in Britain coped with the fundamental changes to the system which had been created after the Second World War. The story of how hubris led to nemesis in 2008, and how the institutions of the world economy were reshaped, is a topic for another occasion when greater historical distance offers a chance for reflection.[1]

What was the Washington consensus? The phrase was coined by John Williamson in 1990 to refer to 'the lowest common denominator of policy advice being addressed by the Washington-based institutions [that is, the International Monetary Fund (IMF), the World Bank and the US Treasury] to Latin American countries as of 1989'. In many ways, it was an extrapolation of what the Thatcher and Reagan administrations adopted domestically in the late 1970s and early 1980s before being applied to other parts of the world, starting with Latin America, continuing with the former Soviet Union and its dependants, and informing responses to the Asian financial crisis of 1997. Williamson did not mean to imply that the reforms were *imposed* by the Washington-based institutions, but rather claimed that there was intellectual convergence on free-market economics and a major shift in attitudes towards the role of the state in the economy. The Washington consensus was characterised by a number of policies: fiscal discipline; redirection of public expenditure to areas offering high economic returns and improved income distribution such as primary health care, primary education and the infrastructure; tax reform to reduce marginal rates and broaden the tax base; interest rate or financial liberalisation; competitive exchange rates; trade liberalisation; inflows of foreign direct investment; privatisation; deregulation of business in order to remove barriers to entry and exit; and secure property rights. Williamson argued that these policies emerged over the previous twenty years and were widely seen as sensible. He objected to the use of the term 'Washington consensus' as a synonym for neo-liberalism or what George Soros called 'market fundamentalism' which implied a minimal state and monetarism. In Soros's opinion,

> we are once again in danger of drawing the wrong conclusions from the lessons of history. This time the danger comes not from communism but from market fundamentalism. Communism abolished the market mechanism and imposed collective control over all economic activities. Market fundamentalism seeks to abolish collective decision making and to impose the supremacy of market values over all political and social values. Both

---

[1] These Presidential Addresses on Britain's role in the international economy will be incorporated into a book on the wider issue of how the economy of the world was governed from the Second World War to the present which I am currently writing.

extremes are wrong. What we need is a correct balance between politics and markets, between rule making and playing by the rules.

Williamson feared that applying the term 'Washington consensus' to a more dogmatic approach based on the assumption that markets would solve everything would discredit the policies that he wished to see adopted.[2] An entire lecture could be devoted to discussing these policies and their application around the world. We might note that growth in some countries, and above all China, occurred without adopting these policies, and that growth has not always been achieved where the policies have been pursued. Indeed, even before the recent financial collapse, the Washington consensus was strongly criticised by Joseph Stiglitz who complained that it concentrated on growth in the Gross Domestic Product rather than improving living standards or democratic and sustainable development.[3] Certainly, the emergence of the Washington consensus was a remarkable shift in policies from the 1950s and 1960s, and marked the end of a number of intellectual approaches. It ended the earlier decoupling of development economics from mainstream economics which had been at the heart of the conflict between the IMF and General Agreement on Tariffs and Trade (GATT) and their critics in the Group of 77 and the United Nations Conference on Trade and Development which had been so serious in the 1960s and 1970s. Dependency theories which stressed the creation of 'under-development' by the advanced industrial economies were weakened, and there was a move away from centralised planning on a large scale by the developing countries.[4] More particularly, in the case of Britain it meant the demise of the fixed exchange rate system of 1944, the abandonment of the sterling area, a shift to floating exchanges, the adoption of financial liberalisation and the removal of capital controls, all

[2] J. Williamson, 'What Washington Means by Policy Reform', in *Latin American Adjustments: How Much Has Happened?*, ed. J. Williamson (Washington, 1990), and 'What Should the Bank Think about the Washington Consensus?', *World Bank Research Observer*, 15 (2000), 251–64; G. Soros, *The Crisis of Global Capitalism* (1998), xx, xxvi. For a recent overview of the shift in the economics profession, see R. E. Backhouse, 'The Rise of Free Market Economics: Economists and the Role of the State since 1970', *History of Political Economy*, 37 annual supplement (2005), 355–92.

[3] M. Naim, 'Fads and Fashions in Economic Reforms: Washington Consensus or Washington Confusion?', at www.imf.org/external/pubs/ft/seminar/1999/reforms/ Naim.HTM, last accessed 7 Mar. 2005; J. Stiglitz, *Globalization and its Discontents* (New York, 2002); T. N. Srinivasan, 'The Washington Consensus a Decade Later: Ideology and the Art and Science of Policy Advice', *World Bank Research Observer*, 15 (2000), 265–70; R. Wade, 'US Hegemony and the World Bank: The Fight over People and Ideas', *Review of International Political Economy*, 9 (2002), 215–43.

[4] J. Toye and R. Toye, 'How the UN Moved from Full Employment to Economic Development', *Commonwealth and Comparative Politics*, 44 (2006), 16–40, and *The UN and Global Political Economy: Trade, Finance, and Development* (Bloomington, 2004).

of which had major consequences for domestic economic policies such as wages policy, the control of inflation and labour relations. My focus is on the political debates over these major shifts in Britain's position in the international economy and their domestic implications.

In the first of these addresses, I utilised the organising concept of the trilemma – the trade-off between the three variables of exchange rates, capital movements and domestic monetary policy. When exchange rates are fixed, as on the gold standard, and capital is allowed to move freely, an active domestic monetary policy is not feasible: a reduction in interest rates to stimulate the domestic economy would lead to an outflow of capital and pressure on exchanges; or a high demand of capital from abroad as between 1905 and 1914 would force up domestic interest rates and hit domestic recovery or investment in the social infrastructure. In the 1930s, the trade-off was different: the pursuit of low interest rates to stimulate the domestic economy was associated with floating exchanges and capital controls. Of course, the attempt of the British and other governments to stimulate their domestic economies resulted in beggar-my-neighbour policies and serious strains in the international economy from which everyone suffered. After the Second World War, an attempt was made to combine domestic employment and prosperity with international stability through fixed exchange rates (with some scope for variation to protect domestic welfare), and controls over capital movements so that interest rates could be varied for purely domestic reasons without a fear for the international consequences. By the early 1970s, this particular trade-off was no longer sustainable and policies changed towards floating exchange rates and freer capital movements, with major consequences for domestic economic policies.[5] The change was fraught and contested, with many domestic repercussions and disputes over what sort of economic policy should be pursued. It is one of the major changes in British history in the last quarter of the twentieth century, and is still being worked out.

The shift in international economic policies was intimately connected with domestic policies. Under fixed exchanges after the Second World War, it was not possible to allow the exchange rate to take the pressure of generous wage settlements and inflation: if domestic costs were allowed to rise, British goods would be expensive in foreign markets, the balance of payments would deteriorate and action would be needed to protect the value of the pound. The outcome was the so-called 'low-effort bargain'. In order to mitigate wage increases through voluntary restraint, industrialists agreed to limit their dividends and the government agreed to improve welfare entitlements, with the result that modest wages and

---

[5] For the trilemma, see M. Daunton, 'Britain and Globalisation since 1850: Creating a Global Order, 1850–1914', *Transactions of the Royal Historical Society*, sixth series, 16 (2006), 6–10.

profits were combined with a lack of incentive to improve productivity. This institutional package had a longer history, back to the recognition of trade unions in the last quarter of the nineteenth century and their exceptional legal privileges in the Trade Disputes Act of 1906, and it was confirmed in the post-war bargain between capital, labour and the state. The bargain could only survive so long as British industry was sheltered from competition at home through price-fixing agreements, and from abroad through import controls and tariffs. As soon as competition appeared with the reduction of tariffs, and above all membership of the European Economic Community (EEC), industrialists were threatened with a loss of market share unless they could be more efficient and productive which placed pressure on the institutional structure that developed after the war. Although a variant of this institutional structure was found in other European countries, the British system had some distinctive features. Unions were recognised but they (and their employers) were not bound by contractual obligations: any bargain could be broken without penalty. Further, bargaining remained adversarial, based on a zero-sum game rather than collaboration to raise productivity to benefit wages and profits.[6] By the late 1960s and 1970s, this pattern was under serious pressure and its dissolution was closely connected with debates over the future shape of Britain and international economic policies.

By the end of the 1960s, the trade-off negotiated at Bretton Woods was under threat. Capital controls were permitted by the Bretton Woods agreement so that countries could preserve the fixed exchange rate and allow an active domestic monetary policy, and this possibility was used by the Kennedy administration in response to the deterioration in the American balance of payments. In his advice to Kennedy, the economist J. K. Galbraith insisted that restrictions on capital flows were the least damaging option available to the president. Another possibility was to reduce overseas military spending which was opposed by the State Department; or to deflate the domestic economy which was clearly not politically desirable. In Galbraith's view, the Treasury's preference for free capital movements was a serious case of 'bankers' syndrome'. It made more sense to retain investment at home in order to improve the efficiency of the American economy and so solve the balance of payments

[6] S. N. Broadberry and N. F. R. Crafts, 'British Economic Policy and Industrial Performance in the Early Post-War Period', *Business History*, 38 (1996), 65–91; B. Eichengreen, *The European Economy since 1945: Co-ordinated Capitalism and Beyond* (Princeton, 2006), 31–47; B. Eichengreen and J. Braga de Macedo, 'The European Payments Union: History and Implications for the Evolution of the International Financial Architecture', *OECD Development Centre, Paris*, Mar. 2001 at http://docentes.fe.unl.pt/~jbmacedo/oecd/triffin.html, last accessed 20 Nov. 2007. On the origins of this system, see R. McKibbin, 'Why Was There No Marxism in Great Britain?', *English Historical Review*, 99 (1984), 297–331; and W. Lazonick, *Competitive Advantage on the Shop Floor* (Cambridge, MA, 1990).

problem. The initial outcome was the Interest Equalization Tax of 1963 rather than actual controls: the cost of borrowing in America was raised for foreigners above the domestic rate. In 1965, President Johnson adopted direct controls which Richard Nixon pledged to abolish if elected. In fact, he could only moderate rather than abolish the interest rate differential and controls. Henry Kissinger, as Nixon's adviser on national security, realised, as had Galbraith before him, that free movement of capital would have serious strategic repercussions. The weakening of the balance of payments as a result of a greater outflow of funds would lead to criticism by European governments of irresponsibility, so undermining American strategic influence. Kissinger argued that it was better to retain controls than cut military spending or to force allies to pay more for defence which would alienate them.[7] Nevertheless, controls were much more difficult to enforce with the widespread adoption of convertibility. Capital could move via the current account, and controls could be evaded by holding dollars off-shore through the emerging Euro-dollar market. Although capital mobility was still lower than in the 1920s let alone prior to 1914, and far from the levels reached by the 1990s, capital controls were already facing greater pressure.[8]

Furthermore, the trade-off between international and domestic economic policies was unstable. In the 1930s, the pursuit of national economic policies was widely seen as destroying international economic stability; by contrast, the fixed exchange rates of the gold standard were believed to have sacrificed domestic prosperity and inspired a nationalistic backlash. The trade-off in 1944 tried to hold a balance: the pursuit of international stability should not be at the expense of domestic prosperity by allowing a degree of flexibility in exchange rates. However, there was a basic problem in the Bretton Woods agreement. There was nothing to require a country to revalue an under-valued currency which led the assistant director of the Office of Management and Budget, James Schlesinger, to complain that under-valuation of the yen and Deutschmark in order to 'engross' international trade 'are clearly beggar-my neighbour policies ... There is no reason that the United States

---

[7] See for example, *Foreign Relations of the United States, 1961–1963: IX: Foreign Economic Policy*, 30: letter from John Kenneth Galbraith to President Kennedy, Washington, 28 Aug. 1963 at http://dosfan.lib.uic.edu/ERC/frus/frus61–63ix/03_Section_3.html, last accessed 2 Aug. 2004; *Foreign Relations of the United States, 1969–1976: III: Foreign Economic Policy, 1969–1972: International Monetary Policy, 1969–1972*, 12: memorandum from the president's assistant for national security affairs (Kissinger) to President Nixon, Washington, 17 Mar. 1969, and 60: memorandum from the under-secretary of the Treasury for monetary affairs (Volcker) to the president's assistant for international economic affairs (Peterson), Washington, 1 Apr. 1971 at www.state.gov/r/pa/ho/frus/nixon/iii/53336pf.htm, last accessed 31 July 2004.

[8] For the development of capital flows, see E. Helleiner, *States and the Re-emergence of Global Finance from Bretton Woods to the 1990s* (Ithaca, 1994); and M. Obstfeld and A. M. Taylor, *Global Capital Markets: Integration, Crisis and Growth* (Cambridge, 2004).

should be willing graciously to tolerate such a condition.'[9] Equally, other countries complained that the Americans were behaving irresponsibly as their balance of payments weakened and the dollar came under pressure. There was nothing in the Bretton Woods agreement to require the Americans to devalue, any more than that there was any requirement for the Japanese and Germans to revalue, and it would be difficult for the Americans to do so given that the dollar was fixed at a gold price of $35 per ounce, and all other currencies were pegged to the dollar. The Americans covered their deficit by paying in dollars which was in many ways beneficial to the world economy by providing liquidity.

Here was Robert Triffin's dilemma: the world economy needed liquidity if it were to continue to grow, and this was provided by the dollars created by the American deficit; but the deficit put the dollar under pressure. This situation was not sustainable. If the Americans took action to solve the Triffin dilemma by deflating the US economy, it might well harm the world economy by cutting off the flow of dollars. In the opinion of General De Gaulle, this was no bad thing for he argued that the Americans were indulging in 'greenback imperialism', using their ability to issue dollars in order to finance military adventures and to purchase European firms, as well as creating inflation which was politically dangerous. His preferred solution, and that of the French economist Jacques Rueff, was to return to the gold standard. Others were more sceptical and feared a loss of liquidity from a return to gold or from a rectification of the American balance of payments.[10]

Would the Americans be able to improve their balance of payments? Kennedy tried to make the American economy more efficient and productive through a programme designed to create faster economic growth and to utilise capacity to the full, through tax breaks on depreciation in order to stimulate investment, improved welfare benefits and minimum wages, investment in human resources, as well as the differential between domestic and overseas interest rates. By these policies, he aimed to stimulate the domestic economy and improve the balance of payments. Although he accepted capital controls as compatible with Bretton Woods, in other respects he took steps to liberalise the world economy through the 'Kennedy Round' of GATT and his advocacy of

---

[9] *Foreign Relations of the Unite States, 1969–1976: III*, 161: memorandum from the assistant director of the Office of Management and Budget (Schlesinger) to the president's assistant for international economic affairs (Peterson), Washington, 20 July 1971, at www.state.gov/r/pa/ho/frus/nixon/iii/53336pf.htm, last accessed 31 July 2004.

[10] R. Triffin, *Gold and the Dollar Crisis: The Future of Convertibility* (New Haven, 1960); J. Rueff, *The Monetary Sin of the West* (New York, 1972); C. S. Chivvis, 'Charles De Gaulle, Jacques Rueff and French International Monetary Policy under Bretton Woods', *Journal of Contemporary History*, 41 (2006), 701–20.

the 'UN Development Decade' to encourage growth in the developing economies (and halt the spread of communism).[11]

Nixon took a somewhat different line, shifting the trade-off to give more attention to domestic political considerations at the expense of the international economy. He was deeply concerned about the possibility of domestic recession in the run-up to the election of 1972, and he wished to build a new electoral alliance with the South and blue-collar workers in a new form of Republicanism. Consequently, he was unable to respond to the continued weakening of the US balance of payments and the appearance of the first post-war trade deficit by deflating the domestic economy. Instead, his answer was to force currency realignment by the under-valued currencies of Germany and Japan.[12]

The regime of fixed exchange rates was therefore under pressure by the late 1960s. The American administration was facing a weakened trade position and mounting costs of war in Vietnam, and did not wish to devalue the dollar by changing the price of gold from $35 per ounce. Rather, it preferred forcing other countries to revalue, above all the yen and the Deutschmark. For its part, the Labour government devalued in 1967 after a considerable delay, and faced continuing problems in maintaining sterling as the second reserve currency. Was the attempt any longer feasible and if not, should British monetary policy abandon the sterling area and shift to Europe? The issues that had troubled the Labour government over the European Payments Union were now more pressing. What forum could be used to deal with these major shifts in the world's monetary regime? It might be thought that the obvious venue for re-negotiating the exchange rates was the IMF, but this did not prove feasible as a result of political tensions. The head of the IMF had always been a European, and the European governments had enough votes to block changes they did not like. The United States had the largest single vote but not sufficient to impose reform – and of course any attempt to use its economic clout would create political animosity. The IMF failed to make any serious proposals for reform, spending a considerable amount of time and effort in proposing minor changes that failed to command assent. Should the solution come from an international conference as in 1944, which the US proposed at one stage to the annoyance of the IMF which felt it would be marginalised; or should it come from the advanced

---

[11] T. W. Zeiler, *American Trade and Power in the 1960s* (New York, 1992); J. W. Evans, *The Kennedy Round in American Trade Policy: The Twilight of GATT?* (Cambridge, MA, 1971); *Public Papers of the President of the United States: John F. Kennedy*, I: *1961* (Washington, DC, 1962), no. 17, 'Special Message to the Congress: Program for Economic Recovery and Growth', 2 Feb. 1961; no. 23, 'Special Message to the Congress on Gold and the Balance of Payments', 6 Feb. 1961; no. 136, 'Special Message to the Congress on Taxation', 20 Apr. 1961.

[12] A. J. Matusow, *Nixon's Economy: Booms, Busts, Dollars and Votes* (Lawrence, 1998).

economies of the Group of 10 (G-10) which would challenge both the IMF and American leadership? Meanwhile, the developing countries were asserting their voice, and they produced their own report through the United Nations Conference on Trade and Development in 1965 which pressed for long-term aid rather than liquidity as the main issue. Reform of the Bretton Woods system was frustrated by institutional difficulties, by conflicts between the US, Europe and developing countries; and by serious disagreements over the appropriate solution, whether it be wider margins between currencies, a 'crawling peg', floating, realignment of currencies with fixed rates, or the introduction of a new form of liquidity less dependent on the dollar.[13]

Meanwhile, the EEC started to move towards its own solution at The Hague in 1969, when the members agreed to consider Economic and Monetary Union (EMU). This ambition was formalised in the Werner Report of October 1970 which set out the steps towards EMU, starting with a reduction in the margin of fluctuation between member currencies as a stage towards fixed rates, integrated financial markets and coordinated budgets.[14] This plan led to considerable tension within the EEC (in particular between France and Germany) as the Bretton Woods system collapsed – and placed the British government in a dilemma as it prepared for entry. It intensified fundamental issues about British monetary policy that had been apparent since the war: could the pound remain a reserve currency; should Britain adopt an Atlanticist policy; should it throw in its lot with EMU; or could it continue to steer its own path between these options in order to retain a degree of autonomy?

The solution adopted by the Nixon administration was 'benign neglect', allowing a crisis to develop without taking action to avert it, in the hope that it would create the opportunity to realign currencies. The moment came on 15 August 1971 when Nixon announced that he was suspending the convertibility of the dollar into gold, without consultation with the IMF or any other country. At the same time, Nixon set out his New Economic Policy, a programme of price and wage controls to limit inflation – an approach strongly criticised by Milton Friedman who

---

[13] See M. G. de Vries, *The International Monetary Fund, 1966–1971: The System under Stress* (Washington, 1976); F. J. Gavin, *Gold, Dollars and Power: The Politics of International Monetary Relations, 1958–1971* (Chapel Hill, 2004); H. James, *International Monetary Cooperation since Bretton Woods* (Washington and Oxford, 1996).

[14] 'Integral Text of the Final Communiqué of the Conference of the Heads of State or Government on 1 and 2 December 1969 at The Hague' and 'Report to the Council and the Commission on the Realisation by Stages of Economic and Monetary Union in the Community [Werner Report]', supplement to bulletin of the European Communities 11 – 1970, both at http://europa.eu.int/comm/economy_finance/euro/origins/origins_2_en.htm, last accessed 25 Apr. 2009. For an account of EMU, see P. Ludlow, *The Making of the European Monetary System: A Case Study of the Politics of the European Union* (London, 1982).

feared that Nixon was moving from the true path of free markets. 'Sooner or later, and the sooner the better, it will end as all previous attempts to freeze prices and wages have ended, from the time of the Roman Emperor Diocletian to the present, in utter failure and the emergence into the open of suppressed inflation.' George Shultz, the secretary of the Treasury and a colleague and disciple of Friedman at the University of Chicago, realised that failure would indeed come sooner rather than later: 'a freeze will stop when labor blows it up with a strike. Don't worry about getting rid of it – labor will do that for you.'[15] His prediction had resonance on the other side of the Atlantic, as the government of Edward Heath was to discover.

Nixon's decision marked the end of sterling–dollar diplomacy between Britain and the United States. It led to considerable uncertainty about what would happen, for the US administration did not have a plan for major reform now that the crisis had arrived. Did it want anything more than a realignment of currencies before returning to the existing order of Bretton Woods; or would the trilemma be fundamentally changed with a new trade-off? In December 1971, Nixon and President Georges Pompidou of France met on the Azores and agreed on a package of realignments which was modified and confirmed by other members of G-10 in the Smithsonian agreement. This agreement was predicated on the assumption that realignment would permit the survival of the Bretton Woods system of fixed but variable exchange rates. Although Nixon had previously opposed devaluation of the dollar, he now agreed that this should be done by changing the price of gold from $35 to $38 per ounce. Germany agreed to revalue the Deutschmark by 13.57 per cent and Japan to revalue the yen by 16.9 per cent, so that there was an overall devaluation of the dollar against other G-10 currencies of 10 per cent. In addition, an attempt was made to introduce an element of reform. The Smithsonian agreement introduced a wider band of variation in exchange rates: instead of allowing a fluctuation of 1 per cent either side of the central rate, the new figure was 2.25 per cent. The result, it was hoped, would be more flexibility within the system of fixed but variable rates, so that stability could be combined with adjustment to changed circumstances. Nixon welcomed the Smithsonian agreement as 'the most significant monetary agreement in the history of the world'.[16] The Bretton Woods system seemed to have been reestablished and floating rejected – but the agreement did not hold and floating rates were soon introduced in the early 1970s. Why did the Smithsonian agreement fail?

[15] Matusow, *Nixon's Economy*, 157.
[16] *Ibid.*, ch. 6, quote at 178; see also James, *International Monetary Cooperation*.

An intellectual case for floating rather than fixed rates was made by Milton Friedman as long ago as 1950 in a memorandum for the Economic Cooperation Administration in Europe; it was published in 1953. Friedman argued against the entire assumption of the Bretton Woods conference in favour of fixed exchange rates, claiming instead that floating rates were 'absolutely essential for the fulfilment of our basic economic objective: the achievement and maintenance of a free and prosperous world community engaging in unrestricted multilateral trade'. Multilateral trade was the main aim of policy, but there had been little success in removing trade barriers because of the commitment to 'an essentially minor goal' of rigid exchange rates. He felt that a country could respond to changes in its balance of payments in four different ways. One was to adjust reserves, which was not possible given their low level after the war. A second possibility was to alter internal prices and incomes, as happened after the First World War when Britain tried to force down wages and costs. Friedman accepted that such an approach was no longer politically feasible as a result of the general commitment to internal stability.

The third approach was favoured by Friedman: the adoption of flexible exchange rates where any move in the balance of payments immediately affected the exchange rate, and at once prompted corrective action. By contrast, the existence of fixed exchange rates meant that steps to correct the balance of payments could be delayed and when something was eventually done, it was by administrative action such as controls on capital flows or prices rather than automatic market forces. Friedman argued that flexible exchange rates were not so much rejected as ignored without any explicit consideration as a result of a misinterpretation of the history of the 1930s. On the one hand, traditionalists who wanted to return to the certainties of the gold standard and its ability to constrain domestic policies had no sympathy with floating rates. On the other hand, reformers distrusted the price mechanism in all forms. The result, Friedman remarked, was a 'curious coalition of the most unreconstructed believers in the price system, in all its other roles, and its most extreme opponents', with the result that floating exchanges were not even considered in the debates leading to the Bretton Wood conference.

By default, a fourth option was adopted, which Friedman believed was the least desirable: direct controls over foreign exchange. Friedman's support for flexible exchange rates did *not* mean that he expected rates would in fact be unstable, for 'the ultimate objective is a world in which exchange rates, while *free* to vary, are in fact highly stable. Instability of exchange rates is a symptom of instability in the underlying economic structure.' In his opinion, fixed exchanges 'froze' the economy by requiring various controls in order to protect the rate; if everything were flexible, the economy could respond to changing conditions and exchange rates would consequently remain stable as a result of the free play of market forces.[17]

Of course, Friedman's case for floating rates was linked with his wider neo-liberal agenda, but there was also support for the policy from different ideological positions. In 1955, James Meade set out a democratic socialist case for floating. As he pointed out, fixed exchange rates meant that a country facing a balance of payments deficit would have to deflate with an increase in unemployment, which was unthinkable. Consequently, domestic deflation would soon be abandoned in favour of direct controls on imports. 'Free trade and fixed exchange rate are incompatible in the modern world; and all modern free traders should be in favour of variable exchange rates.' Such a claim seemed like apostasy on the part of one of the founders of the Bretton Woods system, with its assumption that stable rates were crucial to ending beggar-my-neighbour policies of currency depreciation which had led to a collapse of trade in the 1930s. But Meade felt that times had changed, so that the risk of competitive depreciation was no longer present and could therefore be discounted in devising policies. In the 1930s, deflation and unemployment meant that competitive devaluation appealed to politicians as a way of reducing imports and stimulating exports in order to boost employment at home. In the 1950s, the problem was one of inflation which removed the attraction of competitive devaluation which would only make the problem worse by increasing the price of imports and stimulating exports at a time when capacity was already under pressure. Hence the historical problem leading to the adoption of the fixed exchange rate regime in 1944 was no longer applicable.[18]

Despite this scepticism about the virtues of fixed exchanges, the system became firmly entrenched in the minds of British policy makers. Although the case for floating was made in Operation Robot in 1952, the intellectual case of Friedman and Meade attracted little interest amongst officials or politicians: the issue seemed to have been closed, and the adoption of convertibility in 1958 marked the successful completion of the transition to the principles of 1944.[19] Fixed exchanges were sacrosanct, and the occasional need for devaluation was a major policy decision that entailed considerable anxiety in 1949 and 1967. The Bretton Woods system was validated by the rapid economic growth of western Europe up to the early 1970s. However, the pound started to float in June 1972 and by February–

[17] M. Friedman, 'The Case for Flexible Exchange Rates', in his *Essays in Positive Economics* (Chicago, 1953), 157–203.
[18] J. E. Meade, 'The Case for Variable Exchange Rates', *Three Banks Review*, 27 (Sept. 1955), 3–27.
[19] The debate over floating at the time of Operation Robot is discussed in M. Daunton, 'Britain and Globalisation since 1850: III, Creating the world of Bretton Woods, 1939–58', *Transactions of the Royal Historical Society*, sixth series, 18 (2008), 23–33.

March 1973 floating was widespread throughout the world. Two questions follow. The first question is whether ideas led to change, such as through Friedman's influence on members of Nixon's administration or a growing turn to monetarism and neo-liberalism; or whether the driving force was political contingencies? The second question is whether floating, when it did come and for whatever reason, did indeed have the outcome suggested by Friedman, or something rather different and disruptive?

Ideas were not the major driver of change, for acceptance of the case made by Friedman and Meade was slow and largely followed changes introduced by the pressure of circumstances. In 1971, most officials and politicians still assumed that a realignment of rates was needed rather than floating. In the final stages of the pegged system of exchanges, the only open advocate of floating was Karl Schiller (the German finance minister) who allowed the Deutschmark to float on 9 May 1971 in response to an influx of dollars looking for a safe home and a possible gain from revaluation. It seemed better to stop the influx by floating than by reducing interest rates which would undermine the tight monetary policy favoured by Germany. The Europeans were united in their hostility to the damage and uncertainty caused by American 'benign neglect' but were also divided amongst themselves, which threatened progress with the Werner plan to create a haven of stability or 'benign regionalism'. The French were horrified by Schiller's action, preferring to maintain parities through the use of exchange controls, and the Commission of the EEC was alarmed that the decision of the Germans undermined plans for EMU. The division between France and Germany posed a real threat to the EEC, and after Nixon announced the suspension of convertibility of the dollar into gold on 15 August 1971, the two countries came together in support of a realignment of European currencies and devaluation of the dollar. At this point, floating seemed to have been rejected and fixed exchanges rescued.[20]

In 1972, Shultz favoured floating exchanges, at least in private. However, he could not express his views in public, and the eventual collapse of the Smithsonian agreement and the emergence of floating was a defeat rather than a conscious policy decision. In the words of the economist Gottfried Haberler – the intellectual father of benign neglect – it was a 'non-system'. In June 1972, Arthur Laffer (the chief economist to the Office of Management and Budget) explained that the view in the administration was not that 'a floating rate system would be a preferred

[20] See Eichengreen, *European Economy*, 242–51, on European responses to the end of Bretton Woods; there is an account in The National Archive (hereafter TNA), T267/36, Treasury Historical Memorandum 30, 'The collapse of the Bretton Woods system, 1968–73', chapter 1 section D; James, *International Monetary Cooperation*.

alternative but rather that it might not be such a bad alternative'.[21] Why, then, did the Smithsonian agreement collapse if it were not the result of a conscious decision and the power of economic analysis?

Domestic American politics played a crucial role, for Nixon's concern for reelection meant that he was unwilling to take action to support the balance of payments and the exchange rate which might lead to a recession and deflation. As a result, the American trade balance deteriorated, and Nixon pursued an expansive monetary policy as much out of a miscalculation as cynicism. Nixon's economic team assumed that capacity was idle and that boosting demand would bring it into use without creating inflation. In reality, there was no idle capacity so that fiscal and monetary expansion led to a surge in prices. Herbert Stein of the Council of Economic Advisers remarked, 'We misinterpreted.' Meanwhile, the government hoped that prices and wages could be controlled to stop inflation and allow growth. The policy worked for a time, but the controls were only temporary and there was an obvious danger that once they were removed, Friedman's warning would prove correct: prices would rise in order to restore profits and unions would demand higher wages.[22]

The failures of American policy had international ramifications in two different ways. On the one hand, the US trade deficit meant that countries with a trade surplus (such as Germany) had an in-flow of dollars which created inflationary pressures and placed the exchange rate under strain. On the other hand, countries with a balance of payments deficit – such as Britain – could follow the American example and embark on rapid monetary growth, with an attempt to control inflation through a prices and incomes policy. Not surprisingly, there was continued concern in Europe about the decline in the dollar, with a clear sense that the Americans had no intention of supporting the value of the dollar agreed at the Smithsonian meeting. Mutual mistrust meant that the attempt to reestablish the Bretton Woods system was not likely to last for very long.

One response to these continued concerns was the creation of the European currency 'snake' in the Basle agreement of April 1972, in the aftermath of the crisis caused by the floating of the Deutschmark by Schiller and in response to the Smithsonian agreement which created the possibility of too wide a variation between currencies of the members of the EEC. The Smithsonian agreement permitted any currency to move within a band of 2.25 per cent either side of the dollar or a total of 4.5 per cent, and this meant that two non-dollar countries could move against each other by a greater margin. If country A was at the bottom of its band against the dollar and country B was at the top of its band, then A could

---

[21] James, *International Monetary Cooperation*, 234–5.
[22] Matusow, *Nixon's Economy*, chs. 7 and 8; quote from Stein at 186.

appreciate by 4.5 per cent against the dollar and B could depreciate by 4.5 per cent; and if both happened simultaneously, they could move against each other by 9 per cent. Such a large change in exchange rates was unlikely, but the potential range of fluctuation was too wide for members of the EEC which wished to converge in EMU. In April 1972, the Basle agreement created the 'snake in the tunnel' for the six members of the EEC and the three countries (including Britain) that were about to join. Their currencies were to move within a band of 2.25 per cent of the dollar, so that the maximum fluctuation between any two member currencies would be 4.5 per cent.[23]

Even before the closing of the gold window, Lord Cromer – the former governor of the Bank of England – argued in October 1970 that Britain should take the lead in a new European monetary initiative, as a way of preserving an element of autonomy which had effectively been lost:

> we could still use our influence to bring about the creation of a European Monetary System in which the sovereignty, which we have effectively lost due to our chronic Short Term Indebtedness, would be at least equated with that of the other European Powers and build a System of materially greater stability for all those who form part of it. Without some initiative of this nature, brought to a successful conclusion, the future of the United Kingdom in the economic world of to-day looks bleak.

The Treasury and Bank of England were more cautious, arguing that there was no advantage in taking the initiative at a time when the members of the European Community were engaged on their own deliberations; at most, the British government should express interest without taking a position which would be politically dangerous in supporting one side against another.[24] However, Cromer had raised the fundamental point: could Britain retain a semblance of monetary sovereignty outside the European system, and would membership replace purely theoretical sovereignty by an element of real sovereignty? Britain was moving away from its earlier adherence to the sterling area and dollar diplomacy to a new relationship with Europe, and on 1 May 1972 Britain joined the snake.[25]

---

[23] Eichengreen, *European Economy*, 247–8; Treasury Historical Memorandum 30, ch. 5; James, *International Monetary Cooperation*, 239–40. Details and documents are available at www.ena/lu, 'Historical Events: 1969–79, Crisis and Recovery: The European Currency Snake', last accessed 6 Apr. 2009.

[24] TNA, PREM15/53, and W. S. Ryrie to R. T. Armstrong, 23 Oct. 1970, covering 'Paper on Proposals regarding United Kingdom Participation in a European Monetary System', Aug. 1970, and 'Paper on "Proposals regarding United Kingdom Participation in a European Monetary System"'.

[25] This point is being developed by Kyoshi Hirowatari in his Ph.D. thesis at the University of Cambridge. My analysis follows R. Roberts, 'Sterling and the End of Bretton Woods', paper presented at the International Economic History Conference, Helsinki, at www.helsinki.fi/iehc2006/papers1/Roberts/pdf, last accessed 8 Apr. 2009.

The experiment was short-lived, for on 23 June 1972 Britain left the snake and floated the pound which was clearly a politically sensitive matter given the country's imminent membership of the EEC. The decision seems surprising given Edward Heath's strong commitment to Europe, but the policy of his administration was somewhat inconsistent. Membership of the snake was obviously complementary to Heath's desire to show Britain's European credentials but at same time, his administration expanded the monetary supply and did not feel itself limited by exchange rate considerations. As in the United States, domestic and international considerations were in tension. The Treasury was doubtful about membership of the snake, for the obligation to defend exchange rates within narrower bands would constrain policies to reduce unemployment and to set interest rates for domestic reasons. This approach was apparent in Anthony Barber's budget of 21 March 1972 when he proposed a 'dash for growth' aimed at reducing unemployment and increasing investment with higher public spending and cuts in personal taxes. The budget was expansionary and consciously rejected international considerations:

> The lesson of the international balance of payments upsets of the last few years is that it is neither necessary nor desirable to distort domestic economies to an unacceptable extent in order to maintain unrealistic exchange rates, whether they are too high or too low. Certainly, in the modern world I do not believe that there is any need for this country, or any other, to be frustrated on this score in its determination to sustain economic growth and to reduce unemployment.[26]

In terms of the trilemma, domestic considerations had trumped international commitments.

Barber's approach was welcomed by Peter Jay, the economics editor of *The Times*, who remarked that these were 'the most important words to be spoken by any Chancellor for a decade'. Jay was a supporter of floating and saw the implication of Barber's approach: the exchange rate could not be held within the limits of the snake.[27] Robert Solomon of the Federal Reserve later explained the reaction to the budget speech:

> Although an economist could not quarrel with one word in this statement, it was not the sort of thing that foreign exchange market operators expected to hear from a finance minister. It was interpreted to signify that, should sterling come under pressure, Barber would not wait long before changing its value.[28]

Sterling was indeed soon to come under pressure, for the balance of payments was in deficit; price and wage inflation were mounting; and labour disputes were threatened, with a possible dock strike triggering speculation against the pound. There was a general assumption in Europe

---

[26] Parliamentary Debates, Commons, 5th series, 1971–2, 21 Mar. 1972, col. 1354.
[27] P. Jay, 'A Half-Hearted Jump at the Four Big Hurdles', *Times*, 22 Mar. 1972, 25.
[28] R. Solomon, *The International Monetary System, 1945–76* (New York, 1977), 221.

that the pound needed to be devalued if Britain were to be competitive. Dennis Healey, the shadow chancellor, pointed out on 19 June 1972 that devaluation was widely expected prior to British membership of the EEC: 'The fact that the Chancellor has given warning that he will devalue rather than deflate when he thinks he will be in trouble means that all foreigners will want to pre-empt the devaluation.'[29] Barber denied that he had any intention of devaluing the pound, arguing that the pound was not at an un-realistic rate, that the IMF debt had been paid off for first time since 1964 and that reserves were strong.[30] In fact, sterling was sold and the exchange rate fell below its floor. Although interest rates were raised and the Bank intervened to support the pound, the attempt to support the rate failed.

The government had two options: it could devalue and try to hold the new rate; or it could float the pound. Heath's government opted for floating, ostensibly because it was less disruptive to the international financial system (which was true) but in reality because the weakness of its incomes policy and the deterioration in labour relations meant that it could not guarantee its ability to hold a new fixed rate. The post-war institutional system was failing as increased competition at home and from abroad threatened the 'low-effort bargain' between wages and profits. The level of profit was squeezed and it was increasingly fraught to pay higher wages demanded by the unions.[31] In this difficult economic situation, sterling was floated on 23 June 1972. In principle, the government remained committed to fixed exchanges, and claimed that floating was a temporary measure to deal with the speculative movement of what Heath called 'the vast masses of highly mobile funds which can be switched out of one currency into another at very short notice and in enormous volume'.[32] At the same time, the government extended exchange controls to the sterling area. Here was a crucial moment in defining Britain's identity. Heath's government was retreating ever more from the sterling area which had been so important since the 1930s, but at the same time was raising doubts over its European identity.

The decision to float the pound was generally welcomed as a mark of realism. Supporters of floating were delighted, and not least Friedman who saw it as the beginning of the end of the Smithsonian agreement.[33] His wish was soon realised, for the dollar was under continued pressure in 1973. Trade figures showed a large American deficit and German surplus, and American wage and price controls were about to expire with

[29] Quoted by Healey in *Parliamentary Debates, Commons*, 5th series, 1971–2, vol. 839, 29 June 1972, col. 1723, from Standing Committee E, 19 June 1972, col. 1080.

[30] Barber's interview on the BBC's *Panorama*, quoted in Roberts, 'Sterling', 16–17.

[31] A. Glyn and B. Sutcliffe, *British Workers, Capitalism and the Profits Squeeze* (Harmondsworth, 1972).

[32] Quoted by Roberts, 'Sterling', 18.

[33] *Ibid.*, 19, quoting his article in *Newsweek*.

the threat of inflation; consequently, there was a flight from the dollar into the Deutschmark and other strong currencies. Paul Volcker, a leading official concerned with international monetary policy at the US Treasury, tried to negotiate new parities to save the Smithsonian system, pressing Japan to revalue the yen by at least 10 per cent and seeking a devaluation of the dollar by 10 per cent against European currencies. The dollar was therefore devalued for a second time in 1973. Shultz was sceptical and did nothing to defend the new rate by raising interest rates as the Europeans were demanding; instead, he opted to float the dollar. In March 1973, the EEC council of ministers agreed to a collective float against the dollar – with Britain remaining outside with its own independent float against both the dollar and the European currencies. The Smithsonian agreement expired in February–March 1973, finally undermined by the oil price shock which created divergences between economies' ability to adjust. The rule-based system of 1944 came to an end, with a variety of outcomes: some countries still pegged their currencies to the dollar, which was now floated with no link with gold; some countries were members of joint floats, such as the European scheme; and others, including Britain, floated independently.[34]

Floating had arrived, less as a result of intellectual conversion than in response to political exigencies. Friedman and Meade had provided arguments which suggested that the change might be beneficial for the economy, which brings me to my second major question: were the consequences of floating as positive as they believed, or did it lead to new difficulties and problems? Whatever the theoretical advantages of floating in creating a flexible and responsive economy based on free trade, reality was very different as a result of the political circumstances which had led to the adoption of the new policy. Floating the pound removed the need for monetary discipline, for the money supply could now be expanded with less concern for the constraints imposed by the exchange rate. The strain of any balance of payments deficit could now be taken by a decline in the exchange rate, so that there was less need to limit wage demands in order to maintain competitiveness in export markets. The consequence was inflation caused by monetary expansion and wage demands which led to the freezing of prices and wages controls which culminated in 1974 with Labour's 'social contract' of voluntary wage restraint in return for food subsidies and rent controls. Far from leading to stable exchanges and a free, flexible economy, floating led to instability and controls.

Heath was anxious that Britain should rejoin the snake as soon as possible and become part of the collective float of European currencies against the dollar in order to show the country's commitment to the

[34] James, *International Monetary Cooperation*, provides an account of the demise of the Smithsonian agreement.

EEC. In the meantime, he wished to manage the sterling float to stay within the 2.25 per cent band. Despite the concern of Barber and the Treasury for domestic growth and unemployment, Heath gave considerable importance to rejoining the snake. The apparent loss of monetary sovereignty with the demise of the sterling area led Heath to see European monetary cooperation as a way of regaining it within Europe. He believed that economic integration with Europe would reimpose external discipline, so overcoming some of the dangers posed by a lack of monetary constraints under a floating regime with the consequent need to control wages and prices. Membership of the collective float of European currencies would reinstate the discipline of preserving the balance of payments.[35] The Bank of England working party on the sterling exchange rate agreed, arguing that 'the idea of external discipline has now been revived in the context of the movement towards EMU in Europe'.[36]

The problem was that the collective float was not obviously compatible with the government's domestic economic policy of fast growth, lower unemployment, higher industrial investment, reduction of inflation and avoidance of serious industrial disruption. A commitment to staying within the 2.25 per cent band might threaten this policy by requiring higher interest rates to protect the pound, or limiting wage demands to maintain competitiveness. The tension between the two policies was well put by a Treasury working party in 1973:

> All of these objectives [in domestic economic policy] could be affected by a decision to join the collective float, i.e. to refix the pound in relation to the other EEC currencies. Domestically the decision to float implied a higher priority for employment and growth than for our commitments to fixed parity and European monetary arrangements; conversely a decision to refix implies a reversal of these priorities.

The Treasury was deeply sceptical that the snake and collective float were compatible with domestic policies. The commitment to maintain the exchange rate implied no weakening of counter-inflation policy so that British inflation remained in line with its competitors, and it also required that there be no serious industrial disruption. But the Treasury doubted that it was possible to strengthen counter-inflation policy 'without provoking industrial dislocation'. Measures designed to hold the exchange rate would have a harmful effect on domestic policies: a decision to cut public spending would undermine government proposals to improve the infrastructure; the introduction of higher indirect taxes to reduce demand would increase prices and undermine counter-inflation measures; higher

[35] See Hirowatari's prospective thesis.

[36] Bank of England Archive OV44/128, Working Party on the Sterling Exchange Rate, 7 Sept. 1972. I owe this reference to Kyoshi Hirowatari.

interest rates would hit investment and raise prices. Consequently, the Treasury feared that

> measures which reduced demand could, in the context of joining the float, be particularly damaging to our counter-inflation policy . . . If the unions felt that we were deflating solely in order to be able to join the collective float (i.e. that we were sacrificing growth in order to conform to Community ideas about the merits of a fixed parity) their reaction might be very damaging to the prospects for the counter-inflation policy.

Membership of the collective float entailed deflation and restraining demand to hold down prices, which was politically difficult to achieve without alienating the unions and so weakening counter-inflation policies.[37] Of course, Britain might enter the collective float at a lower exchange rate, which would be more easily defended. But the Treasury doubted the wisdom of this course of action. The Treasury seemed to be locked into the existing institutional system of wage restraint through agreements with the trade unions, and was unwilling to overturn it for the risky venture of fixing the exchange rate. Devaluation would increase prices with serious consequences for counter-inflationary policies. It

> could be the last straw as far as the unions were concerned and thus give a disproportionate boost to the domestic inflationary spiral which might even offset all its good effects on long-term competitiveness. It would certainly put more strain on the counter-inflation policy; and success with the counter-inflation policy is critical to all our objectives, including joining and staying in the Community float.[38]

The collective float was intimately connected with the deterioration in industrial relations that was to prove Heath's undoing in 1974.

Meanwhile the Treasury turned to a number of ways of reconciling membership of the European monetary snake and its external discipline with the pursuit of domestic policies. Treasury officials came up with a number of complex proposals which married technical ingenuity and desperation with political difficulties in securing support from the rest of the Community. As one official put it with a sense of realism, 'It would look altogether as if we had concocted a potion which would be palatable to the United Kingdom and were trying to prescribe it for the rest of the Community.' The schemes were examples of 'gamesmanship' or how to win without actually cheating which would lead to deep suspicion of British sincerity in rejoining. The 'flexible skinned snake' allowed wider margins of fluctuation between currencies; the 'crawling peg snake' removed a set band with an upper and lower limit and permitted a succession of small parity changes. These ideas were opposed by the French, and D. J. Mitchell of the Treasury was 'pretty certain that in

---

[37] TNA, T355/78, PCC(73)2, 19 Mar. 1973, Treasury Policy Co-ordinating Committee: 'Joining the Community Float: Economic Policy Implications', note by the secretary.

[38] TNA, T355/78. 'Joining the community float: economic policy implications', 29 Mar. 1973.

relation to the French any suggestions which dilute what they regard as the purity of the fixed EEC relationships would be anathema; and we should simply be regarded as preparing for further back-sliding on our part'.[39] In any case, there were serious reservations about the wisdom of joining the collective float at all. Meade was doubtful, arguing that priority should be given to other measures to harmonise the economies of the EEC. He pointed out that harmonisation would necessarily have a differential impact on the balance of payments of the member countries, and that rigid exchange rates would be a barrier to change. He argued that floating would allow more flexibility.[40] Barber was sceptical about the desirability of joining, for he felt that there was a wider issue of political presentation and acceptability:

when we make the move we must be in a position to convince public opinion at home that it is a sensible one and that it will assist and not jeopardise our domestic policies. It is going to be difficult to pull this off...

I believe that most people – including the CBI and the TUC in our current talks – would think it extraordinary if in circumstances anything like the present we were to tie our hands by rejoining the snake.[41]

The problem was not only the apparent incompatibility between domestic and international policies: a further concern was the lack of adequate support from France and Germany for sterling balances.

There had been a fundamental shift in attitudes to the sterling area in the 1960s. In 1962, the chancellor of the Exchequer, Reginald Maudling, remarked that 'I regard it as a major aim of policy to free the UK economy from the inhibitions of reserve currency status', and the Bank of England also accepted the desirability of ending the reserve role for sterling while maintaining it as a trading currency.[42] Of course, the change in status for sterling posed serious problems as a result of commitments to sterling holders, and would take a great deal of skill to negotiate. The process started prior to the devaluation of 1967 and even more in its aftermath when other countries diversified their reserves. The Bank of International Settlements (BIS) coordinated a package of support in the Basle agreement of 1968 which offered guarantees for the value of

[39] These schemes are outlined at great length in TNA, T355/77. The quotes are from: 'Rejoining the Snake: Alternative Solutions', D. J. Mitchell, 18 May 1973, and 'Rejoining the Snake: A Scheme for Small Parity Changes', J. G. Littler, 18 May 1973.

[40] TNA, T355/281, 'Meade on EMU', H. H. Liesner, 22 Feb. 1973.

[41] TNA, T355/78, A. Barber to prime minister, 19 June 1973.

[42] C. R. Schenk, 'Managing the Decline of Sterling, 1960–73: A Multilateral Approach', paper presented to the International Economic History Conference, Helsinki, at www.helsinki.fi/iehc2006/papers1/Schenk.pdf, last accessed 9 Apr. 2009, quoting Bank of England Archive, OV47/63, Myners, 3 Jan. 1963, and OV53/30, J. S. Fforde to L. Thomson-McCausland, 2 Dec. 1964.

sterling in return for creditors holding a specified proportion of their reserves in sterling. The result of this agreement was that sterling remained part of the reserves of other countries on a voluntary basis, with joint responsibility for a managed decline in the reserve position of sterling. The British government preferred to proceed through informal multilateral discussions at the BIS (which mainly involved central banks) rather than through the more rigid, interventionist approach of the IMF, which wanted domestic measures to contain demand, limit domestic lending and constrain government borrowing. However, the Basle agreement was coming to an end in 1973 at the very time that Britain was considering its options with regard to the collective float.[43]

Discussions over EMU therefore connected with the need to secure continued agreement to manage the decline of sterling as a reserve currency. The British wanted the Europeans to offer unlimited and unconditional support for sterling, but the Treasury felt that the support fund would not be

> large enough to give protection even against a speculative movement unrelated to our true underlying position. Others were going to insist that support was limited in amount, limited in duration and subject to conditions, including moves to constrain our domestic policies. This created a totally different situation from the one in which we were thinking of 'unlimited and unconditional' support. Since we would never want to draw on this kind of support . . . we would have to rely on the right to change our parity relative to other EEC currencies.[44]

Not surprisingly, the Treasury's Working Party on EMU reported against joining the collective float:

> Until the real conditions for a viable union are met, it would be dangerous and wrong for the UK to surrender any significant degree of its economic autonomy. The real conditions in question are either a very substantial measure of economic convergence between the member countries, or an evident political will to underwrite the massive resource transfers necessary to offset imbalances resulting from different levels of national productivity, inflation etc. Neither of these conditions is even remotely met at present, nor seems likely to be for many years to come. Until they are, the UK government will remain primarily responsible for the economic well-being of the UK, and will need to retain the necessary powers.[45]

Britain did not join the collective float – and in any case it soon collapsed. The snake slithered to an end, starting with France's departure in 1974, and by 1977 only five of nine members of EEC remained within a collective float based on the Deutschmark.

[43] Schenk, 'Managing', 14–20; G. Toniolo, *Central Bank Cooperation at the Bank for International Settlements, 1930–1973* (Cambridge, 2005), 423–6; TNA, T355/78, 'Rejoining the EEC Snake: Support Facilities', 17 Apr. 1973; T355/84, 'Sterling Agreements and the Basle Facility', Bank of England, 9 July 1973.

[44] TNA, T355/78, D. J. Mitchell, 18 June 1973.

[45] TNA, T355/281, L. Airey to D. Allen, 'Report of the Working Party on Economic and Monetary Union', 6 Feb. 1973.

The snake perished as a result of the divergences in the economic policies of its members. Clearly, if two countries wished to maintain a stable exchange rate, they should follow similar monetary policies. However, Germany maintained a tight monetary policy and refused to accommodate the rise in oil prices. By contrast, France opted for an expansionary monetary policy in an attempt to prevent higher unemployment. The result was wide inflation differentials as a result of differing domestic political considerations. Meanwhile, Britain left the snake and declined to join the collective float because of its concern for domestic growth, the need to reduce unemployment, and the desire to boost investment. However, Barber's 'dash for growth' proved to be a disaster, resulting not in growth so much as inflation and an increase in the supply of money. Floating had not worked, and neither had the attempt to impose some form of external discipline by joining the snake. By the time that Heath left office in the aftermath of the three-day week and the challenge from the miners, Britain's international economic policy remained muddled and confused. Would the new Labour government have any more success?

An immediate problem facing Wilson's administration in 1974 was how to respond to the weak balance of payments. Although the Treasury argued for depreciation in order to help export competitiveness, Healey and Wilson were not in favour and the consequent confusion in policy led to a loss of confidence which triggered a capital outflow. The crisis was caused less by the scale of the balance of payments deficit than by uncertainty over the best strategy which would, in the words of Healey, 'get the economy into balance without social breakdown'.[46] The cabinet had to choose between two highly divergent approaches: deflation or the Alternative Economic Strategy. A deflationary policy was urged by the IMF which had shifted its policy towards current account deficits, away from the weakening of conditionality that had been adopted in response to the oil shock in order to prevent a serious economic downturn towards stricter conditions obliging deficit countries to resolve their economic problems.[47] Dennis Healey felt that the government had no option except to follow the advice of the IMF:

> Unless we can do this, we shall not be able to cover the deficit at anything like the present exchange rate. Our only course then would be to hope to achieve equilibrium by allowing the rate to fall to levels at which there might be some chance of foreigners stepping in to buy sterling so as to acquire a lot of United Kingdom assets – British firms and property, as well as financial assets – very cheaply. This, despite the effect that the fall in the exchange rate would have on our own cost of living, is still an optimistic scenario. The pessimistic scenario is one of continuous and probably accelerating depreciation,

---

[46] TNA, CAB128/60, CM(76), 25th conclusions, minute 3, 7 Oct. 1976.
[47] James, *International Monetary Cooperation*, 317, 322–3.

leading to South American-style inflation, with higher import prices feeding through to wages and vice versa.[48]

On his view, floating could lead to a sinking pound and to economic disaster. The general sentiment of the City and industry supported Healey's assessment of the situation.

The opponents of deflation had their 'alternative economic strategy' or planned expansion with direct control over imports. Above all, Tony Benn opposed the government's existing policy of controlling inflation and improving the balance of payments through a combination of a social contract with the Trades Union Congress; exchange rate depreciation; growth in manufacturing; borrowing from abroad to cover the deficit; controls on the domestic economy by a tight fiscal policy; a reduction in public spending; and a tight monetary policy. In his view, there were serious flaws in this approach. Exchange rate depreciation might be so fast that it did not achieve the intention of faster growth and a balance of payments surplus but might instead lead to high inflation which would threaten the social contract. Equally, the social contract might collapse as a result of a higher rate of unemployment. A weak home market and high interest rates might mean that investment in industry would not increase sufficiently to stimulate manufacturing output and productivity, and workers would not accept the need to raise productivity when unemployment was high.

In Benn's view, Britain's relative economic decline occurred in the context of trade liberalisation, and other economies achieved faster rates of growth because they rebuilt industry with modern equipment after the war (as in Germany) or developed new industries behind protective barriers (as in Japan). In these countries, strong balance of payments surpluses led to fast growth of output, high levels of investment and improved productivity. The situation was different in Britain, where the capital stock was run down, domestic markets were open to foreign competition and debt repayment, exports and rearmament were given priority over industrial reequipment. In Benn's opinion, the fixed exchange rate and a weak balance of payments led to constraints on growth: output rose only slowly, with little incentive to invest, a high level of import penetration and cumulative economic decline. In order to break out of this downward spiral, Britain needed to raise the growth rate of industrial capacity, modernise its factories and improve the utilisation of labour with more capital per worker. The aim was uncontentious; his solution was not.

---

[48] TNA, CAB129/193, CP(76)123, 30 Nov. 1976, cabinet, economic policy and the IMF credit, memorandum by the chancellor of the Exchequer.

Benn aimed to reverse the trend towards trade liberalisation which characterised policy since the war. The Central Policy Review Staff explained his case that attempting to break free of the cycle of economic deterioration

> with an open economy in the context of increasing world competition and a slow-growing home market suffering severe import penetration, would be extremely difficult. The weakness of much of British industry, in the face of competition both from more advanced high productivity industries (especially in Japan and some of the countries of the EEC) and from cheap labour countries elsewhere, is now so great that free trade is ceasing to be of benefit to the United Kingdom. It is essential to have a period during which industry can expand and invest without the fears (i) that balance of payments constraints will require the Government to deflate; and (ii) that increasing foreign competition will lead to the continued loss of export markets and higher levels of import penetration will steal the home market. The historical record shows that no country has ever made a major industrial leap forward while, at the same time, leaving its economic frontier continually open to penetration by its more advanced competitors.

In Benn's view, 'the price we must pay for borrowing to finance a free trade policy is too high because it involves unacceptable levels of unemployment, unacceptably low levels of investment and a progressive deterioration of our manufacturing capacity'. In the cabinet discussion of the alternative economic strategy, one minister – probably Benn himself – remarked that 'the economy was bleeding to death, and that only the adoption of a protectionist policy could save the situation':

> Protectionism had been described as a siege economy; but if this was the case, it would be preferable to have the trade unions inside the citadel during the siege rather than the international bankers. It would not be possible to win the support of the people of the country for policies which were needed simply to satisfy bankers. Protectionism was not an easy course and would involve sacrifices; but it presented the best way to gain support of the British people.

The alternative economic strategy marked a fundamental rejection of the policy of multilateralism pursued since the Second World War in favour of economic autarchy. Benn proposed a national recovery plan based on imposing import quotas on manufactures; exchange controls to prevent speculative outflows; control of capital issues and bank advances. Investment would be directed towards a secure home market made possible by import controls; lower interest rates would provide an incentive to investment and employment; and planning agreements would be implemented with more funds for the National Enterprise Board. Such a policy entailed a fundamental realignment of the 'inconsistent quartet'.[49]

---

[49] TNA, CAB128/60, CM(76), 25th conclusions, minute 3, 7 Oct. 1976; 35th conclusions, 1 Dec. 1976; CAB129/93, CP(76)117, 29 Nov. 1976, cabinet, the real choices facing the cabinet: memorandum by the secretary of state for energy; CP(76)116, 30 Nov. 1976, cabinet, the alternative strategy: the case for import controls.

The alternative economic strategy led to one of the most significant debates in the economic history of post-war Britain. Healey and Callaghan were deeply sceptical of Ben's strategy, arguing that IMF support was crucial: without it, confidence would collapse and there would be an 'uncontrollable slide' in the value of sterling which would destroy the social contract. Import controls were illegal under Community law and would also expose Britain to retaliation under GATT. Above all, the strategy would mean a complete *volte face* in policy:

> The whole philosophy behind our international policies – both political and economic – has been based on the assumption that our future lies in membership of the Atlantic Community. This takes the form of membership of the EEC and the free trade and political co-operation which that implies; co-operation in trade and payments policies in OECD; and a major commitment to NATO. A decision to introduce QRs [quantitative restrictions] implies going back on this whole philosophy. It would be damaging to the EEC, damaging to international co-operation in trade and payments policy, and damaging to NATO. Once this damage had been done, it would be extremely difficult to re-establish ourselves in the Atlantic Community. Our former partners would be reluctant to trust so unreliable an ally again, and we would be liable to find ourselves left economically protectionist, and politically isolated.

Healey and Callaghan were far from certain that the alternative economic strategy would work, for Britain could only become more efficient 'by facing up to the competition' rather than hiding behind tariff walls. Rather than industrial regeneration might the siege economy lead to industrial ossification? In their opinion, there was no reason to think that protection would lead industry to develop new and internationally competitive products; rather, management and labour could avoid the need to change, becoming more reliant on the home market which had no choice but to accept whatever quality of goods was offered. When import controls were eventually removed, British industry would be just as uncompetitive as in the past.[50]

The outcome was the adoption of the IMF approach, which many commentators saw as the start of monetarism to impose discipline on the domestic economy. But the reimposition of discipline was more complicated than acceptance of the IMF package. Another approach to the creation of stability was the European Monetary System (EMS), an initiative proposed by Roy Jenkins (at this time president of the European Community) in October 1977 to reactivate EMU. His suggestion was taken up by Schmidt and Giscard in 1978, and came into force in March 1979. The initiative rested on joint policies between members of the

[50] TNA, CAB129/193, CP(76)111, 22 Nov. 1976, cabinet. IMF negotiations: memorandum by the chancellor of the Exchequer; CP(76)116, 30 Nov. 1976, 'The alternative strategy: the case against'; CP(76)123, 30 Nov. 1976, cabinet, economic policy and the IMF credit: memorandum by the chancellor of the Exchequer. Further detail at TNA, PREM16/800–805.

EEC to use the *ecu* as a unit of account between themselves, with a European Monetary Cooperation Fund which could intervene against the dollar and other currencies. The aim was to marginalise the dollar and international financial institutions. Both Schmidt and Giscard preferred fixed parities, but at the very least the EMS would reduce fluctuations and discipline national governments and labour and business interests. By fixing exchange rates between European economies, the consequences of high pay settlements would be much more apparent, and inflation would be constrained.[51]

What were British views on the EMS? The case for membership rested on the need to maintain the exchange rate of sterling through wage restraint and control over the money supply; in other words, it imposed external discipline over domestic policy. Not everyone was convinced. Was there any reason for thinking that linking the exchange rate of a high-inflation country such as Britain with a low-inflation country such as Germany would result in convergence on the lower rate? External discipline would not automatically force the government to persevere with unpopular policies designed to create low inflation. Indeed, Callaghan and Healey feared that a strong Deutschmark would force sterling to rise in value, so reducing competitiveness and leading to unemployment and deflation which would be politically disastrous. They wanted symmetrical adjustment for strong and weak economies, and feared that membership of the EMS could impose discipline only on weaker members such as Britain. Perhaps the benefits of price competitiveness from floating exchanges were more important. Of course, the risks of floating downwards also posed a threat of inflation, for a decline in the exchange rate meant that imports became more expensive, and there was less incentive to take politically difficult action to restrain wages since the exchanges could take the pressure. Such considerations meant that the Labour cabinet and party were generally opposed to joining the EMS. Business organisations such as the Confederation of British Industry tended to agree that stable exchanges were less important than a more competitive exchange rate which would allow industry to benefit from lower interest rates and export prices. Jenkins believed that Callaghan still favoured an Atlanticist policy based on the dollar and the pound, working with the IMF, in preference to the EMS.[52]

[51] Ludlow, *Making of the European Monetary System*; for documents, see www.ena.lu, the EMS, last accessed 8 Apr. 2009.

[52] J. Stalter, 'British Foreign Policy to 1985: The European Monetary System from Conception to Birth', *International Affairs*, 55 (1979), 220–1; R. Jenkins, *A Life at the Centre* (London, 1991), 477; D. Healey, *The Time of My Life* (London, 1989), 440; J. W. Young, *Britain and European Unity, 1945–1999* (London, 2000), 133; Parliamentary Papers 1978–9 XV, Expenditure Committee, *First Report: The European Monetary System* (1978); Parliamentary Papers 1978–9 VI, *The European Monetary System* (Green Paper), presented to parliament by

In the United States, the dollar continued to weaken in the second half of the 1970s, with serious inflationary pressures which led to price and income controls in an attempt to limit political risks, both at home from those who were hit by inflation, and internationally from Germany and other countries who complained of the lack of discipline in American monetary policy. The result was a major shift in American economic policy. On 16 October 1979, the new chairman of the Federal Reserve, Paul Volcker – a man with deep experience as a leading Treasury official at the time of the Nixon *débâcle* – embarked on a policy of tight domestic money and high interest rates to stabilise the dollar. The so-called 'Volcker shock' squeezed inflation out of the American economy: in 1981, inflation reached 13.5 per cent but by 1983, it was down to 3.2 per cent. However, this reduction of inflation came at the cost of a severe recession and high unemployment at home, and a debt crisis in developing countries. At the same time, the World Bank shifted from funding projects to an insistence on structural adjustments in less-developed countries to allow the repayment of debt and to make economies more competitive.[53]

Similarly, the new Thatcher government in Britain adopted the Medium Term Financial Strategy (MTFS) which set firm limits to the growth of the monetary supply. Nigel Lawson argued that the new policy 'represents a belated unlearning of what were mistakenly believed to be the lessons of the war' – a rejection of the Bretton Woods consensus that fixed rates were the cure to the problems of competitive devaluation and beggar-my-neighbour policies which had characterised the 1930s. His view, following Friedman's monetary history of the US, was that the real lesson of the depression was that the Federal Reserve made a serious mistake in reducing the monetary supply in 1929–33, so turning a financial problem into a serious disruption of the economy. The correct lesson, he argued, was that the Federal Reserve should have ensured stable monetary growth. After the war, excess monetary growth was held in check by fixed exchange rates and the pursuit of non-inflationary policies in the States, but the strategy was then fatally undermined by floating rates. The solution was not to return to fixed rates in order to reimpose order: it was to return to monetary orthodoxy.[54] At the same time, the ability of trade unions to demand large wage increases was constrained by higher levels of unemployment and by changes in legislation. The

the chancellor of the Exchequer, Nov. 1978. See also Hirowatari. On US attitudes to the EMS, see Joint Economic Committee, Congress of the US, *The European Monetary System: Problems and Prospects* (Washington, DC, 1979).

[53] D. Kapur, J. P. Lewis and R. C. Webb, *The World Bank: History*, I: *History* (Washington, DC, 1997), 506–7; also D. Harvey, *A Brief History of Neoliberalism* (Oxford, 2005).

[54] N. Lawson, *The New Conservatism: Lecture to the Bow Group* (1980), and *The View from Number 11: Memoirs of a Tory Radical* (London, 1992), 8–9 and ch. 7.

social contract and controls over wages and prices were abandoned and castigated.

By 1985, a renewed effort could be made to balance international stability and domestic welfare. In 1985, the seven leading industrial economies issued a declaration in favour of sustained growth, noninflationary growth and higher employment. Inflation was at the lowest level for twenty years, interest rates had fallen and their economies were growing. However, there were still serious imbalances in the external positions of their economies as a result of variation in growth rates, the debts of developing countries and the appreciation of the US dollar so that it was now seriously over-valued. Action was therefore needed to adjust exchange markets in order to prevent the revival of protectionism in response to disequilibrium between economies. In the Plaza accord in September 1985, the US, Britain, France, German and Japan agreed on domestic policies to resist protectionism, control inflation through monetary policies, liberalise financial markets and reduce taxation and public expenditure. Above all, they agreed that 'exchange rates should play a role in adjusting external imbalances. In order to do this, exchange rates should better reflect fundamental economic conditions than has been the case', and that 'some further orderly appreciation of the main non-dollar currencies against the dollar is desirable'.[55] As a result, the dollar did depreciate against other currencies. In 1987, the Louvre accord between the members of the Group of 6 (G-6), including Britain, aimed to achieve sustainable and non-inflationary economic growth through an open economy and stable exchange rates. The realignment of exchanges in 1985 meant that currencies were 'broadly consistent with underlying economic fundamentals', and the policy commitments of the members of G-6 should allow this to continue to be the case. The Louvre accord concluded that 'further substantial exchange rate shifts among their currencies could damage growth and adjustment prospects in their countries. In current circumstances, therefore, they agreed to cooperate closely to foster stability of exchange rates around current levels.'[56] The aim was to stop any further devaluation of the dollar against the Deutschmark and yen which might threaten economic recovery. Rates would not be fixed but neither should they float in a way that disrupted both international and domestic prosperity.

Meanwhile, Lawson was reconsidering his economic policies. By October 1985, he was disillusioned with monetarism and announced the end of

---

[55] 'Plaza accord, September 22, 1985', www.g7.utoronto.ca/finance/fm850922.htm, last accessed 3 Apr. 2009.

[56] 'Statement of the G6 finance ministers and central bank governors (Louvre accord)', Paris, 22 Feb. 1987, at www.g7.utoronto.ca/finance/fm870222.htm, last accessed 3 Apr. 2009.

the MTFS, for the appreciation of the pound was harming manufacturing industry, and the monetary targets were in any case difficult to hit. He saw the attractions of the Exchange Rate Mechanism (ERM) as a way of linking Britain to low-inflation countries, disciplining financial policy and reducing exchange rate variability. In 1987, Lawson opted to 'shadow' the Deutschmark without informing Thatcher, not as a step towards eventual membership of the ERM so much as to provide a sense of commitment to the exchange rate in anticipation of any future pressure on the pound. The experiment did not last long, for Lawson cut interest rates in response to the stock market crash in late 1987 which led to a return of inflation. The policy of shadowing the Deutschmark was abandoned, and interest rates were raised to reduce consumer spending and contain inflation.[57] Subsequently, the pound was pegged to the ERM in 1992, a short experiment which came to an ignominious end on 'Black Wednesday' (16 September 1993) when even an increase in interest rates to 15 per cent could not stop the pound from falling below its lower margin with the Deutschmark. Pegging is only a 'conditional commitment', and markets realised that it would be broken when the cost of defending the exchange rate was larger than the cost of realignment – and the British authorities were reluctant to raise interest rates sufficiently early or by a large enough amount, so that when action was taken, it smacked of panic. Further, Britain could not use capital controls: these had been almost entirely removed within the EC, and were no longer available to protect the currency. As we know from the analysis of the trilemma, an autonomous domestic monetary policy is not compatible with pegged exchanges in the absence of capital controls – and 1993 is a clear example of the proposition. In 1992/3, British commitment to pegged exchanges lacked credibility, and Britain returned to floating the pound, where it remains.[58]

The two episodes of pegging the pound against other currencies in 1987 and 1992 failed for the same reason: managing the exchange rate entailed domestic economic policies that were inconsistent with domestic political needs. In the first episode, shadowing the Deutschmark stimulated a domestic boom; in the second, Britain was obliged to follow a tight monetary policy as a result of Germany's need to deal with the problems of reunification, which intensified the recession. The attempt to create stability in the exchanges back-fired, for in both cases the result was increasing domestic instability. Eddy George, the governor of the Bank

---

[57] N. W. C. Woodward, *The Management of the British Economy, 1945–2001* (Manchester, 2004), 178–80; D. Kavanagh, *Thatcherism and British Politics: The End of Consensus?* (Oxford, 1987), 301–2.

[58] M. Zurlinden, 'The Vulnerability of Pegged Exchange Rates: The British Pound in the ERM', at http://research.stlouisfed.org/publications/review/93/09/Pegged_Sep_Oct1993.pdf, last accessed 3 Apr. 2009.

of England felt that the issue was not merely the choice of the rate at the time of British entry into the ERM; it was a wider problem involving any attempt to peg the currencies of countries with different domestic policies. His assessment of the different approaches to domestic economic stability and the exchange rate regime – whether floating, an adjustable peg, a fixed rate or monetary union – was that there was no ideal solution. Floating seemed to offer the advantage of a buffer to insulate the domestic economy from shocks from abroad; but he pointed out that the floating rate could reflect market sentiment rather than the real economy, with serious consequences for costs and prices, and for the competitiveness of domestic and foreign goods and services. In autumn 1996, for example, the pound appreciated by 20–5 per cent against European currencies as a result of market concerns about the single currency, which hit exports of British goods. Consequently, 'the insulation provided by a floating exchange rate may prove to be more apparent than real'. The governor was also wary of full membership of the European Monetary Union: it might allow more efficient allocation of resources throughout Europe, but might equally force Britain to follow a European monetary policy that did not meet its domestic needs. His conclusion was sensibly pragmatic, that 'there is no clear best solution, applicable at all times for all currencies, to reconciling the inherent problem of potential conflict between the needs of domestic and external stability'. In his opinion, floating was applicable to an economy with

> a small tradeable sector relative to the size of its domestic economy, but in that case it will need an effective nominal domestic anchor, such as a money supply or inflation target; and it will need an institutional structure – typically an independent central bank – to reinforce the credibility of the commitment to that nominal anchor.

By contrast, fixed rates made more sense in

> smaller, more open, economies or where a credible domestic macro-economic framework is difficult to establish, for example, for historical or political reasons. But in this case it is crucial to recognise that domestic policy must be totally and unreservedly committed to maintaining the fixed exchange rate.

As he pointed out, other options between the two poles of an actively managed float and pegged rates should be rejected as an 'unviable middle ground', lacking 'sufficient discipline on policy' and serving 'to intensify market tensions when a divergence between the policy needs of domestic and external stability does in fact arise'.[59] These words sum up the debate over fixed and floating rates, and their implications for domestic monetary

---

[59] Speech by the governor, 'Leading the way towards sustainable economic growth', speech at the Central Banking Policies Conference, Macau, 14 Aug. 1999, at http://www.bankofengland.co.uk/publications/speeches/1999/speech40.htm, last accessed 3 Apr. 2009.

policy, capital controls and trade policy over the century and a half covered by these lectures. The certainties of the gold standard and of Bretton Woods have given way to a sense of flux and uncertainty.

As I revise this lecture for publication, the Group of 20 has just met in London, and the themes I have considered in these addresses are more relevant than anticipated at the time I decided on the subject of my Presidential adddresses in 2003. What seemed then to be a technical and rebarbative subject is now the topic of daily news broadcasts and conversation on the future of the world economy and domestic prosperity. The governor of the Central Bank of China has recently called for a new supra-currency to replace the dollar somewhat on the lines of Keynes's 'bancor' that was rejected by the Americans in the negotiations leading to Bretton Woods. The plea implies criticism of American handling of dollar's position as the world's reserve currency.

Indeed, there has been talk of 'Bretton Woods II', a fundamentally misguided historical analogy. Unlike in 1944, there is a lack of expert consensus, for not everyone agrees on the solution to be pursued. In the opinion of some commentators, international regulation is not possible, for clever financiers will outwit regulators; others feel that improved, even international, regulation is imperative. This lack of consensus is a major difference from the 1940s when experts were broadly in agreement over the solution, especially through the work of economists attached to the League of Nations. Neither is it clear who can provide leadership. The Bretton Woods agreement of 1944 was the result of a deal struck by Britain and the USA, which was then accepted by the other forty-two countries meeting in 1944. Although the Keynes and White schemes had different assumptions, there was also considerable common ground – and the US had the financial power to impose its own views. There were serious failings with the Bretton Woods agreement, and it was modified after the war in the light of economic realities, but it did provide a basis for post-war financial recovery. The prospects for an agreement are now very different.

The US is widely seen as the problem and not the cure, and consequently has problems in providing leadership. China is the world's major creditor, but its currency is not fully convertible and cannot as yet provide an alternative to the dollar; if it were to become convertible, it would probably appreciate which would reduce its export markets with serious domestic consequences as well as difficulties for the world economy. Equally, if the US took action to improve its balance of payments, reduce its budget deficit and improve domestic savings, it would buy fewer Chinese goods: ending American import-led growth would damage Chinese export-led growth. In both countries, readjustment poses serious domestic problems and could provoke protectionism. Can the Americans and Chinese reach agreement on how to manage this disequilibrium without mutual recriminations; and if they can, how can their decision be legitimated given the 'democratic deficit' in international bodies? Whether international bodies can provide a solution to the financial problems of the world is open to question, and at the very least raises issues about their representation of all interested parties. Will the G-7's Financial Stability Forum be forced to widen its membership to emerging countries; can G-20 find agreement among its own members and secure support from those who are not represented? At present, the signs are as much of tension as agreement.

The task of finding a solution to the international financial crisis is difficult enough, and will only be compounded by attempting to deal with trade at the same time. The financial deal at Bretton Woods was easier to strike than a deal on trade. Bretton Woods dealt with a more technical issue and the agreement was determined by two countries; the conference on trade was much more problematic, running from the initial proposals at the end of 1945 to the closing of the Havana conference in 1948 and the subsequent failure of the International Trade Organization (ITO). Many other countries had voice, and there were deep divisions over issues of development and distributive justice in the world economy which led to the failure of the ITO. Is there any reason to think that agreement will be easier to reach in the near future? In fact, there might be reasons for thinking it might be harder to achieve, despite the promises to restart the stalled talks of the Doha round of the World Trade Organization. By mixing together financial reforms and trade, it might be more difficult to resolve either set of problems: might it make more sense to compartmentalise them? Or does the financial crisis provide the incentive to resolve the deadlock at Doha and to prevent the emergence of protectionism which most countries see as a serious problem?

There are grounds for pessimism. The financial crisis has led to disillusion with open world economies and has intensified anti-globalisation sentiments. Joseph Stiglitz's critique of the Washington consensus in *Globalization and its Discontents* argues for reform of international economic institutions such as the World Bank and World Trade Organization which will be fairer to developing countries. He argues that institutional reform should be complemented by a shift in the 'mindset' of globalisation to take more account of cultural identity and values, in order to create 'globalization with a more human face'. More recently, he has argued for a new approach to debt and a system of global reserves, proposals derided by his critics as utopian and implausible.[60] At the very least, these wider concerns will make solution of immediate

---

[60] Stiglitz, *Globalization and its Discontents*, and *Making Globalization Work* (New York and London, 2006).

issues very difficult. A serious recession threatens to intensify economic nationalism: a FT/Harris poll in July 2007, even before the crisis became so acute, found that in every country surveyed – whether liberal market economies in the US and the UK or in more controlled European economies – more people felt that globalisation was harmful than positive, with the possibility that populist politicians could exploit anti-globalisation rhetoric.[61] The main ground for optimism is that politicians will realise the dangers posed by a collapse of the global economy; it remains to be seen if their actions follow their statement of good intent.

In the first of these four addresses, I referred to the question of whether globalisation might go into reverse in the future as it did between the world wars. Commentators noted various concerns. Might currency misalignment between China and the US lead to the same sort of problems as occurred in 1971 when the dollar was out of line with the Deutschmark and yen? Was there a need to pay more attention to issues of global justice and to reforming the institutions of the IMF and World Bank, and World Trade Organization? Might economic nationalism again appear as a result of widening income inequalities? The general view of commentators when I started these lectures in 2004 was that there was no imminent prospect of a collapse of globalisation as occurred between the wars. Most economists were sanguine that international institutions would stop the worst excesses of beggar-my-neighbour policies which characterised the 1930s. They argued that there was nothing like the coherent oppositional ideology to globalisation of the interwar years, and no Asian equivalent of General De Gaulle who might use financial power to undermine the dollar. But were they being too confident? What Greenspan saw as creating more efficient markets – securitisation and financial liberalisation – has actually spread problems throughout the world and might lead to a backlash of economic nationalism. Larry Summers talked of the balance of financial terror: American budget and trade deficits and lack of savings were made good by Chinese holdings of US Treasury bonds. An optimist might hope that the Chinese holdings of American Treasury bonds are on such a scale that China could not allow the dollar to collapse, and the two countries might cooperate in action to resolve the problem by revaluing the Reminbi and reducing the American budget deficit and increasing domestic savings. But Summers was concerned that the trade deficit might lead to protectionism in America and to dependence on the political discretion of another country. The stakes in this game are now higher than ever, for China fears a loss of its export markets and consequent social instability; and the US has still greater problems in balancing its budget. Will mutual interest lead to a cooperative solution, or might there be a return to economic nationalism?

[61] 'Globalization Generates Dark Thoughts', *Financial Times*, 23 July 2007.

Summers warned in 2004 that American reliance on import-led growth could not continue indefinitely, and hence the export-led growth of other countries could not continue. He warned that 'the consequences of these adjustments being mismanaged are likely to be profound for the global integration process' – and his warning is even more relevant as I deliver this lecture. What the outcome will be remains a topic for future members of this Society to consider.[62]

---

[62] 'Speech by L. Summers, 'The United States and the Global Adjustment Process', at http://www.petersoninstitute.org/publications/papers/paper.cfm?ResearchID = 200, last accessed 3 Apr. 2009.

Transactions of the RHS 19 (2009), pp. 37–55 © Royal Historical Society 2009
doi:10.1017/S008044010999003X

REPRESENTATION *c.* 800: ARAB, BYZANTINE, CAROLINGIAN

By Leslie Brubaker

READ 9 MAY 2008

ABSTRACT. What could or should be visually represented was a contested issue across the medieval Christian and Islamic world around the year 800. This article examines how Islamic, Byzantine, Carolingian and Palestinian Christian attitudes toward representation were expressed, and differed, across the seventh and eighth centuries. Islamic prohibitions against representing human figures were not universally recognised, but were particularly – if sometimes erratically – focused on mosque decoration. Byzantine 'iconoclasm' – more properly called iconomachy – was far less destructive than its later offshoots in France and England, and resulted in a highly nuanced re-definition of what representation meant in the Orthodox church. Carolingian attitudes toward images were on the whole far less passionate than either Islamic or Orthodox views, but certain members of the elite had strong views, which resulted in particular visual expressions. Palestinian Christians, living under Islamic rule, modulated their attitudes toward images to conform with local social beliefs. Particularly in areas under Orthodox or Islamic control, then, representation mattered greatly around the year 800, and this article examines how and why this impacted on local production.

Across the Mediterranean basin, the ways representation was thought about changed across the long eighth century. Beginning around 680, the transformation was more or less complete by *c.* 830. This paper is about why this happened, and what it meant, to the two dominant powers of the Mediterranean in the seventh, eighth and ninth centuries: the Islamic caliphates and, especially, the Byzantine empire. For comparative purposes, I will also look briefly at the Carolingian empire in the west, and the Christian population in Palestine, a region that from the mid-seventh century was ruled by the caliphate from Damascus and then, after 762, from Baghdad.

Talking about representation is complicated, because the word has multiple meanings, and multiple registers within each of these meanings. My focus here will be on only two forms of representation, but even within these two broad definitions we can – and in one case will – find multiple registers of meaning. What one might call social representation is, at the most basic level, about how people display or present or project themselves, both to themselves and to others. (This is the representation that anthropologists and socio-cultural historians talk about.) What one might call a cultural sense of representation is about how authors and artisans present themselves or usually, in the Middle Ages, others, to an audience. This type of representation is governed by what is traditionally called genre: the conventions ruling the particular type of text or image in question. (This is what literary and art historians, and some archaeologists, talk about.) Both understandings of representation – self presentation, on the one hand, and literary or visual images, on the other – are critical for our understanding of the long eighth century, because this is one of the few historical periods in which social and cultural representation, which of course often overlap in practice, were overtly linked, and seriously considered in relation to each other.

I will start with a brief consideration of representation in the Arab world. The 'Islamic conquests' (as they are often called by western historians) followed the death of Mohammed in 632, so that by the middle of the century, Syria, Palestine (including, of course, Jerusalem), the Jazira (between the middle Tigris and the Euphrates), Egypt and the bulk of the former Persian empire was under the control of the Islamic caliphate; by 715, the Arabs also dominated North Africa, Spain and eastward to the Indus valley.[1]

Our main early text for this period, the Koran, maybe dating as a collection from the mid-seventh century and certainly in existence in some form by 690, barely mentions representation and certainly does not make any categorical statement about the right-ness or wrong-ness of literary or visual imagery. But the hadith – a collection of stories concerning the life of Mohammad, the various versions of which are extremely difficult to date with any precision – address the issue of visual representation, and condemn pictures and, especially, makers of pictures. The hadith include statements such as 'the angels will not enter a house in which there is a picture or a dog' or 'those who will be most severely punished on the day of judgement are the murderer of a prophet, one who has been put to death by a prophet ... and a maker of images or pictures'.[2]

This verbal condemnation of imagery and image-makers is, however, moderated by the physical evidence. The early Islamic mosaic panels of unpopulated river landscapes with buildings from the Great Mosque of

---

[1] For a good overview, see H. Kennedy, *The Prophet and the Age of the Caliphates* (1986); F. Donner, *The Early Islamic Conquests* (Princeton, 1981).

[2] For good introductions to this subject see K. Creswell, 'The Lawfulness of Painting in Early Islam', *Ars Islamica*, 11/12 (1946), 159–66, repr. in *Early Islamic Art and Architecture*, ed. J. Bloom, The Formation of the Classical Islamic World 23 (Aldershot, 2002), 101–8; O. Grabar, *The Formation of Islamic Art* (New Haven, 1973), 75–103. For the passages quoted, see *ibid.*, 86.

Figure 1 Damascus, Great Mosque, mosaic of river landscape (photo, Mosaics on the West portico, eighth century The Bridgeman Art Library Nationality/copyright status: out of copyright).

Damascus (Figure 1) – one of the earliest and most sacred buildings of Islam, dating to *c.* 715 – suggest that the real evil was not imagery *per se*, but representations of living creatures, including human beings. Even that was conditional: the material culture preserved from the long eighth century makes it very clear that it was only in the most holy areas of mosques that the prohibition was strictly applied. Baths (as, for example, in the eighth-century complex at Qusayr Amra) were exempt; animals and people certainly appear in the decoration of royal residences (as, for example, in the well-known floor mosaic of a lion attacking gazelles at Khirbat al-Mafjar, also of the eighth century: Figure 2); and images of animals (though not of people) appear in the more peripheral areas of several mosques, including those in the eighth-century complexes at (or formerly at) Mshatta and Qasr al-Hayr. And while the mosaics of the Dome of the Rock are dominated by decorative motifs, cityscapes and rural villa scenes, although unpeopled, appear a decade later, in the courtyard mosaics of the early eighth-century Great Mosque of Damascus, and look remarkably like contemporary and earlier Byzantine work.[3]

---

[3] For the Dome of the Rock, see *The Dome of the Rock*, ed. S. Nuseibeh and O. Grabar (1996); for Qasr Amra, M. Almagro *et al.*, *Qusayr 'Amra. Residencia y baños omeyas en el desierto*

Figure 2 Khirbat al-Mafjar, mosaic of lion attacking gazelles (photo courtesy of the Israel Antiquities Authority).

We may conclude that Arab attitudes toward visual representation discouraged the depiction of living beings, and particularly humans, in specific contexts, notably the mosque. This is a position that does not disdain imagery, but rather acknowledges and respects the ideological power of representation.

The Byzantines also acknowledged and respected the ideological power of representation, and this became particularly important in the late seventh and early eighth centuries, at more or less the same time as the Islamic monuments just noted were conceived.

de Jordania (Madrid, 1975); for Kirbit al-Mafjar, R. Hamilton, *Khirbat al-Mafjar. An Arabian Mansion in the Jordan Valley* (Oxford, 1959); for the Great Mosque, F. Flood, *The Great Mosque of Damascus. Studies on the Makings of an Umayyad Visual Culture* (Leiden, 2001). More generally, see G. Fowden, 'Late Antique Art in Syria and its Umayyad Evolutions', *Journal of Roman Archaeology*, 17 (2004), 282–304.

Before this time, and more specifically, until *c.* 680, images made by human hands were only rarely – and usually problematically – ascribed power. From the fourth century onward, in both Byzantium and the Latin west, relics were believed to convey the real presence of a saint, and thus had miraculous powers to heal and protect, but in the Orthodox east sacred portraits – what we now usually call icons – remained largely commemorative, honouring the memory of the saint portrayed or, in the case of *ex voto* imagery, thanking the saint himself or herself for interceding with Christ on the donor's behalf.[4]

The earliest references to a holy portrait addressed as if it were the saint himself was related by Arculf (who went on pilgrimage to the Holy Land in 683/4) to Adamnán (who recorded the account sometime before 688), as a story he had heard from story-tellers in Constantinople. In brief, a man about to set off on a great military expedition stood before a portrait of the confessor George, and 'began to speak to the portrait as if it were George present in person'; he asked 'to be delivered from all dangers by war'. Adamnán tells us that many died, but the soldier 'was preserved from all misadventure by his commendation to the Christ-loving George, and by the grace of God came safely back. . .and spoke to St George as though he were present in person' again.[5] This is a story, of course, and Arculf and Adamnán made no bones about it having been related by story-tellers. The point is not whether or not the man or the icon actually existed, but rather that this was evidently a story circulating in Constantinople in the 680s, by which time it was, for the first time, thinkable that a saint was actually present in his portrait – that is, that the 'real presence' of the saint reposed in his or her icon. Shortly thereafter, at the Council in Trullo of 691/2, the Orthodox church responded with the first canonical legislation concerning religious imagery;[6] and soon after that, around the year 700, Stephen of Bostra's *Against the Jews* – the earliest anti-Jewish polemic to mention images – notes that 'Veneration is the outward sign by which honour is given' to icons, the oldest secure reference to what appears to mean *proskynesis* (prostration) before images.[7] A generation later, in the 720s, various churchmen condemned the holy portraits, and,

---

[4] P. Brown, *The Cult of the Saints. Its Rise and Function in Latin Christianity* (Chicago, 1981); L. Brubaker, 'Icons before Iconoclasm?', *Morfologie sociali e culturali in europa fra tarda antichità e alto medioevo*, Settimane di Studio del Centro Italiano di Studi sull'Alto Medioevo 45 (Spoleto, 1998), 1215–54.

[5] Ed. L. Bieler, in *Itineraria et alia geographica*, Corpus christianorum, series latine 175 (Turnhout, 1965), 231–2; Eng. trans. J. Wilkinson, *Jerusalem Pilgrims before the Crusades* (Warminster, 1977), 114–15.

[6] L. Brubaker, '*In the Beginning Was the Word*: Art and Orthodoxy at the Councils of Trullo (692) and Nicaea II (787)', in *Byzantine Orthodoxies*, ed. A. Louth and A. Casiday (Aldershot, 2006), 95–101.

[7] The text is known only through later citation in John of Damascus and the iconophile florilegia; John of Damascus, *Against Those Who Attack the Divine Images*, III, 73: ed. B. Kotter,

ultimately, the movement we call iconoclasm (the destruction of images) – but which the Byzantines called, more accurately, iconomachy (the struggle about images) – was officially declared in 754.[8] The critical issue is why sacred portraits became widely accepted as means of accessing the divine comparable to relics around the year 680. Why was 680 the tipping point?

The seventh century was not a happy period for the east Roman empire. Its first quarter was occupied with Persian and Avar invasions, culminating in the siege of Constantinople of 626, when a relic-icon of Christ was famously credited with saving the city.[9] Though the Constantinopolitan repulsion of the siege basically ended the Avar threat, the Persians continued to occupy the empire's military attention for another year, until Herakleios defeated them in 627/8. Seven years later, however, Syria and Palestine were in the hands of a new rival, the Arabs, and, with the battle of the Yarmuk in 636, the Arab conquests began seriously to affect the empire; within the next decade, Byzantium lost its richest province, Egypt. By 650, Byzantium was halved in size, had lost its major agricultural base and, with few financial or military resources in reserve and its infrastructure severely shaken, was presumably low in morale. All of this had, as one might expect, a profound impact on the empire, and it has been rightly argued by many that the seventh century witnessed a decisive shift in Byzantine social, political and cultural interests.[10] The impact of these socio-political events was accentuated – and rhetorically overshadowed – by the heresy (in Byzantine eyes) of the instigators of these problems, Islam.

The Byzantines saw the Arab invasions as God's punishment for their sins. In a sermon delivered in 634, for example, the patriarch of Jerusalem told his audience that 'We have only to repent, and we shall blunten the Ishmaelite sword...and break the Hagarene bow, and see Bethlehem again.'[11] But by the end of the century, it was no longer possible to

Die Schriften des Johannes von Damaskos, III: *Contra imaginum calumniatores orationes tres*, Patristische Texte und Studien 17 (Berlin, 1975), 174; Eng. trans. D. Anderson, *St John of Damascus, On the Divine Images, Three Apologies against Those Who Attack the Divine Images* (Crestwood, NY, 1980), 96.

[8] The history of iconomachy is discussed at length in L. Brubaker and J. Haldon, *Byzantium in the Era of Iconoclasm* (Cambridge, forthcoming). For the terminology, see J. Bremmer, 'Iconoclast, Iconoclastic, and Iconoclasm: Notes toward a Genealogy', *Church History and Religious Culture*, 88 (2008), 1–17.

[9] B. Pentcheva, 'The Supernatural Protector of Constantinople: The Virgin and her Icons in the Tradition of the Avar Siege', *Byzantine and Modern Greek Studies*, 26 (2002), 2–41.

[10] For details to flesh out this cursory summary, see J. Haldon, *Byzantium in the Seventh Century: The Transformation of a Culture*, rev. edn (Cambridge, 1997).

[11] See S. Brock, 'Syriac Views of Emergent Islam', in *Studies on the First Century of Islamic Society*, ed. G. Juynboll (Carbondale, IL, 1982), 9–21, 199–203 (trans. at 9), esp. 10–11, 16–17; repr. in *idem*, *Syriac Perspectives on Late Antiquity* (1984), study 8.

expect that Islam and the Arab threat was going to be overcome by force, diplomacy or an act of God.[12] Already in 686, John of Phenek wrote that 'the end of the world has arrived',[13] and this feeling was strengthened by the consolidation of Arab power under 'Abd al-Malik in the years up to 692. Though the eastern front remained relatively secure across the last fifteen years of the century, the social and cultural instability of the last quarter of the century is clear, and is particularly well expressed in the *Apocalypse* of pseudo-Methodios (written in Syria, probably in 691),[14] and the records of the Council in Trullo of 691/2, which as we have just seen are also distinguished by the earliest canonical legislation about imagery.[15]

The *Apocalypse* of pseudo-Methodios was written in the expectation and hope that the end of the world was about to begin with the fall of the Arabs. Sebastian Brock has compellingly argued that the *Apocalypse* was inspired, at least in part, by 'Abd al-Malik's census (or rumours about it) preparatory to imposing a new taxation system in Mesopotamia; as Muslims, including newly converted former Christians, were exempt from the poll tax, the underlying fear seems to be that the church would lose considerable numbers to the mosque.[16] Gerrit Reinink has expanded this thesis in a number of articles, most recently concluding that 'Undoubtedly this fear was rooted in the awareness that the recovery of Islamic power, going hand in hand with the frustration of apocalyptic hopes and greatly increased taxation of Christians, created circumstances highly favourable to conversion to Islam.'[17] In short, in areas under Arab control, the critical

---

[12] The most important contemporary sources are a history attributed to a certain Sebeos (J. D. Howard-Johnston and F. Thomson, *The Armenian History Attributed to Sebeos* (2 vols., Liverpool, 1999)), the church councils of 680 and 691 and a series of apocalyptic texts, the most important of which is that of pseudo-Methodios: W. E. Kaegi, 'Initial Byzantine Reactions to the Arab Conquests', *Church History*, 38 (1969), 139–49; Brock, 'Syriac Views'; and the articles collected in *The Byzantine and Early Islamic Near East*, I: *Problems in the Literary Source Material*, ed. A. Cameron and L. Conrad, Studies in Late Antiquity and Early Islam 1 (Princeton, 1992).

[13] See Brock, 'Syriac Views', 15–17; R. Hoyland, *Seeing Islam as Others Saw It. A Survey and Evaluation of Christian, Jewish and Zoroastrian Writings on Early Islam*, Studies in Late Antiquity and Early Islam 13 (Princeton, 1997).

[14] G. Reinink, 'Ps.-Methodius: A Concept of History in Response to the Rise of Islam', in *The Byzantine and Early Islamic Near East*, I, ed. Cameron and Conrad, 149–87; *idem, Die syrische Apokalypse des Pseudo-Methodius*, Corpus scriptorium christianorum orientalium 541 (Louvain, 1993); Brock, 'Syriac Views', 19. For an overview of the political situation, see Haldon, *Byzantium in the Seventh Century*, 69–78.

[15] *The Council in Trullo Revisited*, ed. G. Nedungatt and M. Featherstone, Kanonika 6 (Rome, 1995).

[16] Brock, 'Syriac Views', 19; Reinink 'Ps.-Methodius', esp. 178, 181, with additional literature.

[17] Reinink, 'Ps.-Methodius', 181. It now appears unlikely that this conversion was substantial till the ninth century, but the fears were nonetheless real.

destabilising factors expressed by local Christians at the end of the century were eschatological, driven by fear of apostasy and financial insecurity.

The anxieties expressed by the churchmen who recorded the deliberations of the Trullan Council of 691/2 were somewhat different. In addition to providing the first Byzantine canonical legislation about religious images – which, as we have seen, appears to have been a response to the surge in the powers of sacred portraiture a decade earlier – many of the canons expressed concern for the first time about long-standing practices (for example, the 'hellenic' festival of Brumalia, condemned in canon 62) that had never before exercised the religious establishment.[18] What the canons seek above all is a means to purify the church, and like most purification rituals they are more symbolic than practical: the Brumalia, to return to the example just cited, continued to be observed in Constantinople until the twelfth century.[19]

The attempt to regulate and cleanse is equally apparent in one of the canons about imagery, which is, oddly, rarely discussed by Byzantinists. Canon 100 instructed 'that those things which incite pleasures (hēdonē) are not to be portrayed on panels'. After a paraphrased citation of Proverbs 4:23–5, it continued: 'for the sensations of the body all too easily influence the soul. Therefore, we command that henceforth absolutely no pictures should be drawn which enchant the eyes, be they on panels or set forth in any other wise, corrupting the mind and inciting the flames of shameful pleasures.'[20] Canon 100 was overtly concerned with issues of corruption and purity; and it was particularly focused on the distinction between good and bad images. This same theme was the concern of the better-known canon 82, where the historical portrait of Christ was preferred to the symbolic lamb. In Canon 100, however, the distinction is not between the historical and the symbolic, but between images that incite pleasure and other, unspecified images. It is only in the eighth century that we will learn that the aim of good pictures, Orthodox pictures, is to elicit the tears of purifying sanctity, and to induce the emulation of saintly virtues.[21] In 691/2, this has not yet become a standard trope, and it was enough to stress that imagery had a distinct purpose, and that purpose was not aesthetic pleasure. It is clearer here than in any other section of

---

[18] See J. Herrin, '"Femina Byzantina": The Council of Trullo on Women', *Dumbarton Oaks Papers*, 46 (1992), 97–105; Haldon, *Byzantium in the Seventh Century*, 333–7.

[19] *Oxford Dictionary of Byzantium*, I, ed. A. Kashdan *et al.* (Oxford, 1991), 327–8; M.-F. Auzépy, *La vie d'Étienne le Jeune par Étienne le Diacre. Introduction, édition et traduction*, Birmingham Byzantine and Ottoman Monographs 3 (Aldershot, 1997), 262 n. 393.

[20] *Council in Trullo*, ed. Nedungatt and Featherstone, 180–1; an extended version of this argument appeared in Brubaker, 'Art and Orthodoxy'.

[21] See, e.g., L. Brubaker, *Vision and Meaning in Ninth-Century Byzantium. Image as Exegesis in the Homilies of Gregory of Nazianzus*, Cambridge Studies in Palaeography and Codicology 6 (Cambridge, 1999), 19–58.

the Trullan canons that the churchmen are using words about one thing (in this case, images) to talk about something else entirely (in this case, purity).[22] But it is also clear that they are interested in controlling what can be represented, a point to which we shall return shortly.

The attempts of the Trullan churchmen to standardise and cleanse Orthodox practice stemmed from a sense of uncertainty and anxiety that is continued in Anastasios of Sinai's *Questions and Answers*, probably composed at the very end of the seventh century,[23] where Anastasios writes quite plainly that the 'present generation' is enduring a period of spiritual crisis.[24] His work on struggles against demons (the *Diēgēmata stēriktika*, probably composed in its original formulation around 690) continues the purification theme.[25] Indeed, from the late seventh century, the need for internal purity becomes a constant theme of both theological and 'state' rhetoric.[26]

In short, by the later seventh century, Islam and the Arabs had become a permanent fixture, and by the end of the century the surviving texts document the impact this had on the circumstances of Christian life. It is in this context that we must understand the emergence of holy portraits as a means to access divine presence around the year 680. As we have seen, the earliest reference to a holy portrait addressed as if it were the saint is the story about the soldier and the icon of St George recorded by Adamnán. The soldier, we saw, asked 'to be delivered from all dangers by war', and Adamnán tells us that 'It was a war full of danger, and there were many thousands of men who perished miserably. But he...was preserved from all misadventure by his commendation to the Christ-loving George, and by the grace of God came safely back.'[27] The unidentified war of the story can only have been against the Arabs, and so we find the first clear indication of the absorption of 'normal' icons into the cult of relics firmly located in the context of the Islamic conquests of the later seventh century.

---

[22] For discussion of this phenomenon, see Brubaker, 'Art and Orthodoxy'.

[23] J. Haldon, 'The Works of Anastasios of Sinai: A Key Source for the History of Seventh-Century East Mediterranean Society and Belief', in *The Byzantine and Early Islamic Near East*, I, ed. Cameron and Conrad, 107–47.

[24] *Ibid.*, 132.

[25] See B. Flusin, 'Démons et sarrasins. L'auteur et le propos des Diègèmata stèriktika d'Anastase le Sinaïte', *Travaux et mémoires*, 11 (1991), 380–409, but on the problems with the text see also L. Brubaker and J. Haldon, *Byzantium in the Iconoclast Era (ca 680–850): The Sources*, Birmingham Byzantine and Ottoman monographs 7 (Aldershot, 2001), 254 n. 41. On the role of icons in the treatise, see Brubaker, 'Icons before Iconoclasm?', 1250 n. 114.

[26] Similarly, the focus of much popular theological literature was about the nature of divine authority, the relationship between right belief and human experience, and the extent to which divine intervention in human affairs could be demonstrated. See further Haldon, *Byzantium in the Seventh Century*, esp. 144–5.

[27] Ed. Bieler, *Itineraria*, 231–2; trans. Wilkinson, *Jerusalem Pilgrims*, 114–15.

To cut a long story short, the shift in the way sacred portraits were received in Byzantium was, I think, a product of late seventh-century insecurities. God was punishing the Byzantines, and the Arabs were not going to disappear anytime soon. The state, the church and the individual Orthodox believer – all in a state of spiritual crisis – needed help, in the form of new channels of access to divinity. Investing real presence into sacred portraits painted by living people allowed virtually limitless multiplication of direct intermediaries between humans and the holy, in the same way as, centuries earlier, contact relics had solved the problem of limited human remains of saints. The critical issue is the transference from physical presence (the power of relics) to representation (the power of icons), and to that we will now turn.

As noted earlier, social representation (self presentation) and cultural representation (visual imagery) were overtly linked in our period, and the connection between late seventh-century Byzantine self presentation – with all of its expressions of personal and institutional crisis – and changes in the role of visual imagery bring this out nicely. But just as in the Arab world, where as we saw earlier there was a kind of hierarchy of image appropriateness (human figures are fine in a bath house but not in a mosque), so too in Byzantium there are several registers of representation.

Indeed, the erudite Byzantine churchmen who have left us records of their thoughts were quite clear on the distinction between different types of representation, especially as they applied to the theological arguments of iconomachy. These theological arguments are important for understanding the intellectual history of the Byzantine empire, but they are largely beside the point for its social or even cultural history. Just as the Trullan Council followed and responded to a new role for the sacred portrait, so too the theology of the veneration of icons followed along and either codified changes in social practice or attempted to limit them. By systematising the role of sacred portraits in Orthodoxy, eighth- and ninth-century theologians created the *cult* and the *theology* of icons, but they did not create the desire to access the holy in a new way: they justified and codified existing realities. Legislation about images followed changes in custom; theory, in short, followed practice.

This takes us back to Canon 100 of the Trullan Council, where the churchmen instructed that 'things which incite pleasures are not to be portrayed on panels'. As we have seen, this is about purification, but it is also an attempt to control sacred imagery, and to ensure that the newly powerful images were painted in an Orthodox manner. What is important here is that the churchmen did not yet know quite how to explain what 'good' painting was: this once again demonstrates that theology was responding to (rather than leading) changes in practice. But the Trullan churchmen were nonetheless well aware that the significance of representation was changing, and they wanted to ensure that representation remained Orthodox and that they maintained a level of control over it. This hope was only partially fulfilled. The theology of icons that developed across the eighth and ninth centuries has been explored in considerable depth, and the major Byzantine players – particularly from the second Council of Nicaea in 787 onwards – have left lengthy accounts of the significance of representation in the Orthodox world that allow us to understand in some detail how the Byzantines saw.[28] But the problems with relying too heavily on the theology of icons for our understanding of issues of representation in Byzantium are well brought out by a recent analysis of the former patriarch Nikephoros's discussion of the relationship between a portrait and the one portrayed, written shortly after 815, which summarised Nikephoros's conclusions as follows: 'Thus, when an icon is destroyed, it is an offence against the formal, that is to say, visible, properties of the one shown. One does not destroy Christ when one destroys his icon, rather one destroys the possibility of his becoming available to vision.'[29] What Nikephoros meant by this was that the icon, made by human hands, was a manufactured artefact, and the portrait was therefore distinct from its subject – this is a portrait of Christ, it is not Christ himself. When Orthodox viewers looked at the icon of Christ, they could then concentrate their minds on the contemplation of Christ himself. The icon – understood as a manufactured artefact – functioned as an aide-mémoire.

This argument, which demonstrates a good grasp of Aristotelian logic, was developed by Orthodox churchmen in the later eighth and ninth centuries to demonstrate that an image *was* an image, different from its subject, and not to be confused with it: that is, the two levels of representation involved were distinct. From this reasoning it followed that icons were acceptable – even 'truthful' – precisely *because* they were manufactured.[30] But comparison of this theologically correct passage with accounts of how people responded to icons in daily life also demonstrates the sharp contrast between the theology of learned churchmen (the 'theory' of icons) and the response to images considered appropriate in accounts of people in everyday situations (the 'practice' of icons).

[28] See L. Brubaker, 'Byzantine Art in the Ninth Century: Theory, Practice, and Culture', *Byzantine and Modern Greek Studies*, 13 (1989), 23–93; R. Nelson, 'To Say and to See: Ekphrasis and Vision in Byzantium', in *Visuality Before and Beyond the Renaissance. Seeing as Others Saw*, ed. R. Nelson (Cambridge, 2000), 143–68.

[29] C. Barber, *Figure and Likeness. On the Limits of Representation in Byzantine Iconoclasm* (Princeton, 2002), 122.

[30] P. Alexander, *The Patriarch Nicephorus of Constantinople. Ecclesiastical Policy and Image Worship in the Byzantine Empire* (Oxford, 1958), 189–213; Barber, *Image and Likeness*, 107–23, both with additional bibliography.

For the properties of the sacred portrait so carefully distinguished in learned theological treatises disappear in other contexts, even in letters written by the same elevated churchmen who were careful to maintain an Aristotelian balance when writing icon theory. Theodore of Stoudion (759–826), for example, was as commited as was Nikephoros to the Orthodox theological position that expressed the relative relationship between a portrait and the person portrayed; but when writing a letter to the *spatharios* John, he nevertheless praised him for replacing a human godfather with an icon of St Demetrios for 'here the bodily image took the place of its model' and 'the great martyr was spiritually present in his own image and so received the infant'.[31] Here, and even more visibly in hagiographies and miracle accounts, the icon *was* the person represented, and respect to the one was, directly, respect to the other.

On one level, this distinction simply exemplifies the importance of context: theological treatises require the careful formulation of image theory; letters to friends are less formal. But the contrast between the theological understanding of the sacred portrait and the day-to-day reception of the same image is not only about discrete registers of response: it is also, and more importantly, about different understandings of representation.

To Theodore of Stoudion and his fellow churchmen, an icon of St Demetrios could be both an artefact, an object made by human hands, differentiated from the saint, and sharing with Demetrios only likeness, not essence,[32] *and* a manifestation of the saint, standing in for the real Demetrios, who is 'spiritually present in his own image'. The first, theological, understanding of the icon – the icon as artefact – kept holy portraits from being idols and gave the Byzantines arguments with which to counter the Islamic critique of Orthodox imagery, which claimed that the Christians venerated wood. The second understanding of the icon – the sacred portrait as a window to the saint – allowed the image to stand in for the saint pictured; this understanding of the icon presented the saint himself or herself to the worshipper and it is this icon that the faithful kiss when they enter a church, and which became part of Byzantine self-identity. The artefactual, theological icon is a panel painting; in Charles Barber's phrase, 'a signpost whose insistent presence directs us elsewhere' not 'a self-effacing doorway that opens upon another place'.[33] The Byzantines did not interact with an icon understood in this way, they contemplated it. But the second way of understanding an icon – as an

---

[31] Theodore of Stoudion, letter: *Theodori Studitae Epistulae*, I, ed. A. Fatouros, Corpus fontium historiae byzantinae 31/1–2 (Vienna, 1992), 17; trans. C. Mango, *The Art of the Byzantine Empire 312–1453* (Englewood Cliffs, 1972), 174–5.

[32] See, e.g., Barber, *Figure and Likeness*, 122–3.

[33] *Ibid.*, 137.

embodiment of real presence – *is* 'a self-effacing doorway', leading to the saint depicted; and the Byzantines collaborated with icons understood in this way, through veneration. Such collaboration with the image – through kissing or venerating it in other ways, through installing it as a godfather – allowed the Byzantines to interact on a deeply personal level with the icon/saint, so that even today the medium most commonly associated with the Byzantines is the icon. This level of representation was developed by practice, not by theological theory, which indeed never fully caught up with it.

The acceptance of sacred portraits as mediators between the earthly and the divine did not need this dual understanding of representation, it only required the second, a belief in the icon as real presence. The desire for additional and enhanced access to the holy was, as we have seen, a product of the serial crises of the seventh century. But, as at least some churchmen were quick to realise, accepting real presence in icons had the potential to unleash uncontrolled, and uncontrollable, rights to the sacred, for icons were infinitely reproducible. The Trullo Council began the process of regulating Orthodox imagery, but it was really only after the iconoclast backlash instigated in the 720s, and especially during the debates about imagery across the eighth and ninth centuries, that rules and regulations – the Orthodox theory of representation – were fully developed, and the theological icon was born.

Arab and Byzantine ideas about representation have, we can see, many differences, but some similarities. Most significantly, across the long eighth century, both Islam and Orthodox Christianity accepted the power of representation: this is why, in one way or another, both religions tried to regulate its use. Carolingian ideas about representation were very different, and we will briefly turn to these, with a focus on how the Carolingians presented themselves in relationship to what they understood about Byzantium.

I will concentrate on the Frankish response to the Byzantine Council of Nicaea, which in 787 temporarily restored icon veneration. Shortly thereafter, Frankish theologians drew up the *Capitulare adversus synodum* (preserved only in Pope Hadrian I's point-by-point refutation of it), which criticised the decisions taken at Nicaea. The Frankish theologians challenged the evidence adduced in support of icon veneration as an established and ancient Christian tradition, and insisted that the Bible never supported the making or veneration of images. In response to Pope Hadrian's denunciation of this critique, Charlemagne ordered a detailed review of the issues raised, which resulted in what was in effect an independent and autonomous Frankish theological position.[34]

---

[34] For a good overview, see D. Ganz, 'Theology and the Organisation of Thought', in *New Cambridge Medieval History*, II, ed. R. McKitterick (Cambridge, 1995), 758–85, esp. 773–5.

This was the *Opus Caroli Regis contra synodum*, better known as the *Libri Carolini*, compiled between 791 and 793 by the leading theologians at the Frankish court, predominantly Theodulf of Orléans. From the point of view of the theology of images, the *Libri Carolini* adopt a position quite similar to the iconoclast council of 754, with the same emphasis on the traditions of the Old Testament (though unlike any Byzantine commentary on images, the *Libri Carolini* follow the standard western view of images as texts for the illiterate, a tradition inaugurated roughly two centuries earlier by Pope Gregory the Great). According to the *Libri Carolini*, and the synod of Frankfurt which followed, the image held its status by virtue of its ability to recall, remind and instruct. But there should be no cultic practices associated with it: these were a novelty of recent times, an argument which is, again, very close to that of the iconoclast council of 754 (and which was, in fact, as we have seen, true).[35]

The arguments about representation in the *Libri Carolini* are embedded in more overtly political issues concerning the relationship between Aachen and Rome, and Theodulf's particular views about religious art were quickly dropped from Charlemagne's agenda. But we can see how they worked in practice in Theodulf's own oratory at Germigny-des-Prés, constructed in the 790s shortly after the *Libri Carolini* were written. The oratory is a small building with non-figural sculptural decoration and an apse mosaic focused on an image of the ark of the covenant (Figure 3).[36]

The ark of the covenant is described several times in the Old Testament, and the salient passage is Exodus 25:18–20, where, despite the second commandment forbidding graven images, God ordered Moses to decorate the tabernacle with cherubim. To the Byzantines, God's command to produce and decorate the ark and the tabernacle was the ultimate defence of Christian imagery. Theodulf, in contrast, argued that the ark did not justify the mundane production of religious images because it was not a human commission: God commanded Moses to have it made. Against the Byzantine belief that the ark supplied a rationale for Christian representation, Theodulf understood the ark as a pale Old Testament prefiguration, now surpassed by the realities of the New.[37]

Theodulf's mosaic shows two angels, mimicked by two smaller cherubim, actively gesturing toward the empty ark and, below that, toward the altar itself; a hand of God in the centre of the composition is marked by the stigmata of the risen Christ. Unlike Greek images of the

---

[35] A. Freeman, 'Carolingian Orthodoxy and the Fate of the *Libri Carolini*', *Viator*, 16 (1985), 65–108; *eadem*, 'Scripture and Images in the Libri Carolini', *Testo e immagine nell'alto medioevo*, Settimane di Studio del Centro Italiano di Studi sull'Alto Medioevo 41 (Spoleto, 1994), 163–88.

[36] See A. Freeman and P. Meyvaert, 'The Meaning of Theodulf's Apse Mosaic at Germigny-des-Prés', *Gesta*, 40/2 (2001), 125–39.

[37] *Ibid.*

Figure 3 Germigny-des-Prés, oratory of Theodulf, apse mosaic (photo, author).

ark of the covenant, which show the ark of Exodus, Theodulf's version demonstrates how the prophesies of the Old Testament, represented by the ark, have been replaced by the historical reality of Christ, whose incarnation fulfilled the promises of the old laws, and whose death and resurrection superseded them. The ark is now empty; Christ is present at the altar in the form of the eucharist.[38]

Theodulf's ideas are striking, but they did not have a marked impact on Carolingian thought, perhaps because, apart from Claudius of Turin in the 820s, no one aside from a tiny handful of intellectuals – mostly of Spanish origin – thought that theories of representation were an urgent issue at all.[39] Images were not, and never became, integral to western theology. So while Theodulf's ideas are radically different from those we have seen in Islamic and Byzantine Orthodox circles, we cannot really

[38] *Ibid.*

[39] See Ganz, 'Theology and the Organisation of Thought'; and for Claudius J. van Banning, 'Claudius von Turin als eine extreme Konsequenz des Konzils von Frankfurt', in *Das Frankfurter Konzil von 794, Kristallisationspunkt karolingischer Kultur*, II: *Kultur und Theologie*, ed. R. Berndt (Mainz, 1997), 731–49; M. Gorman, 'The Commentary on Genesis of Claudius of Turin and Biblical Studies under Louis the Pious', *Speculum*, 71 (1997), 279–328.

generalise about Carolingian attitudes toward representation from them. The lack of attention paid to Theodulf's work, however, suggests that religious imagery simply did not have the potential to be as powerful in the Carolingian west as it did in the Arab and Byzantine worlds, and indeed in the hybrid world of Christian Palestine.

Palestine was part of the Roman and then the Byzantine empire, and was predominantly Christian when it was conquered by the Arabs. As one of the wealthier provinces of Byzantium, it had hundreds of well-built, lavishly decorated and large churches. The Christian inhabitants of what became Islamic Palestine were allowed to retain their churches and their religion, without any apparent restrictions, and probably remained a majority there for the whole period under consideration here. Nonetheless, figural decoration apparently died out in the churches used by Christians living under Islamic rule: the latest dated floors with figural mosaics seems to be those in St Stephen's church at Umm al-Rasas (718), the church on the Acropolis in Ma'in (719/20) and the church of St George at Deir al-'Adas in southern Syria (722). All subsequent eighth-century churches in the region reveal only floral and geometric ornament.[40]

At the same time, we find a new phenomenon: during the second quarter of the eighth century, people and animals inhabiting church floor mosaics were replaced, or partially replaced, by non-representational motifs. A good example is provided by the mosaic floor of St Stephen's basilica at Kastron Mefaa (modern Umm al-Rasas), which is dated by an inscription to 718. The donors of the mosaic (Figure 4) were originally portrayed on either side of the inscription, and it is still evident where the donors were pictured – but the greater part of each figure has been reconstructed by removing the tesserae and replacing them at random This scrambled cube technique was also later applied to the animate motifs in the mosaics of the main body of the nave, which shows a vine scroll that was once filled with figures and animals. Around this is wrapped a river scene, also disfigured, but with intact representations of ten cities along the Jordan river.[41]

A second, and well-known, example was excavated in Ma'in, which is about 35 km away from Kastron Mefaa, where an inscription dated the floor mosaics of the church on the Akropolis to 719/20. Here a panel which once illustrated Isaiah 65:24, 'And the lion shall eat chaff like the ox'

[40] R. Schick, *The Christian Communities of Palestine from Byzantine to Islamic Rule: A Historical and Archaeological Study*, Studies in Late Antiquity and Early Islam 2 (Princeton, 1995); Brubaker and Haldon, *Byzantium in the Iconoclast Era: The Sources*, 30–6.

[41] M. Piccirillo and E. Alliata, *Umm al-Rasas/Mayfa'ah*, 1:0 *Gli scavi complesso di Santo Stefano*, Studium biblicum franciscorum, Collectio major 28 (Jerusalem, 1994); Schick, *Christian Communities of Palestine*, 472–3.

Figure 4 Umm al-Rasas, St Stephen's church, donor mosaics (photo courtesy of †Michele Piccarillo).

now shows a tree and an urn with bits of the ox protruding anarchically (Figure 5); the lion has not survived at all.[42]

Clearly, Palestinian responses to imagery were not the same as those within the Byzantine empire. Byzantine theories of representation focused on holy portraits while Palestinian Christians were concerned with representations of any living creature; and for this reason Susanna Ognibene has coined the label 'iconophobia' for the Palestinian phenomenon.[43] In fact, the Byzantine rulings against the veneration of images at the Council of Hieria in 754 were not accepted by the Christian church hierarchy in the east: the Council was condemned in 760, 764 and 767 by eastern synods and patriarchs, and two of the strongest voices against the Byzantine position were raised by the eastern monks John of Damascus and Theodore Abu Qurrah.[44] Iconophobia in Palestine was neither inspired

[42] M. Piccirillo, *The Mosaics of Jordan* (Amman, 1992), 196–201; Schick, *Christian Communities of Palestine*, 398–9.

[43] S. Ognibene, *Umm al-Rasas: la chiesa di Santo Stefano ed it 'problema iconofobico'* (Rome, 2002).

[44] See Schick, *Christian Communities of Palestine*, 210–11.

Figure 5 Ma'in, church on the Akropolis, mosaic (photo courtesy of †Michele Piccarillo).

by Byzantine anti-image legislation (or iconoclast beliefs) nor, it seems, was it spurred by any official Islamic policy: the edict against Christian images supposedly issued by the caliph Yazid II in 721 is now generally discounted as an anti-Islamic invention of later Christian writers (it is first mentioned in 787 at the seventh ecumenical Council of Nicaea).[45] Furthermore, many churches that were assuredly still in use in the mid-seventh century were not affected, and, most notably, there is no evidence of *hostile* destruction. As Robert Schick has argued forcefully, the disfigurement, when it appears, is so carefully done we must assume that the people who used and respected the buildings affected were responsible – in other words, the Christian congregations modified their own church floors.[46]

---

[45] See *ibid.*, 215–17.

[46] S. Griffith, 'What Has Constantinople to Do with Jerusalem? Palestine in the Ninth Century: Byzantine Orthodoxy in the World of Islam', in *Byzantium in the Ninth Century: Dead*

In fact, Palestinian 'iconophobia' was more similar to Islamic prohibitions than to the imperial iconoclasm generated in Constantinople, and I have argued elsewhere that that the cultural to-and-fro between Palestinian Christians and their Islamic neighbours – local neighbourhood politics; peer pressure, really – inspired Palestinian Christians to remove (mostly) human, animals and birds from their church floors.

'Mostly' is the operative word here, for just as the Roman *damnatio memoria* (the cutting out of names of disgraced people on statuary) usually left the viewer with just enough information to identify the figure being damned, so too the Palestinian Christians often left just enough of the figure or animal to make it clear what had been removed. I would guess that this is because the process of accommodation (of their neighbours' attitude toward images) was what was important here, rather than agreement with Islamic beliefs about representation.

To conclude: 680 was a turning point in attitudes toward representation in the Orthodox Christian world and, if we accept a date in the late seventh century for the emergence of the early hadith, also for Islam. The coincidence here is striking, especially given the absence of any evidence for a comparable shift in the Christian west. In is also significant that the impact of the turning point appears to enter another register when it hits the Palestinian Christian community – here practice continued to lead where theory (the words of John of Damascus and Theodore Abu Qurra) never follows – but the process of accommodation is quite distinct from either the hierarchy of representation we see in Islam or the two coexisting understandings of representation that we see in Byzantium.

And this takes us back to the beginning – to the two levels of representation with which we began: the social (self presentation) and the cultural (visual imagery). At the end of the seventh century, Byzantine self presentation was, as we have seen, dominated by a sense of personal and institutional crisis; by the end of the image struggle in 843 – indeed already by *c.* 800 – Byzantium had its self-confidence back. At the end of the seventh century, Byzantine attitudes toward images changed radically; by *c.* 800 these shifts had been codified and canonised. In the process, two registers – the theological icon and the icon as real presence – had been created and, in the Orthodox church, they still remain.

Transactions of the RHS 19 (2009), pp. 57–93 © Royal Historical Society 2009
doi:10.1017/S0080440109990041

HUMANISM AND REFORM IN PRE-REFORMATION ENGLISH MONASTERIES

By James G. Clark

READ 8 FEBRUARY 2008

ABSTRACT. It is commonly understood the old monastic order in England confronted the King's Reformation unreformed: the houses of the Benedictines, Cistercians and Cluniacs were seemingly untouched by the spirit of renewal that charged continental congregations in the conciliar era, and their conventional patterns of observant life persisted in the face of a fast-changing world beyond the precinct walls. This paper reexamines this view. There was no formal process of congregational reform in England and the effectiveness of the order's governing bodies faltered over the course of the fifteenth century. Yet the responsiveness of the monks to contemporary trends in learning and teaching and in patterns of personal and corporate devotion may be traced in many of their manuscript records. This is indicative, certainly, of the lively engagement of individual brethren but in a number of instances it can be read as part of a collective impulse for reform that animated the house as a whole, and perhaps even networks of houses. It was an impulse that owed much to a generation of (generally, graduate) monks that rose to prominence against the background of the great church councils; their influence allowed it to flourish, albeit briefly, in the triennial sessions of the Benedictine chapters. Their interest in humanism passed to the next generation of superiors, some of whom appear to have transformed their conventual *curricula*. Their pioneering work perhaps also stimulated a refined conception of the monastic profession which blossomed in the half-century before the suppressions, one suffused with a sharp, one might say, antiquarian sense of the heritage of early English monasticism, and the scholarly calibre and spiritual purity of its celebrated fathers. The energy that emanated from a number of these houses in the reigns of Henry VII and his son attracted like-minded seculars into collaborations that were not necessarily claustral in focus but certainly reformist in tone. Of course, such extra-mural interest and interaction did little to defend the monastic redoubt from the assault of the Cromwellian commissioners.

In the early medieval centuries of conversion and colonisation the fortunes of the monastic communities of England and mainland Europe were interwoven: they were animated by a common impulse for worship, work and study, undermined, if not extinguished, by parallel patterns of invasion and (re)conquest, and reinvigorated by the same phases of reform. The ascendancy of the monasteries of Benedictine origin between 1050 and 1200 was derived to a degree from their bonds of observance, spirituality and scholarship which seemed to reach so readily across regional and political boundaries. Yet in the later Middle Ages, and perhaps in particular in the period after the Black Death (1348–50) and the outbreak of papal schism (1378), it seems the common fraternity of monks began to fragment: the transmission of ideas, books and brethren dwindled and supra-national corporate structures and their legislative supervision it seems were all but forgotten.

The Benedictines of northern, central and (some) southern states emerged from the flux of this period reorganised into regional congregations – Bursfeld, Melk, Padua – following a mode of monastic life which had been reformed in the light of the spiritual and theological renewal stimulated by the general councils of the church and the intellectual revival of the Italian humanists.[1] At the heart of their programme was a refined conception of monastic learning, not only as a disciplinary adjunct to the *Opus Dei* (as Benedict himself had conceived it), or as a necessary preparation (as papal reformers had presented it) for monks to fulfil their pastoral and priestly obligations, but as the sole foundation on which the *professus* might raise their pursuit of spiritual perfection: a learning that led them to a true understanding of their vocation, the *vera eruditio monasticae* of earlier times.[2] The syllabus of study fused the *studia humanitatis* with a form of scriptural exposition which the reformers believed to be an evocation of the pure *lectio divina* of their founder. The priority which the humanists placed upon proficiency in language would provide an ideal preparation for a lifetime's reflection on *verbum Dei*: 'the orators, philosophers and poets [of the pagans] and all other cultivators of the good arts', counselled Abbot Johann von Trittenheim (Johannes Trithemius) of the reformed convent of Sponheim, 'may greatly help to lead us into [a] knowledge of the holy scriptures'.[3] The study of letters at Sponheim was so pervasive there was even said to be a dog that understood Greek. 'Whatever you command of it in Greek', claimed Conrad Celtis, 'it willingly obeys.'[4]

The *studia litterarum* was a perennial theme in the monastic discourse of reform. Cassiodorus (d. *c.* 585) had challenged Benedict's *cenobium*,

[1] There is no modern comparative study of the Benedictine congregations: a summary survey was offered by Philibert Schmitz's *Histoire de l'ordre de Saint Benoit* (7 vols., 1942–56), III.ii, 157–269 (du Concile du Constance à la Réforme). For a lively account of Bursfeld, Melk, Padua and the reform of St-Sulpice de Bourges see G. G. Coulton, *Five Centuries of Religion*, IV: *The Last Days of Medieval Monachism* (Cambridge, 1950), 165–95, 208–34, 386–99. For Padua see also B. Collett, *Italian Benedictine Scholars and the Reformation: The Congregation of Santa Giustina of Padua* (Oxford, 1985). For the learning of the monks of these congregations in the later fifteenth and sixteenth centuries see now F. Posset, *Renaissance Monks: Monastic Humanism in Six Biographical Sketches*, Studies in Medieval and Reformation Traditions, 108 (Leiden, 2005).
[2] N. Brann, *The Abbot Trithemius (1462–1516). The Renaissance of Monastic Humanism*, Studies in the History of Christian Thought, 24 (Leiden, 1981), 107–203, 218.
[3] *Ibid.*, 227.
[4] *Ibid.*, 243.

where the only licit *cultus* was the liturgical labour of the daily office (and the vogue for lettered exchanges was expressly forbidden), with a vision of Vivarium, a living synthesis of secular and sacred learning.[5] The Carolingian reformers reinvested this model with their own imperatives of mission and the promotion of a common cultural and political identity; in turn their curriculum was restored in the century after 1050 as Benedictine houses became the hub of a spiritual and intellectual renaissance.[6] A form of monastic humanism flourished, one that did not condone the consumption of secular literature for its own sake but sought 'to enrich not only their style, their intellectual capital but also their very being', and perhaps (like seculars of the same period) recognised the power of 'man and human experience as a means of knowing God'.[7] The monastic reformers of the fifteenth century did not aim to reprise the humanism of the high Middle Ages, although they would surely affirm the aspiration to enrich style, substance and the sense of being. Their movement represents rather an early (pre-Erasmian) compact of the scholarly values of the humanists and the objectives of the generation of churchmen that presided over the ending of the schism and the (un)settled consequences that followed.

It has always been thought that England's monasteries remained unaffected by this pre-Reformation phase of recovery and renewal. A prospect of the monastic order in post-Black Death England invariably presents an image of institutional stasis and intellectual and spiritual lethargy. Their separation from the European mainstream was apparently a symptom of the country's steady drift into a cultural and devotional backwater. The reception of humanist values was retarded, or so it appears in comparative terms.[8] The reformed monastic and mendicant orders made only modest progress: a Celestine monastery that foundered, a Brigittine double house whose intellectual and spiritual distinction never matched the undoubted riches of its library, and half a dozen

---

[5] Cassiodorus, *Institutiones divinarum et saecularium litterarum*, ed. R. A. B. Mynors (Oxford, 1937). See also G. Picasso, 'Tradizione monastica e cultura umanistica all'alba del Medioevo. *Scienter nescius et sapienter indoctus* (S. Gregorio Magno, Dialogi 2,1)', *Benedictina*, 45, 2 (1999), 259–67. For the prohibition of letters see *Regula Benedicti*, liv.

[6] For the place of learning in the Carolingian reform see *Carolingian Culture: Emulation and Innovation*, ed. R. McKitterick (Cambridge, 1994); D. Ganz, *Corbie in the Carolingian Renaissance*, Beihefte der Francia, Bd. 20 (Sigmaringen, 1990). For the ecclesiastical background see R. McKitterick, *The Frankish Church and the Carolingian Reforms, 789–895*, Royal Historical Society Studies in History (1977).

[7] J. Leclercq, *The Love of Learning and the Desire for God* (New York, 1982), 133; R. W. Southern, *Medieval Humanism and Other Studies* (Oxford, 1970), 59.

[8] See, for example, J. R. Hale, *England and the Italian Renaissance: The Growth of Interest in its History and Art* (1966); *England and the Continental Renaissance: Essays in Honour of J. B. Trapp*, ed. E. Chaney and P. Mack (Woodbridge, 1990).

poorly patronised houses of Observant Friars.[9] Only the Carthusians it seems responded to the continental climate of change. Modern scholars have underlined their role in the transmission of vernacular theology; they were also key agents in the (late) dissemination of *devotio moderna* spirituality.[10] Their achievement can be attributed to three principal convents: London, Hinton (Somerset) and Mount Grace (Yorkshire). There was an abundance of hounds in the precincts of the greater abbeys and priories but it appears there was no Hellenist amongst them.[11]

The isolation of monastic England, and the unreformed condition of its institutional structures and internal mode of life, is a story that originates in the order itself. When expatriate Benedictines prepared for a mission into Jacobean England, they laid claim to an unbroken tradition of monastic observance. The governors of the order cast doubt on the status of their former monasteries, observing that England had never formed a congregation comparable to those on the mainland and had been 'in an earlier stage of evolution' (as one modern authority delicately expressed it) when its house surrendered to the Henrician regime.[12] The expatriates did not secure papal recognition for an English congregation for a dozen years (1619) and the reverberations of the dispute determined the tone of the first post-medieval history of English monasticism, Clement Reyner's *Apostolatus Benedictinorum in Anglia* (1626).[13]

[9] For the failed Celestine foundation of Henry V see J. I. Catto, 'Religious Change under Henry V', in *Henry V: The Practice of Kingship*, ed. G. L. Harriss (Oxford, 1985), 97–115. For the Brigittine abbey of Syon see V. Gillespie, *Syon Abbey*, Corpus of British Medieval Library Catalogues, 9 (2001), *idem*, 'Syon and the New Learning', in *The Religious Orders in Pre-Reformation England*, Studies in the History of Medieval Religion, 18 (Woodbridge, 2002), 75–95. For the Franciscan Observants see *Medieval Religious Houses*, ed. D. Knowles and R. Hadcock (1971); J. Moorman, *A History of the Franciscan Order from its Origin to the year 1517* (Oxford, 1968), 444.

[10] For the Carthusians see E. M. Thompson, *The Carthusians in England* (1930); M. Aston, 'The Development of the Carthusian order in Europe and Britain: A Preliminary Survey', in *In Search of Cult: Essays in Honour of Philip Ratz*, ed. M. O. H. Carver (Woodbridge, 1993), 139–51. For their role in the writing and transmission of devotional and spiritual texts see R. Lovatt, 'The *Imitatio Christi* in Late Medieval England: The Alexander Prize Essay', *Transactions of the Royal Historical Society*, fifth series, 18 (1968), 97–121 at 107, 110; *idem*, 'The Library of John Blacman and Contemporary Carthusian Spirituality', *Journal of Ecclesiastical History*, 43 (1992), 195–230; M. G. Sargent, 'The Transmission by the English Carthusians of Some Late Medieval Spiritual Writings', *Journal of Ecclesiastical History*, 27 (1976), 225–4.

[11] For reports of hunting hounds, terriers and other canines in the precincts of English monasteries in this period see A. Jessopp, *Visitations of Religious Houses in the Diocese of Norwich*, Camden Society, new series, 43 (1888), 21 (Wymondham Abbey, 1492), 264 (Norwich Priory, 1532), 279–80 (St Benet Hulme).

[12] D. Knowles, *The Religious Orders in England* (3 vols., Cambridge, 1949–59), III, 449.

[13] For background see *ibid.*, 445–9. See also G. Sitwell, 'The Foundation and Recruitment of the English Benedictine Congregation', *Downside Review*, 102 (1984), 48–59; *idem*, 'The 1617 Constitutions of the English Benedictine Congregation', *Downside Review*, 98 (1980), 291–7.

To date modern historians have done little to displace the old narrative. In a famous phrase, David Knowles wrote of the 'indefinable spiritual rusticity [which] took hold of a majority of houses', the professed men of this period were 'several degrees more distant from fervour than they had been in 1300'.[14] The culture of the cloister was correspondingly homespun: 'England was far from Italy', Knowles declared, 'and the abbeys were not rich enough in manuscripts to give an imaginative impulse to any young scholar.'[15] His view of the learning of the monasteries, or their lack of it, was shaped by the researches of Roberto Weiss, who regarded his sources with the hauteur that continental observers traditionally reserve for manifestations of English culture. Weiss's verdict was that England's religious orders achieved no 'particular distinction' in this period'.[16] Knowles served as the sole guide for the next generation which drew in greater detail the picture he had sketched for them, of a great graduate enterprise and a standard of life 'humanely speaking easier' than in the preceding centuries.[17]

Over the past decade, the prospect of monastic England in this period has been transformed. Documents and texts unknown to, or unused by, Knowles and his disciples have been (re)discovered through new catalogues, critical editions and *repertoria*; in fact this is true not only for monastic records but also for the intellectual life of this period in general and, in particular, the early reception of humanism.[18] Moreover,

---

[14] Knowles, *Religious Orders*, II, 218, III, 460.

[15] D. Knowles, 'The Cultural Influence of English Medieval Monasticism', *Cambridge Historical Journal*, 7, 3 (1943), 146–59.

[16] R. Weiss, *Humanism in England during the Fifteenth Century*, 2nd edn (Oxford, 1957), 10.

[17] Knowles, *Religious Orders*, III, 460. R. B. Dobson, *Durham Priory, 1400–1450* (Cambridge, 1973); idem, 'English Monastic Cathedrals in the Fifteenth Century', *Transactions of the Royal Historical Society*, sixth series, 1 (1991), 151–72; R. B. Dobson, 'The Monks of Canterbury in the Later Middle Ages, 1220–1540', *A History of Canterbury Cathedral*, ed. P. Collinson, N. Ramsay and M. Sparks (Oxford, 1995), 69–153; J. Greatrex, 'Monk Students from Norwich Cathedral Priory at Oxford and Cambridge, c. 1300 to 1530', *English Historical Review*, 106 (1991), 555–83; idem, J. Greatrex, 'Rabbits and Eels at High Table: Monks of Ely at the University of Cambridge, c. 1337–1539', in *Monasteries and Society in Medieval Britain*, ed. B. J. Thompson, Harlaxton Medieval Studies, 6 (Stamford, 1999), 312–28; B. F. Harvey, 'The Monks of Westminster and the University of Oxford', in *The Reign of Richard II: Essays in Honour of May McKisack*, ed. F. R. H. DuBoulay and C. M. Barron (1971), 108–30; idem, *Living and Dying in England: The Monastic Experience, 1100–1500* (Oxford, 1993).

[18] Prominent among these new research tools are: *English Benedictine Libraries: The Shorter Catalogues*, ed. R. W. Sharpe, J. Carley, K. Friis Jensen and A. G. Watson, Corpus of British Medieval Library Catalogues, 4 (1996); R. W. Sharpe, *A Handlist of the Latin Writers of Great Britain and Ireland to 1540* (Turnhout, 1997); R. M. Thomson, *A Descriptive Catalogue of the Medieval Manuscripts in Worcester Cathedral Library* (Cambridge, 2001); S. Wenzel, *Latin Sermon Collections from Later Medieval England* (Cambridge, 2005). For new light on the reception of humanism see D. G. Rundle, 'On the Difference between Virtue and Weiss: Humanist Texts in England during the Fifteenth Century', in *Courts, Counties and the Capital in the Later Middle Ages*, The Fifteenth-Century Series, 4 (Stroud, 1996), 181–203.

a new outlook on late monasticism has unfolded. There has been a determination to penetrate the institutional structures (and the sources that reflect them) to recover the experience of the individual religious, their 'mentality', 'how they lived and consorted together. . .what they thought and believed' that earlier historians thought elusive.[19] There has also been something of a conceptual shift, a greater willingness to recognise that the cultural, religious and social dynamics of the monasteries were shaped not only by the disciplinary demands of the rule and the socio-economic imperatives of the institution, but also in a process of continuous exchange with the world beyond their walls.[20] Within the personal and permeable culture of the pre-Reformation monk it is possible to see more clearly signs of a response to contemporary intellectual and religious trends of which earlier authorities considered them incapable.

In fact the monastic order in England was never wholly cast adrift from the clerical and ecclesiastical mainstream. Indeed the contribution of the Benedictines to the causes that exercised the clerical establishment, and their pastoral subjects, in the period between the Black Death and the Break with Rome, has been consistently underestimated. To contemporaries, and in particular at moments of perceived crisis, members of these orders were among the most conspicuous and vocal contributors both to public debates and to learned discourse. Certainly in the half-century after 1349, it would appear that the Benedictines were in advance of their secular colleagues in their awareness of and responsiveness to currents of thought passing through the institutional church. The greater matters of the time, the schism in the papacy, the emergence of clerical heterodoxy and the apparent resurgence of popular heresy, elicited a response from the Black Monks that appears to have been coordinated throughout their network and, in the early stages at least, was not matched by any other community of clergy. The president of the

[19] D. Knowles, *The Monastic Order in England* (Cambridge, 1940), 691; Dobson, 'English Monastic Cathedrals', 153. For research that has reached towards this goal see, for example, A. J. Piper, 'The Names of the Durham Monks', in *The Durham Liber vitae and its Context*, ed. D. W. Rollason, Regions and Regionalism in History, 1 (Woodbridge, 2004), 117–25; J. Greatrex, "Who Were the Monks of Rochester?', in *Medieval Art, Architecture and Archaeology at Rochester*, ed. T. Ayers and T. W. T. Tatton-Brown, British Archaeological Association, Conference Transactions, 28 (Leeds, 2006), 205–17; B. Collett, 'Holy Expectations: The Female Monastic Vocation in the Diocese of Winchester on the Eve of the Reformation', in *The Culture of Medieval English Monasticism*, Studies in the History of Medieval Religion, 30 (Woodbridge, 2007), 147–65. Prosopographic studies have served to open up this perspective, notably J. Greatrex, *A Biographical Register of the English Cathedral Priories, c. 1066–1540* (Oxford, 1996); and *The Heads of Religious Houses in England and Wales, III. 1377–1540*, ed. D. M. Smith (Cambridge, 2008).
[20] This perspective is apparent in recent work on women religious: P. Lee, *Nunneries, Learning, and Spirituality in Late Medieval English Society: The Dominican Priory of Dartford* (York, 2001); M. Erler, *Women, Reading and Piety in Late Medieval England* (Cambridge, 2002).

General Chapter encouraged, and perhaps selected, Benedictine scholars to confront Wyclif in formal disputation at Oxford.[21] It seems the same president led at least one scholar to tackle the schism in a treatise intended for a general clerical audience.[22] Surviving examples of Benedictine sermons from this period suggest there was also some attempt to coordinate a campaign of preaching on these themes. From the style and tone of these texts, it would appear they were not composed for conventual consumption alone: the macaronic character of the recorded transcript or digest might reinforce the impression of a general clerical context for their subsequent (if not initial) reception.[23] It was a natural continuation of such a campaign that the Benedictines should secure representation among the English delegates attending at the general councils at Pisa (1409), Constance (1414–18) and Basel (1431–8); once more the monks displayed a greater degree of interest in, and enduring hope for, these *fora* than their counterparts in the secular clergy and episcopacy.[24] In his *Granarium*, John Wheathampstead compiled an essay on *Concilium* that culminated with an account of the achievements of Constance, the condemnation of Wyclif and execution of Hus and the recognition of the authority of the council itself 'in spiritu sancto legitime congregatum potestatem a Christo immediate habeat'.[25] Abbot William Curteys of Bury corresponded with

[21] J. I. Catto, 'Wyclif and Wyclifism at Oxford, 1356–1430', in *A History of the University of Oxford*, II: *Late Medieval Oxford*, ed. J. I. Catto and T. A. R. Evans (Oxford, 1992), 175–261 at 206, 228–9. See also *Documents Illustrating the General and Provincial Chapters of the English Black Monks, 1215–1540*, ed. W. A. Pantin, Camden Society Third Series (3 vols., 1931–7), III, 76–7; M. Harvey, 'Adam Easton and the Condemnation of John Wyclif, 1377', *English Historical Review*, 113 (1998), 321–54

[22] The *quaestio* on the schism composed by the St Albans monk, Nicholas Radcliff, preserved in British Library (BL), Royal MS 6 D X, may have been commissioned by his abbot (and capitular president) Thomas de la Mare. See also A. B. Emden, *A Biographical Register of the University of Oxford to AD 1500* (*BRUO*) (3 vols., Oxford, 1957–9), III, 1539.

[23] Wenzel, *Latin Sermon Collections from Later Medieval England*, especially, 278–87. See also *A Macaronic Sermon Collection from Late Medieval England: Oxford MS Bodley 649*, ed. P. J. Horner, Pontifical Institute of Mediaeval Studies, Studies and Texts, 153 (Toronto, 2006).

[24] Prior Thomas Chillenden of Christ Church, Canterbury, Abbot John Chinnock of Glastonbury and Thomas Clare of Bury and Thomas Rome of Durham Priory attended the council at Pisa; Abbot Richard Salford of Abingdon was present at his own expense; Abbot Thomas Spofford and Abbot William Colchester of Westminster Abbey attended Constance, where Abbot Chinnock may also have been present; Abbot Nicholas Frome of Glastonbury was at Basel. See M. Harvey, 'English Views of the Reforms to be Undertaken at the General Councils, with Special Reference to the Proposals Made by Richard Ullerston' (D.Phil. dissertation, University of Oxford, 1964), 262–3, 277–8. See also G. Masni, *Sacrorum conciliorum...Collection* (31 vols., Florence, 1759–62), XXVII, col. 349. See also Mavis E. Mate, 'Chillenden, Thomas (d. 1411)', in *Oxford Dictionary of National Biography* (Oxford, 2004), 38470; *Memorials of King Henry VI. Official Correspondence of Thomas Benkynton, Secretary to Henry VI and Bishop of Bath and Wells*, ed. G. Williams, Rolls Series, 56 (1872), II. 259.

[25] BL, Arundel MS 11, fos. 34r–40v at 40r. It is worth noting Wheathampstead did not continue his essay beyond the calling of the Basel council.

one English delegate at Basel on the matter of monastic privilege treated there.[26] Thomas Rudborne of Winchester Cathedral Priory filled five folios with reflections on the historical background of the East–West union that resurfaced at the Council of Ferrara-Florence (1438–45).[27] The Black Monks of this period were also sensitive to the internal tensions of identity that animated the regular and secular clergy. In the last quarter of the fourteenth century they appointed themselves the unsolicited champions of Archbishop Richard Fitzralph of Armagh, whose *De pauperie saluatoris* had reignited academic and popular debate over the purpose of the mendicant friars; here there are also signs of coordination across the Benedictine network.[28] Clearly they were also conscious of the clamour over the parochial clergy and the problem of pastoral care. The sermons of the Durham Priory preacher Robert Rypon, a proportion of which were probably presented to a mixed clerical audience, display a recurrent concern for the challenges of contemporary clerical (and diocesan) practice.[29] Perhaps it was inevitable that the Black Monks should respond to these very public controversies since their social origins, their seigniorial and pastoral obligations, positioned them in the orbit of national and regional elites. Yet there are also signs of an awareness of currents of thought and religious practice that were somewhat *avant garde*. Manuscript evidence recently re-analysed suggests that some Benedictine readers of the period were drawn to Joachimite revelations which had attracted public condemnation in academic and Episcopal injunctions.[30] Perhaps the most prominent Benedictine chronicler of the period was fascinated by the fleeting presence of the Flagellants in England and their popularity in Italy.[31] Henry Kirkstead, the Bury novice-master, confronted Hildegardian prophecy through the *Pentachronon* of Gebeno of Eberbach which he copied for himself.[32] Adam Easton, Benedictine of Norwich Cathedral Priory and cardinal priest of Saint Cecilia, attached himself to the cause of Birgitta of Sweden, founder of the order of St Saviour; he composed an apologia, *Defensorium sanctae Birgittae*, in 1389 and in 1391 addressed a letter to the abbess and convent of the order's mother

---

[26] *Memorials of St Edmund's Abbey*, ed. T. Arnold, Rolls Series, 96 (3 vols., 1890–6), III, 252–7.

[27] J. G. Greatrex, 'Thomas Rudborne, Monk of Winchester, and the Council of Florence', in *Schism, Heresy and Religious Protest*, ed. D. Baker, Papers Read at the 10th Summer Meeting and the 11th Winter Meeting of the Ecclesiastical History Society (Cambridge, 1972), 171–6.

[28] K. Walsh, *A Fourteenth-Century Scholar and Primate: Richard Fitzralph in Oxford, Avignon and Armagh* (Oxford, 1981), 446–7.

[29] M. Harvey, *Lay Religious Life in Late Medieval Durham* (Woodbridge, 2006), 29–31, 33.

[30] K. Kerby-Fulton, *Books under Suspicion: Censorship and Tolerance of Revelatory Writing in Late Medieval England* (Notre Dame, 2006), 102.

[31] *Thomae Walsingham, quondam monachi S. Albani, Historia Anglicana, 1272–1381*, ed. H. T. Riley (2 vols., 1863–4), I, 275, II, 242–3.

[32] Kerby-Fulton, *Books under Suspicion*, 202–3.

house at Vadstena. Easton expressed a personal devotion to Birgitta and attributed to her his delivery from papal custody in 1385.[33]

It might be objected, of course, that the activities of a handful of high-profile monastic prelates, scholars and preachers are not indicative of the mood of the network as a whole. The career of Adam Easton carried him far from the house of his first profession into a pattern of life and a perspective that bore the imprint of the secular priest.[34] The presence of texts, or para-textual discourse, connected with these themes in the book collections of a cross-section of convents, however, does suggest that some trace of this engagement had penetrated the monastic enclosure and perhaps the consciousness of the ordinary cloister monk. While they had first passed into monastic hands from the personal collection of a monastic prelate, the common library at Westminster Abbey held a selection of treatises on the schism and councils.[35] The accuracy and completeness of the conciliar *acta* incorporated in Thomas Walsingham's *Chronica maiora* is suggestive not only of direct ties to the English delegates but the presence at St Albans of a now-lost anthology.[36] William Curteys referred to *cedula* recording the Basel discussions; it has been suggested that Thomas Rudborne secured a collection of conciliar *acta*.[37] The Latin works of Wyclif appear to have been a part of the official provisions of some major monastic collections.[38] The textual background to the Fitzralph affair was also widely available in Benedictine collections: glosses in a Norwich manuscript are evocative of a lively reader response.[39] An engagement with popular, reformist and radical patterns of thought can also be glimpsed in surviving and recorded manuscripts; it is possible that there are more such traces to be identified. When the reformer Peter von Rosenheim entered Melk in 1418 he confronted a monastic community apparently unaware of the currents of reform that were palpable – only

[33] J. Hogg, 'Adam Easton's *Defensorium Sanctae Birgittae*', in *The Medieval Mystical Tradition*, 6, ed. M. Glasscoe (Woodbridge, 2003), 213–40. For Easton's career see also M. Harvey, *The English in Rome, 1362–1420: Portrait of an Expatriate Community* (Cambridge, 1999), 188–212.

[34] Harvey, *The English in Rome*, 188–212.

[35] *English Benedictine Libraries*, ed. Sharpe *et al.*, B108. 9–13 (632). This sequence of texts, works of John Acton, John Colt, Thomas Parker and Nicholas Ryssheton, dating from 1378, 1395–6, which may have been bound together in a single codex, was recorded at the abbey by John Leland in the 1530s but may have entered the book collection a century or more before. It is tempting to connect them with the intellectual legacy of Cardinal Simon Langham and the abbacy of William of Colchester (1387–1420).

[36] See especially *The St Albans Chronicle, 1406–1420*, ed. V. H. Galbraith (Oxford, 1937).

[37] *Memorials of St Edmund's Abbey*, ed. Arnold, III, 255; Greatrex, 'Thomas Rudborne', 174.

[38] See, for example, Oxford, Oriel College, MS 15, a compilation made for Nicholas Fawkes of Glastonbury Abbey: J. I. Catto, 'Some English Manuscripts of Wyclif's Latin Works', in *From Ockham to Wyclif*, ed. A. Hudson and M. Wilks, Studies in Church History, Subsidia, 5 (Oxford, 1987), 353–59 at 354, 357.

[39] Oxford, Bodl., Bodley MS 144, fo. 34r.

300 miles from Constance – in the region at large. By contrast, there can be little doubt the Black Monks of England were fully conscious of the climate of reform.

The greater public and popular engagement of the monastic order between the death of Edward III and the deposition of Richard II bequeathed a powerful, if not unproblematic, legacy to the generations that followed. It is possible that their prominence in the crises of the recent past contributed to the Benedictines renewed stature in the clerical hierarchy, not only on the Episcopal bench but also among the handful of regular religious that now attracted the attention and counsels of the crown.[40] Internally, the experience of preceding decades appears to have stimulated a spirit of reflection not only on the place of the monastic order in *patria cleri*, but also on the appropriate forms of the professed life itself. Moreover, there arose a cadre of monk whose education and formation had occurred between 1378 and 1417 that was committed it would appear, to the conversion of these impulses into a systematic process of reform. As men of good (or at least middling) birth professed in early adulthood after a respectable grammar schooling, they were representative of the career monk of this period, but their extended exposure to the academic community, in a syllabus of study that generally culminated in a doctorate, and occasionally a period of regency, set them apart from the majority of their brethren. Their academic prowess projected them early (perhaps prematurely) into ecclesiastical and public affairs: Dr Simon Southerey of St Albans was summoned to the Council of Stamford in 1392 only three years after he had been *prior studentium* at Oxford; William Weld of St Augustine's Canterbury was among those summoned to a council in January 1399 convened to address the schism.[41] Their reputations raised largely outside the monastic precincts also led them with remarkable alacrity to the head of their communities. Between 1400 and 1425 a succession of these comparatively youthful candidates of wide academic, administrative and, in some cases, cosmopolitan, experience succeeded as superiors of England's premier abbeys and priories. It seems that contemporaries recognised the distinction of this rising generation and the potential danger it posed to the forces of tradition both sides of the monastic enclosure. The chronicler Walsingham interpreted the Westminster injunctions issued to the Benedictines in 1421 as a defensive response to the advent of new and youthful leadership.[42]

---

[40] Knowles, *Religious Orders*, II, 178–84, 280–3, 369–70. Knowles doubts the influence of the Black Monks under the Lancastrians, but his account of Henry V's monastic foundations and his tally of monastic prelates in some way supports a counter-argument.

[41] Emden, *BRUO*, III, 1734, 2007.

[42] *Historia Anglicana*, ed. Riley, II, 337: 'quod major pars praelatorum ac seniorum eiusdem ordinis defecisset effraenata juverntus eius tempore successisset'.

The significance of this constituency in the monastic network should not be overstated but there are grounds for suggesting that it did form an identifiable interest group in the Benedictine General Chapters, the governing body of the order in the northern and southern provinces of England in the first, and perhaps the second decade of the fifteenth century. It was a group that numbered not only the superiors of several principal houses but a selection of successful graduate monks employed in the capacity of proxy delegate to the chapter, or diffinitor, or visitor, in the triennial cycle of capitular visitations.[43] The surviving accounts of capitular sessions suggest these men cultivated a self-conscious style that distinguished them from other delegates. When called upon to preach, they delivered their collation *in Latinis*, a format no longer universal either at the general or indeed the daily, conventual chapter. Frequently, the redactor recorded the tone of the sermon as *fructuose*, or similar terms which might be dismissed as formulaic were it not that surviving sermons have been shown to be replete with the *florida verborum venustas* connected with the classicising writers of the period.[44] Moreover, on more than one occasion between 1421 and 1444, members of this apparent group appear associated with proposals for reform. It cannot be coincidental that three of the six representatives selected to treat with the king's advisers after the council at Westminster in 1421 were from the rising generation of graduates already associated, in regional, national and international arenas,with measures of reform.[45] Prior John Wessington (Washington) of Durham had already invested in learning, completing a purpose-built library by 1418; Abbot Thomas Spofford of St Mary's Abbey, York, had collaborated with secular clergy in the province in the revision of the abbey's liturgical regime; he had also served in the English delegation at the Council of Constance (1414–17); Abbot John Wheathampstead, by some margin the most junior member of this group, had already initiated internal reforms in the network of monasteries under the parental supervision of St Albans.[46] A fourth member of the group

[43] For the role of graduates in the work of the chapters see, for example, those named as capitular visitors in 1393 and those selected as electors for the next chapter, Prior John Braby of Selby, William Islep, Thomas Merk and Thomas Shrewsbury, all Oxford men, while Braby and four further theologians, Thomas Bekenham, Thomas Camme, Thomas Grantham and Simon Southerey, were selected as electors for the next chapter: *Chapters*, ed. Pantin, II, 92–3.

[44] See, for example, the preacher William Walden: 'verbum Dei ibidem fructuose proposuit in Latinis': *Chapters*, ed. Pantin, II, 135. For the style of such sermons see S. Wenzel, 'The Classics in Late Medieval Preaching', in *Medieval Antiquity*, ed. A. Welkenhuysen, H. Braet and W. Verbeke, Mediaevalia Lovaniensia, Series 1, Studia XXIV (Louvain, 1995), 127–43.

[45] *Chapters*, ed. Pantin, II, 107–8.

[46] For the careers of these three superiors see Emden, *BRUO*, III, 1744, 2032–4. For Wessington see also Dobson, *Durham Priory*, 81–113. Although Wessington was forty-five at

of six was Thomas Elmham, a former Benedictine of St Augustine's Canterbury, who had transferred to the Cluniac congregation and, with royal patronage, taken the priorate of Lenton (Nottinghamshire). Elmham was a formidable scholar and arguably a more accomplished Latinist than these three superiors.[47]

The common intellectual hinterland of these representatives should also be underlined. By the time of the Westminster council each of these monks was well known for their scholarly enthusiasm. Both Wessington and Wheathampstead had embarked on book projects that over the course of their career would transform their conventual collections.[48] Spofford appears to have been among the earliest English enthusiasts for the literary culture of the Italian humanists, an enthusiasm perhaps initiated at York where the Minster treasurer, John Newton, was also an enthusiast, and possibly fuelled at Constance, where the secular delegates from England are known to have forged connections with continental *litterateurs*.[49] There can be little doubt that their commitment to learning was a cornerstone of their own plans for monastic renewal.

The link between intellectual activities and the reinvigoration of observant life was openly articulated only two years after Westminster at the Northampton Chapter of 1423. Alan Kirton, proctor of the Abbot Charwelton of Thorney, a graduate who surely can be counted among the like-minded learned members of the chapter, addressed the delegates on the decline of daily scriptural *lectio* in the houses he visited regularly (*quod in locis per ipsum regulariter visitatis*): 'the life of Martha [i.e., the *vita active*] is in many ways commendably observed but not that of Mary (*vita contemplativa*).[50] Another chapter, the account of which is undated (but perhaps fell before 1426), addressed the analogous issue of appropriate conduct and discourse in the cloister hours and the levity, and non-Latinity, of conventual conversation.[51] Although Wessington served as capitular president in 1426, and, in turn, Wheathampstead also held the office, it seems subsequent sessions did not return to these themes. Yet the inclinations of this generation were also cultivated outside the chapter. In

his election, he was younger than many of his predecessors in office and was promoted above the heads of elder colleagues: *ibid.*, 89.

[47] For a summary of Elmham's career see S. E. Kelly, 'Elmham, Thomas (b. 1364, d. in or after 1427)', in *Oxford Dictionary of National Biography*, 8734. His university career was apparently brief.

[48] Dobson, *Durham Priory*, 378–86; *English Benedictine Libraries*, ed. Sharpe *et al.*, B88, B89, B90 (563–84).

[49] Newton was one of two commissioners appointed to supervise the reform of observance at Spofford's abbey in 1390. For Newton in York diocese see J. Hughes, *Pastors and Visionaries: Religion and Secular Life in Late Medieval Yorkshire* (Woodbridge, 1988), especially 178–83.

[50] *Chapters*, ed. Pantin, II, 142.

[51] *Ibid.*, 180–2 at 182.

1423 Abbot Richard de Boxore of Abingdon sought an Episcopal licence to leave his monastery for three years for further study (at an appropriate *studium generale*, perhaps abroad) 'for the defence of the Catholic faith', barely a year after his election to the dignity. Abbot Wheathampstead also evinced an evangelical zeal and his patronage of the library at Gloucester College, the order's Oxford *studium*, between 1420 and his death, was perhaps intended to nurture another generation of defenders of orthodoxy.[52] A trace of continental influence in shaping these impulses should not be discounted. There was no formal business between the Benedictine networks, and international correspondence is scarce in monastic archives, Abbot Spofford attended the reformist chapter at Peterhausen while at Constance, and there is no doubt the venerable Abbot Wheathampstead engaged warmly with Cluniac representatives during their ill-fated English mission in 1458.[53]

A discourse of reform flourished in the Cluniac network, at least for a generation, in the first quarter of the fifteenth century. As Prior of Lenton Thomas Elmham served twice as vicar general for their houses in England (two terms, 1415–19) and appears an advocate, of some impatience, for a process of reform. He began (and perhaps completed) a visitation of convents subject to Cluny in the summer of 1415 and reported: 'I have found many things that need to be cut away, some to be cured by healing medicine, a few to be strengthened and cherished.' Briefly, the different branches of the network in England became united under a common cause.[54] In the decades that followed, the English Cluniacs were diverted by their mother house into a fruitless struggle for the recovery of properties and rights overlooked during the long years of the Anglo-French war; the enmity between England and France also stifled a final attempt at systematic reform initiated by Cluny in 1458.[55]

The English Cistercians shared this restorative impulse although it appears the stimulus came from outside the congregation in the General Chapter at Cîteaux and the actions of the English superiors were in response to capitular supervision: the scrutiny and reform of the order's Oxford *studium* was ordered as early as 1411; plans for a purpose-built house of studies were initiated but were not advanced until Archbishop

---

[52] Notable among his donations was a deluxe copy of Thomas Netter's *Doctrinale*, now BL, Royal MS 8 G X *ex dono* identifying Gloucester College at fo. 204v.

[53] Emden, *BRUO*, III, 1744; *Registra quorundam abbatum monasterii S. Albani, qui sæculo XVmo. Floruere*, ed. H. T. Riley, Rolls Series, 28/6 (1872–3), *Registrum abbatiae Johannis Whethamstede*, I, 317–22.

[54] R. Graham, 'The English Province of the Order of Cluny in the Fifteenth Century', *Transactions of the Royal Historical Society*, fourth series, 7 (1926), 98–130.

[55] Graham, 'English Province of the Order of Cluny', 109–20.

Chichele proffered a site in 1437.[56] A general reform of the congregation was promulgated in 1488 but it remains too poorly documented to trace its course and effects.[57] The infrastructure of the Oxford *studium* did not develop sufficiently to support a succession of student monks before the close of the fifteenth century, which may explain the signs of a surge in book provisions and scholarship in a number of houses in the decades that followed.[58]

There is no doubt that the force and frequency of the discourse of renewal among delegates to the Benedictine chapters had diminished by the middle decades of the fifteenth century. Mid-century chapter meetings record only routine business; and it may be significant, and not merely the random pattern of manuscript preservation, that the flow of sermons runs dry. The injunctions issued by the General Chapter in 1444 were in large measure a recapitulation of those promulgated a century earlier and, significantly, did not return to matters not fully addressed following the Council of Westminster.[59] The fading of the early fervour for reform must be seen as the consequence of an inevitable generational shift: the young and energetic superiors of the reign of Henry V were spent by the time of the Yorkist ascendancy over his son. It also brings into sharp focus the failure of the capitular governance to stimulate systematic change. The provincial and general chapters had always struggled to be properly representative: Christ Church Cathedral Priory never recognised their authority and the presidency passed between an unchanging roster of elite abbeys.[60] The dominance of an elite group of graduates in its deliberations and its delegated roles only increased the degree of detachment from the daily rhythm of observant life in provincial houses.

Yet the absence of a significant measure of reform at the structural centre of monastic England masks the extent to which the learned superiors (and other seniors) of the early and mid-fifteenth century effected change in their own and affiliate communities. The surviving *comperta* of Episcopal visitations – their capitular counterparts are preserved only as reports delivered *in capitulo* – are rigid in their formulaic questions and responses and convey no sense of measurable change over time. Where they are preserved, the *acta*, *dicta* and *gesta* of this

---

[56] For the provision of the Oxford *studium* see J. I. Catto, 'The Cistercians in Oxford, 1280–1539', in *Benedictines in Oxford*, ed. H. Wansbrough and A. Marett-Crosby (1997), 108–15.

[57] *Letters from the English Abbots to the Chapter at Cîteaux, 1442–1521*, ed. C. H. Talbot, Camden Fourth Series, 4 (1967), 112–13.

[58] One of the last graduates of the Cistercian *studium* was also the most prominent: Gabriel Dunne of Stratford Langthorne progressed from Oxford to Louvain, to the abbacy of Buckfast, and, after the Dissolution, to a prebendary of St Paul's: Nicholas Orme, 'Dunne, Gabriel (c. 1490–1558)', in *Oxford Dictionary of National Biography*, 7818.

[59] *Chapters*, ed. Pantin, II, 187–220.

[60] Knowles, *Religious Orders*, II, 43–5 at 45.

generation give a glimpse, although a highly partial one of the dynamic transformation, if not reform, of conventual life that many of the greater abbeys and priories witnessed in this period.[61] The experience of these years is best explored perhaps in the books, both liturgical and 'library' volumes, and the original writings, which can be connected with these communities.

A palpable change brought into focus by these books, and one which may have been part of a wider programme of reform, concerned the curriculum of study followed by the younger monks. In the later Middle Ages those entering the cloister could expect to remain under the tutelage of a mature monk for as much as a decade after their profession.[62] The extended period of custody addressed pragmatic concerns over the unrestricted expansion of the monastic community in a context of diminished resources and also provided the scope for recruits to complete the training in the 'primitive sciences' required under capitular and papal canons as the prerequisite for a period of university study.[63] The syllabus of primitive sciences is scarcely documented either in official legislation or domestic records but in the first century or so of the programme it appears to have adhered closely to the demands of the university arts course. Yet from the first quarter of the fifteenth century, the brethren were provided with a greater diversity of authorities. There appears to have been a change of emphasis, from a curriculum founded on the precepts of Latin grammar and the principles of logic and philosophy, to one that privileged the finer points of language, rhetoric and metre and their possible application in poetry and prose. The profusion of preceptive manuals on rhetoric, anonymous and authored, in monastic anthologies of the period is evidenced in a variety of contemporary library catalogues.[64] It was perhaps telling of the approach that an

---

[61] The most lengthy and perhaps the liveliest accounts are those recording the first and second abbacies of John Wheathampstead of St Albans: *Annales monasterii S. Albani a Johanne Amundesham monacho ut videutr consripti AD 1421–1440*, ed. H. T. Riley, Rolls Series, 28 (2 vols., 1870–1); *Registrum quorundam abbatum monasterii S. Albani qui seaculo XVmo floruere*, ed. H. T. Riley, Rolls Series, 28/6 (2 vols., 1872–3).

[62] B. F. Harvey, 'A Novice's Life at Westminster Abbey in the Century before the Dissolution', in *The Religious Orders in Pre-Reformation England*, ed. J. G. Clark (Woodbridge, 2002), 51–73.

[63] For the background to these canons see Knowles, *Religious Orders*, II, 15. It was *Summi magistri* of Benedict XII that placed particular emphasis on the 'primitive sciences' of grammar, logic and philosophy, although the decretal *Ne in agro* had raised the matter as early as 1311: *Chapters*, ed. Pantin, I, 173–4.

[64] *English Benedictine Libraries*, ed. Sharpe *et al.*, B30.7, B55.142a, B86.14A, B89.6a (139, 287, 553, 573); M. R. James, *Ancient Libraries of Canterbury and Dover. The Catalogues of the Libraries of Christ Church Priory and St. Augustine's Abbey at Canterbury and of St. Martin's Priory at Dover. Now First Collected and Published with an Introduction and Identifications of the Extant Remains* (Cambridge, 1903) nos. 1408, 1412, 1415 (360–1), 1420, 1422 (367), 1456 (366), 1492 (376).

(apparently) Benedictine sermon preached in the early fifteenth century placed 'the colours of rhetoric' among the liberal arts.[65] At the greater monasteries it appears that the student monks were now provided with structured readings in these linguistic and literary modes just as, in earlier generations, they had been set to a course in the old and new logic and natural philosophy of Aristotle.[66] The sequence of texts that opens a collection compiled at Christ Church, Canterbury, may have been prepared for this purpose: two pairs of elementary guides to rhetoric and metre are joined by a selection of orations and epigrams presumably intended to exemplify the principles which the guides introduce.[67] The literary emphasis of these manuals encouraged the return to the cloister *studium* of a wide range of Latin 'readers', poetry and prose texts of classical and early medieval *auctores*, which had not been a predominant feature of monastic reading patterns since the twelfth century.[68] In a number of cases these books were quite literally returned to the cloister from the remote custody, or state of disrepair, in which they had been placed after academic authorities had entered conventual collections. The monks of Worcester Priory recommissioned a tenth-century grammar primer containing the staple authorities of the Carolingian monastery, Priscian's *Institutiones grammaticae* and Bede's *Ars metrica*; an anonymous annotator added snatches of verse in a humanist script.[69] This literature was also the subject of lively activity in new acquisition and production which in some communities may have been coordinated but frequently was furthered by the independent initiative of individual monks. The graduate monks were particularly active in the provision of these texts, recognition perhaps that these readings were the foundation of their higher studies. Hugh Legat, a graduate monk of St Albans Abbey, purchased what appears to have been a series of early *quaterni* which contained, among other texts, a copy of Ovid's *Heroides*, comparatively rare in England.[70] The university environment was the likely source of some of these 'finds', perhaps not

---

[65] Oxford, Bodl., Bodley MS 649, fo. 128r.

[66] For an impression of the authorities in arts employed in earlier generations see the fifteenth-century catalogue of the library of St Augustine's Abbey, Canterbury: *Ancient Libraries*, 349–59, 361–3 (nos. 1279–1392, 417, 423). The same catalogue contains no fewer than six copies of Cicero's *De officiis* (pp. 304–5, nos. 1010–11, 1015, 1016, 1018) now perhaps more prominent in the linguistic preparation of the monks.

[67] BL, Royal MS 10 B IX, fos. 46v–52v, 53r–55r (there are further epigrams to fo. 55v).

[68] A volume recorded again at St Augustine's, Canterbury, may serve to exemplify the shift at least in the greater houses: owned by John Hawkhurst (d. by Feb. 1430), it held glosses on Horace's Odes, Epodes and Epistles and on Sallust: James, *Ancient Libraries*, no. 1451 (365) see also his books at nos. 1013 (304), 1477, 1479–80 (368). See also Emden, *BRUO*, II, 890–1.

[69] Worcester Cathedral Chapter Library, MS Q5 (fo. 78r).

[70] Oxford, Bodl., Rawlinson MS G 99. Legat's inscription is at flyleaf ix ult. v, the *Heroides* at 21r–65v. Legat also acquired copies of Cicero's *De inventione* and the pseudonymous *Ad Herennium*, which he had bound: BL, Harley MS 2624, fo. 2r.

the collections of the secular university and colleges, which remained small and utilitarian, but the general pool of books that grew between the institutional boundaries constantly renewed through the operation of loan-chests, a vigorous second-hand market and (at least at Oxford) the presence of productive workshops on the city periphery.[71] This remained a rewarding hunting-ground for monastic readers at the turn of the century and the pre-Reformation period and perhaps a principal source for classical and humanist literature: a note in another Worcester manuscript appears to bear witness to the exchange of books between the brethren and secular clerks at Oxford: among the books recorded are the works of Cicero, Seneca and an unspecified *Liber poetrie*.[72]

The prominence of the *ars dictaminis* in the monastery might also be seen as a symptom of the 'literary turn' in the cloister curriculum. *Dictamen* had always been regarded as a valuable tool, and in the fourteenth century, if not before, the composition of conventual letters, indentures and other *diplomata* had been taught at least to those identified as future administrative officers. Between 1400 and 1450, however, there was a change in the character of the manuals and paradigms that were read and replicated by these students of *dictamen*. The utilitarian modes of the previous century were replaced by texts that were markedly more literary in character.[73]

From the middle years of the century, and perhaps earlier at a number of the greater abbeys and priories, these established, if previously overlooked, exemplars of Latin poetry and prose were supplemented by contemporary exponents of the new literary culture of the continent. The appearance of these texts in manuscripts both surviving and recorded is suggestive of a wider exposure to early humanism than modern scholars have allowed. Moreover, it was an assimilation that appears to have begun at least as early as any learned community in England. A collection of humanist Latin that entered the library at St Mary's York under the hand of Abbot Spofford is likely to have been completed before his death in 1453. The volume contains orations from a formidable roll call of pioneer and contemporary humanists, Gasparino Barzizza, Poggio Bracciolini, Leonardo Bruni, Leonardo Giustiniani, Antonio Loschi and Francesco

[71] For background see M. B. Parkes, 'The Provision of Books', in *The History of the University of Oxford*, II: *Late Medieval Oxford*, ed. Catto and Evans, 407–83.

[72] Worcester Cathedral Chapter Library, MS F 69 (fo. 363v).

[73] An instance of this novel approach to the *ars dictaminis* is offered by the Canterbury anthology, BL, Royal MS 10 B IX. For the teaching of *dictamen* in this period see *Medieval Rhetorics of Prose Composition: Five English Artes dictandi and their Tradition*, ed. M. Camargo (Binghamton, NY, 1995); M. Camargo 'Beyond the *libri catoniani*: Models of Latin Prose Style at Oxford University, *c.* 1400', *Mediaeval Studies*, 56 (1994), 165–87. For the trend in contemporary library catalogues see James, *Ancient Libraries*, 298 (nos. 951–66), 299–300. The range of authorities here (St Augustine's, Canterbury) ran from Geoffrey of Vinsauf's *Poetria nova* to the letter book of the Canterbury monk John Mason, of which there were three copies available nos. 953–4, 966.

Petrarca.[74] The Christ Church manuscript, compiled at intervals from the 1430s or 1440s to at least the 1460s, contains a selection of humanist *encomia* and epistles, the exemplars for some of which must have been held at the priory not later than the middle of the century.[75] The Latin works of Boccaccio and Leonardo Bruni appear to have been known well enough at St Albans to be referenced and summarised by compilers active between 1420 and 1465.[76]

In the next generation these *ad hoc* acquisitions and compilations appear to have cohered at a number of houses into a coordinated scheme in which the authorities of earlier centuries were substituted with more modish authors and texts. At Worcester there was perhaps a policy of filling conspicuous literary *lacunae*; a number of manuscripts show signs of restructuring in the last quarter of the fifteenth century; in one case excerpts from Cicero's *De amicitia* was added to an earlier anthology and annotated in a script displaying humanist features.[77] John Sucley and Nicholas Hanbury acquired a manuscript containing Bruni's translation of Aristotle's *Ethica* and *Politica* which they proffered to their own priory at Worcester 'ad usum proficuum futurorum'.[78] William Sellyng's purchases in Italy were made not solely out of personal interest but with the intention of renewing the resources of the priory and its members; a Latin Plutarch was dispatched to Oxford; other texts he acquired served as the exemplars for home-grown compilations.[79] The sequence of catalogues of the library at Canterbury College, Oxford, from 1501 to 1524 appears to record the systematic replacement of the scholastic *textus* with representatives of the new learning: the editor of these inventories identifies the Latin text of Aristotle's *Politics* with the translation of Leonardo Bruni. The catalogue of 1521 also records a sequence of Cicero's rhetorical works and the verse of Horace and Virgil, to reflect perhaps what were now the reference works of the typical college fellow: the personal library of Thomas Goldwell, whose early career spanned the last quarter of the century, matches closely

[74] BL, Harley MS 2268, fos. 3r-117r.

[75] BL, Royal MS 10 B IX. The manuscript was acquired by the Christ Church monk, Henry Cranbrook, in 1452, from one J. Hynder, who may also have been a monk of the house.

[76] Wheathampstead cited *De claris mulieribus* under the heading 'Amor coniugalis' in BL, Cotton MS Tiberius D V, Pt I, fo. 6r. His *Palearium poetarum* (partially preserved in BL, Add. MS 26764) was apparently modelled on Boccaccio's *Genealogia deorum gentilium*. A compilation for which Abbot Wheathampstead was at least partially responsible contains a brief *accessus* on Bruni which precedes an epitome of his *De primo bello Punico*: BL, Arundel MS 11, fo. 92r–99v at 92r.

[77] Worcester Cathedral Chapter Library, MS fos. 124, 203v–206v.

[78] Worcester Cathedral Chapter Library, MS Add X (11), a slip of parchment removed from MS F 140 (Ludolphus of Saxony).

[79] *Canterbury College, Oxford*, ed. W. A. Pantin, Oxford Historical Society, New Series, 6–8, 30 (4 vols., 1942–85), I, 21 (1501 catalogue).

the new accessions to the college library.[80] Certainly, towards the turn of the century, it was commonplace – and perhaps an expectation – that monks in the early stages of their career might have access to some of the most significant classical and contemporary authorities in the *studia humanitatis*. Perhaps the most popular primer in early Tudor England, John Holt's *Lac puerorum* (STC 13604), was provided for the brethren at Norwich Priory; Holt was himself an *alumnus* of Magdalen College School, an associate of Grocyn and a correspondent of Thomas More.[81] It is tempting to connect the prints of Agostino Dato (1479) and Lorenzo Traversagni (1480) from the so-called schoolmaster press of St Albans not only, as is often suggested, to the demands of the curriculum at distant Cambridge but also to the needs of the monastic syllabus at the nearby abbey.[82]

The presence of these books is not itself unequivocal proof that patterns of teaching in these communities had changed over the course of the fifteenth century. Yet some corroboration can be found elsewhere. It may be significant that particular collections of texts were provided not only as *usum conventus* but also more precisely as *opus claustralis*.[83] The appearance of a French (presumably) master, Pierre Corré, at Christ Church, Canterbury, as early as the priorate of Thomas Chillenden (d. 1411) may be a sign of a new approach to elementary teaching.[84] One of the first conventual acts of Abbot Wheathampstead was to revise the terms of employment for an elementary master.[85] Perhaps the most tangible measure of the cultural shift is the changing character of monastic writing itself. There can be no doubt that in the half-century after 1425 the Black Monks rediscovered forms and genres of Latin writing which had attracted few practitioners within their precincts in the recent past. Most notable was the renewed enthusiasm for epistolography; not only were the classical, medieval and humanist masters consumed but many brethren, and not only the well-connected superiors, entered into correspondence of their own. The collections of John Wheathampstead and Robert Joseph, knowledgeable, if also often clumsy, evocations of the work of (among others) Cicero, Peter of Blois, Petrarch and Bruni are

---

[80] *Ibid.*, 60–2 (1521 catalogue), 81 (Goldwell inventory), 105 (Bruni: catalogue of 1510).

[81] *English Benedictine Libraries*, ed. Sharpe *et al.*, B59. 24 (306).

[82] See also J. G. Clark, 'Print and Pre-Reformation Religion: The Benedictines and the Printing in England, c. 1470–1550', in *The Uses of Script and Print, 1400–1700*, ed. J. Crick and A. Walsham (Cambridge, 2004), 71–92.

[83] An early example is the Tewkesbury book Oxford, Trinity College, MS 50 'ad utilitatem claustralium ibidem studentium'. See also, from St Albans, Cambridge, Corpus Christi College, MS 5 'in libraria conventus ad opus claustralium voluit remanere'.

[84] BL, Royal MS 10 B IX, fo. 44v. He was removed when war resumed.

[85] To be paid an annual rate of 13s 4d: *Annales*, ed. Riley, I, 110.

well known,[86] but the manuscripts of the period also preserve the work of modest grafters in the genre: the anonymous Canterbury, Durham and Glastonbury monks who transmitted personal letters to and from their respective academic *studia* in the first half of the fifteenth century;[87] the authors of the satirical model letters who appear to have been connected with seasonal celebrations at the Benedictine Gloucester College;[88] and the concise letters of friendship copied (and perhaps composed) by the mid-century Worcester monk, John Lawerne, that filled the few blank spaces in his commonplace book.[89] Versification was also reinvigorated. The revision of monastic verse of the high Middle Ages witnessed in many monastic anthologies of this period should surely be read as a consequence of the renewed emphasis on metre: at Glastonbury, a monk who may be identified with John Matthew, recast and extended the twelfth-century *De professione monachorum*; at Durham John Wessington (or an anonymous monk working under his influence) returned Lawrence of Durham's verse-exegesis, the *Hyponosticon*.[90] The renewed sensitivity to verse is evoked with equal colour in the far from polished couplets frequently found in margins and on pastedowns. It would be wrong to dismiss this doggerel too hastily; many of the most complete examples are commemorative or obituary verses and their acrostics and cryptic dates represent an accurate recreation of an early form.[91]

In the half-century before the Henrician Reformation the literary character of the cloister syllabus can be brought into sharper focus. Here the appointment of secular masters to direct the elementary studies of the brethren is not only glimpsed but fully documented. Here also we have the distinct advantage of the direct witness of a monk that

---

[86] For Wheathampstead's letters see *Registrum*, ed. Riley. For Joseph see *The Letter Book of Robert Joseph, Monk-Scholar of Evesham and Gloucester College, Oxford, 1530–3*, ed. H. Aveling and W. A. Pantin, Oxford Historical Society, New Series, 19 (Oxford, 1967).

[87] *Formularies which Bear on the History of Oxford, c. 1204–1420*, ed. H. E. Salter, W. A. Pantin and H. G. Richardson, Oxford Historical Society, New Series 4–5 (2 vols., Oxford, 1942), I, 238, II, 304–6, 312–14, 317, 321; *Chapters*, ed. Pantin, III, 27, 30–1, 53–5. These last were letters of business but in style and tone are no dissimilar from those of either Wheathampstead or Joseph.

[88] See, for example, the trilogy of letters, attributed to identifiable scholar monks, preserved in BL, Harley MS 5398, fos. 128r–131v. The incomplete satire of Canterbury College preserved in BL, Royal 10 B IX (fos. 32v–33v) might also be seen in the same mould: *Canterbury College, Oxford*, ed. Pantin, III. 68–72.

[89] For Lawerne's model letters see Oxford, Bodl. Bodley MS 692, fos. 29v, 65r, 84r among others.

[90] The 'expanded' text of the *De professione* is now Oxford, Bodl., Bodley MS 496, fos. 207r–214r. The early fifteenth-century extract from Lawrence of Durham is found in BL, Add. MS 6162, fos. 8v–10v, a codex which may be connected with Wessington. For both see Sharpe, *Latin writers*, 108, 282, 360.

[91] Perhaps inevitably, Abbot Wheathampstead's commonplacebooks are replete with commemorative verses of this kind. See, for example, Cambridge, Gonville and Caius College, MS 230, fos. 24v, 41r, 52v, 56v.

was himself a teacher of novices and juniors. Robert Joseph passed the period from 1521 to 1528 as master of the novices at Evesham Abbey. His letter book contains not only a continuous, reflective commentary on his occupation, but also samples of the *lecturae* and texts that he prepared for his charges. Clearly the elementary curriculum at Evesham was founded on contemporary and humanist manuals whose precepts were applied and tested with reference to an array of ancient and modern authors. One lecture addressed the *Comoediae* of Terence.[92] In correspondence with colleagues and pupils Joseph so frequently echoes the verse of Baptista Mantuanus it seems scarcely credible he was not also a syllabus author.[93] Joseph expected his pupils not only to study the masters but to emulate them in compositions of their own. He condemned those that 'follow the *Regula Benedicti* so superstitiously that they keep their subjects away from letter writing as though from a brothel. Is not this the quickest way to keep good letters away from their monks?'[94]

The level of Latinity in the greater abbeys and priories of this period was high indeed. Here a comparison with the most accomplished humanist authors, or the use of adjectives such as 'medieval' and 'euphusitic', is unhelpful: it is the contrast their compositions offer to their immediate predecessors that is more meaningful.[95] These monks were schooled in a style of Latin that was informed by a greater knowledge of the mechanics of the language and the models of classical past than perhaps any generation since the Gregorian reform.

There are fragments that suggest this facility with language extended to experimental forays in Greek. There is a shadowy tradition of Greek at Reading Abbey as early as the thirteenth century; there was an (apparently elementary) guide to Greek in the library at Ramsey Abbey in the early fourteenth century; it has been suggested that a century later at least one monk of Durham Priory was familiar with some Greek vocabulary.[96] From the middle years of the fifteenth century the evidence is more substantive. A number of Greek texts now entered both conventual and individual book collections. At St Augustine's Canterbury a bi-lingual Greek–Latin psalter was recorded in the late fifteenth-century library

---

[92] *Letter Book of Robert Joseph*, ed. Aveling and Pantin, 56–9 (Letter 47).

[93] See, for example, *ibid.*, 23, 33, 124–7 (Letters 15, 25, 83).

[94] *Ibid.*, 35–6 (Letter 28).

[95] E. F. Jacob, '*Florida verborum venustas*: Some Early Examples of Euphuism in England', *Bulletin of the John Rylands Library, Manchester*, 17 (1933), 264–90.

[96] For Reading see A. Coates, *English Medieval Books: The Reading Abbey Collections from Foundation to Dispersal* (Oxford, 1999), 108–9. Ramsey also held a guide to Hebrew: *English Benedictine Libraries*, ed. Sharpe *et al.*, B67, 53, 54 (337). For the Durham possibility see Dobson, *Durham Priory*, 372 and n. Dobson doubts a connection between the Durham monk, Robert Emyldon, and a page of Greek preserved in Cambridge, Fitzwilliam Museum, McLean MS 169.

catalogue.[97] Durham Priory procured a copy of Suda's Greek glossary made by the Byzantine scribe Emmanuel of Constantinople.[98] A Latin–Greek dictionary was among books held by brethren of the Cluniac priory of Monk Bretton (South Yorkshire).[99] An anonymous monk of Reading secured a Greek Josephus (*De bello Judaico*, books 9–14) perhaps in the final quarter of the century.[100] In advance of these houses, and many secular communities of learning, Christ Church, Canterbury, appears to have become a centre of active learning in the ancient language. A manuscript that passed through the hands of mid-century monk Henry Cranbrook contains a leaf bearing notes on the alphabet and vowels in Greek.[101] It would seem William Sellyng mastered Greek in Italy, probably in Bologna.[102] It is likely he returned to the priory with Greek texts: in 1488 he completed a Latin translation of Chrysostom's *Sermo ad populum consolatorius* (*Homilia quinta*) which is preserved in a Canterbury manuscript; William Ingram's catalogue of 1508 also recorded a *Liber grecorum*.[103] There is also a hint that he taught Greek at Canterbury: in a compilation owned by William Worcester (but containing various contemporary writings of monastic origin) are brief notes on Greek grammar, 'per doctorem Sellyng'.[104] Whatever its origins, there are some grounds for suggesting that Greek was also alive at Reading Abbey at the turn of the fifteenth century. The sojourn there (for as much as a decade) of the Hellenist scribe Johannes Serbopoulos has been treated as nothing more than an act of cultural patronage on the part of Abbot John Thorne II, and the monastery served merely as a clearing house for codices intended for readers of Greek at Oxford and elsewhere. Yet not all of the intended recipients of Serbopoulos's books have been identified and the sustained patronage seems extraordinarily altruistic if there was no concomitant benefit for the monastery itself.[105] It is worth noting there was also a notable thirst for Greek learning among those with no training in the language. The Canterbury monk Henry Cranbrook

[97] James, *Ancient Libraries*, 201 (no. 92). There was also a Hebrew psalter (no. 89) three volumes apart in the same section of the library.

[98] BL, Harley MS 3100.

[99] *English Benedictine Libraries*, ed. Sharpe *et al.*, B55.104 (282): Ambrosius Calepinus.

[100] Leiden, University Library, MS Bibl. Publ. Gr. 16. See also Coates, *English Medieval Books*, 109, 143.

[101] Oxford, Bodl., Selden Supra MS 65, fo. 146r. See also Weiss, *Humanism in England*, 131.

[102] For a summary biography see Emden, *BRUO*, III, 1666–7; Weiss, *Humanism in England*, 153–9 at 154.

[103] BL, Add. MS 15673, fos. 3r–28v ascription on fo. 28v; James, *Ancient Libraries*, 163 (no. 284). See also p. 81 below.

[104] BL, Cotton MS Julius F VII, fo. 118r. See also Weiss, *Humanism in England*, 157; J. W. Bennett, 'John Morer's Will: Thomas Linacre and Prior Sellyng's Greek Teaching', *Studies in the Renaissance*, 15 (1968), 70–91.

[105] Coates, *English Medieval Books*, 110–12.

copied Latin translations of, among others, Basil, Plutarch and Xenophon in his portion of a codex that passed through other Canterbury hands.[106] At St Albans John Wheathampstead plundered the Latin Plutarch and Xenophon in Bruni's translation, although the same scholar's rendering of Aristotle's *Politics* may not have reached him.[107] The level of linguistic novelty did not rise to Hebrew, however.[108]

The syllabus of the cloister *studium* in England evolved therefore in a manner that was not dissimilar to the more instrumental reform of Benedictine convents in Austria, Padua and the Rhineland. For their part the brethren of Bursfeld became so immersed in Greek and Latin literature that the General Chapter intervened to keep them in rational bounds. Here, and in their affiliate houses and congregations, the purpose of the *studia litterarum* was to provide a foundation for the study of scripture. In particular, the linguistic training of the brethren, in Latin, Greek and, at Padua, Melk and possibly Bursfeld, also in Hebrew, was to prepare them for a purer sort of exegesis. These studies were fostered in a formal school structure not unlike the higher faculties of the university: the brethren were under the direction of lectors that expounded on the biblical languages and the commentary tradition.

There is little to suggest that the *studia litterarum* in English houses was channelled in a coordinated way towards higher studies in scripture at least before the close of the fifteenth century. The surviving and recorded books of scripture and scriptural commentary display few, if any, of the dynamics found in respects of grammar, rhetoric, the *ars dictaminis* and Latin literature. Library catalogues suggest that collections of patristic and academic authorities were consolidated and, in a number of cases incrementally enlarged, but their character did not significantly change. The scope and use of the scriptural resources at Durham Priory in this period has been analysed in depth:[109] here the different traditions of commentaries and glosses, together with the sermon collections, were re-shuffled during the library reorganisation of the mid-fifteenth century. Yet no one mode of study was privileged above another, although the deployment of some thirty volumes of sermons to the cloister cupboards does suggest a particular steer on the independent reading of the brethren during the cloister hours. New accessions to the collection were sporadic

---

[106] BL, Royal MS 10 B IX, fos. 64v–67r, 68r–70v, 75v–79v.

[107] For Wheathampstead's references to these newly translated authorities in sections of his *Granarium*, see, for example, (BL, Cotton MS Tiberius D V, fos. 140r–v, 169v). See also Weiss, *Humanism in England*, 35–6; C. E. Hodge, 'The Abbey of St Albans under John Whethamstede' (Ph.D. dissertation, Manchester University, 1934), 234–460.

[108] The residual reference works in the greater conventual libraries do not reflect a working knowledge of the biblical language. Even Abbot Wheathampstead did not master it.

[109] A. J. Piper, 'The Durham Monks and the Study of Scripture', in *The Culture of Medieval English Monasticism*, ed. J. G. Clark (Woodbridge, 2007), 86–103.

but nonetheless determined by conventual priorities, the most important of which appears to have been to fill known lacunae, whether in early, academic or contemporary exegesis. If there was an overriding theme, it was an 'appetite for the unusual'.[110] The Durham inventories show scriptural studies managed much as they had been in the fourteenth century (although in different spaces), and perhaps earlier. There were competing demands: the needs of the student monks, at the priory, and at their academic *studia*, the pastoral responsibilities of the brethren, both internally (in a large cathedral priory) and beyond the precinct, the personal interests of individual readers, and a lingering attachment to the notion of meditative *lectio divina*. There is no sign that resources, and patterns of reading and study, were refocused to create an exegetical school in the style of the reformed congregations. Though not nearly so well documented as Durham, there is no reason to suppose that at other houses the scene was significantly different.

Yet it is possible that a new approach was adopted at a number of houses in the decades either side of 1500. The anonymous account of Abbot Richard Kidderminster's reign at Winchcombe (Gloucestershire) first noticed by W. A. Pantin evokes a scriptural *schola* that seems *prime facie* reminiscent of those pioneered in the reformed congregations.[111] Lectures were also delivered at Winchcombe although since the Sentences of Peter Lombard was the principal focus the prevailing atmosphere was surely closer to the academic schoolroom. A better match for the Bursfelders is the brief glimpse of scriptural teaching at Evesham Abbey (some twenty years after Kidderminster's arrival at Winchcombe) captured in the letter book of Robert Joseph. Here there appears to have been a tradition of lectures or *lectiones* on scriptural topics; in the somewhat idiosyncratic (and perhaps untypical) example preserved in Joseph's manuscript the fusion of the linguistic and literary expertise with scriptural exegesis is explicit.[112] The liberal references in Joseph's letters to the latest examples of scriptural scholarship – Jacques Lefevre d'Etaples, Erasmus – perhaps can be read as an index of the authorities familiar to his pupils.[113]

If their formal training in scripture fell short of the reformed model there was nonetheless a responsiveness in English cloisters to the currents of contemporary theology. Perhaps most striking is the surge of interest in John Chrysostom. The Council of Florence (1431–45) reawakened Western interest in the Greek fathers, a revival to which a

---

[110] *Ibid.*, 99.
[111] W. A. Pantin, 'Abbot Kidderminster and Monastic Studies', *Downside Review*, 47 (1929), 198–211.
[112] *Letter Book of Robert Joseph*, ed. Aveling and Pantin, 15–18 (Letter 13).
[113] *Ibid.*, 26 (Letter 18).

substantial corpus of surviving and recorded manuscripts bear witness.[114] Chrysostom was perhaps the prime focus of these studies in both southern and northern communities: Pope Nicholas V (1447–55) commissioned a translation of the *Homiliae* from the humanist George of Trebizond.[115] The English monks seem conscious of the trend at an early stage: copies of Chrysostom and the pseudonymous *Opus imperfectum super Mattheum* are prominent among new accessions to conventual collections. Thomas of Horstede presented a manuscript containing the homily on Matthew 15:21 to Rochester Priory.[116] Chrysostom's homilies were among the texts that Prior Sellyng brought to Canterbury from Italy. The subject of his only known translation was one of Chrysostom's homilies and Prior Gladstone had it reproduced, perhaps for wider circulation.[117] A manuscript of the pseudo-Chrysostom homilies on Matthew which was at Worcester Priory carries readers' remarks in English, such as 'loke' and 'loke wel'.[118]

It is worth noting that there are hints of a similar response to these trends in (at least) the greater houses of their Cistercian colleagues. A copy of Francesci de Rovere's (Pope Sixtus IV) *Tractatus de sanguine Christi* bears the *ex libris* of Hailes Abbey (Gloucestershire) together with an inscription naming 'Robertus Crombrek commonachus'; the manuscript may have been acquired in Italy since the flyleaves are formed of fragments from an Italian copy of Terence's *Comoediae*.[119] This taste for contemporary theology is consistent with the pastoral interests reflected in two surviving manuscripts owned by another Hailes monk of the period, John Brystow: a copy of the sermons of Jacobus de Voragine, which Brystow partly copied, and anthology of penitential texts and sermons. Theological and pastoral studies were perhaps promoted by the pre-Reformation abbot of Hailes, Stephen Segar, who in the shadow of the Dissolution countered Cromwell's preferred preacher with 'a great clerk. . .a bachelor of divinity of Oxford to catch [him] in [his] sermons'.[120] It is possible these common patterns of study were reinforced through either personal or institutional collaborations, notwithstanding their corporate differences.

[114] For background see *Christian Unity. The Council of Ferrara-Florence 1438/39–1989*, ed. G. Alberigo, Bibliotheca Ephemeridum Theologicarum Lovaniensium, 97 (Louvain, 1991), especially essays by H. Chadwick (229–39), G. R. Evans (177–85) and M. Harvey (202–23).

[115] For George of Trebizond see C. H. Lohr, 'Metaphysics', in *Cambridge History of Renaissance Philosophy*, ed. C. B. Schmidt, Q. Skinner, E. Kessler and J. Kraye (Cambridge, 1988), 537–638 at 561–3.

[116] BL, Royal MS 5 A X.

[117] Two copies survive: BL, Add. MS 15673. BL, Holkham MS Add. 47675. See also pp. 90, 92 below.

[118] BL, Royal MS 2 E VI, fos. 102r, 129v.

[119] BL, Royal MS 8 D XVII, fos. 3r, 75r.

[120] *Letters and Papers Foreign and Domestic, of the Reign of Henry VIII: Preserved in the Public Record Office, the British Museum, and Elsewhere in England*, ed. J. S. Brewer, J. Gairdener and R. H. Brodie (22 vols. in 35, 1862–1935), IX, 747, 192.

Robert Joseph of Evesham wrote to a 'Brother Evesham' of Hailes regarding the imminent arrival there of Gabriel Clement of Abingdon; whether Clement sought a change of habit, or a period of study, is unrecorded, but at a personal level at least the Cistercian house was held to be part of the same network of its two Benedictine counterparts.[121]

The English monks were also sensitive to the devotional currents of the day. The promotion of the canonisation of Birgitta of Sweden seems to have cast an impression on a number of Benedictine communities. The *Revelationes* are recorded in catalogues compiled barely half a century later. A partial copy of the text was made at the Cluniac abbey of Paisley (Renfrewshire); a copy was also recorded in the hands of their brethren at Monk Bretton (South Yorkshire).[122] Abbot Wheathampstead of St Albans explored the textual background to the *Revelationes* and copied into one of his commonplace books an encyclical that appears to have come from Syon Abbey.[123] Their close watch on the councils led monks of the later fifteenth century to the work of Chancellor Jean Gerson. John Porter alias Smythe of Durham owned a copy of his *De consolatione theologiae*; Robert Holyngbourne of Canterbury had no less than a four-volume edition of the *Opera*.[124] It has been claimed that English interest in the *devotio moderna* was confined to the Carthusians but at least one early manuscript of Thomas von Kempen's *Imitatio Christi* may be of monastic provenance, perhaps another of the commissioned compilations of Abbot Wheathampstead of St Albans; a fragment of the imitation was incorporated in a collection in the possession of an anonymous monk of Tewkesbury.[125]

So far as it may be recovered from these fragments, the intellectual culture prevailing in English houses of the later fifteenth and early sixteenth centuries provides some parallel with continental Europe. At Bursfeld, Melk and Padua these patterns of study were harnessed to the restoration of pure monastic observance as extrapolated from close, critical readings of the *Regula Benedicti* and other early codes. The intellectual dynamics identified in monastic England were too diffuse to

---

[121] *Letter Book of Robert Joseph*, ed. Aveling and Pantin, 33–4 (Letter 25). Joseph's correspondence with six monks of Hailes is preserved in the letter book; the letters also show a familiarity with Abbot Segar.

[122] The Paisley book is now BL, Royal MS 13 E X. The Monk Bretton example appears in the inventory of books held by former brethren after the Dissolution: *English Benedictine Libraries*, ed. Sharpe *et al.*, B55. 22 (271).

[123] BL, Arundel MS 11, fos. 177r–180r. Another of the abbot's commonplace books contains the form of profession of the minoresses: Oxford, Bodl., Bodley MS 585, fos. 48r–72r at fo. 52r.

[124] BL, Add. MS 50856, fos. 49r–69r; *Canterbury College, Oxford*, ed. Pantin, I, 85.

[125] The manuscript that may be associated with Wheathampstead is Oxford, Laud Misc. 215, the *Imitatio* being at fos. 1r–79r. The script, rubrication, decoration and *mise en page* are analogous to books known to have been produced under his supervision. The Tewkesbury manuscript is BL, Royal 8 C VII.

stimulate such a systematic transformation of conventual life, but there are unmistakable signs of a shift in outlook. The teaching and learning of the cloister *studium* engendered in these generations a mood of reflection on the nature and use of the monastic vocation. The impulse to trace the history of their own house was reinvigorated: early foundation histories and *gestae abbatum* were replicated and, in some cases, continued.[126] These researches were extended by some to the history of the monasteries in England, the British Isles and the entire European story of the order.[127] Of course, in these collections and compositions there was more than a trace of the traditional monastic taste for narrative, chronology and the collation of the archival fragments. Yet the selection of sources, and the tone of the commentary connected with them, is suggestive of a different object, to unravel, and understand, the evolution of monastic order and its place and purpose in church and polity. Here there is recognition of the plurality of monastic religion and the relationship of the *Regula Benedicti* to the codes that preceded and followed it. In the longer texts there is also an attempt to locate the monastic tradition in the institutional and theological context of early Christian (and indeed, pre-Christian) history.[128]

These curious compilations have been presented as the death-pangs of the 'monastic tradition of historiography'.[129] They might also be

---

[126] At Durham, John Wessington compiled a narrative of the origins of the see that was ultimately settled at Durham (Oxford, Bodl., Laud Misc., MS 748); at St Albans, John Wheathampstead renewed the abbey's historical collections making fresh copies of such early texts as Matthew Paris's *Vitae duorum Offarum* (Oxford, Bodl., Bodley MS 585). The *acta* of the abbots collected in the *Liber benefactorum* (BL, Cotton MS Nero D VII) since the last quarter of the fourteenth century were continued down to the reign of Abbot Ramridge (1492–1521); at Westminster (John Flete) and Winchester (Thomas Rudborne) new narratives were made, with an emphasis on the formative years of the church and its community. It is worth noting signs of a similar impulse at major Cistercian houses, where early foundation histories were recopied (Fountains, Kirstall) and, in the case of Thomas Burton at Meaux, and John Brompton at Jervaulx, new narratives compiled: A. Gransden, *Historical Writing in England*, II: *c. 1307 to the Early Sixteenth Century* (1982), 356–71, 392–8; N. R. Ker, *Medieval Libraries of Great Britain. A List of Surviving Books*, Royal Historical Society, Guides and Handbooks, 3, 2nd edn (1964), 88, 107; Sharpe, *Latin writers*, 220.

[127] W. A. Pantin, 'Some Medieval English Treatises on the Origins of Monasticism', in *Medieval Studies Presented to Rose Graham*, ed. V. Ruffer and A. J. Taylor (Oxford, 1950), 189–215. See also a Durham compilation connected to Wessington, Oxford, Bodl., Laud Misc. 748, fos. 82r–83r; Wheathampstead's 'essay' *Monachatus* incorporated in his *Granarium*: BL, Arundel MS 11, fos. 107r–113v; Spofford's compilation, BL, Harley MS 2268, fos. 282r (title on 281r)–294r. BL, Cotton MS Cleopatra B II, a composite which may be connected with Winchcombe, contains an anonymous annal of monastic foundations at fos. 42r–58v; there are others in BL, Add. MS 6162, fos. 26r–31v (Durham), and Oxford, Bodl., Bodley MS 832, fos. 180r–184v.

[128] The most striking examples are Wheathampstead (BL, Arundel MS 11, fos. 107r–113v), Andrew Aston at Bury (BL, Cotton MS Claudius A XII, fos. 142r–145r) and John Wessington (Dobson, *Durham Priory*, 381–2).

[129] Gransden, *Historical Writing*, II, 342–424: 'The conclusion cannot be avoided that the chronicle tradition of the religious houses was all but dead well before the end of the fifteenth century' (424).

read as a response to the corporate challenges of the Fitzralph and Wyclif affairs. Their reverberations had faded, however, before a number of these texts were fully developed. It is not entirely implausible to interpret these researches as a response to public discourse on monastic reform initiated at Constance, brought to the English Benedictines at Westminster in 1421, and continued thereafter in the triennial sessions of their chapter: it is worth noting that three of the six that negotiated the Westminster injunctions, Thomas Elmham, John Wessington and John Wheathampstead, were compilers of texts of this kind.[130] It is tempting also to connect the character of these collections with the changing culture of cloister *studium*. Certainly, there was an antiquarianism at work here that was consistent with the priority attached to ancient authorities in the schoolroom. More specifically, the vogue for Latin translations of Greek authorities – Basil, Chrysostom – afforded these compilers fresh insights into, and in the case of some perhaps their first sight of, the world of the monastic pioneers.[131]

Interestingly, there appears to have been a degree of corporate and personal identification with the monastic past uncovered in these compilations. Monastic superiors sought to harness the spiritual – and implicitly at least, the political – power of their historic tradition to the public representation of their own house. In the second half of the fifteenth century, it was perhaps the dominant idiom in their verbal and visual productions, from stained glass to statuary.[132] In the half-century before the Henrician Reformation, there arose a vogue for professed monks to take a name-in-religion rich in historical resonances, perhaps the patron saint of their own house (Alban, Cuthbert), or of a monastic pioneer of English (Bede, Dunstan) or European acclaim (Basil, Benedict).[133] These names were common among scholarly brethren but there were a number of instances where they were adopted throughout the house. They may be seen as a self-conscious celebration of the new historicism which now pervaded the order, but where they were adopted by the cohort as a whole,

[130] For summary details of the known writings of these three see Sharpe, *Latin Writers*, 342–3, 344–5, 653–4.

[131] See, for example, later medieval copies of the *Regula Benedicti*, bound with the rule of Basil: Oxford, Jesus College, MS 42 (Gloucester) and Oxford, Bodl. Lyell MS 19 (Canterbury, Christ Church).

[132] For the superiors of this period animating a 'theatre of memory' with 'visual counterpart[s] to cartularies and chronicles' see J. M. Luxford, *The Art and Architecture of English Benedictine Monasteries. A Patronage History*, Studies in the History of Medieval Religion, 25 (Woodbridge, 2005), 68. For an example of this theatre at Durham see *Rites of Durham*, ed. J. Raine, Surtees Society (1842).

[133] For example, monks of Westminster presented for ordination in 1516 included Robert Bennett, Anthony Dunstan and William Gregory: Register Fitzjames, London, Guildhall Library, 9531/9, fos. 171r, 173r; among the monks of St Albans that signed the surrender on 5 Dec. 1539 were Richard Benett and Robert Gregory.

and combined with corporate references to the monastic past, they might be understood to be the expression of a collective search for a purer form of life.

There are some indications that these aspirations passed into a measure of reform, at least in respect of particular monasteries. It is perhaps an index of the impulse for reform that there were local initiatives for the reinvigoration of the *Opus Dei* at a time that the General Chapter's appetite for such a programme had subsided. Thomas Spofford reorganised the liturgical customs of his community at York as early as 1390.[134] His purpose was partly pragmatic, to resolve the ambiguities and (probably) contradictions that were the legacy of generations of unsystematic accretions. But his code also offered a greater clarity and purity in the daily offices, a reduction of the number of customary psalms, prayers and responses; perhaps a better evocation of Benedict's *Opus*. Prior Wessington appears to have presided over a qualitative change in the observance of his monks but did not make significant changes to the ordinal or customary.[135] There were measures to reinvigorate observance at St Albans under Wheathampstead; in the early sixteenth century at Abingdon under Abbot Thomas Rowland.[136] This continuing investment in their own office offers a valuable counterbalance to accounts of the Benedictines' appropriation of secular modes of liturgical performance.[137]

Another measure of reform that appears to have passed through much of monastic England was the return to the tradition of the *ars scribendi*. Their exposure to humanist scholarship may have underlined the aesthetic and intellectual value of script but it was their reflections on their own past that reminded them of the importance of writing in the monastic life: in Thomas Elmham's *Speculum Augustininesium* history and script were united as he sought to recreate the script of his sources just as he reproduced their substance.[138] In his own, and subsequent, generations,

---

[134] The fruits of Spofford's reform are contained in the customary compiled for use at St Mary's Cambridge, St John's College, MS D 27. The text was printed in *The Ordinal and Customary of the Abbey of Saint Mary, York St. John's College, Cambridge, MS. D.27*, ed. L. McLachlan and J. B. L. Tolhurst, Henry Bradshaw Society, 78 (1936).

[135] Dobson *Durham Priory*, 110.

[136] *Annales*, ed. Riley, I, 101–16 at 102–7. Thomas Rowland appears to have sponsored the production of a printed breviary (STC 15792: 1528) which may reflect a measure of liturgical reform at the abbey.

[137] R. Bowers, 'An Early Tudor Monastic Enterprise: Choral Polyphony for the Liturgical Service', in *The Culture of English Medieval Monasticism*, ed. J. G. Clark (Woodbridge, 2007), 21–54.

[138] Cambridge, Trinity Hall MS 1. For examples of documents copied in 'authentic' script see fos. 21v, 22r, 23r, 24r. See also M. Hunter, 'The Fascimiles in Thomas Elmham's History of St Augustine's, Canterbury', *The Library*, fifth series, 28 (1973), 215–20; Gransden, *Historical Writing*, 353–5.

a greater number of Benedictines practised book-hands than perhaps at any point since the twelfth century. They not only copied books for themselves but also made compilations for presentation to the monastery. Although surviving copies are too scarce to recover clearly the scriptorial practice of any house, there is an impression that a common style of script and *mise en page* was cultivated.[139] These features might be taken to suggest that writing was taught in these houses. If so it was a syllabus that was sensitive to wider currents: a number of monastic manuscripts written, or notated, in the century before 1540 display scripts in humanist style. William Sellyng appears an early exponent of an Italianate hand.[140] Certainly the first generation of Tudor monks seemed confident with its distinctive rounded letter forms: a *nota bene* among marginalia in books of Abbot Richard Kidderminster is a model of a humanist N B ligature.[141] The continental congregations had placed particular emphasis on the *ars scribendi* in their reform of conventual life: in the Melk network writing manuals were circulated to assist in teaching and ensure commonality.[142] Here the parallels with their English counterparts are striking. Although there are no analogues to the Melk manual(s), clearly the production of texts was promoted by the monastic superiors of the fifteenth century, and later, and although customaries are too few to document it, it must be that the *horarium* (and perhaps the space of the monastery) was adapted to create opportunities for students and practitioners of the art.

Neither these signs of change, nor the strain of thought that seems to have stimulated them, cohered into a synthetic movement for reform. The stasis of the General Chapter in the second half of the fifteenth century, and the first decades of the sixteenth, was surely a contributory factor. There is no trace of the engaged and experienced graduates that had animated its sessions between Constance and Basel; such men were still to be found in monastic England, indeed they were the mainstay

---

[139] See, for example, J. G. Clark, *A Monastic Renaissance at St Albans: Thomas Walsingham and his Circle, c. 1350–c. 1440* (Oxford, 2004), 111–20. Books made at Worcester Priory between the late thirteenth century and the Dissolution were uniform both in their appearance and their low production values: Thomson, *Descriptive Catalogue*, xxv. Antonia Gransden has suggested that at Bury the brethren contributed only to the copying of 'unpretentious' books: A. Gransden, 'Some Manuscripts in Cambridge from Bury St Edmunds Abbey: Exhibition Catalogue', in *Bury St Edmunds: Medieval Art, Architecture, Archaeology and Economy*, ed. A. Gransden, British Archaeological Association Conference Transactions, XX (1998), 228–85 at 239.

[140] Humanist scripts have been identified in the text and rubrics of several manuscripts held at Worcester Priory: F104 (*ex libris*); F124 (annotations in section six); F142 (titles). For Sellyng's hand see *Canterbury College, Oxford*, ed. Pantin, IV, 84.

[141] For Kidderminster's books see, for example, Oxford, Bodl., Inc. d.G.5.2.1494/1 (Augustine: Basel, 1494); Oxford, Rawl. Q.d.12 (*Vitas patrum*: Lyon, 1502).

[142] S. H. Steinberg, 'Instructions in Writing by Members of the Congregation of Melk', *Speculum*, 16/2 (1941), 210–15.

of its exposure to the intellectual currents from the continent, but the very opportunities the new learning presented to them proved more diverting than the sterile discourse of the triennial chapter. None of the cosmopolitan scholars of this period played a role in the governance of the order, and, of course, the *praeceptor* of many of them – William Sellyng – presided over a monastery that still refused to recognise their authority. It might also be argued that the attitude of the secular (clerical and royal) authorities in the century before 1540 was less congenial even than it had been in 1421. At Westminster, Henry V may have diverted the rising generation of graduates from any programme of change they might have envisaged but the maladroit affair nonetheless generated further discussion of reform. Seventy years on, however, the campaign of Henry VII and Cardinal Morton on exemption pushed the premier abbeys and priories into a defensive position from which they had barely advanced before Wolsey's monition of 1520.[143] Of course, there are grounds for suggesting that the structure of monastic England militated against any general process of reform. As the opponents of the expatriate Benedictines alleged in 1607, there had never been an English congregation. Even when the network had been smaller, under Dunstan, say, or Lanfranc of Bec, a common pattern of observance had proved elusive.

It was not perhaps a deliberate acknowledgement of this fact but in the half-century before the Dissolution, the modish impulses of the monastic order turned increasingly outward, to explore and express their interest in humanism and reform in collaboration with like-minds beyond the precinct walls. Their interest in intellectual novelties had led them into scholarly interactions with seculars, clerks and patrons, at least from early in the fifteenth century. John Wheathampstead of St Albans cultivated a wide circle of correspondents; he courted (unsuccessfully) the interest (and learned counsel) of Piero del Monte but secured the patronage of Humfrey, duke of Gloucester, to whom he presented books of the abbey and his own collection.[144] These contacts were not confined to the superiors and well-travelled graduates. By contrast with his superiors, Henry Cranbrook of Christ Church, Canterbury, appears to have followed a modest, and largely unrecorded course, at the priory, yet exchanged epistles with a wide variety of correspondents, amongst whom were the scholarly earl of Worcester,

---

[143] The early Tudor policy towards the monasteries requires further study. Early contributions include J. Gairdner, 'Archbishop Morton and St Albans', *English Historical Review*, 24 (1909), 91–6; D. Knowles, 'The Case of St. Albans Abbey in 1490', *Journal of Ecclesiastical History*, 3, 2 (1952), 144–58. See also C. Harper-Bill, 'Archbishop John Morton and the Province of Canterbury, 1486–1500', *Journal of Ecclesiastical History*, 29 (1978), 1–21.

[144] R. Weiss, 'Piero del Monte, John Whethamstede and the Library of St Albans Abbey', *English Historical Review*, 60 (1945), 339–406.

John Tiptoft, who commended him for his 'stilo Tulliano comptis'.[145] These epistolary friendships, formal and informal, flourished down to the Dissolution: the learned monk of the pre-Reformation period was placed within the select circle like minds that cultivated the interest of Erasmus.[146] It can only be speculated how many letters now lost may have passed between the most prominent scholar monks of this period – John Dygon of St Augustine's Canterbury, Richard Kidderminster of Winchcombe – and some of the most celebrated seculars and their patrons.[147] From the turn of the fifteenth century, these transactions also became notably collaborative. At a number of houses, secular scholars were welcomed as supernumerary members of the monastic community; John Gwynneth, a learned musician and theologian, sojourned at St Albans during the 1530s; at St Augustine's, Canterbury, Abbot John Essex alias Voche (or Vokes) appears to have cultivated a circle of scholarly contacts, among them the antiquarian John Twyne, cultivated in a manner that might be likened to a salon; the circle was warmly recalled by one writer almost half a century later.[148] Abbot Hugh Cook alias Faringdon of Reading offered his patronage to the learned Leonard Cox, whose *The Arte or Crafte of Rhetorycke* (Richard Redman: London, 1532, *c.* 1535; STC 5947 / 5947. 5), a reworking of Philip Melancthon's *Institutiones rhetoricae*, was dedicated to him. During his time at Reading Cox is also said to have translated Erasmus's *De pueris instituendis*.[149]

In a handful of cases these contacts were so well founded that they fostered common enterprises in the interests of intellectual and spiritual renewal. The educational foundations sponsored at Bruton, Milton and Winchcombe might be viewed in this light, the fruit of collaborations between the superiors of these houses and secular patrons that shared their humanist preferences.[150] Interestingly, in these foundations, the monks collaborated not only with like-minded clergy but also laymen. Perhaps the most remarkable of these collaborations was also connected (in a minor way) with Winchcombe, and with the Cistercian abbey of

---

[145] BL, Royal MS 10 B IX, fo. 122r.

[146] Abbot Richard Bere of Glastonbury (1493–1525) was praised as a patron of learning by Erasmus and the prominent English Erasmian and court diplomat, Richard Pace: Emden, *BRUO*, I, 150.

[147] For Dygon see R. Bowers, 'Dygon, John (c. 1482–1566?)', in *Oxford Dictionary of National Biography*, 8355.

[148] For Gwynneth see A. B. Emden, *A Biographical Register of the University of Oxford, 1501–1540* (Oxford, 1974), 253–4. See also J. G. Clark, 'Reformation and Reaction at St Albans Abbey, c. 1530–1558', *English Historical Review*, 115 (2000), 297–328. For John Essex see Emden, *BRUO, 1501–1540*, 193. See also Knowles, *Religious Orders*, III, 95.

[149] S. F. Ryle, 'Cox, Leonard, b. *c.* 1495, d. in or after 1549', in *Oxford Dictionary of National Biography*, 6525.

[150] *VCH Somerset*, II, 136; *VCH Dorset*, II, 61; *VCH Gloucestershire*, II, 420–1.

Hailes.[151] In a period probably between the first and second decades of the sixteenth century, the monks of these houses entered into a rich interaction with local gentleman, Sir John Huddelston, and Christopher Urswick, almoner to Henry VII and subsequently dean of York.[152] The precise nature of their relationship remains obscure, although the abbots of Hailes and Winchcombe acted as trustees of a school foundation at Winchcombe funded through the bequest of Huddelston's (presumably) widow.[153] Perhaps this was the final act of a social and patronal connection that had continued for a decade or more before Sir John's death. It seems it was in memory of his ties to Huddelston and their mutual relationship with the brethren of Hailes that Urswick, as Huddelston's executor, presented the monastery with two manuscript books, exemplars of humanist artistry and scholarship. There may have been other books in the donation, although the decoration of the two survivors does suggest that they were intended as companion pieces; their preservation together might corroborate this. The codices comprised a Latin psalter and a Latin translation of the pseudo-Chrysostom's Homilies on Matthew (i.e., the *Opus imperfectum*).[154] Both had been procured by Urswick; the psalter was copied in 1514 and presented to Hailes three years later (1517); no date of manufacture is recorded for the Chrysostom but it was donated to the monastery a year after the psalter. The script of both was the work of Pieter Meghen whose skills were employed by a number of English patrons at this date, amongst them Henry VIII. It is likely that Urswick commissioned them for his own use before selecting them for the Hailes donation: both carry illuminated title pages which depict Urswick in decanal robes knelt in prayer before, respectively, the psalmist and Chrysostom at his books (see Figures 1 and 2). There is no indication that Sir John Huddelston was himself a scholar or a commissioner of books,

---

[151] *VCH Gloucestershire*, II, 420–1.

[152] For Urswick see J. B. Trapp, 'Urswick, Christopher (1448?–1522)', *Oxford Dictionary of National Biography*, 28024. See also P. I. Kauffmann, 'Polydore Vergil and the Strange Disappearance of Christopher Urswick', *Sixteenth-Century Journal*, 17, 1 (1986), 69–85. Urswick's interest in the Cistercian tradition may have been initiated at Furness (Cumbria) where he is said to have received his early education (Huddelston was also a native of the region); Furness Abbey held the parish of Urswick, fewer than five miles distant. The prior of Hailes was Huddelston's confessor, the abbot his executor, and when he made his will he was resident in the precinct: The National Archives, PCC, Prob. 11/17, f. 164r.

[153] Stratford on Avon, Shakespeare Birthplace Trust, Leigh of Stoneleigh MSS, DR18/31/5. The first four unnumbered folios contain a copy of an indenture dated 7 Sept. 1521 detailing the obligations of the abbots of Hailes and Winchcombe to the school at the latter and the celebration of an obit for Lady Huddelston at the former. See also *VCH Gloucestershire*, II, 420–1.

[154] Now held in Wells Cathedral Library, MSS 5 and 6. See *Medieval Manuscripts in British Libraries*, ed. N. R. Ker, I. C. Cunningham and A. J. Piper (5 vols., Oxford, 1969–2002), IV, 561–3.

Figure 1. The Chrysostom presented to Hailes Abbey by Christopher Urswick, here featuring the donor, Wells Cathedral MS 6, fo. 1r.

but clearly Urswick considered them a fitting memorial of his connection with the monks of Hailes, and perhaps a symbol of his role in their school foundation.

This was not the only instance in which Urswick involved himself in the provision of monastic books. He appears to have collaborated in – and perhaps offered his patronage to – a project undertaken by Prior Thomas Goldstone of Canterbury to reproduce William Sellying's translation of Chrysostom's homily, 'ad populum'; two manuscripts were made, also the work of Pieter Meghen and perhaps Urswick's role was to secure his services. It is possible, though not proven, that both books entered the monastic collection at Christ Church, although one came into the personal possession of Archbishop William Warham at an unspecified point before 1532.[155] Goldstone also requested a text from Urswick, a copy

---

[155] Now BL, Add. MS 15673 and BL, Holkham Add. MS 46575, Warham's book. See also Kauffmann, 'Polydon Vergil', esp. 75–85; J. B. Trapp, 'Notes on Manuscripts Written by Pieter Meghen', *The Book Collector*, 24, 1 (1975), 80–96.

Figure 2. The psalter presented to Hailes Abbey by Christopher Urswick, Wells Cathedral MS 5, fo. 1r.

of Celsus's *Dissuasoria*, a defence of ecclesiastical possessions and privilege also incorporated in both manuscripts. Urswick was drawn to Goldstone and his community not only for their learning but also, it would appear, for their common outlook on church affairs. His correspondence with the prior showed him to be suspicious of the radical champions of reform and implicitly a staunch supporter of the monasteries. His assistance in the reproduction of humanist scholarship was surely intended as a contribution to this cause.

It is a reflection of the enduring dynamics of English monasticism at the end of the Middle Ages that measures of reform should have been formulated in collaboration with their own clerical and lay patrons. The hereditary founders may have cast off the care of their houses in the shadow of the Dissolution[156] but many monasteries still maintained a close and often constructive interaction with the clergy and laity of their immediate catchment. Indeed it might be suggested that with the proliferation of provincial schools (in which the monasteries had a patronal interest), the elaboration of the parochial worship (the preference for pricksong polyphony which the monastic churches had pioneered), and the penetration of print culture, there was greater common ground between the cultural and devotional tastes of the brethren and the social community beyond their precinct walls. In the new environment of the pre-Reformation *urbs* perhaps it was natural for men such as John Essex, Richard Kidderminster and Robert Joseph to live out their humanist values under local horizons, where now there were men of various conditions with whom to share them. Such, of course, were the centrifugal forces that undermined the capitular structures of the order. In the century before 1540, the General Chapter retained its role as supervisor of the monasteries and continued its cycle of triennial visitations (at least to 1527) and its meetings (to January 1532);[157] but it could not recover the common purpose that briefly animated its sessions in the early fifteenth century. The absence of any capitular canons in the early Tudor period, and the mounting pressure for regulation from the crown and episcopacy, should not obscure the appetite for reform and renewal still to be found in particular houses. In the reigns of Henry VII and his son, the greater abbeys and priories of the Benedictines, and perhaps a number of their Cistercian counterparts, continued the reinvigoration of the claustral syllabus which had begun as much as a century before; so far as can be deduced from a handful of manuscript fragments, their approach to the liberal arts and to scripture bore some resemblance

---

[156] For this trend in the later Middle Ages see B. J. Thompson, 'Monasteries and their Patrons at Foundation and Dissolution', *Transactions of the Royal Historical Society*, sixth series, 4 (1994), 103–25.

[157] *Chapters*, ed. Pantin, III, 124–36 (visitation of Malmesbury Abbey), 218–19, 262.

to the curricula cultivated in the congregations of Bursfeld, Melk and Padua. Where they survive, their writings suggest that they also shared their conception of the monastic vocation, as the pursuit of Christ-like perfection through cerebral as well as devotional service. When they challenged the claims of English expatriates in the early seventeenth century, the Europeans were too hasty to cast their former houses as wholly unreformed. Perhaps they were right to argue that the lack of a true congregational structure – the historic devolution and individuality of England's monasteries – had left them vulnerable in the face of a hostile king.

Transactions of the RHS 19 (2009), pp. 95–116 © Royal Historical Society 2009
doi:10.1017/S0080440109990053

LORD BURGHLEY AND *IL CORTEGIANO*: CIVIL AND MARTIAL MODELS OF COURTLINESS IN ELIZABETHAN ENGLAND*

By Mary Partridge

The Alexander Prize Essay

ABSTRACT. William Cecil, Lord Burghley, is not usually characterised as a courtier. He has traditionally been cast as a grave, hard-working statesman. Historians today recognise that almost every Elizabethan politician of national stature was, to a certain extent, a courtier. However, the epithet 'courtly' is still largely reserved for the self-styled chevaliers of Elizabeth's entourage. The courtliness of men such as Burghley, whose public persona was based predominantly on 'civil' rather than chivalric values, is rarely acknowledged. Yet Balthazar Castiglione's celebrated dialogue, *Il libro del cortegiano*, explored civil and martial ideals of courtly conduct. Burghley can be (and was) depicted as a model Castiglionean courtier. His friends and early biographers credited him with *il Cortegiano*'s signature characteristic, *sprezzatura*. They also emphasised his social versatility – another attribute associated with *il Cortegiano*. Moreover, Burghley shared Castiglione's monarchocentric political agenda. He served his commonwealth by cultivating a personal relationship with his prince. This relationship licensed him to counsel Elizabeth, encouraging her to rule wisely and virtuously. He thus embraced the Castiglionean paradigm whereby public service was identified with personal service to a particular monarch. Burghley's adoption of this paradigm has arguably been overlooked as a result of the historiographical climate of the past twenty years. Patrick Collinson's enormously influential concept of monarchical republicanism has encouraged historians to conceptualise Burghley as a republican who happened to live in a monarchy. This may have obscured his approximation to Castiglione's ideal courtier, who was specifically designed to operate in a monarchical context.

In 1598, Elizabeth I's chief minister, William Cecil, Lord Burghley, died at Cecil House in Westminster. Shortly after Burghley's death, a former member of his household composed a biography of the great man. The work was known as the *Anonymous Life of William Cecil*, until Alan Smith

* I am very grateful to Peter Lake, and (as always) Richard Cust for commenting on drafts of this paper. I also received helpful feedback from Elisabeth Cawthorn and Malcolm Smuts, who responded to a shorter version at the Western Conference on British Studies in San Antonio (2008), and the North East Conference on British Studies in Boston (2008). Finally, I would like to thank the reviewer of the paper, for many constructive suggestions.

convincingly attributed it to Michael Hickes. Hickes, the author, had been working for Cecil since 1573. In 1580, he became one of Burghley's secretaries.[1] He evidently liked and admired his master, and the biography was a tribute *in memorandum*. It was intended to demonstrate that Burghley had been everything a man in his position ought to be. Hickes paid tribute to Burghley's indisputably statesmanlike qualities. He saluted him as a 'grave and wise councillor' – indeed, 'the wisest and gravest councillor of this age'.[2] Yet Hickes was careful to point out that 'what business soever was in [Burghley's] head, it was never perceived at his table where he would be so merry as one would imagine he had nothing else to do'.[3] Burghley has often been cast (with justification) as the packhorse of Elizabethan government. He frequently reminded his correspondents that the best years of his life were 'faythfully paynfully and dangerously spent' in the service of his queen and country.[4] His phenomenal work ethic, and capacity to transact voluminous quantities of political business, never ceases to impress his biographers.[5] It is consequently difficult to envisage him behaving as if 'he had nothing else to do' but be merry.

Hickes, however, evidently felt that the capacity to simulate leisureliness was an important part of Burghley's public persona. Cicero identified this skill as an admirable attribute for a statesman. Setting the scene for his dialogue *De oratore*, he described how Lucius Crassus projected an aura of easy-going 'geniality' to guests at his villa, despite his concern about the terminal crisis enveloping the Roman republic.[6] Burghley's reverence for Cicero was well known, and Hickes may have intended to compliment his former master by depicting him as a model Ciceronian politician.[7] However, in the late sixteenth century, the art of studied relaxation was generally identified with Balthazar Castiglione's perfect courtier. Castiglione drew heavily on *De oratore* when composing *Il libro del cortegiano* (a dialogue set at the court of Urbino, in which the protagonists resolve 'to shape in woordes a good Courtyer').[8] Nonetheless, it would be

---

[1] Alan G. R. Smith, 'Introduction', in Michael Hickes, *The Anonymous Life of William Cecil, Lord Burghley*, ed. Smith (Lewiston, NY, and Queenston, ON, 1990), 10.

[2] Hickes, *Life of Cecil*, 70, 73.

[3] *Ibid.*, 121–2.

[4] British Library (BL), Lansdowne MS 102, fo. 10r.

[5] See, for example, Stephen Alford, *Burghley: William Cecil at the Court of Elizabeth I* (New Haven and London, 2008), 315.

[6] Cicero, *On the Ideal Orator*, trans. James M. May and Jakob Wisse (Oxford and New York, 2001), 63.

[7] According to Henry Peacham, Burghley 'would alwaies carry [Cicero's *De officiis*] about him, either in his bosome or pocket'. Henry Peacham, *The Compleat Gentleman* (1622), 45.

[8] Thomas Hoby, *The Covrtyer of Count Baldessar Castilio*, trans. Thomas Hoby (1561), sig. Ci r. All subsequent references to this edition. For Cicero's influence on Castiglione, see Jennifer Richards, 'Assumed Simplicity and the Critique of Nobility: Or, how Castiglione Read Cicero', *Renaissance Quarterly*, 54, 2 (Summer 2001), 460–86.

a mistake to equate Ciceronian geniality with Castiglionean *sprezzatura*.[9] The former was a skill; the latter, a science.[10] The concept of *sprezzatura* was central to Castiglione's vision of 'what in Court a Courtier ought be'.[11] One of the principal interlocutors in his dialogue, Ludovico Canossa, suggested that a courtier 'ought to accompany all his doinges, gestures, demeaners, finally al his mocions with a grace, and this, me think, ye put for a sauce to euery thing, without the which all his other properties & good condicions were litle woorth'.[12] When pressed, Canossa elaborated:

> But I, imagynyng with my self ofterntymes how this grace commeth, leaving a part such as have it from above, fynd one rule that is most general which in thys part (me thynk) taketh place in all thyngs belongyng to a man in worde or deede above all other. And that is to eschew as much as a man may, and as a sharp and dangerous rock, Affectation or curiosity and (to speak a new word) to use in every thing a certain Reckelessness, to cover art withal, and seeme whatsoever he doth and sayeth to do it wythout pain, and (as it were) not myndyng it.[13]

Sprezzatura became inextricably associated both with Castiglione, and with Renaissance ideals of courtly conduct.[14]

The Burghley who emerges from the pages of Hickes's *Life* thus possesses the signature characteristic of a Castiglionean courtier. Initially, we might be tempted to dismiss this as an inconsequential detail. Elizabeth's long-serving, long-suffering Lord Treasurer seems like an improbable disciple of *il Cortegiano*. For centuries, historians refused to acknowledge that he was, in fact, a courtier. They preferred to define him as a statesman. This epithet was applied to other politicians associated with the group that Winthrop Hudson named 'the Cambridge connection' (also known as the Athenian tribe).[15] However, an examination of contemporary sources suggests that courtly conduct literature significantly influenced the representation of men such as

---

[9] As Peter Burke observes, the word *sprezzatura* is difficult to translate. The first English translator, Thomas Hoby, translated it as 'Reckelessness', and 'disgracing'. Peter Burke, *The Fortunes of the* Courtier: *The European Reception of Castiglione's* Cortegiano (Cambridge, 1995; repr. University Park, Pennsylvania, 1996), 68–71.

[10] Sidney Anglo, 'The Courtier: The Renaissance and Changing Ideals', in *The Courts of Europe: Politics, Patronage and Royalty 1400–1700*, ed. A. G. Dickens (1977), 33–53 (36).

[11] The quotation comes from Thomas Sackville, Lord Buckhurst's commendatory sonnet, published with Hoby's *Covrtyer*, sig. Aiiv.

[12] Hoby, *Covrtyer*, sig. Eir. The passage quoted above is Cesare Gonzaga's paraphrase of Ludovico Canossa's argument.

[13] *Ibid.*, sig. Eiir.

[14] In Lorenzo Ducci's *Ars aulica*, for example, aspiring royal attendants were advised 'to shunne a most dangerous rocke [note the appropriation of Canossa's metaphor], that is *curious and open affectation*'. Lorenzo Ducci, *Ars aulica: Or the Courtiers Arte*, trans. [Edward Blount?] (1607), 88.

[15] Winthrop S. Hudson, *The Cambridge Connection and the Elizabethan Settlement of 1559* (Durham, NC, 1980), 46–60.

Burghley, Sir Francis Walsingham and Sir Walter Mildmay. In the late sixteenth and early seventeenth centuries, these politicians were recognised as models of Castiglionean civility.

The tradition of portraying the Athenians as statesmen not courtiers – and the assumption that the two roles should be differentiated – enjoys a long pedigree. In 1641, Robert Naunton published his *Fragmenta Regalia, or, Observations on the Late Queen Elizabeth, her Times and Favorits*. He divided the men at Elizabeth's court into three basic types: *Togati*; Martialists or *Militiae*; and courtiers. He distinguished courtiers (such as Sir Christopher Hatton) from *Togati* (such as Burghley and Walsingham). The latter were accredited with the gravitas of Roman senators. The former were dismissed as 'meer vegetable[s] of the Court'.[16] The historiographical climate of the mid-twentieth century was conducive to such characterisations. Historians emphasised the bureaucratic features of Tudor government. Geoffrey Elton, in particular, portrayed the 'statesmen of the age' as 'somewhat humdrum but very sound civil servant[s]'.[17] Elton acknowledged that such men were 'no strangers to the Court', but insisted that they were not 'its creatures' (or vegetables). His solution to the obstinate refusal of 'statesmen' and courtiers to differentiate themselves was to propose that court politics be stripped of all its cultural paraphernalia: 'We need no more reveries on accession tilts and symbolism, no more pretty pictures of gallants and galliards; could we instead have painful studies of Acatry and Pantry, of vicechamberlains and ladies of the Privy Chamber?'[18] Such 'painful studies' would identify the real politicians who had (literally) been masquerading as courtiers.

Socio-economic historians also chronicled the rise of the 'middling sort' and the 'new gentry'. These proto-bourgeois classes featured prominently in contemporary analyses of the British civil wars. The upheavals of the mid-seventeenth century were interpreted as a forceful demonstration of their agency.[19] R. H. Tawney traced the activism of the commercially minded *nouveau riche* back to the early Elizabethan era.[20] Lawrence Stone developed Tawney's hypothesis when he argued that a 'crisis in the affairs of the hereditary *elite*, the aristocracy' meant that 'For a time this group

---

[16] Robert Naunton, *Fragmenta regalia* (1641), 27.

[17] Thomas Cromwell was Elton's archetypal statesman. See G. R. Elton, 'Tudor Government: The Points of Contact. III. The Court', *Transactions of the Royal Historical Society*, fifth series, 26 (1976), 211–28 (215). The epithet 'a somewhat humdrum but very sound civil servant' was applied to Walter Mildmay. Burghley was similarly described as 'rather drabber' than his mistress, 'the brilliant queen'. Geoffrey Elton, *England under the Tudors* (1955; 2nd edn 1974), 263, 410.

[18] Elton, 'Tudor Government', 225.

[19] See, for example, Christopher Hill, *The English Revolution: 1640* (1940; 3rd edn 1955; repr. 1985), 11–20.

[20] R. H. Tawney, 'The Rise of the Gentry, 1558–1640', *Economic History Review*, 11, 1 (1941), 1–38.

lost its hold upon the nation, and thus allowed political and social initiative to fall into the hands of the squirearchy.'[21] Such theories suggested that 'middling' men had been playing an increasingly important part in public affairs for at least a century before the crisis of the Caroline regime. The combined effect of Elton's bureaucratic emphasis and Tawney's neo-Marxist analysis was to generate considerable interest in a particular type of individual within the Tudor and Stuart political establishments. This was the self-made arriviste. His origins were non-aristocratic (he 'sprung from that middle class from which the Tudors drew their best servants').[22] He usually demonstrated his precocity at grammar school, and subsequently at Oxford or Cambridge. On leaving university, he was drafted into the service of an expanding state. Every stage of his career was marked by hard work, aspiration and achievement. Members of the Athenian tribe conformed rather nicely to this stock-type. The assumption that a courtier's role was essentially decorative impeded recognition of the possibility that the Athenians might have functioned in such a capacity.[23]

Over recent decades, the courtier's stock has been reappraised. In 1985, David Starkey demonstrated the extent to which Henry VIII's personal attendants wielded genuine power within the English body politic.[24] Courtliness could no longer be dismissed as a purely recreational pastime for men of aptitude, and a serious pursuit for mediocrities only. The prizes available to proficient disciples were enticing enough to attract the most talented individuals. Moreover, Starkey argued that ability to court was not a luxury but a necessity for early modern 'statesmen':

> to survive, the minister had to have the aptitudes of a courtier and the favourites had to have the skills of a politician and often the techniques of an administrator as well. For both, in fact, the goal they strove for was the same: influence, or, in the sixteenth century's own language, the favour of the prince.[25]

[21] Lawrence Stone, *The Crisis of the Aristocracy: 1558–1641* (Oxford, 1965; repr. 1966), 13.

[22] J. E. Neale made this comment about Cecil. J. E. Neale, *Queen Elizabeth I* (1934; repr. 1952), 62.

[23] Conyers Read's conception of a courtier can be gauged from *Mr Secretary Cecil*, in which he summarised the career of Cecil's father Richard. Having described Richard's 'painfully slow' promotion at Court (from Page of the Chamber to Groom of the Wardrobe to Yeoman of the Wardrobe), Read wrote: 'He never got beyond that [Yeoman of the Wardrobe]. But always he remained close the royal person. Probably he should be classified among the courtiers. Henry VIII evidently thought well of him in that role, took him along to the Field of the Cloth of Gold and later to the siege of Boulogne. But the King made nothing more of him.' Read added that 'Henry VIII had too keen an eye for a good man to have missed Richard if Richard had had the qualities which won for his son a unique position beside Henry's great daughter.' Conyers Read, *Mr Secretary Cecil and Queen Elizabeth* (1955; repr. 1965), 20. Courtiers, we infer, were simply royal attendants who lacked the capacity to be serious politicians.

[24] David Starkey, *The Reign of Henry VIII: Personalities and Politics* (London, 1985; repr. 2002), esp. xi–iii.

[25] *Ibid.*, 21.

He took issue with Elton's attempt to maintain 'the distinction between courtier and councillor', on the grounds that 'Not only were courtiers and councillors pursuing (and achieving) similar goals and using similar methods, *they were often the same person.*'[26]

The notion that some Elizabethan ministers were 'mere' politicians and bureaucrats has also been challenged as a result of new, interdisciplinary approaches to history and biography. It has been argued that the personae of Elizabeth's councillors were shaped, not merely by their political and social circumstances, but by the cultural influences to which they were exposed. Historians have analysed the personal and professional impact of their classically inspired education. Markku Peltonen highlighted the ubiquity of 'the classical humanist vocabulary' in Elizabethan political discourse.[27] Patrick Collinson drew attention to the ease with which humanistically schooled politicians adopted classical republican solutions to monarchical problems.[28] Collinson's concept of monarchical republicanism has not only generated invaluable insights into episodes such as the Bond of Association (1584); more generally, it has encouraged early modern historians to contextualise politics by seeking out the texts that shaped the mental worlds of policy makers. Yet the fact that it has loomed so large in Elizabethan historiography for the past two decades may help to explain why Castiglione's contribution to political discourse has attracted relatively little attention. *Il libro del cortegiano* is not a republican text. It presupposes a personal monarchy, and its primary concern is to explore the ways in which an individual can flourish and do good in that environment. Its eponymous hero is certainly no apparatchik. He plays an active part in public affairs; he offers counsel candidly; and he is ready, if necessary, to reprove his prince's errors and vices. Several interlocutors even argue that *il Cortegiano* is not bound to serve a tyrannical lord (although they do not discuss the possibility of active resistance).[29] None of this alters the fact that Castiglione's dialogue is essentially about personal monarchies – the opportunities they present and the challenges they pose.

Scholars such as David Starkey and Jennifer Richards have emphasised Castiglione's indebtedness to *De oratore*.[30] *Il Cortegiano* and the Ciceronian

[26] David Starkey, 'Court History in Perspective', in *The English Court: From the Wars of the Roses to the Civil War*, ed. David Starkey *et al.* (Harlow, 1987), 1–24 (12–13).

[27] Markku Peltonen, *Classical Humanism and Republicanism in English Political Thought: 1570–1640* (Cambridge, 1995), 7.

[28] Patrick Collinson, 'The Monarchical Republic of Queen Elizabeth I', in his *Elizabethan Essays* (London and Rio Grande, 1994), 30–57.

[29] Hoby, *Covrtyer*, sigs. Oiir–Oiiiv.

[30] David Starkey, 'The Court: Castiglione's Ideal and Tudor Reality: Being a Discussion of Sir Thomas Wyatt's Satire Addressed to Sir Francis Bryan', *Journal of the Warburg and Courtauld Institutes*, 45 (1982), 232–9; Richards, 'Assumed Simplicity'.

orator share an underlying agenda – to persuade those around them to act virtuously in the interest of the commonwealth – and Castiglione was undoubtedly inspired by Cicero.[31] Starkey suggested that Castiglione's great achievement lay in the fact that he 'successfully transplanted Cicero from the forum to the Renaissance court'.[32] Yet he would scarcely have needed to reinvent Cicero's orator if the latter had proved fit for purpose in a courtly environment. The whole point of *il Cortegiano* is that he is *not* a republican orator, and can therefore exploit a political paradigm that disarms a Brutus or a Demosthenes.[33] He does not belong in a republic, monarchical or otherwise, and has consequently played a relatively peripheral part in many recent analyses of late sixteenth-century political culture. It is worth noting that literary scholars, who are perhaps less preoccupied with the concept of monarchical republicanism, have done far more than historians to highlight Castiglione's relevance to the Elizabethan political scene.[34]

Cultural historians have argued that Elizabethan politicians did not only derive certain ideas and attitudes from the intellectual training they received during their formative years; they were also endowed with distinctive approaches to policy-making and self-presentation. Mary Crane has explored how the processes of gathering and framing (gathering knowledge or wisdom from a text or scenario, and framing it in a culturally and socially acceptable format), shaped the methodology and ideology of humanist councillors.[35] Stephen Alford has examined memoranda drafted by Cecil during the early years of his tenure as Elizabeth's secretary. Alford highlights the extent to which Cecil's thought processes and political tactics were influenced by the techniques of classical rhetoric – techniques that he could hardly have avoided internalising during the course of his studies.[36] Like the concept of monarchical republicanism, this rhetorical methodology appears irrelevant, if not inimical, to *il Cortegiano*. It deliberately illuminates the processes whereby decisions are made and desirable outcomes achieved. It requires the politician to show his working out – which is something *il Cortegiano* prefers not to do. Yet, as Quentin Skinner has demonstrated, the arts of

[31] Mary Augusta Scott, 'The Book of the Courtyer: A Possible Source of Benedick and Beatrice', *Publications of the Modern Language Association (PMLA)*, 16, 4 (1901), 475–502 (485).

[32] Starkey, 'Castiglione's Ideal and Tudor Reality', 233.

[33] See the comparison between Aristotle and Calisthenes in Hoby, *Covrtyer*, sig. Ssiiv.

[34] Jennifer Richards, *Rhetoric and Courtliness in Early Modern Literature* (Cambridge, 2003), 43–54. See also Daniel Javitch, *Poetry and Courtliness in Renaissance England* (Princeton, 1978), 18–49.

[35] Mary Thomas Crane, *Framing Authority: Sayings, Self and Society in Sixteenth Century England* (Durham, NC, 1960), 12–38.

[36] Stephen Alford, *Early Elizabethan Polity: William Cecil and the British Succession Crisis* (Cambridge, 1998), esp. 14–24.

courtliness and rhetoric were closely aligned in the minds of early modern commentators. Renaissance courtiers deployed rhetorical strategies to manipulate their audiences. This fact was widely acknowledged, not least by critics who doubted the capacity of some courtiers to use their powers of persuasion responsibly.[37] There was nothing inherently anti-Castiglionean about Burghley's overtly rhetorical approach to decision-making. Indeed, it can be regarded as a thoroughly courtier-like device to win the trust of his prince, by persuading her that he offered a balanced, reliable and well-informed perspective on the issues that confronted her.

Despite the insights of the past twenty-five years, we still find it difficult to conceptualise the Athenians as courtiers in anything other than a technical sense. The Elizabethan politicians whose courtliness we acknowledge are those who embraced athletic and chivalric ideals of courtly conduct. These include the earl of Leicester (Master of the Horse and Elizabeth's general in the Netherlands); the second earl of Essex (jouster, Master of the Horse, Master of the Ordnance and military commander); Philip Sidney (the Protestant war hero); and Christopher Hatton (an excellent dancer).[38] Elizabeth's gender surely affects our perception of who did, and not, count as a courtier during her reign. We assume that the primary role of the queen's male courtiers was to court her – in the lists, on the dance floor and through the medium of love poetry. This has focused our attention upon the men in her entourage who cast themselves as courtly lovers and chevaliers.

However, an overtly chivalric persona was by no means the only acceptable image for a Castiglionean courtier. *Il libro del cortegiano* delineates both civil and martial ideals of courtliness. As Sidney Anglo has observed, the Urbino Courtier resembles a cut-and-paste conglomeration of humanist truisms, and values associated with the feudal nobility.[39] Renaissance humanism and medieval chivalry are often deemed immiscible. The Pilgrimage of Grace (1536–7) and the Northern

---

[37] For example, Skinner explores the anxieties of some commentators about the rhetorical technique of *paradiastole*, and its deployment in the political sphere. *Paradiastole* involved the identification of vices with corresponding virtues. According to moralists, it enabled unscrupulous men and women to present wicked traits as positive qualities. Roger Ascham complained that this pernicious trick was routinely used by contemporary courtiers. Quentin Skinner, *Visions of Politics: Hobbes and Civil Science* (Cambridge, 2002), 90–115; Roger Ascham, *The Scholemaster* (1570), fos. 14v–15r. I am grateful to Susan Brigden for referring me to Skinner's work on *paradiastole*.

[38] Leicester, Hatton and Sidney have all been identified with the Urbino prototype. See Walter Schrinner, *Castiglione und die englische Renaissance* (Berlin, 1939); Daniel Javitch, 'The Philosopher of the Court: A French Satire Misunderstood', *Comparative Literature*, 23, 2 (Spring 1971), 97–124 (107–8); Katherine Duncan-Jones, *Sir Philip Sidney: Courtier Poet* (1991), 156.

[39] In his inaugural lecture as Professor of History at the University College of Swansea, Sydney Anglo (playing devil's advocate) asked his audience: 'what is the *Libro del Cortegiano*

Rebellion (1569) have been interpreted as reactions by the socially conservative north of England against the ascendancy of educated, ambitious 'new men' in London.[40] The Essex revolt (1601) has been presented as the final whimper of an aristocratic cult of honour, rendered obsolete by a newer 'synthesis' of 'humanistic wisdom', reformed religion and law.[41] It is certainly valid to analyse these episodes (and other, less dramatic developments) in terms of a culture clash. Yet Castiglionean courtesy literature provided a platform upon which both cultures could be accommodated. It encouraged aspiring courtiers to cannibalise both value systems, appropriating attributes strategically and selectively.

The Urbino interlocutors discuss martial models of courtliness in Book I of *Il libro del cortegiano*. According to Canossa, the perfect courtier should aspire to 'vnderstandyng in all exercises of the bodie, that belonge to a man of warre', and skill 'on those weapons that are vsed ordinarily emong gentlemen'. He should surpass representatives of all nations in martial sports:

> And because it is the peculyer prayse of us Italians to ryde well, and to manage wyth reason, especiallye roughe horses, to runne at the rynge and at tylte, he shall bee in this amonge the beste Italyans. At tourneymente, in kepyng a passage, in fightinge at barriers, he shall be good emonge the best Frenchemen. At *Joco di canne*, runninge at Bull, castinge of spears and dartes, he shall be amonge the Spaniardes excellent.

Hunting is 'one of the chiefest' activities fit for a courtier, 'for it hath a certaine lykenesse with warre'. Yet Canossa – one of the brightest stars of Duke Guidobaldo's glittering court – admits that he lacks expertise in various war-like exercises.[42] Federico Fregoso subsequently confirms that a courtier may specialise in non-military accomplishments:

> I will haue our Courtier therfore, if he find himself excellent in anie thinge beeside armes, to sett out himselfe, and gete him estymatyon by it after an honest sorte, and be so dyscreete and of so good a iudgement, that he maye haue the vnderstandinge after a comelye maner, and with good pourpose to allure men to heare or to looke on that he supposeth himselfe to be excellente in: making semblant alwaies to doe it, not for a bragge and to shewe it for vainglory, but at a chaunce, & rather praied by others, then commyng of his owne free will.[43]

Fregoso's words effectively license politicians such as Burghley to develop a brand of courtiership that emphasises other skills and attributes 'beeside armes'.

---

but an elegant amalgam of medieval and Renaissance commonplaces?'. Sydney Anglo, *The Courtier's Art: Systematic Immorality in the Renaissance* (Swansea, 1983), 2.

[40] See, for example, G. R. Elton, 'Politics and the Pilgrimage of Grace', in *After the Reformation: Essays in Honor of J. H. Hexter*, ed. Barbara C. Malament (Manchester, 1980), 25–56; and Stone, *Crisis of the Aristocracy*, 251–3.

[41] Mervyn James, 'At a Crossroads of the Political Culture: The Essex Revolt, 1601', in *Society, Politics and Culture: Studies in Early Modern England* (Cambridge, 1986), 416–65 (459).

[42] Hoby, *Covrtyer*, sigs. Diiir–Eiv.

[43] *Ibid.*, sig. Qiiiir–v.

The Urbino interlocutors insist that knightly proficiency should be complemented by a comprehensive grounding 'in those studyes, which they call Humanitie'. Canossa recommends just such a grounding for 'oure Courtier',

> whom in letters I will haue to bee more then *ind*yfferentlye well seene . . . and to haue not only the vnderstandinge of the Latin tunge, but also of the Greeke, because of the many and sundrye thinges that with greate excellencye are written in it. Let him much exercise hym selfe in poets, and no lesse in Oratours and Historiographers, and also in writinge bothe rime and prose, and especiallye in this our vulgar tunge.[44]

It is worth noting that, whilst Castiglione's protagonists imply that a courtier need not master all the skills pertaining to soldiery, there is no suggestion that his learning can be, or appear, even slightly deficient. The scholarly prowess of the Athenians is, of course, beyond dispute.[45] If courtliness could be reduced to a checklist of essential accomplishments, Burghley and his Cambridge associates would clearly tick all of the academic boxes. *Il Cortegiano*'s education is not restricted to book learning. 'I am not pleased with the Courtyer', observes Canossa, 'if he be not also a musitien, and beside his vnderstanding and couning vpon the booke, haue skill in lyke maner on sundrye instruments.' The count also endows his courtly paragon with '*the* cunning in drawyng, and the knowledge in the very arte of peincting'.[46]

The Renaissance courtier could thus aspire to mastery of 'civil' or chivalric arts (or both). Castiglione reinvented the medieval knight as a Renaissance commonwealthsman, without entirely subsuming the former into the latter. His dialogue explored martial and humanist ideals of excellence, appealing to soldiers and scholars alike. His interlocutors' project of describing the perfect courtier was undertaken in a genuine spirit of inquiry, and their ideas were sufficiently catholic to engage representatives of more than one culture. As a non-prescriptive, Ciceronian dialogue, *Il libro del cortegiano* does not seek to pit one code of conduct against another. Neither, in the final analysis, does it encourage the reader to endorse one particular *modus vivendi* and discount alternative options. It rather facilitates synthesis, suggesting that various skills and ideals can be yoked together in pursuit of a benevolent agenda.[47] It offered viable models of courtly conduct to a range of individuals and groups – including the Athenians.

[44] *Ibid.*, sigs. Hiiiv–Hiiiir.

[45] Hudson, *Cambridge Connection*, 54.

[46] Hoby, *Covrtyer*, sigs. Iiir–Iiiiv.

[47] Dialogues constructed according to the Ciceronian model (such as *Il libro del cortegiano*) tended to be open-ended. By contrast, the authors of Socratic dialogues (such as the 'Courtier and Cuntry-Gentleman') steered their readers towards a particular conclusion. See K. J. Wilson, *The Formation of English Renaissance Dialogue* (Washington, 1985), 23–44.

Castiglione's dialogue was sufficiently open-ended to foster various styles of courtiership. However, all Castiglionean courtiers shared two crucial characteristics. First, all were committed to the ultimate 'ende' of a courtier, as defined by Ottaviano Fregoso:

> The ende therfore of a perfect Courtier . . . I beleaue is to purchase him, by the meane of the qualities whiche these Lordes haue giuen him, in such wise the good will and fauour of the Prince he is in seruice withall, that he may breake his minde to him, and alwaies enfourme hym francklye of the trueth of euerie matter meete for him to vnderstande, without feare or perill to displease him.[48]

The model courtier deploys his talents, not for selfish ends, but to encourage his prince to govern wisely and well. At first glance, this mission statement reads like a reiteration of the maxim that men must be willing 'not so much to serue their owne turnes as their Prince and Countrey'.[49] Such exhortations were underpinned by Cicero's prolifically quoted injunction that 'we be not borne for our selues alone: but somedeal of our birth our countrey, somedeal our parentes, somedeal our frendes do claime'.[50] Cicero, of course, failed to mention any obligation to princes. It is tempting to suppose that his sixteenth-century admirers were equally unconcerned with the responsibilities of a subject. Hence, when early modern authors invoke the duties owed to 'prince-and-country', we tend to assume that they are actually acknowledging a debt to the commonwealth. Yet Ottaviano explicitly states that (in temporal matters) a courtier should concentrate first and foremost upon serving his prince. Whilst the country will obviously benefit if the prince is nudged along the path of virtue, this strategy is undeniably monarchocentric.

Burghley's dedication to the common weal is often regarded as a quasi-republican trait. His attempts to force Elizabeth's hand over the issue of the succession, and his readiness to override her wishes concerning the fate of Mary Stuart, suggest a tendency to champion the interests of the country over the will of the queen, whenever the two seemed to diverge.[51] Yet Burghley defined his agenda in terms that are strikingly similar to those employed by Ottaviano. Towards the end of his life, in a letter to his son Robert, he wrote that

> I do hold and will allwayse this course in such matters as I differ in opinion from hir Majesty as long as I may be allowed to gyve advise; I will not chang my opinion by affirmyng the Contrary for that war to offend God to whom I am sworn first, but as a servant I will obey hir Majesties commandment, and no wise contrary the same, presvming

[48] Hoby, *Covrtyer*, sig. Ssiiv.

[49] Anon., 'The English Courtier, and the Cuntry-Gentleman: A Pleasaunt and Learned Disputation, betweene Them Both', in *Inedited Tracts: Illustrating the Manners, Opinions, and Occupations of Englishmen during the Sixteenth and Seventeenth Centuries*, ed. W. C. Hazlitt (1868; repr. New York, 1964), 1–93 (16).

[50] Cicero, *Marcus Tullius Ciceroes Three Bokes of Duties to Marcus his Sonne* (1556), fo. 9v.

[51] See Collinson, 'Monarchical Republic', 48–55; Alford, *Burghley*, 286–92.

that she being Gods cheff minister hear it shall be Gods will to have hir com*m*and*m*ents obeyed after *that* I have performed my dvtye as a Councillor and shall in my hart wish, hir Com*m*and*m*ents to have such good successes, as I am sure she inte*n*deth.[52]

Burghley thus insisted that his role was to capitalise on the favour and trust that Elizabeth reposed in him by counselling her freely and frankly. He also affirmed that his devotion to Elizabeth overrode all other considerations, except the fear of God. Like *il Cortegiano*, he apparently believed that he could best serve his commonwealth by serving his prince. He endorsed Castiglione's equation of public service with disinterested royal service.

The second characteristic common to all Castiglionean courtiers was *sprezzatura*. The concept of *sprezzatura* is often regarded as quintessentially aristocratic, and antithetical to pains-taking humanists such as Burghley.[53] After all, it proclaims that a gentleman's talents are innate, not acquired; he is brilliant because he was born that way, and because it befits one of his status to be brilliant. The value of hard work and discipline, in which Burghley firmly believed, is implicitly discounted. *Il Cortegiano* is even advised not to aspire to anything other than a modest competence at chess, because everyone knows how much effort is required to become 'couning at it'.[54] By contrast, as Mary Crane has observed, sixteenth-century humanist literature tended to emphasise the moral worth of diligent busyness, and the corrosive effects of idleness ('What bringeth ruste to Iron smothe?').[55] Crane also argues that ambitious English humanists of non-aristocratic origins sought to justify their participation in public affairs by identifying themselves and their aspirations with pre-validated, uncontentious truisms. Their conspicuous subscription to a 'common culture' was designed to allay fears that their values and ambitions were innovative, self-promoting, and would ultimately undermine the social order.[56] Crane regards individualism as the prerogative, or privilege, of the nobility.[57] A nobleman's social preeminence was uncontroversial, and his political activism was taken for granted. He was consequently placed under less pressure to authorise his exercise of power. According to this analysis of Tudor political culture, *sprezzatura* represented an unambiguous assertion of aristocratic identity. The 'reckless' courtier does not seek to explain himself through reference to the 'common culture';

[52] Cambridge University Library (CUL), MS Ee. iii. 56, no. 85.
[53] See, for example, Eduardo Seccone, '*Grazia, sprezzatura, affetazione* in the Courtier', in *Castiglione: The Real and the Ideal in Renaissance Culture*, ed. Robert W. Hanning and David Rosand (New Haven and London, 1983), 45–67 (60).
[54] Hoby, *Covrtyer*, sig. Piiiv.
[55] Crane, *Framing Authority*, 94; 119. Nicholas Bacon, *The Recreations of his Age* (Oxford, printed *c.* 1903, issued 1919), 3.
[56] Crane, *Framing Authority*, 12–38.
[57] *Ibid.*, 10–11.

such explanation would demystify him. He prefers not to demonstrate how he has constructed himself. Instead, he assumes the persona of a conjurer, unveiling accomplishments as if they were scarves drawn from his sleeves, or rabbits pulled out of his hat. *Sprezzatura* accentuates his individualism by obscuring the cultural context of his actions and abilities – whereas the essence of humanist 'framing' is contextualisation.

Yet *il Cortegiano* arguably occupies a halfway house between the poles of 'transcendent dilettantism' and studious self-referencing.[58] The Urbino interlocutors agree that he should practise *sprezzatura*, but they also deconstruct the concept. Cesare Gonzaga acknowledges that some individuals are lucky enough to be born with a God-given capacity for nonchalant grace. However, on behalf of 'such as of nature haue onely so much, that they be apte to beecome gratious in bestowinge labour, exercise, and diligence', he 'would faine knowe what art, with that learning, and by what meane they shall compasse this grace'.[59] To highlight the need for 'labour, exercise, and diligence' is, of course, to explode the mystique of *sprezzatura* entirely. Canossa, who is charged with revealing the tricks of the trade, suggests that 'euen as the bee in the greene medowes fleeth alwayes aboute the grasse chousynge out flowres: so shall our Courtyer steale thys grace from them that to hys seming haue it, and from ech one that parcell that shal be most worthy praise'.[60] As Crane has observed, the metaphor of the bee flitting from flower to flower in a meadow, extracting the sweetest nectar from each bloom, was frequently deployed by humanist scholars to describe the process of 'gathering' wisdom to which one would subsequently frame oneself.[61] The key to *sprezzatura*, it would seem, is for *il Cortegiano* to 'source' his behaviour in precedents and examples. Moreover, the protagonists proceed to justify this 'art that appeereth not to be art', by citing other circumstances under which it has conventionally been practised. Canossa recalls having read 'that there were some excellent Oratours, which among their other cares, enforced themselues to make euery man beleve that they had no sight in letters, and dissemblinge their conning, made semblant their orations to be made very simply, & rather as nature and trueth lead them, then study and arte'. De Medici adds that

> This in like maner is *verified* [my italics] in musicke: where it is a verye great vice to make two perfecte cordes, the one after the other, so that the verye sence of our hearing abhorreth it, and often times deliteth in a seconde, or in a seuen, which in it selfe is an vnpleasaunt discord and not tollerable: and this proceedeth because the continuance in the perfit tunes engendreth urksomenesse and betokeneth a to curious harmonye.

---

[58] The phrase 'transcendent dilettantism' is Sydney Anglo's. Anglo, 'The Courtier', 36.
[59] Hoby, *Covrtyer*, sig. Eir.
[60] *Ibid.*, sig. Eiir.
[61] Crane, *Framing Authority*, 58.

Canossa invokes 'a proverbe emonge some most excellent poincters of old time, that *To muche diligence is hurtfull*.[62] *Sprezzatura* is thus thoroughly contextualised. Castiglione addresses concerns about its morally subversive potential by highlighting its cultural ubiquity and well-established antecedents. His treatment of the concept exemplifies the humanist techniques of 'gathering' and 'framing'; and his repeated warnings about how hard *il Cortegiano* must work to sustain the illusion of aristocratic dilettantism are couched in the humanist vocabulary of diligence, endeavour and pains-taking. As Sidney Anglo perceptively remarks, 'amateurism is stressed throughout *Il Cortegiano* to such an extent that, in the end, it creates a profession of itself'.[63]

Returning to the issue of Burghley's deceptively carefree demeanour at the dinner table, it is worth noting that Hickes was not the only early modern biographer to identify the Lord Treasurer as a skilful practitioner of *sprezzatura*. John Clapham made the same point in his *Certain Observations concerning the Life and Reign of Queen Elizabeth*. Clapham, like Hickes, was a long-term member of Burghley's establishment: 'a great part of my time, even from my tender age, I spent in his house and about seven years in attendance upon his own person'.[64] Like Hickes, he made no secret of his regard for Burghley ('It is a hard matter for a man strongly possessed with affections . . . to retain a true measure in speaking or writing').[65] Having prepared his readers for a flattering portrait, Clapham praised the easy *sprezzatura* of Burghley's manners: 'surely to him that had seen his behavior only at his table, with what pleasant, familiar and ordinary talk he passed the time, Cecil might have seemed a man free from all care and business'.[66] The historian William Camden, a Cecilian protégé, also commended his mentor for eschewing verbal 'Affectation or curiosity'. Camden described the Lord Treasurer's speech as 'fluent and elegant . . . not affected, but plaine and easie'.[67] Such comments are not confined to posthumous character sketches of Burghley. In the opening years of Elizabeth's reign, Roger Ascham observed that his friend, then 'M. Secretarie' Cecil, 'hath this accustomed maner, though his head be neuer so full of most weightie affaires of the Realme, yet, at diner time

[62] Hoby, *Covrtyer*, sigs. Eiir–Eiiiv.

[63] Anglo, 'Courtier: Changing Ideals', 36.

[64] John Clapham, *Elizabeth of England: Certain Observations concerning the Life and Reign of Queen Elizabeth by John Clapham*, ed. Evelyn Plummer Read and Conyers Read (Philadelphia, 1951), 71.

[65] *Ibid.*, 70.

[66] *Ibid.*, 83.

[67] William Camden, *Annals, or, the Historie of the Most Renowned and Victorious Princesse Elizabeth*, trans. R. N. (1635), 494. For Camden's relationship with Burghley, see Patrick Collinson, 'One of Us? William Camden and the Making of History', *Transactions of the Royal Historical Society*, sixth series, 8 (1998), 139–63 (158).

he doth seeme to lay them alwaies aside: and findeth euer fitte occasion to taulke pleasantlie of other matters'.[68] Hickes, Clapham, Camden and Ascham were all close associates and admirers of Burghley. It is telling that all of them credited him with a courtier-like capacity 'to cover art . . . and seeme whatsoever he doth and sayeth to do it wythout pain, and (as it were) not minding it'.

Social versatility was an essential component of *sprezzatura*. The nonchalant courtier was required to appear at ease with all sorts of companions, in various scenarios and situations.[69] The Urbino interlocutors suggested that a courtier should learn 'To frame himself to the company' – in other words, to modify his conduct according to the character and tastes of those around him.[70] The ability to read, and adapt to, the temperament of his prince was obviously an invaluable political asset.[71] However, he was also expected to interact successfully with a wide range of constituencies. Philibert de Vienne's *Philosopher of the Court* referred to 'a certayne framing and agreeing in all our actions, to the pleasing of the worlde' habitually practised by competent courtiers.[72] Prefatory verses published with the *Covrt of Ciuill Courtesie* promised that the handbook would show a young gentleman 'at all assays how he himselfe shall frame' to best effect.[73] Giovanni della Casa's courtesy manual, *Galateo*, instructed the reader 'to frame and order thy doings . . . to please those with whom thou lyuest'.[74]

According to Hickes, Burghley possessed all the skills of a courtly chameleon. He was a highly adaptable raconteur:

> His ordinary speeches were commonly cheerful, merry, and familiar, but witty, sharp, and pithy, without dullness or sourness. And whatsoever company he came into, either old, young, men or women, great or mean, he could talk aptly and delightfully, and withal so merrily as was much pleasing to all hearers, and yet not without gravity nor unfit for a great councillor.[75]

Compare this with Canossa's description of *il Cortegiano*'s social versatility: 'Likewise in company with menne and women of all degrees, in sportinge in laughyng, and in iestynge he hath in hym a certayne sweetenesse, and so

---

[68] Ascham, *Scholemaster*, sig. Bjr.

[69] Hoby, *Covrtyer*, sig. Ciiir.

[70] *Ibid.*, sig. Diiiir.

[71] Starkey, 'Court History in Perspective', 7.

[72] Philibert de Vienne, *The Philosopher of the Court*, trans. George North (1575), 95.

[73] S[imon] R[obson], *The Covrte of Ciuill Courtesie: Fitly Furnished with a Pleasant Porte of Stately Phrases and Pithie Precepts* (1577), sig. Aiiiv. The phrase 'at all assays' suggests a wide range of scenarios.

[74] Giovanni della Casa, *Galateo: Or Rather, a Treatise of the Manners and Behauiours, it Behoueth a Man to Vse and Eschewe, in his Familiar Conuersation*, trans. Robert Peterson (Newbery, 1576; facsimile reproduction Amsterdam and New York, 1969), 4.

[75] Hickes, *Life of Cecil*, 123.

comely demeanours, that whoso speaketh with hym or yet beholdeth him, muste nedes beare him an affection for ever.'[76] This passage from Thomas Hoby's translation of *Il libro del cortegiano* reminded Gabriel Harvey of Sir Thomas More – another model of 'civil' courtliness.[77]

Hickes, Clapham and Ascham cast Burghley as an expert practitioner of *sprezzatura*. They also deconstructed his care-free demeanour. Like the Urbino interlocutors, they highlighted both the façade of easy nonchalance, and the prodigious effort that lay behind it. Their pointed references to the 'business', 'care' and 'weightie affaires' that Burghley successfully concealed might seem to contravene the ethos of *sprezzatura* – until we appreciate that *sprezzatura* was, in fact, a clever synthesis of insouciance and industry. Its fusion of aristocratic and humanist ideals reflected Castiglione's integrative agenda.

This agenda validated Burghley's own political style. Throughout his career, the Lord Treasurer experimented with the cross-fertilisation of patrician and professional modes of expression. As architectural historians have recognised, his great houses of Burghley and Theobalds reflected this magpie approach to self-fashioning. He transformed both buildings from relatively simple manor houses into palaces fit for his queen.[78] Conspicuous construction was a preoccupation (disapproving contemporaries called it a vice) of the early modern socio-political elite.[79] Great houses testified to the wealth, status, taste and familial identity of their owners. The instincts that they gratified – display and dynastic ambition – were hardwired into the aristocratic psyche. Burghley's lavish building projects can thus be construed as traditionally aristocratic enterprises, undertaken by a parvenu peer determined to create a convincingly 'noble' identity. This was certainly the view of those who claimed 'in a rash and malicious mockry *tha*t England is beco*me* Reg*nu*m Cecilia*nu*m'.[80] Jill Husselby has demonstrated that the inner courtyard of Burghley House was designed to impress newly arrived guests with its nonchalant magnificence.[81] James Sutton cites the Middle Court of Theobalds as a similar example of 'architectural *sprezzatura*'.[82] At Burghley House, the iconography associated with the Order of the Garter

[76] Hoby, *Covrtyer*, sig. Ciiir.

[77] Caroline Ruutz-Rees, 'Some Notes of Gabriel Harvey's in Hoby's Translation of Castiglione's *Courtier* (1561)', *PMLA*, 25 (1910), 608–39 (616–17).

[78] Alford, *Burghley*, 142–3, 228–9.

[79] Felicity Heal and Clive Holmes, *The Gentry in England and Wales, 1500–1700* (Basingstoke, 1994), 137–8.

[80] The National Archives, SP 12/181, fo. 159r.

[81] Jill Husselby, 'The Politics of Pleasure: William Cecil and Burghley House', in *Patronage, Culture and Power: The Early Cecils, 1558–1612*, ed. Pauline Croft (New Haven and London, 2002), 32–6.

[82] James M. Sutton, *Materializing Space at an Early Modern Prodigy House: The Cecils at Theobalds* (Aldershot, 2004), 42.

reminded visitors that the Lord Treasurer was a fully initiated member of the chivalric elite. The genealogies displayed at Theobalds attested that Burghley was just as interested in lineage, and his own dynastic heritage, as any member of the ancient nobility. A gallery of ancestral portraits conveyed the same message.[83]

However, the Cecilian portraits did not simply advertise Burghley's affinity with the old aristocracy. Baron Waldstein, who visited Theobalds in 1600, recorded that the portraits were supplemented by 'an account of the notable acts of each [Cecil] under different reigns'.[84] Burghley thus constructed a genealogy of diligent service. The idea that nobility could be earned as well as inherited is discussed in Book I of *Il libro del cortegiano*. Of course, Castiglione was not the only sixteenth-century author to address this issue. The humanist thesis that 'a righte gentleman is sooner séene by the tryall of his vertue then blasing of his armes' was surely one of the most widely debated propositions of the early modern era.[85] As Felicity Heal and Clive Holmes have pointed out, most social commentators brokered a compromise between the competing claims of lineage and merit. They argued that noble birth was highly conducive to greatness, but that it needed to be substantiated by virtue and wisdom to realise its true potential.[86] The Urbino interlocutors appear to favour this Aristotelean mean.[87] Canossa initially asserts that he 'wyll haue this our Courtyer therfore to be a Gentleman borne & of a good house'. Pallavicino contends that 'this noblesse of birthe is not so necessarie for the Courtyer'. He seems to anticipate a degree of conservative scepticism: 'And if I wiste that any of you thought it a straunge or newe matter, I would alledge vnto you sondrye, who for all they were borne of most noble bloude, yet haue they been heaped full of vyces: And contrarywise, many vnnoble that haue

---

[83] Alford, *Burghley*, 299–302.

[84] *The Diary of Baron Waldstein*, ed. G. W. Groos (1981), 85.

[85] John Lyly, 'Euphues to a Young Gentleman in Athens Names Alcius, who Leauing his Studie Followed All Lyghtnes and Lyued both Shamefully and Sinfully to the Griefe of his Friends and Discredite of the Vniuersitie', in *Euphues: The Anatomy of Wyt* (1578), fos. 83v–85r (fo. 84r). For analysis of the debate about the relative merits of lineage and virtue, see Peltonen, *Classical Humanism*, 35–9.

[86] Heal and Holmes, *The Gentry in England and Wales*, 30–3. Thomas Hoby's widow Elizabeth described her second husband, John Russell, as 'Right noble twice, by virtue and by birth'. *Chronicles of the Tombs: A Select Collection of Epitaphs*, ed. Thomas Joseph Pettigrew (1857; repr. New York, 1968), 348. The Elizabethan minister John Bridges observed that 'true Nobilitie consisteth not so much in the goodes of fortune, gorgeous apparell, and prowde and hauty lookes and behauior, as in courteous countenance, and other virtuous qualities of the minde, the verye true implements and furniture of a right Courtier'. Rudolf Gwalther, *An Hundred, Threescore and Fiftene Homelyes or Sermons, vppon the Actes of the Apostles, Written by Saint Luke*, trans. John Bridges (1572), sig. a2v.

[87] Aristotle himself argued that men 'become good and excellent through three things. These three are nature, habit, and reason'. Aristotle, *The Politics*, trans. Carnes Lord (Chicago and London, 1984), 218.

made famous their posteritie.' However, illustrious ancestry is presented as a facilitator, rather than a guarantee, of worthiness. Canossa highlights the usefulness of pedigree as an incentive, or admonition, to virtue:

> For noblenesse of birth (is as it were) a clere lampe that sheweth forth and bringeth into light, workes both good and badde, and enflameth and prouoketh vnto vertue, as wel with the feare of slaunder, as also with the hope of praise . . . the noble of birthe counte it a shame not to arriue at the leaste at the boundes of their predecessours set foorth vnto them.

He also advises that a well-born courtier will find it easier to establish himself socially and politically:

> For where there are two in noble mans house which at the first haue geuen no proofe of themselues with woorkes good or bad, assoone as it is knowen that the one is a gentleman borne, and the other not, the vnnoble shall be muche lesse estemed with euerye manne, then the gentleman, and he muste with much trauaile and long time imprint in mennes heades a good op[i]nion of himselfe, which the other shal geat in a moment, and onely for that he is a gentleman.[88]

The arguments in favour of lineage are thus pragmatic, and implicitly acknowledge the supremacy of virtue.[89]

The Urbino interlocutors contribute nothing particularly original or startling to the debate about the nature of true nobility. Nonetheless, *il Cortegiano* represents a carefully calibrated amalgam of hereditary and desert-based constructs of nobility. In the portrait gallery at Theobalds, Burghley effected a similar amalgamation. He used an aristocratic device (the illustration of ancestry) to associate himself and his forebears with the humanist ideal of virtuous endeavour. He transformed the Cecils' history of service into a pedigree. The concept of a service aristocracy appealed to other associates and off-shoots of the Athenian tribe – including Burghley's nephew, Francis Bacon. In 1580, whilst still a nineteen-year-old student at Gray's Inn, Bacon was apparently persuaded that Elizabeth had immediate plans for his advancement. He wrote to Burghley, thanking his uncle for the 'comfortable relation of her Majesty's gracious opinion and meaning towards me':

> It must be an exceeding comfort and encouragement to me, setting forth and putting myself in way towards her Majesty's service, to encounter with an example so private and domestical of her Majesty's gracious goodness and benignity; being made good and verified in my father so far forth as it extendeth to his posterity, accepting them as commended by his service, during the non-age, as I may term it, of their own deserts.

He added that he would be

> well content that I take least part of either his abilities of mind or of his worldly advancements . . . yet in the loyal and earnest affection which he bare to her Majesty's

[88] Hoby, *Covrtyer*, sigs. Ciiv–Ciiiir.
[89] See Richard Cust, 'Catholicism, Antiquarianism and Gentry Honour: The Writings of Sir Thomas Shirley', *Midland History*, 23 (1998), 40–70 (48–53).

service, I trust my portion shall not be with the least, nor in proportion with my youngest birth. For methinks his precedent should be a silent charge upon his blessing unto us in all our degrees, to follow him afar off, and to dedicate unto her Majesty's service both the use and spending of our lives.[90]

Bacon was not a scion of the old aristocracy; by default, his claim to office rested solely on humanist ideals about the elevated function of able and conscientious commonwealthsmen. Yet his letter to Burghley suggests that he regarded this claim as hereditary. His sense of entitlement, like that of a nobleman, derived from his assumption that he would automatically be given the opportunity to serve his queen and country as his father had done. He did not merely cite the achievements of Sir Nicholas Bacon as a 'precedent' that he was bound to emulate. He used the specific vocabulary of dynastic transmission, describing the appetite and aptitude for worthy employment as his 'portion'. The ancestral portraits at Theobalds no doubt reminded Burghley's second son and political heir, Robert Cecil, that service was also his portion. Burghley's expectations for his son, like Bacon's hopes of preferment, were based upon a genuine fusion of lineal and meritocratic definitions of nobility. *Il Cortegiano* embodied this fusion – and so, ostentatiously, did Burghley.

Theobalds and Burghley House also displayed their owner's scholarly credentials. As Stephen Alford observes, the Great Gallery at Theobalds was 'something like an instruction manual for classical and contemporary history'.[91] Waldstein noted that it contained

coloured portraits of the Roman Emperors from Julius Caesar to Domitian, busts of the 12 Caesars sculpted in some special material, a terrestrial globe which is 12 spans in circumference, pictures of some of the Knights-Commander of the Golden Fleece, and also of the following Kings: Richard III, Henry IV, Edward IV, Henry V, VI, VII. On the opposite wall are portraits of Don John of Austria, the Duke of Parma, Count d'Egmont, the Admiral of France, the Prince of Conde, and the Duke of Saxony; in addition there are views of a number of important cities.[92]

The artefacts were gathered and framed to highlight Burghley's encyclopaedic knowledge base and cultural savoir-faire. They emphasised the fact that the lordly designer of Theobalds was more than a wealthy *magnifico*; he was also a conscientiously educated and well-informed politician. He conformed to the Urbinese ideal of a humanist courtier.

It is generally recognised that 'chivalric' courtiers could, and did, subscribe to the image of the serious and scholarly royal acolyte.[93] It

[90] Bacon to Burghley, 18 Oct. 1580, in *The Letters and Life of Francis Bacon*, ed. James Spedding (7 vols., 1861–74), I (1861), 13–15.

[91] Alford, *Burghley*, 301–2.

[92] *Diary of Waldstein*, ed. Groos, 85.

[93] Roland Mushat Frye, '"Looking Before and After": The Use of Visual Evidence and Symbolism for Interpreting Hamlet', *Huntingdon Library Quarterly*, 45, 1 (Winter 1982), 1–19 (15).

is less frequently acknowledged that humanist politicians could adopt aristocratic modes of behaviour, if the occasion demanded it. As English ambassador in Paris, Francis Walsingham knew how to behave like a seigneur (when his finances permitted).[94] In 1571, for example, he rode into the French capital with Lord Buckhurst and the earl of Rutland, accompanied by a well-turned-out retinue of stout compatriots.[95] This is a practice that the archetypal countryman, Vincent, identifies as characteristic of the old-fashioned, landed nobility and gentry in the dialogue *Of Cyuile and Vncyuile Life* ('our seruingmen . . . follow vs in the streetes, when wee bee at London, or any other great Towne').[96] Thomas Nelson's epitaph to Walsingham presents the secretary as a munificent practitioner of traditional hospitality and charity. Walsingham 'pittied euery strangers sute that came vnto his gate'; he 'did good to rich and poore that came vnto [his] gate'; and he was 'the comfort of the poore, that to them almes did giue'.[97] It is noteworthy that Nelson describes suitors and paupers congregating at Walsingham's gate, instead of fighting their way through the mêlée at court. It may be no more than a figure of speech, but it implies an aristocratic paradigm for virtuous conduct.

Mary Crane has argued that sobriety of dress distinguished humanist councillors from aristocratic courtiers, noting that Cecil was 'famous for his plain dress and would have made a clear visual contrast to the leaders of the opposing factions of courtiers (Leicester, Hatton, Essex)'.[98] According to Crane's analysis, a George Clifford, third earl of Cumberland (resplendent in his azure jousting armour) self-consciously projected himself as a courtier, whereas a Francis Walsingham (simply attired in black) deliberately disavowed the cult of courtliness.[99] In Book II of the *Il libro del cortegiano*, however, Federico Fregoso argues that the appearance of a royal acolyte should 'bee rather somewhat graue and auncient, then garishe. Therefore me thinke a blacke coulour hath a better grace in garmentes then any other, and though not throughly blacke, yet somwhat darke.' He concedes that 'vpon armour it is more meet to haue sightly and meery coulours, and also garmentes for pleasure, cut, pompous and riche. Likewise in open showes about triumphes, games, maskeries, and suche other matters, because so appointed there is in

---

[94] Walsingham, like most other ambassadors, was perennially short of funds. On 22 June 1572, he notified Cecil that 'my diet is thin, my family reduced to as small a portion as may be, and my horse being onely twelve'. Dudley Digges, *The Compleat Ambassador* (1655), 213.

[95] See Rivkah Zim, 'Dialogue and Discretion: Thomas Sackville, Catherine de Medici and the Anjou Marriage Proposal 1571', *Historical Journal*, 40, 2 (June 1997), 287–310 (294).

[96] Anon., 'Courtier, and the Cuntry–Gentleman', 34.

[97] Thomas Nelson, *A Memorable Epitaph, Made vpon the Lamentable Complaint of the People of England, for the Death of the Right Honorable Sir Frauncis Walsingham Knight* (1590).

[98] Crane, *Framing Authority*, 119.

[99] See Roy Strong, *Nicholas Hilliard* (1975), 46.

them a certein liuelinesse and mirth.' Generally, however, he 'coulde wishe they should declare the solemnitie that the Spanyshe nation muche obserueth'.[100] This visual 'solemnitie' reinforced *il Cortegiano*'s 'sober, & circumspecte' demeanour.[101] It was an image to which many Tudor courtiers aspired. Referring to Holbein's portrait of a sombrely clad Anthony Denny (one of the chief gentlemen of Henry VIII's Privy Chamber), W. A. Sessions observed that 'Although this early courtly model of Puritan humanism appears to lack Burgundian chivalry or Castiglione's *sprezzatura* . . . he certainly possesses the gravitas Castiglione in the first book of the *Courtier* requires.'[102] Sessions is right to detect shades of *il Cortegiano* in Denny's grave and studiously unpretentious image. In fact, the suggestion that Denny does not evince *sprezzatura* can be challenged. Well-cut and coloured black clothes did not flaunt themselves in the eye of the beholder, but they were expensive.[103] They were thus ideally suited to create the impression of unostentatious but authentic elegance.

Since the 1980s, it has generally been acknowledged that the distinction between courtiers and councillors is rather artificial. However, this insight has presented us with a new problem. The political style of a Leicester or a Hatton appears very different to that of a Burghley or a Walsingham. Hence, although we accept that they were all, in some sense, courtiers, it seems impossible to treat them as a single, homogeneous group. We overcome this obstacle by persuading ourselves that Leicester and Hatton were court*ly*, whereas Burghley and Walsingham were not. Leicester and Hatton embodied the cultural ideal of the courtier, whereas Burghley and Walsingham were simply skilled practitioners of court politics. Instead of discriminating between 'courtly' courtiers and their professionally competent counterparts (which essentially resurrects the old courtier/councillor division), we should recognise that there were different models of courtliness. Some Elizabethan courtiers favoured the traditional knightly paradigm, whilst others subscribed to more modern, humanistic and 'civil' codes of conduct. These models were intended to complement each other, and could easily be interchanged or integrated. In *Il libro del cortegiano*, neither is accorded precedence. The courtliness of the Athenians was just as valid and authentic as that of their more flamboyant colleagues. To paraphrase Patrick Collinson, they were statesmen who happened also to be *cortegiani*; or vice versa.[104]

[100] Hoby, *Covrtyer*, sigs. Oiiiiv–Pir.

[101] *Ibid.*, sig. Dir.

[102] W. A. Sessions, *Henry Howard, the Poet Earl of Surrey: A Life* (Oxford, 1999), 364.

[103] Leslie Ellis Miller, 'Dress to Impress: Prince Charles Plays Madrid, March–September 1623', in *The Spanish Match: Prince Charles' Journey to Madrid, 1623* (Aldershot, 2006) 27–50 (31–2).

[104] Collinson, 'Monarchical Republic', 43.

Collinson's concept of monarchical republicanism has arguably distracted attention from the fact that it was imperative for leading Elizabethan politicians to develop successful strategies for interacting with the queen on a personal basis. Elizabeth's councillors were able to envisage England without a monarch, to the extent that they planned for an emergency interregnum in the event of the queen's assassination. Yet they never forgot that their political influence depended on their access to, and management of, their royal mistress. In 1586, when Elizabeth blamed Burghley for engineering the execution of Mary Stuart, the temporarily disgraced Lord Treasurer acknowledged that he was politically impotent whilst 'barred' from the royal entourage. Pleading for rehabilitation, he wrote to Elizabeth: 'I know not w*h*at man*n*er of ~~speche~~ wordes to direct...to your Ma*j*esty.'[105] The deletion of the word 'speche' is significant; the problem was precisely that Burghley could not speak to the queen, or engage with her face-to-face. Such engagement was crucial to the brand of politics he practised. He flourished in the intimate, supremely monarchical milieu of the court. Moreover, throughout his career, he defined himself through reference to his personal relationship with the queen. He was her servant first and foremost, saving only the honour of God.[106] His emphasis on individual service to a particular prince is more reminiscent of *Il libro del cortegiano* than *De oratore*. He was the creature of a personal monarchy – a model Renaissance courtier.

---

[105] BL, Lansdowne MS 102, fo. 6r.
[106] CUL, MS Ee. iii. 56, no. 85.

Transactions of the RHS 19 (2009), pp. 117–138 © Royal Historical Society 2009
doi:10.1017/S0080440109990065

COMMUNICATING EMPIRE: THE HABSBURGS AND THEIR CRITICS, 1700–1919*

The Prothero Lecture

By R. J. W. Evans

READ 2 JULY 2008

ABSTRACT. In the vibrant current debate about European empires and their ideologies, one basic dichotomy still tends to be overlooked: that between, on the one hand, the plurality of modern empires of colonisation, commerce and settlement; and, on the other, the traditional claim to single and undivided *imperium* so long embodied in the Roman Empire and its successor, the Holy Roman Empire, or (First) Reich. This paper examines the tensions between the two, as manifested in the theory and practice of Habsburg imperial rule. The Habsburgs, emperors of the Reich almost continuously through its last centuries, sought to build their own power-base within and beyond it. The first half of the paper examines how by the eighteenth century their 'Monarchy', subsisting alongside the Reich, dealt with the associated legacy of empire. After the dissolution of the Holy Roman Empire in 1806 the Habsburgs could pursue a free-standing Austrian 'imperialism', but it rested on an uneasy combination of old and new elements and was correspondingly vulnerable to challenge from abroad and censure at home. The second half of the article charts this aspect of Habsburg government through an age of international imperialism and its contribution to the collapse of the Dual Monarchy in 1918.

It is proper on an auspicious occasion like this to invoke the memory of the man whose name adorns our proceedings. (Sir) George Prothero was a typical British historian of the Victorian and Edwardian age, best known as a pioneering Cambridge tutor, then as long-serving editor of the *Quarterly Review*. So surely he is quite irrelevant for my purposes today? But wait! Prothero's education – not unusually for one of his generation

* The first ideas for this paper were stimulated by the request to form a panel at the 2005 Anglo-American Conference, on the theme of 'Empires', when the original call for papers had entirely failed to elicit any on the central-European imperial tradition. Those ideas were reworked for a paper in Czech which has been published as 'Císaři bez říše: Habsburkové a *Reichsidee* v 19. století', in *Per saecula ad tempora nostra. Sborník / Festschrift Jaroslav Pánek* (2 vols., Prague, 2007), II, 619–24. In more or less its present form the lecture was delivered during the proceedings of the 2008 Anglo-American Conference, which was devoted to the topic of 'Communications': hence the line of argumentation here adopted. Annotation in what follows is strictly reserved to literature bearing on the imperial theme as such.

(he was born in 1848) – had included a spell at Bonn; he even translated a work of Ranke's. When the First World War came, the already very senior Prothero found himself, as head of a newly established History Section at the Foreign Office, overseeing investigation and judgement on the (recent) past of the belligerent enemy powers in central Europe.[1] At the end of hostilities, Austria-Hungary was in fact extremely prominent (comprising all of its first fourteen items) in the long series of Peace Handbooks, which, under the general editorship of Prothero, were issued to explain and justify the international decision to liquidate the Habsburg Monarchy and deprive its last ruler, Charles, recent successor to the venerable Francis Joseph, of his imperial title.

The Habsburgs had evidently lost the battle for publicity as well as the military contest. Long before the war they had often been associated with a style of secretive, unaccountable rule which seemingly set much store by the traditions of *arcana imperii* and tricked itself out with ponderous and (out)dated ceremonial. As monarch, Francis Joseph (about whom much more later) had still wielded important prerogatives known technically, and suggestively, as *iura majestatica reservata* – as opposed to those which he shared with his legislatures and which were therefore 'communicata'.[2] He was notoriously resistant to novel means of spreading information, notably the telephone.[3]

Perhaps the Habsburgs simply embodied the wrong kind of 'empire', as then understood and prized? They were not colonialists (likewise in the then current sense), with one exception to be treated near the end of this paper. Nor were they carriers of European values overseas. Indeed, the whole nature of the Habsburgs' imperial credentials is problematic by that point, as we shall see, for other reasons. Yet at the same time the Habsburgs were the oldest 'imperialists' of all: members of the family had borne the title of emperor, with little interruption, for over six centuries. In the present context, the years around 1700 are the place to begin.[4]

At that time two preconditions were set for the shift of Europe's one and only imperial dynasty to a modern exercise of its powers. Both involved both loss and profit. First, and very specifically in 1700, the extinction of the Spanish branch of the family meant a rupture with their Mediterranean-based globalism; but it allowed a concentration of

---

[1] C. W. Crawley, 'Sir George Prothero and his Circle', *Transactions of the Royal Historical Society*, 20 (1970), 101–27. This was the first Prothero lecture. It is very brief on wartime; for that see Erik Goldstein, *Winning the Peace. British Diplomatic Strategy, Peace Planning, and the Paris Peace Conference, 1916–20* (Oxford, 1991), 30–47.

[2] László Péter in *Die Habsburgermonarchie, 1848–1918*, VII: *Verfassung und Parlamentarismus*, ed. P. Urbanitsch and H. Rumpler (2 vols., Vienna, 2000), 239–540, at 253–4.

[3] Jean-Paul Bled, *Franz Joseph* (Oxford, 1992), 201.

[4] An Appendix at the end of this paper supplies an overview, for convenience, of the principal stages in the narrative which follows.

lands and ambitions in the centre of Europe. Secondly, as a looser process around that date, what proved to be the definitive defeat of the previously chronic Ottoman menace would gradually deprive the Habsburgs of their ideological weapon of crusade; but, again in compensation, it brought vast territorial gains. Henceforth the extended 'hereditary lands' (*Erblande*) of the house of Austria would be nicely balanced, about half within and half outwith the Holy Roman Empire, of which they were long-time sovereigns. The nature of *imperium* in that Reich was above all unique and in theory universal.[5] The emperor purported to be, on the one hand, 'Roman', i.e. inheritor of the hegemony of ancient Rome; even though now, by fragmentation and by the celebrated theory of *translatio imperii*, he controlled just that relic which was predominantly (as it came to be designated) German: 'deutscher Nation'. On the other hand, he was 'holy', i.e. he embodied the sacred ecumenical role of the church; but that had now likewise become fragmented, and this time internally, by the Lutheran Reformation. The settlements of 1555 and 1648 helped to contain the religious breach in the Reich; while the global Roman idea could long be eked out through the anti-Turkish campaigns of the emperors.

By 1700, Emperor Leopold I had proved remarkably successful in consolidating and representing the powers of his office. Moreover, they were increasingly *communicated* through a heightened 'baroque' repertoire of imperial symbols, rituals and ceremonial. Intensive study of late has revealed the extent of that aulic cultural display – not inferior to, and hardly less influential than, the simultaneous imagery of the Sun King.[6] It rested on multi-media panegyric, in texts, music and theatre, architecture and elaborate decorative schemes. But there was little or no overt court propaganda. That seems to have remained largely true under Leopold's sons, the short-lived Joseph and then Charles VI, who incorporated or reincorporated Spanish traditions (and some of the formerly Spanish lands), as well as the 'Caroline' motif in the history of the Reich, from Charlemagne via the iconic emperors Charles IV and Charles V.

What was actually being conveyed? An inextricable blending of 'German' and 'Austrian' motifs.[7] Thus Catholic patronage and the so-called 'pietas Austriaca' pertained rather more to the Habsburgs as territorial rulers marked by counter-reforming zeal; Roman themes

---

[5] The classic treatment is Richard Koebner, *Empire* (Cambridge, 1961).

[6] Maria Goloubeva, *The Glorification of Emperor Leopold I in Image, Spectacle and Text* (Mainz, 2000); Rouven Pons, '*Wo der gekrönte Löw hat seinen Kayser-Sitz': Herrschaftsrepräsentation am Wiener Kaiserhof zur Zeit Leopolds I* (Egelsbach, 2001); Jutta Schumann, *Die andere Sonne: Kaiserbild und Medienstrategien im Zeitalter Leopolds I.* (Berlin, 2003). Cf. also Jeroen Duindam, *Vienna and Versailles: The Courts of Europe's Dynastic Rivals, 1550–1780* (Cambridge, 2003), esp. 287ff.

[7] Cf. R. J. W. Evans, *Austria, Hungary, and the Habsburgs. Central Europe, c. 1683–1867* (Oxford, 2006), 3–14.

more to their dignity as Kaiser, especially as legends of the family's physical descent from ancient Italy, even from Greek gods, began to fade into the background.[8] The two together are well exemplified by the grand structures which celebrated imperial sovereignty even within some of the great Austrian monasteries, like the ceremonial stairways (*Kaiserstiegen*) at Göttweig and elsewhere. Depictions of authority might tend to emphasise the absolute character of hereditary dynastic power, or the popular mandate vouchsafed by the elective principle which still nominally underlay imperial dominion. And who could say to which side the associated armoury of symbols actually belonged? The double eagle (*Doppeladler*) had been used from the time of Emperor Sigismund of Luxemburg in the early fifteenth century onwards.[9] Then there were the black-and-gold (*schwarzgold, schwarzgelb*) colours; or the crowns and insignia; or the elaborate array of vestments, precious stones and the rest.

The imperial mystique itself still exercised a strong sway. It was not yet challenged directly by ideological rivals, even by the mightiest extra-European 'empire', that of Spain, or by the western monarchies that largely reserved imperial locutions for domestic consumption. Rather it was emulated, especially from Russia, where Peter I took the precise title of 'imperator' (rather than 'tsar') and finally gained grudging recognition from the Habsburgs of some sort of parity for a Russian empire (*Российская империя*), as successor to the Russian tsardom (*Царство Русское*) of Muscovy, resting on an alternative genealogy, via Constantinople, of the same imperial claims and their symbolism, including the two-headed (*dvuglavyi*) eagle.[10]

An event in 1740 undermined all of this: the death of Charles VI, leaving only a daughter, Maria Theresa. The Reich held to Salic law, so there was an enforced separation of the *Kaisertum* from the dynasty of Habsburg, or rather Habsburg-Lorraine, as it became with Maria Theresa's marriage to Francis of Lorraine. The formal but hardly transparent elective procedures threw up a new (Bavarian) emperor who was actually by then at the head of a coalition fighting to dispossess the young queen of most of the rest of her possessions. That put to the test a famous and ineffable document known to history as the Pragmatic Sanction, originally devised back in 1703 as a secret Habsburg family

[8] Marie Tanner, *The Last Descendant of Aeneas. The Hapsburgs and the Mythic Image of the Emperor* (New Haven, 1993); cf. my review in *New York Review of Books*, 17 Feb. 1994, 25–7.

[9] Franz-Heinz Hye, 'Der Doppeladler als Symbol für Kaiser und Reich', *Mitteilungen des Institutes für Österreichische Geschichtsforschung*, 81 (1973), 63–100.

[10] Isabel de Madariaga in *Royal and Republican Sovereignty in Early Modern Europe*, ed. R. Oresko *et al.* (Cambridge, 1997), 351–81. Richard Wortman's authoritative *Scenarios of Power: Myth and Ceremony in Russian Monarchy, from Peter the Great to the Death of Nicholas I* (2 vols., Princeton, 1995–2000) neglects this aspect, along with the wider issue of Russian emulation of Germany and Austria.

inheritance compact ('pactum mutuae successionis') to secure a future
female succession: a transaction of highly dubious validity in imperial
law – but an emperor could carry it through. In the process of gaining
acceptance within and beyond the Austrian lands from 1713 onwards,
it acquired some crucial and portentous extra wording, that the lands
of the house were to be undivided (*unzerteilt*), or held 'indivisibiliter et
inseparabiliter', as the Hungarian statute declared in 1723.[11]
Challenged from abroad, the Pragmatic Sanction held at home. For
us the point is that Maria Theresa needed a new legitimation for her
own lands, independent of any imperial endorsement. Her relation to the
Reich remained awkward, even after 1745, when her husband was chosen
as emperor. Not for nothing was Habsburg dynastic authority vindicated
at just this time by the massive genealogical and medievalist publications of
a Swabian Benedictine historian, with a name that commanded attention:
Marquard Herrgott, in his *Genealogia diplomatica augustae gentis Habsburgicae*
(1737), and *Monumenta augustae domus Austriacae* (in eight volumes from
1750).[12] Yet the chief means of propagating the new goals was a massive
programme of state-building initiated by Maria Theresa, backed by a
reform party among her advisers and administrators, implemented for
the first time by squarely Austrian bodies, and communicated by *printed*
decree, instruction, exhortation and earnest Enlightenment treatise, as
well as by the beginnings of belletristic engagement on behalf of the
government.

Maria Theresa's eldest son, Joseph II, restored the organic bond with
the Empire. Or did he? His coronation, *vivente imperatore*, in 1764 was a
showpiece of the Old Reich, later recalled by Goethe in a celebrated
chapter of his autobiography as one of 'the symbolic ceremonies through
which the German Reich, almost buried in so many parchments, papers
and books, could for a moment be restored to life'. It is a quite homely
event in the poet's extended narration, blending with his own teenage
escapades and his first love for a mysterious girl called Gretchen.[13] For

[11] Edmund Bernatzik, *Die österreichischen Verfassungsgesetze* (Leipzig, 1906), 6–9 (1713), 13–15
(1723). For the question of validity, cf. Joachim Whaley in *Sacrum Imperium: Das Reich und
Österreich, 996–1806*, ed. Wilhelm Brauneder and Lothar Höbelt (Vienna, 1996), 293. The
standard works remain Gustav Turba, *Die Grundlagen der Pragmatischen Sanktion* (2 vols., Vienna
and Leipzig, 1911–12), and *idem* (comp.), *Die Pragmatische Sanktion. Authentische Texte* (Vienna,
1913).

[12] *Genealogia diplomatica augustae gentis Habsburgicae, qua continentur vera gentis hujus exordia,
antiquitates, propagationes, possessiones, et praerogativae . . . opera . . . Marquardi Herrgott* (2 vols.,
Vienna, 1737); *Monumenta augustae domus Austriacae, in quinque tomos divisa* (4 vols. in 7, Vienna
and Freiburg.i.B., 1750–72). Cf. Josef Peter Ortner, *Marquard Herrgott, 1694–1762. Sein Leben
und Wirken als Historiker und Diplomat* (Vienna, 1972); Andrew Wheatcroft, *The Habsburgs:
Embodying Empire* (1995), 216–18.

[13] Johann Wolfgang von Goethe, *Werke*, IX: *Aus meinem Leben. Dichtung und Wahrheit*, pt 1,
ed. L. Blumenthal (repr. Munich, 1981), 179–216 (quoted at 183), a section written in 1811.

Joseph this introduced a phase of vigorous imperial activity, when he sought to breathe new life into the ancient institutions – he was not yet properly ruler of the hereditary lands anyway. However, he soon began to undermine his own position by headstrong methods and frustration at the limited scope he possessed to assert himself.[14] So Joseph turned to aggressive promotion of the extra- or even anti-imperial cause instituted by his mother: the campaign for an Austrian state and civic nationality. And note: that campaign was non-national or pre-national. There was as yet no sign of ethnic considerations on the governmental side, even though resistance to Joseph's centralising–standardising–regularising innovations contributed greatly to *creating* ethnic agendas in Habsburg central Europe.

Joseph II's self-presentation proceeded accordingly; however, it was also openly imperial. Curiously Joseph could *only* be an emperor – unlike his predecessors, he remained uncrowned in any of his realms, in order not to be hampered by oaths or other restraints on his authority. But he cultivated a markedly populist register as the *Volkskaiser*. Especially in Bohemia, among the Czech peasants, he became such a *lidový císař*; and probably the best-known image of this 'people's emperor' was of Joseph handling the plough there. Although in fact he apparently did so only once, and only for one furrow, at Slavíkovice in Moravia in 1769, the deed was commemorated in a monument and in endless prints and doggerel.[15] Yet (perhaps by the same token) the ideological challenge was to Joseph as ruler of Austria: within Germany, of course, that came mainly from Prussia. There was still little criticism of Kaiser or Reich as such: indeed a particular species of allegiance, *Reichspatriotismus*, spread widely among educated Germans in the later eighteenth century; while changing notions of empire in the wider world hardly impinged (the British especially, via Hanover, continued to be strong supporters of the Reich).[16]

Joseph's death in 1790 introduced two and a half decades of turbulence: the nemesis of the old *Reichsidee* and the birth of a new one, with complex intertwining between the two. In the background there proceeded the dramatic penetration of French armies across the Rhine; deep divisions which opened up among and within the German states as they sought to manoeuvre; and the final assault on imperial institutions spurred by

[14] Derek Beales, *Joseph II*, I: *In the Shadow of Maria Theresa, 1741–80* (Cambridge, 1987), 110–33; Whaley in *Sacrum Imperium*, ed. Brauneder and Höbelt, 299ff.

[15] Metodej Zemek in *Österreich zur Zeit Kaiser Josephs II.*, ed. K. Gutkas *et al.* (Vienna, 1980), 291–3; cf. *ibid.*, 352–4. Cf. also V. M. and V. R. Kramerius, *Kniha Josefova*, ed. M. Novotný (Prague, 1941).

[16] John G. Gagliardo, *Reich and Nation: The Holy Roman Empire as Idea and Reality, 1763–1806* (Bloomington, 1980); Wolfgang Burgdorf, *Reichskonstitution und Nation: Verfassungsreformprojekte für das Heilige Römische Reich Deutscher Nation im politischen Schrifttum von 1648 bis 1806* (Mainz, 1998).

direct or indirect Napoleonic promptings.[17] That is not part of the present analysis, so I move to the caesura itself, as the Habsburgs experienced it: the years 1804 and 1806. I take the latter date first, for convenience of exposition.

After the Reichsdeputationshauptschluss, the battle of Austerlitz and the formation of the Rhine Confederation, the danger grew ever more real that Napoleon would either seize the imperial crown himself or press some client on the electoral college (which now had a Protestant majority anyhow). Therefore on 6 August 1806 a herald in full livery mounted the balcony of the Church of the Nine Choirs of Angels on Vienna's am Hof square (right next to the Austrian war ministry). He was there to communicate, in time-honoured style, an imperial decree of his master Francis II. Having rehearsed his standard titulature (including the claim to be 'at all times augmenter of the Reich'), the emperor announced to the crowd 'that we consider the bond, which has hitherto attached us to the body politic of the German Reich, to be dissolved'.[18]

This was a unilateral declaration of disbandment (rather than just of abdication), and as such probably *ultra vires* in any case. It remains a subject of contention how much the extinction of the Old Reich actually mattered to contemporaries. Yet the dissolution evidently left a void for many, as well as giving rise to an intensive constitutional debate, which included some significant wider sentiment for a restoration at the end of the Napoleonic wars, before the German Confederation (*Deutscher Bund*) came to be imposed as a fruit of the negotiations at Vienna.[19]

The Habsburgs' own damage limitation was already in place earlier. When Napoleon had proclaimed himself 'empereur des français' in May 1804, he prompted an immediate response from Francis: the announcement, in August of the same year, that he himself would henceforth be a hereditary 'emperor of Austria' – thus (as it happened) automatically promoting himself from Francis the Second to Francis the First. Once again this was an act of highly dubious validity in imperial law (much in the way the Pragmatic Sanction had been); and for the next twenty-four months it created a bizarre spectacle of the same monarch

[17] For a political analysis: Wolf D. Gruner, 'Österreich zwischen Altem Reich und deutschem Bund, 1789–1816', in *Sacrum Imperium*, ed. Brauneder and Höbelt, 319–60.

[18] 'daß Wir das Band, welches Uns bis izt an den Staatskörper des deutschen Reichs gebunden hat, als gelöst ansehen': text at http://de.wikisource.org/wiki/Datei:Niederlegung_Reichskrone_Seite_1.jpg. (accessed 1 Feb. 2009). Cf. the arguments in Heinrich von Srbik, *Das österreichische Kaisertum und das Ende des Heiligen Römischen Reiches, 1804–6* (Berlin, 1927). For the hesitations in Austrian policy, see Adolf Beer, *Zehn Jahre österreichischer Politik, 1801–10* (Leipzig, 1877), 50ff, 228ff.

[19] Wolfgang Burgdorf, *Ein Weltbild verliert seine Welt: der Untergang des Alten Reiches und die Generation 1806* (Munich, 2006); Helmut Tiedemann, *Der deutsche Kaisergedanke vor und nach dem Wiener Kongress* (Breslau, 1932); Heinz Angermeier, *Das Alte Reich in der deutschen Geschichte* (Munich, 1991), 449–521.

reigning over two different but overlapping empires. Moreover, was not Austerlitz in the following year as a consequence really the battle of the Four Emperors? Yet the implications of the *démarche* were less far-reaching than might at first appear. The decree stresses that it is a matter of title only – as if one should call oneself (say) 'king of Jerusalem' (which indeed the Habsburgs did). It confirms the continued existence of a 'united Austrian body of states' (*vereinigter österreichischer Staaten-Körper*), and explicitly introduces no change in governmental relations, so that each domestic 'state' retains its 'existing titles, constitutions, privileges and arrangements' ('daß Unsere sämmtlichen Königreiche, Fürstenthümer und Provinzen, ihre bisherigen Titel, Verfassungen, Vorrechte und Verhältnisse fernerhin unverändert bey-behalten sollen'). A special rescript confirmed that for the Hungarian lands; but it applied elsewhere too, for example in Bohemia.[20] In other words, there was now an Austria *emperor*, but no Austrian *empire*.

These circumstances helped shape the ways in which the new message of empire was conveyed. The watchwords were dynastic legitimacy and a *supra*national Austria. That matched the mood and priorities of the conscientious, but small-minded and chronically suspicious Francis – at least, most of the time. He actually began his 'new' reign by unveiling a great equestrian statue to his revolutionary uncle Joseph II in the main square outside the Hofburg in Vienna. Then he indulged a brief fling with popular patriotism in 1808–9, encouraging a lively exercise in public relations which blended German, Austrian and provincial motifs, masterminded by the court archivist Joseph Hormayr.[21] But the French soon crushed the resultant uprising at Wagram, and Francis reverted to his natural immobility and authoritarian secrecy, especially once Napoleonic dominance had been overthrown and the Vienna Congress could trumpet on his own ground the virtues of legitimate authority.

Yet 'legitimacy' could be a weasel word, even for the Habsburgs. They had, after all, defaulted of late on their long-standing ideological assertion of a purely inherited patrimony, extended only by marriage agreements, as encapsulated in that slightly defensive, yet resonant catch-phrase: 'tu felix Austria, nube'. The acquisition of Galicia in 1772 rested on (specious) medieval claims of Hungarian kings to portions of historic Poland; Bukovina was a naked land-grab from the enfeebled Turks; then Venice a mercenary transfer. In the event, Francis I grew mistrustful of

---

[20] The decree of 1 Sept. 1804 is in Bernatzik, *Die österreichischen Verfassungsgesetze*, 30–2. Cf., for the Bohemian dimension, Bohuslav Rieger, *Drobné spisy* (2 vols., Prague, 1914–15), I, 328–50.

[21] André Robert, *L'idée nationale autrichienne et les guerres de Napoléon: l'apostolat du baron de Hormayr et le salon de Caroline Pichler* (Paris, 1933); Joseph von Hormayr, *Politisch-historische Schriften, Briefe und Akten*, ed. Helmut Reinalter *et al.* (Frankfurt, 2003).

all kinds of territorial allegiance, even the 'Austrian' one his predecessors had fostered. He presented himself as 'father of the fatherland', and expected solely individual loyalty to his imperial person. That went with the paternalist system, associated with Metternich, but at least as much tributary to the emperor himself, with paid informers and apologists, which came to be seriously challenged in the 1820s and 1830s.[22]

We can see the problem if we contemplate the symbols of the new *Kaiserreich.* The Habsburgs could deploy regalia old and new. The venerable insignia of the Reich, headed by Charlemagne's crown, orb, sceptre and lance, had been 'rescued' from Nuremberg in the dark days of the 1790s; but they were not used (rather they were put on public show in Vienna).[23] Instead the resplendent *Hauskrone*, the 'house crown' commissioned by Rudolf II two centuries earlier for no obvious purpose (it had played a merely ancillary role in earlier rituals), was now drafted in as the chief jewel of Austria. It became conspicuous in iconography, as in Amerling's portrait of Francis, a superb depiction of the grandiose, sumptuous exterior and the care-ridden, vulnerable monarch within. Yet – as we shall see – that gained no practical function either. In fact only the imperial mantle for ceremonial wear was newly made.[24] Similarly with other accoutrements. Whereas the *Doppeladler* and the coat of arms, together with the *schwarzgelb* colours, were taken over more or less bodily from the Old Reich, a freshly conceived female figure came to represent 'Austria', evidently on the same lines as the 'Germania' now on display elsewhere in the Confederation and as France's 'Marianne', but usually adorned with a so-called mural crown rather than with any trappings of liberty.[25] Emblem or no, the actual meaning and denotation of 'Austria' remained deeply unclear.

And what of the arts? We have already seen (in roughest outline) the earlier role of the baroque image, then of the enlightened word. Reduced courtly budgets had largely put paid to the first, then censors crabbed the second. It is instructive to notice the Habsburg emperors' relation to the one great creative achievement of this period in their realms:

[22] Márta S. Lengyel, *Reformersors Metternich Ausztriájában* (Budapest, 1969), and *eadem, Egy tévelygő Habsburg-alattvaló a 19. század derekán* (Budapest, 1985), usefully examines two government publicists, Anton Gross-Hoffinger and Julian Chownitz. Another was Joseph Christian von Zedlitz, on whom see Eduard Castle in *Jahrbuch der Grillparzer-Gesellschaft*, first series, 8 (1898), 33–107, 17 (1907), 145–64; Zdeňko Škreb, *ibid.*, third series, 12 (1976), 317–42; Oskar Hellman, *Joseph Christian Freiherr von Zedlitz* (Leipzig, 1910).

[23] Hermann Fillitz, *Die Insignien und Kleinodien des Heiligen Römischen Reiches* (Vienna, 1954), esp. 44–6.

[24] Hermann Fillitz, *Die österreichische Kaiserkrone und die Insignien des Kaisertums Österreich* (Vienna, 1959). Cf. Karel Chytil, *Koruna Rudolfa II. a její autor* (Prague, 1929), for a Czech perspective on this crown.

[25] Selma Krasa-Florian, *Die Allegorie der Austria. Die Entstehung des Gesamtstaatsgedankens in der österreichisch-ungarischen Monarchie* (Vienna, 2007).

music's classical age. On the whole, a sharp decline of patronage can be detected, after Mozart, whom Joseph II still appointed *Kammermusicus* in the 1780s. Mozart's imperial opera *La Clemenza di Tito* was premiered at the Bohemian coronation of Leopold II.[26] But Schubert was just a boy chorister in the court chapel; it was left to Francis's youngest brother Rudolf to try to make up for the rest of his family as maecenas. The young Beethoven composed cantatas on the death of Joseph and on the accession of Leopold II. Yet his response to Napoleon's self-proclamation as emperor (removing the dedication of his 'Eroica' symphony) could hardly have been more different from the Habsburg one; and of course it is only the English-speaking world which, following the whim of a London publisher, labels his last piano concerto the 'Emperor' (though this *is* dedicated to the Archduke Rudolf).

The most notable musical connection was far more straightforward: Joseph Haydn's *Kaiserhymne*, freely offered by the patriotic composer as an imperial anthem, to counter the Marseillaise. However, let us bear in mind that in 1797 this wonderful melody, majestic but intimate, touching and a shade folksy, was still designed, with its trite deferential text, for the whole of the Holy Roman Empire.

By the 1830s the Habsburgs stood more and more in need of ideological support, as their commitment to legitimate dynastic rule dealt them a cruel blow in the practical sphere: Francis's elder son, and therefore inevitable successor, was a simpleton. Ferdinand was duly crowned in the various kingdoms of the Monarchy: in 1830 in Hungary, *vivente rege*; in 1836 in Bohemia; in 1838 in Lombardy-Venetia. The Prague occasion in particular seems to have been a real *Volksfest*, much appreciated throughout the Bohemian lands.[27] There was, however, no *imperial* coronation. Why not? Because the new hereditary principle of rule did not require it? But of course the Habsburgs had been territorial rulers of their so-called *Erblande*, explicitly 'inherited' lands, for centuries, fulfilling the appropriate rites of accession. I suggest two larger reasons: first a clash at the Hungarian diet, on which we need to pause.

This debate of 1835 in Hungary is normally dismissed – if noted at all – as evidence of the triviality of the country's ancien regime; but in fact it reveals a shift in fundamental constitutional realities. It began soon after Francis's death, with a grievance of the patriotic opposition in the Lower House that Ferdinand, though already crowned king as the *Fifth*, is now ruling, in the language of his decrees, as the *First*, i.e. using

[26] Hugh LeC. Agnew, 'Ambiguities of Ritual: Dynastic Loyalty, Territorial Patriotism and Nationalism in the Last Three Royal Coronations in Bohemia, 1791–1836', in *Bohemia*, 41 (2000), 3–22.

[27] Jan Muk, *Poslední korunovace českého krále roku 1836* (Prague, 1936); Milada Sekyrková, *7.9.1836. Ferdinand V., poslední pražská korunovace* (Prague, 2004); Agnew, 'Ambiguities of Ritual'.

his imperial style: an insult to Hungarian independence and status in Europe. The Habsburg side justified the practice with historical examples: Hungary had always recognised the imperial title as senior. It became a central counter-proposition that things were now different: the Holy Roman Empire had commanded respect (it had guaranteed the *jus gentium* and so forth); whereas 'little' Austria, formerly just an archduchy, now 'overshadows' Hungary, 'swallows it up'. The next weeks saw the title issue mixed up with a range of liberal demands for free speech, a separate army, peasant emancipation, and the like. The issue yielded some diverting episodes – as when the loyal address on the new ruler's name-day could not be sent because the diet was locked in an impasse about how to address the envelope – but it also gave rise to major speeches by rising liberals, among them Ferenc Deák, who seized on this pretext to develop his argument that the Pragmatic Sanction involved a mere personal union with 'Austria'. The affair lasted nearly six months and generated over thirty debates. All were precisely recorded and distributed for maximum effect by the skilful and eloquent young lawyer, Lajos Kossuth.[28]

A second uncertainty for the makers of Habsburg ceremonial lay in the still unfinished business of the 'Reich deutscher Nation'. A German dimension of the imperial legacy could not be gainsaid: Austria held the presidency of the German Confederation, and no sort of clear boundary could be drawn in relations between Austria and the rest of Germany (roughly they prefigured what in the post-Second World War situation between West and East would be called 'deutsch-deutsche Beziehungen').[29] Thus cultural influences readily operated in either direction. One instance would be the appropriation in the 1840s of Haydn's *Kaiserhymne* tune for Hoffmann von Fallersleben's stirring text, 'Deutschland Deutschland über alles'. However, in political terms the rest of the Confederation tended to have the better of these interactions, given Austria's tough censorship and conservative ethos. Moreover, acceptable – and permitted – traditions in the latter were broadly Habsburg-dynastic and 'Austrian' in a loose sense (as with the historical dramas of Franz Grillparzer), rather than embracing the larger heritage of the Old Reich as a whole.[30]

[28] Lajos Kossuth, *Összes munkái*, I–V: *Országgyűlési tudósítások* (Budapest, 1948–61), IV, 342–670 *passim*. Commentary in Mihály Horváth, *Huszonöt év Magyarország történelméből 1823-tól 1848-ig* (2 vols., Geneva, 1864), I, 453ff.

[29] The general point is well taken by Robert A. Kann, 'The Dynasty and the Imperial Ideal', repr. in his *Dynasty, Politics and Culture* (Boulder, 1991), 45–67. Peter J. Katzenstein, *Disjoined Partners. Austria and Germany since 1815* (Berkeley and Los Angeles, 1976), 35–96, deploys a striking political-science approach to good effect.

[30] Herbert Seidler, *Österreichischer Vormärz und Goethezeit. Geschichte einer literarischen Auseinandersetzung* (Vienna, 1982); cf. Friedrich Sengle, *Biedermeierzeit. Deutsche Literatur im Spannungsfeld zwischen Restauration und Revolution* (3 vols., Stuttgart, 1971–80), esp. I, 110ff.

The immediate 'pre-March' years confirmed all the weaknesses of Austrian identity and the emotional bankruptcy of the paternalistic *Kaiserreich*.[31] As a leading critic, Viktor von Andrian-Werburg, famously put it in 1843, Austria was a 'purely imaginary name . . . not a people, not a land, not a nation'; its regime had (literally) 'no idea'.[32] When revolution came it resurrected the whole German issue, which flooded (back) into Austria as a national movement and occupied the space left empty there by the stunted domestic literary and intellectual development since the 1820s. And many Germans still hungered for their own Reich, as was evident in the terminology of 1848, whereby the provisional government appointed by the Frankfurt parliament was designated a *Reichsregierung* and its head of state an imperial vicar (*Reichsverweser*) – a post occupied by the maverick liberal Habsburg, Archduke Johann.[33]

The revolution that broke out in March 1848 issued in a series of largely divergent campaigns, constitutional but above all national, which, led by Germans and Magyars, nearly brought down the whole Habsburg edifice. They culminated by October (the month of George Prothero's birth) in a popular uprising in Vienna and civil war in Hungary. One large step towards the recovery of the old order was an out-and-out dynastic stroke: the childless and witless Ferdinand was swept aside (not least for the concessions he had made to Kossuth and others), and replaced by his nephew, the teenage Francis Joseph: shades here of those earlier unilateral, arbitrary and at best only semi-licit acts of the Habsburgs we have already encountered in 1713–23, 1804 and 1806. The vigorous young monarch now set himself to face down his detractors at home and in the rest of Germany, and to reassert a distinctively Austrian idea of Empire. He was helped by the fact that, for all the reprehension of his policies in some quarters abroad, the Monarchy remained a European great-power desideratum: indeed, Russia was willing to step in and help quell the Hungarian rebellion. But the Habsburgs learned one important thing from their revolutionary experience: the old *a*national or *supra*national ways were obsolete; the future would have to be *multi*national.

The 1850s were the sole decade of Austria in its fullest designation.[34] The Sylvester Patent of 31 December 1851, which restored absolute

---

[31] Cf. Wolfgang Häusler in *Was heißt Österreich? Inhalt und Umfang des Österreichbegriffs vom 10. Jahrhundert bis heute*, ed. Richard G. Plaschka *et al.* (Vienna, 1995), 221–54 (though he does not address the 'imperial' deficit as such).

[32] Viktor von Andrian-Werburg, *Oesterreich und dessen Zukunft* (2 vols., Hamburg, 1843–7), I, 8.

[33] For the whole issue, see Heinrich von Srbik, *Deutsche Einheit: Idee und Wirklichkeit vom Heiligen Reich bis Königgrätz* (4 vols., Munich, 1935–42), a powerful analysis in thrall to its own 1920s–1930s agenda.

[34] Overview of the neo-absolutist 'experiment' in Evans, *Austria, Hungary and the Habsburgs*, 266–92.

rule, declared that 'the lands united under old historical or new titles with the Austrian imperial state form the indivisible components of the Austrian imperial hereditary Monarchy'.[35] The ideological programme now launched thus combined authoritarian and multinational themes; and it was underpinned by a much more professional style of official propagation. A typical image of the time was the one illustrated by August Strixner, of the Empire's peoples, in their various costumes, sitting or standing in a boat (filled well beyond health and safety levels!) steered by Francis Joseph and the allegorical figure of 'Austria'. On the sail is the slogan *viribus unitis*, the personal device of the emperor and a further significant manifestation of his purpose, as of the continuing overlap with a legitimation of dynastic rule.[36]

The wider projection was of a 'modern' Austria: a state dynamically transformed by administrative centralisation, as advertised in the colossal statistical compilation by Karl Czoernig, *Österreichs Neugestaltung*, and the complacent compendium entitled *Rückblick* by Bernhard Mayer. Yet the antithetical notion of a 'Catholic great power', indeed the last defender of the universal objectives of the Roman church, also belonged to the public rhetoric.[37] And these messages still needed to be backed by publicity abroad to counter the poison of émigré detractors, and by spies to infiltrate their networks. Quaintly, one of the most effective of those spies, Gustav Zerffi, would go native in Britain and end up at the head of the Royal Historical Society, like Prothero after him.[38]

This Reich, however, continued to eschew communicating by any kind of coronation, even though some plans existed for a consolidated Austrian–Hungarian–Bohemian one.[39] In that, as in other respects, there was an evident French and Napoleonic exemplar for Habsburg stances, as there had been for the declaration of empire in 1804 (even though at that juncture Bonaparte *had* had himself crowned). So it is fitting to cite a typical statement of the regime's purpose as offered to Louis Napoleon in 1858 by Francis Joseph's ambassador in Paris, Baron Alexander Hübner:

---

[35] 'Die unter den alten historischen oder neuen Titeln mit dem österreichischen Kaiserstaate vereinigten Länder bilden die untrennbaren Bestandteile der österreichischen kaiserlichen Erbmonarchie': 'Kaiserliches Patent vom 31. Dezember 1851', in *Reichsgesetz- und Regierungsblatt*, 1852, II, Stück, Nr. 2.

[36] Krasa-Florian, *Allegorie der Austria*, 78–9.

[37] Karl von Czoernig, *Österreichs Neugestaltung, 1848–58* (Stuttgart and Augsburg, 1858); [Bernhard Mayer], *Rückblick auf die jüngste Entwicklungs-Periode Ungarns* (Vienna, 1857); Gottfried Mayer, *Osterreich als 'Katholische Grossmacht': ein Traum zwischen Revolution und liberaler Ära* (Vienna, 1989), is narrower than its title suggests.

[38] Tibor Frank, *From Habsburg Agent to Victorian Scholar: G.G. Zerffi, 1820–92* (Boulder, 2001). Zerffi was chairman of the Society 1880–5, while Lord Aberdare was a fainéant president (1878–92); Prothero was president 1901–5.

[39] Otto Urban, *Česká společnost, 1848–1918* (Prague, 1982), 153ff; Krasa-Florian, *Allegorie der Austria*, 105ff.

'Every power has a moral foundation, a principle from which one cannot turn away with impunity. Austria has as principle the recognition of the unalterable rights of the sovereign and a rejection of the efforts of nationalities to organise themselves in national states.' The French emperor appears to have demurred.[40]

Napoleon III shortly afterwards administered a celebrated open rebuke to that very diplomat, a gesture which initiated for Austria the catastrophes of 1859 and 1866. It lost wars to France and Prussia: as a result of these the new states of Italy and Germany could be established, from which the Habsburgs were wholly excluded. At home the autocratic regime collapsed, and after years of political turmoil Francis Joseph had to concede not only constitutional government throughout his realms, but wide-ranging autonomy to Hungary under the terms of the so-called Compromise law of 1867. In the present context, we need to consider three consequences of this painful adjustment to changing realities.

First, in Hungary Francis Joseph could now at last submit himself to a coronation. It was an occasion of the utmost splendour. Yet in essential respects it took place on the Hungarians' terms. They held it to purge the 'illegal' transaction of December 1848, never recognised in their statutes. Henceforward 'Ferenc József' was their *king*, and no longer their emperor at all. Moreover, since the remaining joint affairs of the whole Monarchy – mainly the army and the diplomatic service – were now managed jointly with Hungary, it soon became a moot point how far those were still imperial either. Thus the terminology of empire was gradually and messily dismantled.

The semantic agenda of the Compromise created a strict parity, with locutions as with institutions: 'Österreichisch-Ungarische Monarchie' or 'Österreichisch-Ungarisches Reich' were initially agreed as alternatives by both parties to describe the totality of the Habsburg realms. But Hungarians soon undermined any 'Reich' usage, for the joint dealings of the Monarchy.[41] The epithet 'common' (*gemeinsam* and *közös*) tended to impose itself (and always in Magyar texts). So too did the famous alliterative abbreviation 'k[aiserlich] *und* k[öniglich]', to differentiate clearly the Habsburgs' styles of rule in the separate halves of their

---

[40] 'Chaque puissance, Sire [to Napoleon III] . . . a une base morale, un principe duquel elle ne peut s'écarter impunément: . . . l'Autriche a pour principe le respect dû aux droits imprescriptibles des souverains, et la non-reconnaissance des prétentions des nationalités de s'établir en états politiques.' 'Ne dites pas cela' m'interrompit l'Empereur, 'l'Autriche et l'Angleterre sont les deux puissances qui n'ont pas de principes, et au fait, c'est ce qu'il y a de mieux.' Hübner, entry for 15 May 1858: *Neuf ans de souvenirs d'un ambassadeur d'Autriche à Paris sous le second empire, 1851–9* (2 vols., Paris, 1904), 164.

[41] Bernatzik, *Die österreichischen Verfassungsgesetze*, 33–4 (decree for locutions); Gerald Stourzh in *Die Habsburgermonarchie*, ed. Urbanitsch and Rumpler, VII, 1177–230, at 1183ff.

dominions.[42] Worse was to follow, for Hungarian politicians were now free to develop further their own ideology of monarchical statehood, the 'theory of the holy crown', which led some of them by the early twentieth century to an assertion of full sovereignty for their country.[43] As one of them put the matter in 1909: 'Austria and Hungary connote therefore, as the dual appellation implies, *not* one Reich, but a lasting union (*Vereinigung*) designed for certain international purposes.'[44]

Alongside this body-blow to imperial thinking, Bohemian frustration about coronations, or the lack of them, might appear trivial. Yet this too, as the second of our considerations, diminished the scope of the Habsburg *Reichsidee*. Unlike Hungarians, Czechs had been happy to call their previous ruler 'Ferdinand *V*'; they made no apparent objection to the accession of Francis Joseph either (indeed, Czech representatives seem to have applauded it at the time as much as the Germans). Nevertheless, that gala in 1836 had raised their expectations: Czechs from then on sang 'God save our dear *king* Ferdinand';[45] and they showed him especial favour when he settled in Prague castle during his long enforced retirement. After the collapse of absolutism, Czech politicians and aristocrats gained four successive promises from Francis Joseph that he would have himself crowned in Bohemia. One of them involved the notable historian Antonín Gindely, who drew up plans for the ceremony on the basis of reliable archivalia. Yet the event never happened, not even during the First World War, when another great historian, Josef Pekař, was associated with a scheme for the coronation of Emperor Charles I.[46]

Whereas Czechs were less obsessed than Hungarians with the idea of the crown as such, it assumed in Bohemia too the attribute of a sort of – frustrated – national mission, as an alternative to the increasingly discredited imperial or Austrian loyalty (connoted by the disparaging

---

[42] The weight rested on the 'and', since there were plenty of 'k[aiserlich] k[öniglich]' institutions within Austria itself, where of course the ruler was also king (of Bohemia etc.) as well as emperor.

[43] An argument first made in Ferenc Eckhart, *A szentkorona-eszme története* (Budapest, 1941); then by László Péter, esp. in 'The Holy Crown of Hungary, Visible and Invisible', *Slavonic and East European Review*, 81 (2003), 421–510.

[44] 'Österreich-Ungarn bedeutet daher, wie es ja auch die Doppelbezeichnung besagt, nicht Ein Reich, sondern eine bleibende, auf gewisse internationale Zwecke abzielende Vereinigung': Albert Apponyi, *Österreich und Ungarn* (Vienna, 1909), 207. Cf. Apponyi in *Erinnerungen an Franz Joseph I, Kaiser von Österreich*, ed. E. v. Steinitz (Berlin, 1931), 113–35.

[45] 'Bože zachovej nám *krále* Ferdinanda mílého': Josef Kalousek, *České státní právo*, 2nd edn (Prague, 1892), 527–8.

[46] The promises were made in 1861, 1865, 1870 and 1871. More on all this in Evans, 'Císaři bez říše'. At issue was not merely the nature of sovereignty over Bohemia proper, but also the Czech state-rights claim, rather akin *mutatis mutandis* to the Hungarian 'holy-crown' doctrine, of the integrity of all the Bohemian lands (i.e. including Moravia and Austrian Silesia too).

term *rakušanství*). That undermined the prospect of any Slav-based *imperial* polity, though such a solution had been advocated by a series of major Czech figures. It was first adumbrated by Joseph Dobrovský, whose pioneering appeal on behalf of the Habsburgs' Slav subjects was delivered on the occasion of the Prague coronation of Leopold II and in the presence of the emperor.[47] Then the theme was taken up by national leaders, from František Palacký, who linked it with what he presented as the authentic Austrian mission of federalism, to Pekař, who saw Bohemia as the true base of Habsburg imperial claims.[48]

Thirdly, there was now a further more direct menace, indeed a rival: a real German Empire, a *Deutsches Reich* and a *Deutscher Kaiser*, laying claim *eo nomine* to the inheritance of the Holy Roman Empire, or at least to the acceptable face of it, which meant its medieval face (and accordingly using the earlier *single*-headed eagle as its emblem), and tracing wholesome Prussian antecedents. Thus Austria was left with the legacy of what was widely perceived, as served up in the master narrative of the Borussian school, to have been the later decay, division and patriotic deficit of the Old Reich.[49] That supreme communicator of Germanic antiquity, Richard Wagner, after all, not only appropriated key episodes from the history of the Reich, beginning with Henry the Fowler, for his national operas, but even relocated the climax of the *Nibelungenlied* on the Rhine rather than the Danube.[50]

Austria limped along as a kind of quasi-Reich. Most of the time it contained only one 'half', or 'Reichshälfte' (though the very locution implied its pair!); and even this half, notoriously, bore no official name, beyond that of being 'the kingdoms and lands represented in the Parliament [*Reichsrat*]'.[51] Or perhaps it was rather one of two separate

---

[47] 'Ueber die Ergebenheit und Anhänglichkeit der Slawischen Völker an das Erzhaus Oesterreich [Prague, 1791]', ed. Flora Kleinschnitzová, in *Listy Filologické*, 45 (1918), 96–104.

[48] Examples in František Palacký, *Radhost. [Sbírka] spisův drobných z oboru řeči a literatury české, krásovědy, historie a politiky* (3 vols., Prague, 1871–3), III, 10–17, 43–58, 210ff *passim*; Josef Pekař, *Z české fronty* (2 vols., Prague, 1917–19), I, 22–9.

[49] For Germany: Elisabeth Fehrenbach, *Wandlungen des deutschen Kaisergedankens, 1871–1918* (Munich, 1969). Erich Zöllner sees the 'Austrian idea' (*Österreich-Begriff*) as being in a 'permanente Krisensituation' after 1867, in *Die Habsburgermonarchie, 1848–1918*, III: *Die Völker des Reiches*, ed. A. Wandruszka and P. Urbanitsch (2 vols., Vienna, 1980), 1–32, esp. 29.

[50] *Die Nibelungen: ein deutscher Wahn, ein deutscher Alptraum. Studien und Dokumente zur Rezeption des Nibelungenstoffs im 19. und 20. Jahrhundert*, ed. Joachim Heinzle and Anneliese Waldschmidt (Frankfurt, 1991); John Evert Härd, *Das Nibelungenepos. Wertung und Wirkung von der Romantik bis zur Gegenwart* (Tübingen,1996); Otfrid Ehrismann, *Nibelungenlied. Epoche – Werk – Wirkung*, 2nd edn (Munich, 2002).

[51] Gerald Stourzh, 'Die dualistische Reichsstruktur, Österreichbegriff und Österreichbewußtsein, 1867–1918', in *Innere Staatsbildung und gesellschaftliche Modernisierung in Österreich und Deutschland 1867/71 bis 1914*, ed. H. Rumpler (Vienna, 1991); cf. Ernst Bruckmüller on the (semantic) crisis of the *Österreich-Begriff* in *Was heißt Österreich?*, ed. Plaschka *et al.*, 255–88.

interconnected Reichs, since Hungarians defined their own country more and more as a distinct empire (*birodalom*). The Austrian state incorporated plenty of imperial terminology, especially conspicuous to describe bodies – Reichsrat, Reichsgericht, etc. – which had introduced genuine constitutionality: shades, it might seem, of the participatory element that had always characterised the Old Reich. And from 1893 Austria had its own imperial history courses: *Reichsgeschichte*, a subject prescribed particularly for law faculties, as an account of the common Habsburg past (and embracing that of Hungary till 1867), which yielded important textbooks by Czech as well as German writers.[52]

The core 'imperial' discourse, inherited from the 1850s, remained that of multinational parity, local autonomies and the furtherance of diversity.[53] This last now included full religious toleration (with the *pietas Austriaca* reduced to the private devotions of the Habsburgs). The aspiration was reflected best of all in a collective ethnology of the Habsburg lands, begun under the patronage and with the active involvement of the heir to the throne, Rudolf, whence its familiar designation as *Kronprinzenwerk*. This huge enterprise: 24 volumes appearing over 16 years, 432 authors, 264 artists, was designed to show the common purpose among the peoples of the Monarchy and to promote strategies of convergence. Yet it tended also to accentuate differences, not least in that it all had to appear simultaneously in a parallel Hungarian version (though this was markedly less successful in marketing terms).[54] Moreover, the old-fashioned official language (of *Volksstämme* and the like) and sentiment which underlay such programmes were increasingly folksy and outmoded. Nor could any real progress be made towards federalism, as the central state bureaucracy was needed at every turn to sustain the political process.[55]

That is a large story, not for today. Suffice it now to note that the weakness of 'Austria' as a symbol or identity left dynastic fealty as the basic focus for imperial allegiance, the more so as the ageing Francis Joseph became a fairly popular and even iconic figure across much

---

[52] Examples in R. J. W. Evans, 'Historians and the State in the Habsburg Lands', in *Visions sur le développement des états européens. Théories et historiographies de l'état moderne*, ed. W. Blockmans and J.-Ph. Genet (Rome, 1993), 203–18.

[53] Maciej Janowski, 'Justifying Political Power in Nineteenth-Century Europe: The Habsburg Monarchy and Beyond', in *Imperial Rule*, ed. A. Miller and A. J. Rieber (Budapest, 2004), 69–82, full of insights.

[54] *Die österreichisch-ungarische Monarchie in Wort und Bild* (24 vols., Vienna, 1886–1902); *Az Osztrák-Magyar Monarchia írásban és képben* (21 vols., Budapest, 1887–1901). Cf. Regina Bendix, 'Ethnology, Cultural Reification and the Dynamics of Difference in the *Kronprinzenwerk*', in *Creating the Other: Ethnic Conflict and Nationalism in Habsburg Central Europe*, ed. Nancy M. Wingfield (New York, 2003), 149–66.

[55] Cf. John W. Boyer, 'The Position of Vienna in a General History of Austria', in *Wien um 1900. Aufbruch in die Moderne*, ed. P. Berner *et al.* (Munich, 1986), 205–20.

of the Monarchy by the end of the nineteenth century. Tales grew of his dedication to the state and to the individual concerns of his subjects, of his military and hunting prowess, of his virtues, notably accessibility, clemency and fairness.[56] As time went on, the display of the emperor's defence of familial values and love of children gained poignancy through the tragedies of his own private life. And during much of his reign Francis Joseph took on the role of a classic *princeps ambulans*, with regular ceremonial visitations to all parts of his realm.[57] Then came more and more anniversaries, centenaries, jubilees. Yet it proved harder and harder for him to line up all his ducks in a row. Thus the great Bohemian exhibition of 1891 took place with only Czech and no German participation; the golden jubilee of 1898 brought frictions in Hungary (hardly surprisingly, since Francis Joseph's reign there only counted from 1867); then the diamond jubilee in 1908 was both ignored by Hungarians and boycotted by the Czechs.[58]

Historians these days have become more sensitive to the reserves of dynastic loyalty in the late Monarchy; as also to the ways in which they were deliberately stage-managed, from the very beginning of the reign onwards.[59] Yet Francis Joseph always remained a reluctant idol: his most penetrating biographer wrote of the emperor's 'contemptuous rejection of every art, great or small, which might have popularized monarchical activity'.[60] And it was a wasting asset, non-transferable. Only later, too late, would distinguished literary versions of the 'Habsburg myth', in the writings of Joseph Roth, Robert Musil, and co., suffuse the vanished

[56] Much evidence in Helmuth A. Niederle, *Es war sehr schön, es hat mich sehr gefreut: Kaiser Franz Joseph und seine Untertanen* (Vienna, 1987). For the general point: Kann, 'The Dynasty and the Imperial Ideal'.

[57] Thus there were, for example, official visits to Prague in 1847, 1849, 1852, 1854, 1858, 1866, 1868, 1880, 1891, etc.: Urban, *Česká společnost, passim*. One particularly important visit is discussed in Daniel Unowsky, 'Political Nationalism, Dynastic Patriotism, and the 1880 Imperial Inspection Tour of Galicia', *Austrian History Yearbook*, 34 (2003), 145–71.

[58] Elisabeth Grossegger, *Der Kaiser-Huldigungs-Festzug, Wien 1908* (Vienna, 1992), surely belittles the significance of the absences.

[59] A good survey by Ernst Hanisch, *Der lange Schatten des Staates: österreichische Gesellschaftsgeschichte im 20. Jahrhundert* (Vienna, 1994), 212ff; cf. *The Limits of Loyalty. Imperial Symbolism, Popular Allegiances, and State Patriotism in the Late Habsburg Monarchy*, ed. L. Cole and D. Unowsky (New York and Oxford, 2007), including my 'Afterword', 223–32. For the first phase, see Daniel Unowsky, 'Reasserting Empire: Habsburg Imperial Celebrations after the Revolutions of 1848–9', in *Staging the Past. The Politics of Commemoration in Habsburg Central Europe, 1848 to the Present*, ed. Maria Bucur and Nancy M. Wingfield (W. Lafayette, 2001), 13–45. And in general, see *idem, The Pomp and Politics of Patriotism. Imperial Celebrations in Habsburg Austria, 1848–1916* (W. Lafayette, 2005).

[60] Josef Redlich, *Emperor Francis Joseph of Austria: A Biography* (London, 1929), 536; but at the same time he allows that the monarch 'did indubitably possess both popularity and the confidence of his people'.

imperial cause with an aura of nostalgia.[61] At the time it was challenged on its own terms by the continuing locus just across the border in Germany of a revived and galvanic *Kaiserreich*. Even the sublimest musical celebration of imperial rule, the younger Johann Strauss's *Kaiser-Walzer* of 1889, was in fact written for the opening of a new *Berlin* concert hall, and originally called 'Hand in Hand' – Francis Joseph firmly attached to the young and fresh-baked William II.

By that time Habsburg sovereignty not only needed German support; it also needed new forms of *communication*. Its final throw was actually to join in the business of 'empire', as conventionally understood in the parlance of the Atlantic world. For in 1878 Austria-Hungary at last acquired a foreign colony, albeit a piece of contiguous territory and well within the bounds of the European continent. The occupation of Bosnia-Hercegovina at one level reversed the Habsburgs' pro-Ottoman policies of most of the nineteenth century (and a positive enthusiasm for the Turks in Hungary), and raised suspicion of a return in the northern Balkans to the domineering Catholicism of 200 years before; though in fact it soon sought conciliation of the local Muslims. The occupation was driven by the usual colonial claims of the day, decked out with a specifically Hungarian piece of flag-waving, since the crown of St Stephen had briefly exercised suzereignty over the territory in the Middle Ages. Here was the standard image of a self-imposed mission of improvement out of duty, flanked by the normal economic calculations of the period.[62] We should also observe, not for the first time in the present account, that the seizure of Bosnia initially attracted more condemnation at home, in both halves of the Monarchy, than it did abroad.

Their engagement with modern 'imperialism', however, would soon lead the Habsburgs down a slippery slope. From the outset the new international posture rested, emotionally and diplomatically, on the Dual Alliance with Germany formally negotiated in the immediate aftermath of the occupation. 'Hand in hand', indeed; but with the Second Reich leading. By 1908, practical necessities, as well as codes of prestige and honour, dictated the full annexation of Bosnia-Hercegovina. That unleashed forces, within the region and beyond, which led directly to 1914: the assassination of the heir to the throne, Franz Ferdinand, in the Bosnian capital Sarajevo and the outbreak of European war. On one hand the war, fought with the combined resources of the 'Central Powers', i.e.

<hr>

[61] The notion has been popularised by Claudio Magris, *Il Mito absburgico nella letteratura austriaca moderna* (Turin, 1963; 2nd edn 1988), esp. in its German version as *Der habsburgische Mythos in der österreichischen Literatur* (1966 etc.)

[62] Evelyn Kolm, *Die Ambitionen Österreich-Ungarns im Zeitalter des Hochimperialismus* (Frankfurt, 2001). For the cultural mission: Robin Okey, *Taming Balkan Nationalism* (Oxford, 2007).

of *Mitteleuropa*, as it now increasingly came to be called, reinforced an old-new *German* centre of gravity and locus for the Habsburg imperial idea. On the other hand, it delivered the destiny of Austria-Hungary over to its military arm.

The Austrian army, albeit less prominent in politics and society than its German equivalent, had retained the local 'Reich' traditions most intensely. The longest terminological survivor of the ancien regime was the war office, the *Reichs*kriegsministerium, only officially renamed as a 'common' ministry in German documents as late as 1911, and then under the protest of Franz Ferdinand, who sought to use it as the nucleus of a restored 'Kaisertum Österreich'.[63] The assassination put paid to that; and then the resulting hostilities soon showed how little Austria-Hungary's fighting services could sustain their position without massive German support. In the end they could not do so at all. It is a crowning irony that on 1 November 1918, the day when the war ended in the Adriatic, the pride of the fleet, greatest battleship in the Habsburg navy, was sunk by a mine with all hands, having never fired a shot against the enemy. Its name was Francis Joseph's imperial motto: *Viribus Unitis*.[64]

By the war years the fabric of imperial allegiance was anyway wearing very thin, thinner still after the death of the veteran Francis Joseph in 1916. Not till the previous year had the last of the symbols of Dual Monarchy been finally agreed, with the promulgation after decades of haggling of a joint coat of arms.[65] Only then too, in 1915, did the non-Hungarian territories gain the official designation 'Austria'. The material as well as the ideological armoury of independent Habsburg imperial rule was exhausted. And that occasioned the reckoning with the entire Habsburg political edifice, as it commended itself to the likes of George Prothero. Which is where – in the old cinema parlance – we came in.

My final task is to indicate, very briefly, what conclusions may be drawn from the narrative and analysis I have essayed here. I communicate them, following the style of today, in six bullet points.

- The imperial issues surrounding the Habsburgs' status and authority formed a significant irritant in themselves. To the end, the most deadly critics of their empire – whether Holy Roman or Austrian – were domestic ones.
- The issues were part of an overall opacity of political culture in Habsburg central Europe, and of the dynastic bond as such in lands

[63] Stourzh in *Die Habsburgermonarchie*, ed. Urbanitsch and Rumpler, VII, 1194. For the protest: Leopold von Chlumecky, *Erzherzog Franz Ferdinands Wirken und Wollen* (Berlin, 1929), 265.

[64] At least the ship has inspired two good websites: www.viribusunitis.ca, and www.geocities.com/tegetthoff66/viribus.html (accessed 1 Feb. 2009).

[65] Franz-Heinz Hye, *Das österreichische Staatswappen und seine Geschichte* (Innsbruck, 1995). Czech criticism: Pekař, *Z české fronty*, I, 5–15, 61–78.

where the imperial dignity never acquired a territorial vis-à-vis. The fate of the magnificent but mothballed *Hauskrone* is a case in point.

- The issues are a sign of the stunted growth of any conception of 'Austrianness', and its profound vulnerability to nation-based identities.
- That all added to an insecurity about the 'imperial' mission, in the age of imperialism, of Europe's oldest imperial dynasty, especially its ever more erratic and excitable stances in the Balkans up to 1914.
- At root there was always the German factor, given the irreducible linkage between the central-European *Reichsidee* and the 'deutsche Nation'. The Habsburgs could never jump over their own shadow; neither could they fill the vacuum left by the termination of the First Reich or thereafter correct the imbalance generated by the instauration of the Second.
- And last but not least, the legacy. The Nazi German Empire, which completed the nemesis of the *Reichsidee*, replicated much of the constellation of *Mitteleuropa* as already established during the First World War. Yet – as would be familiar to readers of *Mein Kampf*, where Hitler vents some of his most venomous tirades against Austrian political traditions[66] – it could only have been erected on the *ruins* of the Habsburg imperium. If for no other reason, I hope that the claims of my subject to have been both an essential precondition for, and a foremost obstacle to, the coming of the Third Reich will leave you persuaded that it has been deserving of your attention.

Appendix: Chief persons and events mentioned (Habsburg emperors in bold)

1657–1705	**Leopold I (Habsburg) H[oly] R[oman] Emperor**
1683–99	relief of Vienna and Turkish wars
1701–14	War of Spanish Succession
1703–23	'Pactum mutuae successionis' ➔ Pragmatic Sanction
1705–11	**Joseph I HREmperor**
1711–40	**Charles VI HREmperor**
1740–2	*interregnum in Reich*
1740–8	**Maria Theresa as ruler of Austria** (till 1780); Prussian seizure of Silesia; war of Austrian Succession: Bavaria, France, Prussia, etc. v. Austria
1742–5	*Charles V (Wittelsbach) HREmperor*

---

[66] E.g. *Mein Kampf* (Munich, 1938), esp. 71ff.

1745–65	**Francis I (Lorraine) HREmperor**
1756–63	Seven Years War: Austria and France etc. v. Prussia
1765–90	**Joseph II (Habsburg-Lorraine) HREmperor**
1780–90	**Joseph II as ruler of Austria**
1790–2	**Leopold II HREmperor**
1792–1806	**Francis II HREmperor**
1792–1801	imperial war against France
1803	Reichsdeputationshauptschluss: secularisation and mediatisation of parts of Reich
1804	Napoleon 'empereur des français'; **Francis (II→I) Emperor of Austria**
1805	Austria defeated by Napoleon at Austerlitz ('battle of Three Emperors')
1806 (6 Aug.)	Francis ('at all times augmenter of the Empire') lays down imperial crown and dissolves Reich
1809	Austria defeated by Napoleon at Wagram
1814–15	Congress of Vienna
1835–48	**Ferdinand I Emperor of Austria**
1836	Ferdinand crowned in Prague
1848–9	revolutions in Habsburg lands; civil war in Hungary
1848 (2 Dec.)	Ferdinand abdicates; **Francis Joseph Emperor of Austria** (till 1916)
1851–9	Sylvester Patent introduces neo-absolutist rule
1859	Austro-French war: Austrian defeats at Magenta and Solferino
1866	Austro-Prussian war: Austrian defeat at Königgrätz
1867	Compromise law (Hungary) and December Constitution (Austria) create 'Austria-Hungary'; **Francis Joseph** crowned **King of Hungary**
1870–1	abortive negotiations for Bohemian compromise
1871	(2nd) German Empire (Deutsches Reich) founded
1878	Austro-Hungarian occupation of Bosnia-Herzegovina
1879	Dual Alliance between Austria-Hungary and Germany
1908	Austro-Hungarian annexation of Bosnia-Herzegovina
1914	assassination of Franz Ferdinand; outbreak of the First World War
1916–18	**Charles I Emperor of Austria = Charles IV King of Hungary**
1918 (Oct.–Nov.)	Collapse of Austria-Hungary; withdrawal of Charles I/IV
1919	post-war (Versailles etc.) settlement: dissolution of Austria-Hungary confirmed

Transactions of the RHS 19 (2009), pp. 139–149 © Royal Historical Society 2009
doi:10.1017/S0080440109990077

THE SLAVE TRADE, ABOLITION
AND PUBLIC MEMORY

By James Walvin

READ 26 SEPTEMBER 2008

ABSTRACT. The bicentenary of the Abolition of the Slave Trade Act in 1807 prompted a remarkable wave of public commemorations across Britain. In contrast to the low-key events of 1907, 2007 saw a sustained and nation-wide urge to commemorate, publicise and discuss the Atlantic slave trade and its abolition. Government interest proved an important influence, and was reflected in a lively educational debate (resulting in changes to the National Curriculum.) This political interest may have stemmed from the parallel debate about modern human trafficking, and contemporary slave systems. Equally, the availability of funding (from the Heritage Lottery Fund) may have persuaded a host of institutions to devise exhibitions, displays and debates about events of 1807. Perhaps the most striking forms of commemoration were in broadcasting and publishing: the BBC was especially active. There were few regions or localities which remained unaffected by the year's commemorations.

But why was there such interest? Was 1807, with the outlawing of an unquestioned evil, seen as a moment of national virtue? But if so, how are we to recall the role played by the British in the *perfection* of Atlantic slavery and the slave trade? The lively debates in 2007, from major national institutions to small local gatherings, revealed the problematic nature of abolition itself. After all, slavery survived, and even the slave trade continued after 1807. So what was important about 1807? The commemorations of 2007 raised public awareness about an important transformation in the British past; it also exposed those intellectual and political complexities about the ending of the Atlantic slave trade which have proved so fascinating to academic historians.

2007 marked the bicentenary of the abolition of the British slave trade, an anniversary characterised by remarkably varied and numerous commemorations. But what happened in 2007 stood in marked contrast to 1907, when the centenary of abolition was a modest affair. Compared to the plethora of events in 2007, the centenary registered only the slightest flicker of remembrance. The leader in *The Times* on 25 March 1907 for example commemorated, not the Act of Abolition, but the Act of Union.[1] Understandably, The British and Foreign Anti-Slavery Society – descendant of the original anti-slavery movement in the 1820s – took up the issue, and recalled that abolition had been 'an event of the

---

[1] *Times*, 25 Mar. 1907.

highest importance' but even that society was more concerned about events in the Congo.[2] It is true that a service was held in Westminster Abbey – and Africans celebrated in Sierra Leone[3] – but the Anti-Slavery Society remained more agitated about contemporary slave systems – and slave-trading routes in and from Africa: the Act of 1807 was mentioned largely in passing, and under the shadow of more momentous, immediate issues.[4]

It was all very different in 2007. The bicentenary of the 1807 abolition prompted a remarkable wave of commemorations across Britain – sometimes in the most unexpected of places. Few major public institutions failed to offer their own, distinctive or local interpretation of the events leading to the Act of 1807. Government departments (and the prime minister and his deputy) took an active interest, and there was even a debate in parliament about the abolition of the slave trade.[5] TV and radio disgorged countless programmes on abolition: the BBC also created a string of excellent websites.[6] Discussions about abolition, essays and commentaries filled the press (including some of the tabloids), and bookshop windows were crowded with new publications devoted to the end of the slave trade. The sheer volume of abolitionist commemorations surprised even those scholars prepared for a busy year.[7] This public interest in abolition was, to a degree, driven forward by the remarkable coverage given to abolition in the press, TV and radio. But whatever the source or inspiration, public interest in abolition was extraordinary, with tens of thousands trooping through various exhibitions and large numbers of school children bussed to those same events. The exhibition in Westminster Hall for example attracted more than 100,000 visitors. The Equiano exhibition in Birmingham attracted 30,000.[8] I had been speaking in public on the topic for years and had never previously met such widespread attention: large, interested crowds, well-informed and critical questions, and a genuine attention to the broader issues.

As the year unfolded, and as the public debate became more voluble (especially towards the end of March 2007 – the actual anniversary of the 1807 Act), it was clear enough that ever more people were not

[2] *The Anti-Slavery Reporter*, fourth series, 27 (1907), 'Annual Report', 1907, 2–12.

[3] *Ibid.*, 41–5.

[4] *Times*, 23 Mar. 1907.

[5] *Parliamentary Debates (Hansard)*, Tuesday 20 Mar. 2007, vol. 458, no. 64, cols. 687–780.

[6] www.bbc.co.uk/history/british/abolition.

[7] I had decided to set aside the year for abolition activities. In the end I did eighty-nine lectures on the topic at a range of gatherings, from local libraries through to national institutions and international venues.

[8] Figures provided by the curators, Melanie Unwin (parliament) and Clare Weston (Birmingham). For parliament see also http://slavetrade.parliament.uk/slavetrade.

only interested in Britain's slaving past, but they were confused and sometimes troubled by it. What had initially seemed, to many people, an opportunity to commemorate – celebrate even – abolition, had broadened into a growing realisation that the slave trade and abolition were more problematic than it appeared at first sight. This realisation was also apparent in the planning of a number of abolition exhibitions.[9] In the necessarily protracted build-up required for major exhibitions (roughly two years to plan and effect the major 1807–2007 displays) the complexities of abolition became clearer. Many of the groups convened to plan for the commemorations felt, at first, that 2007 could provide a 'feel-good' moment: one of those historical remembrances which showed the British at their best. Who could deny that the slave trade was bad – and that abolition was good and that the British had led the way? 1807 could, then, be commemorated as an example of British historical virtue: an episode when all sorts and conditions of British people came together to overthrow an indisputable scourge. Yet scratch the surface of the story of abolition and the slave trade and it is immediately apparent that the story is more complex, more troublesome and in many respects quite different from the popular imagination. Some simple points confirm those complexities.

First, if we were to commemorate the British Abolition Act of 1807, how should we incorporate the story of the British slave trading in the century *before* 1807: the period when the British became the dominant Atlantic slave trader? More than three and a half million Africans had been transported across the Atlantic in British ships in that period. Moreover, by the last years of the British trade, one African in five was carried in a ship from Liverpool.[10] Similarly – though this was often overlooked in the public debate in 2007 – the British slave system continued long *after* 1807. Full emancipation for Britain's slaves did not materialise until 1838, and even then, only at a cost of £20 million paid (not to the slaves) but to the slave holders. Moreover slavery continued to thrive elsewhere, notably in the USA until 1865: in Brazil it was not abolished until 1888.[11] Even then, the British, though flushed by an anti-slavery culture after 1838, and apparently determined to end slavery world-wide, were not averse to the reintroduction of Indian indentured labour into the Caribbean (and other possessions) to fill the labouring gaps created by the departed freed slaves.[12] Nor did the slave trade end in 1807. An 'illicit' slave trade – though hounded by the American and British navies – saw almost three

---

[9] I was adviser/guest curator for the Equiano Exhibition at the Birmingham Museums and Galleries, and at the parliamentary exhibition in Westminster Hall.

[10] See *Liverpool and the Transatlantic Slave Trade*, ed. David Richardson, Suzanne Schwarz and Anthony Tibbles (Liverpool, 2008).

[11] For the broad history of slavery, see David Brion Davis, *Inhuman Bondage* (New York, 2006).

[12] Howard Temperley, *After Slavery: Emancipation and its Discontent* (2000).

million Africans shipped across the Atlantic, mainly to Cuba and Brazil.[13] Stated simply, the Act of 1807 did not stop the Atlantic slave trade, nor did it end slavery in the Americas.

The story of abolition becomes even more confusing when we consider the 1807 Act itself. It is true that the Act represented a remarkable political (and social) change in British political interests. But how should we weigh that transformation in the balance alongside the many dozens of Acts *promoting* slave trading and passed by the British parliament between, say, 1672 and 1800? The British parliament was a confirmed slave-trading legislature long before it established a reputation for its abolitionist impulses.[14] Of course these Acts form a specific example of a more general point: that slave trading was part of the British economic and cultural landscape from the mid-seventeenth century onwards. Any number of major institutions (from the monarchy downwards) had involved themselves in slave trading – and it was easy to see why: the material benefits of the slave trade and slavery could be seen across Britain. Most striking in the buoyant ports which fed and benefited from the trade, from Glasgow to Bristol, the slave trade seeped into the most unusual and unexpected corners of British life. It was most visible in the universal consumption of slave-grown sugar,[15] it could even be detected in a number of stately homes acquired courtesy of the fruits of Atlantic trade and enslaved African labour.[16]

Such simple facts, well known to historians, were often startling to many who first came to discuss abolition prior to 2007 and the ensuing debates served to complicate the process of how to commemorate 1807. How could a gallery or museum present a visiting public with the complexities not merely of the Act of 1807, but of the broader world of slavery and slave trading? Add to this, the problems of physical space, finance and time and it was clear that public historians were faced by a complex brew of decisions. One important decision, taking by a large number of institutions, helped to simplify the problem of how to commemorate 1807. Many agreed not simply to tell the *general* story – not to recite the history of the abolition movement culminating in the Act of 1807 – but

[13] For these and all other details, see the TransAtlantic Slave Trade Data Base, www.slavevoyages.org.

[14] William Pettigrew, 'Parliament and the Escalation of the Slave Trade, 1690–1714', in *The British Slave Trade: Abolition, Parliament and People*, ed. Stephen Farrell, Melanie Unwin and James Walvin, Edinburgh University Press for Parliamentary History Yearbook Trust (Edinburgh, 2007).

[15] James Walvin, *Fruits of Empire. Exotic Produce and British Taste, 1660–1800* (1997), ch. 8.

[16] S. D. Smith, *Slavery, Family and Gentry Capitalism in the British Atlantic. The World of the Lascelles, 1648–1834* (Cambridge, 2006).

to speak to a specific and often a local case study.[17] There seemed little point repeating, in varied settings around the country, the broad history of abolition. Once taken, that decision had the effect of forcing local groups, and local institutions, to find a *specific* or a local *entrée* into the abolition story. Organisers began to ask: let us try to speak, for example, to abolition in Manchester, the north-east or East Anglia. Parliament, quite properly, sought to tell the parliamentary story. In Birmingham, the municipal exhibition concentrated on the remarkable study of one man – the African, Olaudah Equiano. Thus it was that local museums and galleries approached abolition through local or regional interests, or through an engagement with materials which were strongly represented in their holdings. English Heritage for example used Lord Mansfield's home – Kenwood House – as a setting for a discussion of abolition. The Wisbech and Fenlands Museum focused on the life of the local abolitionist hero Thomas Clarkson. Hull inevitably did much the same with Wilberforce. The end result was an extraordinary mosaic of very different activities and commemorations: the Royal Mail issued six abolition stamps (containing two African faces) and the Royal Mint issued a commemorative two pound coin.[18] Small schools displayed pupils' drawings and comments on the slave trade while at the other, grander extreme, the archbishop of Canterbury preached about the slave trade before the queen and prime minister in Westminster Abbey.[19]

Although it was perhaps the nation's major institutions – parliament, the National Portrait Gallery, the British Museum[20] – which inevitably caught the eye, some of the most revealing responses to 1807 were to be found in smaller places: local schools, local authorities and small town libraries.[21] From such local initiatives there emerged an astonishing profusion of printed and graphic materials: pamphlets, posters, booklets, essays, books. And it was there, often far removed from the major ebb and flow of mainstream slave business, in London and the major ports, that some of the most revealing displays were to be found. They also yielded

---

[17] The BBC played an active role, through their local/regional stations in encouraging scrutiny of local slavery connections. See e.g. www.bbc.co.uk/norfolk/abolition; www.bbc. co.uk/Isle of Man; bbc.co.uk/somerset/abolition.

[18] For a list of the major events, see *Bicentenary of the Abolition of the Slave Trade Act, 1807–2007* (HM Government, 2007), 14–15.

[19] *Service to Commemorate the Bicentenary of the Abolition of the Slave Trade Act*, Tuesday 27 Mar. 2007.

[20] The major abolition events for the year can be found in *Calendar of Events, 2007, Bicentenary of the Abolition of the Slave Trade Act*, published by the Dept for Communities and Local Government, 2007.

[21] Among the many pamphlets published by local authorities see Kirklees Council, *The Abolition of the Slave Trade*, 2007, City of Westminster, *Abolition of the Slave Trade Events to Mark the Bicentenary of the 1807 Act of Parliament*, 2007; *Connecting Histories*, Birmingham City Council, 2007.

some of the most original discussions about abolition. Who normally thinks of East Anglia having links with Atlantic slavery? And what sort of connections are normally made between the north-east and the enslaved Atlantic? Yet by dint of committed local effort (and often unflagging application by a small local band of enthusiasts) serious research was undertaken in local holdings, and a persuasive case was made for the importance of local slave-trading connections. Although it may be felt that this merely confirms what we have known for a long time – that Atlantic slavery reached into all corners of British life – such local and regional studies, in support of public exhibitions, confirmed, via careful research, details which are often missing. Local ships heading to the slave colonies, local industries tied to slavery (coal to the plantations for instance) returning planters migrating 'home' to East Anglia. What began as an effort to give 1807 a *local* context thus evolved into an important statement not merely of regional entanglement with slavery, but also helped to fill in some of the gaps in our broader understanding of Atlantic slavery and of abolition.[22]

As if all this were not enough to satisfy the public curiosity about abolition, a major film (*Amazing Grace)* and a number of plays, notably *Rough Crossings* (adapted by Caryl Phillips from Simon Schama's book of the same name) offered theatrical versions of the abolition story. For those in need of still further information, bookshop windows were filled with books aimed at the 'abolitionist moment' of 2007. Publishers had clearly planned to capitalise on the interest in abolition in 2007.[23] The end result was that there was a huge number of access points to the history of abolition, from across the entire British cultural landscape. Most departments of the BBC (including comedy) offered something on abolition. By March 2007 it was as if there was a blanket cultural coverage of the topic, in every conceivable format: publishing, the press, TV and radio, film and theatre, websites, libraries, museums, galleries, archives, churches – and politics. By the end of March, and the actually anniversary itself, it was almost impossible to avoid the public discussion about the abolition of the slave trade. It is hard to think of a comparable historical anniversary attracting such ubiquitous, wide-ranging cultural and social attention. Quite *why* this happened remains perplexing: what is/was so *special* about abolition to spawn such commemorations? Some suggestions are worth considering.

First, there was the prospect of money. The availability of funding, via the Heritage Lottery Fund, to commemorate abolition was undoubtedly

---

[22] For a very good example, see John Charlton, *Hidden Chains. The Slavery Business and North East England, 1600–1865* (Newcastle upon Tyne, 2008).

[23] My own book, *A Short History of Slavery* (2007), delivered to the publishers in 2005, was 'parked' for a year by Penguin in order to hit the abolitionist market in 2007.

a powerful incentive. Institutions assembled abolitionist proposals in the hope of attracting HLF funding, and thereby being able to host an exhibition or display. By March 2008 the HLF had made 270 awards amounting to a total of £15 million.[24] But how far the prospects of HLF funding had *inspired* the initial decision to plan a commemoration of 1807 is impossible to say. The other major 'cultural broker' was the BBC, and there again the key decisions taken within the BBC to address abolition flowed from a variety of sources. Heads of major departments clearly took a policy decision that they should find an appropriate way of discussing abolition (as news, drama or live discussion for example). The build-up to 2007 coincided with a period when the BBC awaited the government's latest decision on the Corporation's licence fee: the need for the BBC to present a socially responsive front was doubtless a factor in discussions within the BBC.

Across all this activity there was cast a political shadow. Tony Blair's government showed a keen interest in the bicentenary of abolition. A committee was established, chaired by the deputy prime minister, John Prescott, and consisting of prominent figures from various bicentenary organisations and institutions. It met regularly to monitor national plans for 2007, and to see in what ways the government might help the process. It was a curious affair: a senior cabinet member (other ministers stood in when Prescott was unavailable) taking time out of a busy schedule to listen to broadcasters, directors, curators, clerics and academics discussing plans for 2007. Yet why should a government have *any* interest in such an arcane historical event?

The prime minister himself provided the best evidence for the government's interest in abolition. In 'A message from the Prime Minister', Blair wrote:

> This anniversary is a chance for all of us to deepen understanding of our heritage, celebrate the richness of our diversity and increase our determination to shape the world with the values we share. I hope you will get involved in some way. There should be something for everyone. This is everyone's bicentenary.[25]

All this came at a time when issues of *contemporary* slave trading were of political concern. Human trafficking had, again, established itself as a major global problem, via a string of incidents, confirming the contemporary enforced movement of people from poor regions to the west, for labour or for prostitution. It was as if the historical example of 1807 offered a beacon of what might be achieved if people of good will and political resolve put their strength behind a campaign. During, 2007, the British government was edging towards signing up to the European

---

[24] Information kindly provided by Dr Fiona Spiers, Head of Heritage Lottery Fund, Yorkshire and Humberside.

[25] 'A Message from the Prime Minister', *Calendar of Events*.

Convention against Human Trafficking. They finally signed in December 2008, to the ringing words of the home secretary 'I strongly believe the trafficking of human beings is one of the vilest crimes to threaten our society.'[26] William Wilberforce would have been happy to hear it.

There was more to Blair's government interest than this however. Here was a government which was openly committed to 'social inclusion', and especially to a concerted effort to ensure that racial equality was observed at all levels of British life.[27] This, in alliance with the influence of a number of prominent black politicians in Blair's cabinet, ensured that the bicentenary had a strong contemporary appeal in Westminster. It was as if the historical events culminating in abolition in 1807 resonated with a number of modern-day political issues. Human trafficking, social inclusion, the drive for racial equality, all came together to provide good reasons to give strong political support to the bicentenary of the abolition of the slave trade.

There were, of course, other factors which lent themselves to the public interest in 1807. British black communities – not a factor in 1907 – had their own interest in the slave trade and abolition, and found a particular voice through local community churches and related organisations. Black churches addressed 1807 in their own distinctive fashion, often via day schools or religious services. When the mayor of London organised a day school devoted to 1807–2007 it concentrated on the role of the churches in the slave trade. The day was, not surprisingly, dominated by black churches and black preachers from across the capital.[28] This community-based interest in abolition was a highly appropriate reminder of what had happened after 1787. Then, the bedrock of popular abolition in its earliest phase (say, 1787–92) had been in British dissenting chapels, notably Methodists and Baptists.[29] And so it was in 2007. There was a neat, and not altogether accidental symmetry here, bringing the original abolition campaign into line with a contemporary campaign of black commemoration.

Throughout 2007, the abundance of abolitionist activities served a number of purposes. It provided a convenient forum for political interest at the centre of government, it offered an ideal opportunity for the allocation of funds from the Heritage Lottery Fund and it presented the BBC with an ideal opportunity to fulfil its obligations as a public service broadcaster. Even so, these factors do not fully explain the depth and ubiquity of activity in 2007. Whatever the *specific* inspiration behind this or that exhibition, there was a genuine groundswell of public interest

---

[26] Home Office, *Press Release*, 17 Dec. 2008.
[27] *Reaching Out. An Action Plan on Social Inclusion*, Cabinet Office, Sept. 2006.
[28] *In God's Name. The Role of the Church in the Transatlantic Slave Trade*, City Hall, Aug. 2007.
[29] Seymour Drescher, *Capitalism and Antislavery* (Pittsburgh, 1986).

in 1807. This may have been merely a particular aspect of that general and broadly based British popular interest in history: in local, family, regional, military or even celebrity history. The culture of lecture-going, the remarkable array of historical-based groups across Britain found a new focus for their curiosity in 2007. But the abolitionist bicentenary went further even than this. What emerged, as the year progressed, was the realisation that behind abolition lay the slave trade and slavery. There was a growing appreciation, among large numbers of people, of an issue which historians themselves had slowly come to accept over, say, the past forty years: that the enslaved Atlantic was central not merely to the Americas or Africa – but to Britain itself.

The story of African enslavement, of the Atlantic slave ships and of the plantation societies of the Americas might seem distant to the British. Viewed from Britain, here are topics which seem designed more for Africanists, naval scholars or historians of the Americas. Yet Atlantic slavery was driven forward by British commercial and political forces. In return, Britain derived huge economic and social benefits. Nor were those interests – or benefits – to be seen merely in the great slave ports (London, Bristol or Liverpool for example). The broader British economy, the financial systems of London (banking, finance and insurance, global credit arrangements and capital accumulation) all were enmeshed with Atlantic slavery.[30] And so too was British social life. What could be more British than a sweet cup of tea? (The Chinese tea made palatable to British tastes by the addition of slave-grown sugar from the Caribbean.) As the abolition debate developed in 2007, it became clear that African slavery was a critical factor in helping the transformation of eighteenth-century Britain. Moreover, slavery in the Americas was itself made possible by the Atlantic slave ships, and the dominant slave-trading power by the mid- and late eighteenth century was Britain. Yet all this raises the enigma which has troubled historians – and more recently a broader public – for years. If all this was true, if slavery and the slave trade were indeed so central, there remains the curious issue of why did the British end it? If the slave trade was so buoyant and profitable (and current data suggests it was) why did the British turn against it? The simple question remains: why *was* the slave trade abolished in 1807? Thus, what had seemed a simple bicentenary, exposed an interested public to a major historical debate and conundrum.

This is a debate which takes us well beyond the slave trade itself, engaging as it does the changes which were at work at the heart of Britain in the late eighteenth century. Any understanding of the politics of abolition in 1807 becomes not merely a parliamentary story, personified in popular memory by Wilberforce, but inevitably turns into a discussion

---

[30] Kenneth Morgan, *Slavery and the British Empire* (Oxford, 2007).

about the nature of abolition itself.[31] Here was a popular movement which was literate, dissenting, radical and often female. It was, equally, influenced by an African voice – an African agency – which helped to shape the origins and development of abolition politics. African voices, and African experiences – most notably the horrors endured in the belly of British slave ships – became a basic element in the campaign against the slave trade after 1783. It began in 1783 with news about the murder of Africans on the Liverpool slave ship *Zong*,[32] and gathered pace in the primary data teased out of the slave statistics, and from the voices of slave sailors, by Thomas Clarkson.[33] This raw, brutal data – first-hand accounts of the sufferings created by the slave ships, widely circulated in cheap or free pamphlet literature, and hammered home in crowded lectures across Britain, was hugely influential in shifting British opinion towards abolition.

In 2007 the complexity of abolition was, at once, appealing and yet difficult. How to grapple with it, present it, simplify it for, say, visitors to a gallery or museum? But the public debate about abolition in 2007 also meant that the British public were confronted not simply by a story about the slave trade and abolition, but by a compelling historical narrative that went right to the heart of British history itself. This, in its turn, struck a chord in the often confusing debate about 'identity'. Older, popular images of a benign British empire which brought the blessings of freedom to all corners of the world seemed hugely tarnished when set alongside the history of slavery and the slave trade. Brutality and violence were not so much an incidental by-product of the Atlantic slave empire, but its very essence. Along with other maritime and imperial Europeans, the British visited extraordinary damage on the peoples and societies of Africa in order to provide cheap labour to tap the potential of the tropical and semi-tropical Americas. The benefits to the British were clear and indisputable. But those benefits were acquired at the cost of staggering levels of suffering endured by millions of Africans.

How, then, are we to blend this story of Atlantic slavery into the broader narrative of Britain's imperial story? Equally, what does the history of slavery reflect on the history of the British in that first phase of imperial expansion and global domination in the eighteenth century? At one level the history of Atlantic slavery seems to be geographically distant. Yet the major thrust of much recent work on the slave trade has been to confirm the degree to which the slave trade (and the slave communities shaped by that trade) was integral to the British experience in the eighteenth century.

---

[31] For the origins of abolition see Christopher Leslie Brown, *Moral Capital* (Chapel Hill, 2006).

[32] This is the subject of my forthcoming book, *The Zong. One Ship in the Age of Slavery* (2010).

[33] Ellen Gibson Wilson, *Thomas Clarkson. A Biography* (1989).

Slavery was, to use a phrase I have employed *ad nauseum*, as British as a sweet cup of tea.

This point was vividly captured in one of the best exhibitions spawned by the bicentenary, in the Museum in Docklands, 'London, Sugar and Slavery' (suitably housed in an old sugar warehouse). Via a careful blend of words, artefacts and images, a complex historical process was presented, illustrating how an exotic produce (sugar) cultivated by enslaved Africans, became an unquestioned and everyday feature of domestic British life.

2007 was, then, a quite remarkable historical commemoration. But unlike most such events, it is destined to leave an important legacy of its own. Two aspects in particular seem destined to survive. First, some of the projects, launched to find a local opportunity to discuss 1807–2007, have spawned on-going, serious research projects into the links between a region and Atlantic slavery. More significantly perhaps, the study of slavery has begun to settle into the National Curriculum. In effect, the study of slavery and the slave trade has shifted from the edges of historical concern to occupy a central location not merely among professional historians, but as a major theme in the British popular historical imagination.

In 1907, the Abolition Act of a century before had seemed a worthy change. By 2007 that same Act represented a massive upheaval which also spoke to a range of present-day British issues. The British abolition of the slave trade seemed more relevant, more resonant and more significant in 2007 than it had a century before. And to explain that fully, we need to engage with British society of the early twenty-first century.

Transactions of the RHS 19 (2009), pp. 151–179 © Royal Historical Society 2009
doi:10.1017/S0080440109990089

CULTURES OF EXCHANGE: ATLANTIC AFRICA IN THE ERA OF THE SLAVE TRADE

By David Richardson

READ 25 APRIL 2008 AT SHEFFIELD HALLAM UNIVERSITY

ABSTRACT. Cultural factors have often been invoked to explain parliament's decision in 1807 to outlaw slave carrying by British subjects but they have only infrequently been cited in efforts to explain why the Atlantic slave trade itself became so large in the three centuries preceding 1807. This paper seeks to redress this imbalance by looking at ways in which inter-cultural dialogue between Africans and Europeans and related adjustments in social values and adaptations of African institutional arrangements may contribute to improving our understanding of the huge growth in market transactions in enslaved people in Atlantic Africa before 1807. In exploring such issues, the paper draws on important theoretical insights from new institutional economics, notably the work of Douglass North. It also attempts to show how institutionally and culturally based developments in transatlantic slave trafficking, the largest arena of cross-cultural exchange in the Atlantic world before 1850, may themselves help to promote understanding of the much broader historical processes that underpin economic change and the creation of the modern world.

The bicentenary of the abolition of the British slave trade has provoked renewed public and scholarly interest in the significance of parliament's decision to outlaw British slave trafficking in 1807 as well as in the mix of factors that induced it to do so.[1] Scholarly debate over the causes of that event has come almost full circle as religious explanations first identified by Sir Reginald Coupland in the 1930s and subsequently challenged by more economically deterministic ones have recently returned to centre-stage as part of broader, culturally based arguments.[2] The extent to which cultural forces influenced the rise of British anti-slavery will doubtless remain a source of discussion. But, insofar as such forces were involved, they reveal

---

[1] For the most recent assessment of the factors involved, see the essays in *The British Slave Trade: Abolition, Parliament and the People*, ed. Stephen Farrell, Melanie Unwin and James Walvin (2007).

[2] See, for instance, Roger Anstey, *The Atlantic Slave Trade and British Abolition, 1760–1810* (1975); Seymour Drescher, *Econocide: British Slavery in the Era of Abolition* (Pittsburgh, 1977); *idem, Capitalism and Antislavery: British Mobilization in Comparative Perspective* (Oxford, 1987); *idem, The Mighty Experiment: Free Labor versus Slavery in the British Emancipation* (Oxford, 2004); David B. Davis, *Slavery and Human Progress* (Oxford, 1984); Christopher L. Brown, *Moral Capital: Foundations of British Abolitionism* (Chapel Hill, 2006).

how non-economic factors have helped to shape market activity and even economic growth and performance. When parliament proscribed slave carrying by British subjects, it denied them involvement in a commercial activity in which in 1807 they remained major stakeholders and from which they could have continued to profit. Moreover, by funding naval and other slave trade suppression policies after 1815, parliament sought to impose its own reformed values on other nations and their slave traffickers. Its campaign to do so met with resistance and evasion internationally.[3] Ultimately, however, it contributed to a more generalised revulsion against and outlawing of slave trading and even slavery itself among European and American powers by the end of the nineteenth century. Given the antiquity and robustness of slavery as an institution, this was a remarkable transformation.[4] Organised anti-slavery provides a dramatic example of how shifts in social values helped historically to change economic behaviour.

In this paper, we shall argue that, if cultural factors were instrumental in outlawing the Atlantic slave trade, they were also central to facilitating its growth and structure through to 1807. Constituents of culture – human perceptions of the world, values, institutions, political and other behaviour – have become integral to what today is commonly known as new institutional economics. Proponents of institutional economic theory recognise that factor endowments are important to economic performance. But they also tend to argue that inter-country differences in economic performance as well as in rates of economic change are linked to the mix of cultural and institutional factors that have increasingly shaped the human environment within which economic activity increasingly takes place. In particular, according to Douglass North, a key architect of this branch of economics, order and disorder need to be placed 'at the center of inquiry' into understanding the process of economic change. As North insists, 'order is a necessary (but not sufficient) condition for long-run economic growth'.[5]

The historical performance of economies has provided an important testing ground for theories of institutional economics. Some of the most revealing findings centre on issues relating to trade, notably long-distance trade or cross-cultural exchange. Both involved high levels of risk, and understanding how risk was managed or mitigated is believed to have

---

[3] David Eltis, *Economic Growth and the Ending of the Transatlantic Slave Trade* (Oxford, 1987); Joel Quirk and David Richardson, 'Anti-slavery, European Identity and International Society: A Macro-historical Perspective', *Journal of Modern European History*, 7 (2009), 68–92.

[4] For reviews and interpretations, see Robert W. Fogel, *Without Consent or Contract: The Rise and Fall of American Slavery* (New York, 1989); David B. Davis, *Inhuman Bondage: The Rise and Fall of Slavery in the New World* (Oxford, 2006).

[5] Douglass C. North, *Understanding the Process of Economic Change* (Princeton, 2005), 103–4.

been crucial to understanding how such activities grew. In one of his earliest studies, North argued that growth in transatlantic trade in the two centuries after 1650 was linked to sizeable improvements in shipping productivity (or reductions in oceanic freight rates). These, in turn, were related to declines in piracy – and concomitant increases in security and order – throughout the Atlantic Basin.[6] Studies by other scholars have linked historical expansion of long-distance trade to improvements in credit security based, among other things, on family and ethnically rooted networking as well as other forms of social capital. Such developments are seen to have been crucial in underpinning the thirteenth-century commercial revolution in the Mediterranean as well as long-distance trade in Africa.[7] They are also seen to have reinforced gains in shipping efficiency to foster growth in transatlantic trades from the seventeenth century onwards.[8]

There has been some acknowledgement of the influence of cultural factors in shaping the Atlantic slave trade after 1500. The reluctance of Christians to enslave fellow believers is seen to have been a critical factor in determining that Africans, not Europeans, would be taken from the Old World as slaves to the Americas.[9] The fact that African slave dealers had no scruples, religious or otherwise, when it came to enslaving members of other sub-Saharan ethnic groups reinforced the pattern.[10] But, while cultural factors were evidently important in explaining the racial character of the Atlantic slave trade, their role in helping to explain how that trade became so large still remains largely understudied. This

[6] Douglass C. North, 'Sources of Productivity Change in Ocean Shipping, 1600–1850', *Journal of Political Economy*, 76 (1968), 953–70.

[7] For the medieval Mediterranean, see Avner Greif, 'Institutions and International Trade: Lessons from the Commercial Revolution', *American Economic Review*, 82 (1992), 128–33; *idem*, 'On the Political Foundations of the Late Medieval Commercial Revolution: Genoa during the Twelfth and Thirteenth Centuries', *Journal of Economic History*, 54 (1994), 271–97. For Africa, see Abner Cohen, 'Cultural Strategies in the Organization of Trading Diasporas', in *The Development of Indigenous Trade and Markets in West Africa*, ed. Claude Meillassoux (1971), 266–81; Paul E. Lovejoy, *Caravans of Kola: The Hausa Kola Trade 1700–1900* (Zaria, 1980); Philip D. Curtin, *Cross-Cultural Trade in World History* (Cambridge, 1986); Janet T. Landa, *Trust, Ethnicity and Identity: Beyond the New Institutional Economics of Ethnic Trading Networks, Contract Law and Gift-Exchange* (Ann Arbor, 1994).

[8] The literature on networking in Atlantic trade has grown rapidly in the last half century. See, for example, Bernard Bailyn, *New England Merchants in the Seventeenth Century* (Cambridge, MA, 1955); David Hancock, *Citizens of the World: London Merchants and the Integration of the British Atlantic Community, 1735–1785* (Cambridge, 1997); Simon D. Smith, *Slavery, Family and Gentry Capitalism in the British Atlantic: The World of the Lascelles, 1648–1834* (Cambridge, 2006).

[9] David Eltis, *The Rise of African Slavery in the Americas* (Cambridge, 2001), ch. 1. A similar pattern helped to shape the much older movement of non-Muslim enslaved Africans into the Islamic world.

[10] As Water Rodney reminded us, legal and judicial processes helped ensure that, in some cases, captives sold to Europeans would come from within the same ethnic group as their enslavers (Walter Rodney, *A History of the Upper Guinea Coast, 1545–1800* (Oxford, 1970), 108).

paper seeks to redress that issue. In it, I propose to explore some of the processes that underpinned transactions in slaves at the African coast. As we shall see, the evolution of these processes involved inter-cultural dialogue, negotiation and creative institutional adaptation. Together, these strengthened the capacity of African coastal trading communities to respond, with varying degrees of effectiveness, to external shifts in demand for captive labour. Whether such developments should be seen as creating a 'middle ground' of Euro-African dealings similar to that suggested for Euro-Indian relations in mainland North America is open to question, not least because Europeans never seriously threatened to settle and thus to claim land in Africa before the nineteenth century.[11] But insofar as institutional change in Atlantic Africa fostered expansion of cross-cultural exchange in captive Africans, it contributed, on the one hand, to wealth accumulation in the Americas and, on the other, to inflicting damage and disorder on those African societies whence captives came. The cultures of exchange in Atlantic Africa that evolved during the era of the export slave trade had, therefore, far-reaching ramifications. These ramifications cannot be explored in detail in this paper, but when considered as by-products of the evolving human environment within which the slave trade was conducted, they shed light on how economic change occurred more generally in the Atlantic world in the early modern period.[12]

I

Slavery is commonly identified with severe exploitation of the labour of the enslaved; the absence of human rights; and the threat of violence, actual or perceived.[13] The relative weight of these identifiers of slavery has varied through history, but all three were prevalent in transatlantic slavery. The severity of exploitation of enslaved Africans in the Americas has sometimes been seen as a vital source of capitalist accumulation in Europe.[14] In Europe, transatlantic slavery came to be justified by the denial of human rights to people of African descent, a situation that some, though not all, abolitionists sought to rectify from the 1780s.[15] In

[11] On the debate over the 'middle ground' in Euro-Indian relations in the Americas, see the exchange between Susan Sleeper-Smith, Richard White and Philip J. Deloria, in the forum, *William and Mary Quarterly*, third series, 63 (2006), 3–22.

[12] On the concept of the Atlantic World and the need to place Africa and Africans at the centre of its development, see *The Atlantic World, 1450–2000*, ed. Toyin Falola and Kevin D. Roberts (Bloomington, 2008).

[13] I do not seek to define slavery here but, rather, to note the conditions under which enslaved people had to live. For a discussion of definitions, see Joel Quirk, *Unfinished Business: A Comparative Survey of Historical and Contemporary Slavery* (Paris, 2009).

[14] On accumulation see Eric Williams, *Capitalism and Slavery* (London, 1944); and Joseph E. Inikori, *Africans and the Industrial Revolution in England* (Cambridge, 2002).

[15] Quirk and Richardson, 'Anti-slavery and European Identity'.

all its facets, from Africa through to the Americas, transatlantic slavery was firmly rooted in violence. Violence was the instrument for enslaving people in Africa; it was instrumental in efforts by their captors to turn Africans into commodities; and it was intrinsic to plantation life in the Americas. Moreover, violence was an element in the resistance of the enslaved to their situation, wherever that resistance occurred and it became an important vehicle by which slavery in the Americas was dismantled in the century after the Saint-Domingue uprising in 1791.[16] From beginning to end, violence was the bedfellow of transatlantic slavery.

Disorder and violence are commonly regarded as enemies of sustained economic growth or commercial performance.[17] At the heart of transatlantic slavery, therefore, lay an apparent paradox: how, given the brutality associated with the capture and transport of enslaved Africans to the Americas, did the trafficking in captive Africans come to assume the scale and durability that it did. Part of the answer may lie within African belief systems. According to some historians, wealth accumulation through trade in some parts of Africa was seen to take place in a zero-sum cosmology within which accumulation through commerce by some groups involved trade-offs against personal or familial health and even social tranquillity. Ironically, slave trading moderated the trade-off between 'wealth' and 'sorrow' by allowing traders to retain some captives as part of their kinship group and thus compensate for any anticipated loss of kin that would flow from commercial success.[18] Others have suggested a different, though not necessarily incompatible, answer to the apparent paradox by pointing to a separation of the internal initial enslavement process, with all its attendant violence and disorder, from the later stages of moving captives to the African coast for sale. In short, a geographical division of labour between enslavement and marketing of captives is said

---

[16] There is a huge and ever growing literature on violence and resistance in transatlantic slavery. Among recent examples, see Stephen D. Behrendt, David Eltis and David Richardson, 'The Costs of Coercion: African Agency in the Pre-Modern Atlantic World', *Economic History Review*, 54 (2001), 454–76; *Fighting the Slave Trade: West African Strategies*, ed. Sylviane Diouf (2003); Laurent Dubois, *A Colony of Citizens: Revolution and Slave Emancipation in the French Caribbean, 1787–1804* (Chapel Hill, 2004); Eric Robert Taylor, *If We Must Die: Shipboard Insurrections in the Era of the Atlantic Slave Trade* (Baton Rouge, 2006).

[17] As North puts it, the 'persistence of disorder [in many societies] is, on the face of it, puzzling because disorder increases uncertainty and typically the great majority of players are losers' (*Understanding the Process*, 103).

[18] See, for example, Robert W. Harms, *River of Wealth, River of Sorrow: The Central Zaire Basin in the Era of the Slave and Ivory Trade, 1500–1891* (New Haven, 1981), 197–215. The concept of the zero-sum was not, of course, peculiar to Africans; it was a feature of some strands of mercantilist thinking in Europe and helps to account for intra-European conflicts for control of land in the Americas and of trade with particular parts of Atlantic Africa, among other things. I shall ignore the latter aspect of the cultures of exchange in Atlantic Africa in this paper and to emphasise instead Afro-European relations.

to have emerged, with African societies absorbing the collateral damage associated with the Atlantic slave trade and slave shippers claiming the benefits from it.[19] Even if we accept that such a geographical separation of processes occurred, it was never wholly complete. Slave narratives and other evidence remind us that those involved in enslaving others by violence might fall victim to the same themselves, even quite close to the coast, and end up on slave ships.[20] There were instances also of European traders raiding African coastal communities for slaves and though such practices may have diminished in relative importance in time, it is evident that violence – or at least the threat of it – remained a powerful weapon in the armoury of coastal sellers and buyers of captive Africans. In this respect, violence was always implicit, as well as being often explicit, in slave trafficking.[21]

Nonetheless, from the earliest stages of European oceanic contact – and in most cases before slaves became the dominant item of exchange – trade quickly became the primary and increasingly predominant mechanism of interaction between African and European along the Atlantic African littoral. Although Africans are often depicted as the weaker of the partners in such engagements, the fact that commercial exchange became the *modus operandi* of interaction reflects, it may be argued, more the strength of African communities in their dealings with Europeans rather than their weakness.[22] Those dealings, of course, involved parties from very different cultural backgrounds and economic worlds, but as the scale

[19] Paul E. Lovejoy, *Transformations in Slavery: A History of Slavery in Africa* (Cambridge, 1983; 2000 edn), 68.

[20] See, for example, the narrative of Venture Smith, who suggests that after seizing him and many others with a view to their sale to Europeans, his own captors were themselves seized near Anomabu on the Gold Coast and subsequently sold into transatlantic slavery (*A Narrative of the Life and Adventures of Venture, a Native of Africa but Resident above Sixty Years in the United States of America* (New London, 1798), 13).

[21] As Richard Hakluyt noted, on his first expedition to Africa for slaves, Sir John Hawkins secured his victims 'partly by the sword, and partly by other means' (Richard Hakluyt, 'The First Voyage of the Right Worshipfull and Valiant Knight, Sir John Hawkins, now Treasurer of Her Majesties Navie Royall, Made to the West Indies 1562', in *The Hawkins' Voyages*, ed. Clements R. Markham, Hakluyt Society, 57 (1878), 6). On the wider issue of African resistance as well as violence in Afro-European relations see Walter Hawthorne, *Planting Rice and Harvesting Slaves: Transformations along the Guinea-Bissau Coast, 1400–1900* (Portsmouth, NH, 2003); and David Richardson, 'Shipboard Slave Revolts, African Authority and the Atlantic Slave Trade', *William and Mary Quarterly*, third series, 58 (2001), 69–92.

[22] Adam Smith, among others, noted the resilience of African polities in dealings with European traders, contrasting this with the collapse of indigenous American communities when faced with Europeans (Adam Smith, *Wealth of Nations* (2 vols., 1776), ed. Edwin Cannan (1961 edn), II, 150). His views are echoed in some recent interpretations of Afro-European relations. See for example, Robin Law, '"Here Is No Resisting the Country": The Realities of Power in Afro-European Relations on the West African "Slave Coast"', *Itinerario*, 18 (1994), 50–64; Eltis, *Rise of African Slavery*, 147; Emma Christopher, *Slave Ship Sailors and their Captive Cargoes, 1730–1807* (Cambridge, 2006), 157.

of European trade with Africa grew, Afro-European dealings in slaves emerged as probably the major international arena of cross-cultural exchange from the mid-seventeenth to the early nineteenth century. The security and efficiency within which that exchange occurred – and the controlled or managed violence on both sides that underpinned it – had important consequences for the growth of transatlantic slavery and the wider Atlantic economy. Moreover, as a form of cross-cultural activity, its development anticipated what was to be a growing and arguably transformative feature of an emergent global economy from the seventeenth century onwards.

As in other exchange relationships, the scale and pattern of slaving activities at the African coast was largely shaped by negotiation or 'dialogue' between the parties concerned. On the European side, those involved included resident traders and their mulatto offspring, many of the former being employees or ex-employees of the corporate trading companies established by most western European nations to represent their interests in the African trade in the seventeenth century.[23] Accordingly, resident traders were more numerous on the ground in regions such as Senegambia, the Gold Coast and West-Central Africa south of the Congo, where Europeans established forts or settlements than at the Windward Coast, the Bight of Biafra and the Loango Coast north of the Congo, where, on the European side, bargaining for slaves was more commonly done by ships' captains. On the African side, slave transactions were usually conducted by merchant communities that were typically subject to political oversight and regulation by local states, which also often

[23] Among the earliest mulattoes were Portuguese renegades and settlers in Upper Guinea (Rodney, *Upper Guinea*, 83–8). Called by contemporaries, *lançados,* after the Portuguese word to throw or cast, they married within the local community, placed themselves under local rule and joined in local ceremonials. Most became traders, throwing in their lot with local Africans. Other Portuguese helped to found the settlement at Luanda and became in time integrated into the local community there (Joseph C. Miller, *Way of Death: Merchant Capitalism and the Angolan Slave Trade, 1730–1830* (1987), 245–314). For other European-mulatto communities, see James F. Searing, *West African Slavery and Atlantic Commerce: The Senegal River Valley, 1700–1860* (Cambridge, 1993), 93–129; Margaret A. Priestley, 'Richard Brew: An Eighteenth Century Trader at Anomabu', *Transactions of the Historic Society of Ghana*, 4 (1959), 29–46; Kwame Y. Daaku, *Trade and Politics on the Gold Coast 1600–1720* (Oxford, 1970), 48–96; Adam Jones, *From Slaves to Palm Kernels: A History of the Galhinas Country (West Africa) 1730–1890* (Wiesbaden, 1983); George E. Brooks, *Landlords and Strangers: Ecology, Society, and Trade in Western Africa, 1000–1630* (Boulder, 1993); idem, *Eurafricans in Western Africa: Commerce, Social Status, Gender and Religious Observance from the Sixteenth to the Eighteenth Century* (Oxford, 2003); Bruce L. Mouser, 'Trade, Coasters, and Conflict in the Rio Pongo from 1790 to 1808', *Journal of African History*, 14 (1973), 45–63; idem, 'Isle de Los as a Bulking Center in the Slave Trade 1750–1800', *Revue Française d'Histoire d'Outre-mer*, 83 (1996), 77–90; idem, 'Continuing British Interest in the Coastal Guinea-Conakry and Fuuta Jaloo Highlands (1750–1850)', *Cahiers d'Etudes Africaines*, 43 (2003), 761–90; *A Slaving Voyage to Africa and Jamaica: The Log of the Sandown 1793–1794*, ed. Bruce L. Mouser (Bloomington, 2002).

served as intermediaries or middlemen between inland suppliers of slaves and European buyers.[24] Buffers to some extent between the violence of the slave procurement zone and the more orderly transactions in slaves of the coast, the trading communities along the Atlantic littoral were the frontline of the cultural interface between Africans and Europeans in the slave trafficking business. It was their strategic position between African supplier and European buyer of slaves as well as their skill in handling dialogue and transactions with Europeans that allowed them to accumulate wealth from the slave export trade.[25] Such wealth sometimes became the envy of inland slave suppliers, encouraging in some instances a military and political 'push to the sea' by inland states. A form of vertical integration in slave supply chains in Africa, such action could destabilise more than improve the efficiency of the Afro-European interface.[26]

The nature of the Afro-European commercial dialogue and the ensuing patterns of economic exchange were shaped by various factors, the importance of which could vary from one trading venue to another or, depending on changes in the 'actors' involved, even at the same venue through time.[27] Three key features of slave trafficking in Atlantic Africa

[24] Studies of such communities include A. J. H. Latham, *Old Calabar, 1600–1891* (Oxford, 1973); Robin Law, 'A Lagoonside Port on the Eighteenth Century Slave Coast: The Early History of Badagri', *Canadian Journal of African Studies*, 28 (1994), 1–21; *idem, Ouidah: The Social History of a West African Slaving 'Port', 1727–1892* (Oxford, 2004), 71–122; Paul E. Lovejoy and David Richardson, 'Trust, Pawnship and Atlantic History: The Institutional Foundations of the Old Calabar Slave Trade', *American Historical Review*, 104 (1999), 333–55; *idem*, '"This Horrid Hole": Royal Authority, Commerce, and Credit at Bonny, 1690–1840', *Journal of African History*, 45 (2004), 363–92; Kristin Mann, *Slavery and the Birth of an African City: Lagos, 1760–1900* (Bloomington, 2007).

[25] Philip D. Curtin, 'The Abolition of the Slave Trade from Senegambia', in *The Abolition of the Atlantic Slave Trade*, ed. David Eltis and James Walvin (Madison, 1981), 83–97; Robin Law, 'Slave-raiders and Middlemen, Monopolists and Free Traders: The Supply of Slaves for the Atlantic Trade in Dahomey, c. 1715–1850', *Journal of African History*, 30 (1989), 45–68; Patrick Manning, *Slavery and African Life: Occidental, Oriental and African Slave Trades* (Cambridge, 1990), 95–6; Eric W. Evans and David Richardson, 'Hunting for Rents: The Economics of Slaving in Pre-Colonial Africa', *Economic History Review*, 48 (1995), 678–99.

[26] Two examples of such moves were Dahomey's conquest of the slave 'port' of Ouidah in the Bight of Benin in 1727 and Asante's conquest of the coastal Fante states of the Gold Coast between 1807 and 1816. Gareth Austen has described the latter as the culmination of a longstanding Asante desire to seize 'the middlemen's rake-off' from their slave sales to European forts (Gareth Austen, 'Between Abolition and *Jihad*: The Asante Response to the Ending of the Atlantic Slave Trade, 1807–1896', in *From Slave Trade to 'Legitimate Commerce': The Commercial Transition in Nineteenth-Century West Africa*, ed. Robin Law (Cambridge, 1995), 93). In neither case, however, did slave exports through the routes in question return to pre-conquest levels, though some exports may have been channelled through alternative routes.

[27] A minority of shipmasters made multiple voyages, often to the same trading venue, and thus became well known to local African traders. In some cases, they identified ships by the master's name not the ship's (*Efik Traders of Old Calabar, Containing the Diary of Antera Duke*, ed. Daryll C. Forde (1956)). Many masters, however, made only one or two voyages

have been highlighted by recent quantitative assessments of the export slave trade.[28] The first was the incorporation of increasing numbers of venues in Atlantic Africa into the slave supply network as the scale of embarkations for the Americas rose from a few thousand captives a year before 1600 to between 40,000 and 60,000 a year by the second half of the eighteenth century. Most of the earliest captives boarded ship at Senegambia and at West-Central Africa south of the Congo, but from the mid-seventeenth century the Gold Coast, the Bight of Benin (or Slave Coast) and the Bight of Biafra became important embarkation centres. They were later joined by the Loango Coast from the early eighteenth century, Sierra Leone and the Windward Coast from the 1740s and South-East Africa from the 1780s. Expansion in slave exports from Africa thus depended on deepening activities in some regions, notably West-Central Africa, and extending their reach to others, notably in the Gulf of Guinea. Each type of activity involved widening the boundaries of Euro-African cross-cultural commerce and thus dialogue or negotiation between slave buyer and slave supplier. In the long run, slave shipments depended heavily on just four regions – West-Central Africa, the Bight of Benin, the Bight of Biafra and the Gold Coast – where four out of five of the 12.5 million captives taken from Africa to the Americas boarded ship.[29] Other regions, nevertheless, became significant participants in the Atlantic slave trade at certain times, further broadening the commercial dialogue between African and European trader.

A second major feature of commercial exchange in Africa was the varying intensity of concentration of activity among different exporters at different regions of slave supply. It is well known that throughout the history of the Atlantic slave trade Portuguese-speakers almost totally dominated shipments of African captives from south of the Congo.[30] This reflected Portugal's investment in Luanda and later Benguela, but

in command, though they may have made earlier voyages in a more junior capacity. On the African side, discord within local communities could result in major changes in local trading personnel. A prime example is a notorious 'massacre' at Old Calabar in 1767, which allowed one emerging trading faction to displace an established one, with the fallout from the event continuing for a decade or more and disturbing external trade relations (Randy J. Sparks, *The Two Princes of Calabar: An Eighteenth-Century Atlantic Odyssey* (Cambridge, MA, 2004); Paul E. Lovejoy and David Richardson, 'Anglo-Efik Relations and Protection against Illegal Enslavement at Old Calabar, 1740–1807', in *Fighting the Slave Trade*, ed. Diouf, 101–21.

[28] The following section draws heavily on evidence contained in www.slavevoyages.com, last accessed 10 Jan. 2009, and *An Atlas of Transatlantic Slavery*, ed. David Eltis and David Richardson (New Haven, forthcoming), which itself relies on the aforementioned dataset.

[29] This is the latest estimate of the total number of captives boarding ship in Africa for the Americas based on www.slavevoyages.com, last accessed 10 Jan. 2009. It is estimated that the dataset contains evidence of at least 80 per cent of all transatlantic slaving voyages dispatched to Africa from the Americas and Europe.

[30] On the dominance of the 'south Atlantic' slave trade by vessels from Brazil see also Miller, *Way of Death*; David B. Birmingham, *Trade and Conflict in Angola: The Mbundu and their*

was underpinned by the fact that, in the age of sail, the southern Atlantic wind and current systems largely favoured traders departing on their slave voyages from Brazil and returning to the same. Brazilian ports under Portuguese control, notably Pernambuco, Bahia and Rio de Janeiro, thus dominated the Angolan slave trade south of the Congo. This did not mean that ships from these ports traded only to Angola. On the contrary, after 1650, they took a large share of the captives leaving from the Bight of Benin. At the same time, ships departing Lisbon developed at various times an active trade with places in Upper Guinea between Senegambia and Sierra Leone. In these parts of Atlantic Africa, therefore, as Afro-European commercial dialogue developed, it became essentially (or at least largely, in the case of the Bight of Benin) one conducted in Portuguese or some pidgin variant thereof.[31]

Few other carriers achieved the level of dominance in slaving or other commercial activities with a particular region or sub-region that Portuguese-speakers did at Angola. But it is now clear that other carriers – almost all of them entrants into the slave trade from the mid-seventeenth century – took disproportionately large shares of their slaves from just a few regions. To give just some examples, largely from the eighteenth century when the slave trade of most carriers reached its peak: the Dutch in the form of the Middelburg Company after 1730 took most of their slaves from Guinea (meaning, in this case, the Windward Coast and Gold Coast) and the Loango Coast; the French largely focused in the same period on the Loango Coast, the Bight of Benin and Senegal; and the British, who rivalled the Portuguese as the principal carriers of slaves in the eighteenth century, largely concentrated on the Gambia and Gold Coast, where London-registered ships centred much of their trade, and at the Bight of Biafra, Sierra Leone and the Windward Coast, from where Liverpool ships embarked over half of all the slaves they carried from Africa in 1720–1807.[32] In short, therefore, while cross-cultural trade in Africa commonly involved more than one European trading nation in dialogue with local African slave suppliers, it was not uncommon for traders from one nation – or even one or two ports from within one nation – to dominate local commercial conversations with indigenous

---

Neighbours under the Influence of the Portuguese 1483–1790 (Oxford, 1966); Jose C. Curto, *Enslaving Spirits: The Portuguese–Brazilian Alcohol Trade at Luanda and its Hinterland, c. 1550–1830* (Leiden, 2004); Mariana P. Candido, 'Merchants and the Business of the Slave Trade in Benguela, c. 1750–1850', *African Economic History*, 35 (2007), 1–30.

[31] As noted earlier, Portuguese-speaking mulattoes were also important in parts of Upper Guinea from an early stage in African-European oceanic contact.

[32] Details of Liverpool's trade pattern are provided in Paul E. Lovejoy and David Richardson, 'African Agency and the Liverpool Slave Trade', in *Liverpool and Transatlantic Slavery*, ed. David Richardson, Suzanne Schwarz and Anthony J. Tibbles (Liverpool, 2007), pp. 43–65. For others, see *Atlas of Slavery*, ed. Eltis and Richardson.

traders. Such concentrations of activity by European slave carriers at particular venues in Africa have yet to be fully explained. In the absence of the natural environmental factors that helped to explain Portuguese dominance south of the Congo, they point towards the importance of networking and social capital as well as local knowledge and coastal 'creole' languages as key factors in promoting cross-cultural exchange in Atlantic Africa. The persistence of such patterns through time also points towards the impact of the human environment in fostering potential barriers to entry among established carriers against new entrants seeking to encroach on trade at particular venues. However one interprets such patterns, commercial dialogue across cultural boundaries involved shifting combinations of African and European parties to such activity at different places. Given that most slave carriers disembarked their human cargoes in American colonies that lay under their own national jurisdiction, the factors helping to shape commercial dialogue in Atlantic Africa were instrumental, too, in promoting connections between specific slave supply regions in Africa and markets for slaves in the Americas. Put another way, understanding the patterns of cross-cultural dialogue in Africa helps to explain the different mix of ethnicities of enslaved Africans arriving in different parts of the Americas.[33]

Accompanying these concentrations of activity by different European carriers at particular regions of Africa was an equally powerful tendency for the export slave trade to become concentrated not just in a few slave supply regions but also at a relatively small number of ports along

---

[33] Attempting to understand these transatlantic connections has been a major aspect of recent research on the influence of Africa and Africans in shaping the cultural history of the Atlantic world. This is not my concern here. Such research, however, is the focus of on-going debates centring on the relationship between African heritage and the American environment in creating new or synthetic cultures in the Americas. For strong claims of African heritage in shaping such cultures, see Michael A. Gomez, *Exchanging our Country Marks: The Transformation of African Identities in the Colonial and Antebellum South* (Chapel Hill, 1998), 11, 38, 150; Gwendolyn M. Hall, *Slavery and African Ethnicities in the Americas: Restoring the Links* (Chapel Hill, 2005), xv, 49, 55–79, 168–9. For other examples, see John K. Thornton, *Africa and Africans in the Making of the Atlantic World, 1400–1800* (1992; repr. New York, 1998); *Identity in the Shadow of Slavery*, ed. Paul E. Lovejoy (2000); *Trans-Atlantic Dimensions of Ethnicity in the African Diaspora*, ed. Paul E. Lovejoy and David V. Trotman (New York, 2003); *Enslaving Connections: Changing Cultures of Africa and Brazil during the Era of Slavery*, ed. José C. Curto and Paul E. Lovejoy (Amherst, 2004); *The Yoruba Diaspora in the Atlantic World*, ed. Toyin Falola and Matt D. Childs (Bloomington, 2004); *Africa and the Americas: Interconnections during the Slave Trade*, ed. José C. Curto and Renée Soulodre-La France (Trenton, 2005); and Judith A. Carney, *Black Rice: The African Origins of Rice Cultivation in the Americas* (Cambridge, MA, 2001). For different emphases, see Sidney Mintz and Richard Price, *An Anthropological Approach to the Afro-American Past: A Caribbean Perspective* (Philadelphia, 1976); and, more recently, David Eltis, Philip D. Morgan and David Richardson, 'Agency and Diaspora in Atlantic History: Reassessing the African Contribution to Rice Cultivation in the Americas', *American Historical Review*, 112 (2007), 1329–58.

the Atlantic coast of Africa. This is a third key finding of the recent quantitative literature on the trade. That literature shows that, especially after the entry of north European nations into the slave trade, scores of places between the Senegal River in the north and the Orange River in the south were embarkation places for African captives at any point in time.[34] But a critical finding of the recently published on-line slave voyages database is that among the numerous embarkation places, ten 'ports' accounted for the dispatch from their home continent of up to two-thirds (or 8 million) of all the enslaved Africans bound for the Americas. Importantly, all were located south-east of the Windward Coast. They comprised Cape Coast and Anomabu (at the Gold Coast); Ouidah (Bight of Benin); Bonny and Old Calabar (Bight of Biafra); and Loango, Malembo, Cabinda, Luanda and Benguela (West-Central Africa). Some, like Ouidah and Luanda, numbered their departing captives in millions, in Luanda's case close to 3 million. The others typically accounted for up to half a million or more.[35] Such places were African equivalents of well-known European slaving ports such as Bristol, Liverpool, London and Nantes or American ones such as Rio de Janeiro, Bahia and Pernambuco. Like their European and American counterparts that are often considered critical to the integration of the Atlantic economy from the sixteenth century onward, Luanda, Ouidah, Cabenda, Bonny and the other leading centres of slave trafficking in Atlantic Africa were equally pivotal to the integration of sub-Saharan Africa into the same. They were the epicentres of the most intensive promotion of cross-cultural dialogue and exchange activity involving oceanic commerce in the Atlantic world. What happened in these African ports helped to shape the scale and pattern of slave exports to the Americas as much as Liverpool, Rio de Janeiro and the other infamous slave ports of the Atlantic world did. Two – Luanda and Benguela – were closely tied to the Portuguese and Brazilian worlds. Cape Coast, Anomabu, Bonny and Old Calabar became vital to British traders, at least until 1807. Of the rest, Ouidah, Loango, Malembo and Cabinda were focal points of competition between different national groups of slave carriers through time. In each of these respects, what transpired in each of these African slaving emporia was a microcosm of much larger processes of cultural interchange throughout the Atlantic seaboard of Africa.

In other respects, too, commercial life in the leading African slave ports was symptomatic of wider patterns. At some, notably Cape Coast,

[34] See also David Eltis, Paul E. Lovejoy and David Richardson, 'Slave-Trading Ports: An Atlantic-Wide Perspective, 1676–1832', in *Ports of the Slave Trade (Bights of Benin and Biafra)*, ed. Robin Law and Silke Stricktrodt (Stirling, 1999), 12–34.

[35] For details of the estimated numbers departing from each of these ports see *Atlas of Slavery*, ed. Eltis and Richardson, table 4.

Anomabu, Ouidah and Luanda, there emerged European and mulatto resident populations, who played an active part in dealing with local traders. At Bonny, Old Calabar, Loango, Malembo and Cabinda, by contrast, exchange depended more on ship-to-shore interaction, though temporary factories might be erected on shore at some places. Everywhere, some form of creole or pidgin language developed as the language of exchange. Whatever format existed, as in other areas of Atlantic trade, transactions in slaves at the key trading emporia in Africa were typically underpinned by investment by Europeans not only in factories and castles (where allowed) but also in networking activities and in other forms of trust-building social capital. Such activities, reinforced by regularities and continuities in commercial dealings and the personnel involved, have been the subject of recent studies of Ouidah, Bonny, Old Calabar, Luanda and Benguela.[36] Investment in social capital in these places took various forms and, commonly involving participation in local cultural activities, was economically important in several ways. It facilitated in particular the growth of credit in coastal slaving transactions, about which there is evidence from as early as the seventeenth century.[37] Advancement of credit by Europeans to Africans became a vital factor in supporting increased commercial interaction between the coast and inland sources of slaves. It is, however, also evident that 'trust' alone was often insufficient to sustain credit-based transactions between European and African traders. In such circumstances, local political and institutional practices – and the values they embodied – were commonly appropriated and adapted by both European and African parties to safeguard such transactions. Among the practices so adapted was human pawnship, where people, including kin, might be pledged as pawns to creditors in return for loans, and local secret societies such as Ekpe, which, among other things, served as local debt enforcement agencies.[38] The adaptation of such institutions to the needs

[36] Law, *Ouidah*; Lovejoy and Richardson, '"Horrid Hole"'; *idem*, 'Trust'; Miller, *Way of Death*; Candido, 'Merchants in Benguela'.

[37] Ray A. Kea, *Settlements, Trade and Polities in the Seventeenth Century Gold Coast* (Baltimore, 1982), *passim*; Paul E. Lovejoy and David Richardson, 'The Business of Slaving: Pawnship in Western Africa, c. 1600–1810', *Journal of African History*, 42 (1999), 25–50.

[38] On pawning in general see *Pawnship in Africa: Debt Bondage in Historical Perspective*, ed. Paul E. Lovejoy and Toyin Falola (Boulder, 1994); and *Pawnship, Slavery and Colonialism in Africa*, ed. Paul E. Lovejoy and Toyin Falola (Trenton, 2003). For its specific relationship to the export slave trade, see Lovejoy and Richardson, 'Business of Slaving'. In terms of secret societies, there are useful discussions of Ekpe (or the Leopard Society) at Old Calabar and adjacent areas in Latham, *Old Calabar*; Donald C. Simmons, 'An Ethnographic Sketch of the Efik People', in *Efik Traders*, ed. Forde; and U. N. Abalogu, 'Ekpe Society in Arochukwu and Bende', *Nigeria Magazine*, 126–7 (1978), 78–97. For the Poro Society, which operated throughout much of what is today Sierra Leone, Liberia and the Cote d'Ivoire, see Kenneth Little, 'The Political Function of Poro: Part I', *Africa: Journal of the International Africa Institute*, 35

of international exchange was the outcome of a truly cross-cultural dialogue in which Europeans appropriated and, in negotiation with their African trading partners, adjusted local institutions to new use. Without such cross-cultural agreement, and the credit transfers that it facilitated, the scale of the Atlantic slave trade would have been much smaller than it was.

II

A fuller appreciation of the role of cross-cultural dialogue in underpinning the development of the Atlantic slave trade requires that we look at other elements in the processes that facilitated the linking of African supply of captives with American demand for slaves. Though a variety of elements were involved, I propose here to concentrate on two, not least because they concern the cultural context of exchange. The first relates to the 'rules of the game' within which negotiation of slave purchases occurred at the African seaboard; the second to the pattern and trends of slave prices at the African coast. Both sets of issues involved buyers and sellers of slaves in cultural and institutional dialogue. How they resolved them throws light on the respective bargaining positions of buyers and sellers of slaves at the African coast and ultimately, I shall argue, the extent to which the export slave trade shaped African economic life between the seventeenth and nineteenth centuries.

For international trade to prosper and grow the parties involved in exchange need to recognise and accept mutually agreed rules of engagement. These comprise part of the 'order' necessary for exchange to prosper. Such 'rules' complement other desirable elements within which commercial interaction takes place, but in important ways provide a framework within which social capital developed. One critical element was mutual respect for the security of the person and property of each of the parties involved and mechanisms for redress if that security was impaired.[39] Another is the establishment of mutually acceptable procedures for conducting trade negotiations and of mechanisms for resolving disputes over their interpretation. Underpinning both is the assumption that each party to any negotiation will benefit from the exchange process by satisfying its own demand for goods or items at competitive prices. As a form of international activity, the trafficking in slaves at the Atlantic coast was naturally subject to such constraints. Indeed, its long-run growth depended on their acknowledgement and

(1965), 349–65; *idem*, 'The Political Function of Poro: Part II', *Africa: Journal of the International Africa Institute*, 36 (1966), 62–72; and Beryl L. Bellman, *The Language of Secrecy: Symbols and Metaphors in Poro Ritual* (New Brunswick, 1984).

[39] For a discussion of this issue on one context at least, see Lovejoy and Richardson, 'Anglo-Efik Relations'.

acceptance, as recent evidence showing a link between the potential for market breakdown and instability in trade activity in Senegambia, Sierra Leone and Gabon underlines.[40] This contrasts with the high and often sustained levels of slave exports from other parts of Atlantic Africa, notably at the leading slave ports mentioned earlier. The evidence suggests, therefore, that the capacity of buyers and sellers to establish the 'rules' under which transactions in slaves could be pursued to mutual benefit varied from one part of Atlantic Africa to another. It could vary, too, at the same place through time, as the political leaders at Old Calabar acknowledged in 1780. In response to the murder locally of two Liverpool shipmasters by one disaffected faction in the community and a subsequent falling away in trade, they sought to reassure Liverpool traders by noting that that they had made 'Great Law about whitemen not hurt' and suggesting that 'Suppose one family Stop any whitemen[,] We Will Brock [i.e. Break] that family because all Country Stand by that Law this time.' The leadership of Old Calabar certainly appreciated the value of safeguarding the personal security of traders at least if slaving activities were to prosper.[41]

Space constraints prevent a full discussion of the evolution of the rules of commercial engagement throughout Atlantic Africa, but three points may be noted. First, trade in Africa rarely occurred in a political vacuum; on the contrary, in most regions and places, the export slave trade became tightly interwoven with local political structures, with competition for the rents accruing from trade providing an important ingredient for political rivalry within states and sometimes even conflict between them.[42] With few exceptions, therefore, trade became surrounded by local political protocols, to which exporters of slaves had to pay appropriate regard. The actual form of protocols varied from place to place, and might involve acknowledging local political authority, following standard bargaining practices and paying bribes. Understanding and respecting local practice

---

[40] On the high incidence of coastal attacks on ships at these places, see Behrendt, Eltis and Richardson, 'Costs of Coercion'; Richardson, 'Shipboard Slave Revolts'.

[41] 24 June 1780, Old Callabar (*sic*), from King Henshaw, Duke Ephraim and Willy Honesty, cited in Paul E. Lovejoy and David Richardson, 'Letters of the Old Calabar Slave Trade 1760–1789', in *Genius in Bondage: Literature of the Early Black Atlantic*, ed. Vincent Carretta and Philip Gould (Louisville, 2001), 109–10. The issue of security worked both ways: nine years later, in 1789, Duke Ephraim, son of the Duke Ephraim who signed the Old Calabar letter to Liverpool merchants in 1780, had cause to write to a Bristol trading firm, demanding the return of two of his canoe men named Abashey and Antegra. He claimed they were 'free men' and had been kidnapped into slavery by one of the Bristol firm's shipmasters. Duke Ephraim reminded his Bristol correspondents: 'I Done very well with Capt Leroach [Laroche] and he to[o]k my people of[f]' (*ibid.*, 111).

[42] Evans and Richardson, 'Hunting for Rents'. For the theoretical basis of this argument, see Anne O Krueger, 'The Political Economy of the Rent-Seeking Society', *American Economic Review*, 64 (1974), 291–303.

was, therefore, an important precondition for successful initiation and conduct of trade. Fractures within local political structures sometimes created short-term opportunities for gain by buyers of slaves, but the instabilities generated by political division within coastal communities or between them and internal suppliers of slaves were rarely beneficial to buyers of slaves in the longer term.[43] Significantly, the export slave trade tended to prosper most in the presence, not the absence, of political order at African coastal venues. Paying due regard to the local political or ceremonial protocols, therefore, was a relatively small price to pay for Europeans as part of the cost of achieving security and expansion in trade relations.

Second, in addition to adjusting to local politics, buyers of captives had, as in other markets, to accommodate local, often culturally or politically determined, preferences for imported trade goods among sellers of slaves. It is sometimes argued that Europeans duped African sellers of slaves by offering shoddy or inferior goods in exchange for human captives. This argument had its roots, among other things, in the late eighteenth-century abolitionist discourse. The allegedly poor quality of firearms, which commonly formed part of the 'bundles' of commodities exchanged for slaves, has been particularly emphasised.[44] Without seeking to deny that attempts at duplicity occurred, it appears, nevertheless, that, as consumers, Africans for the most part called the tune when it came to deciding the composition of the bundles of goods that Europeans had to supply if they wanted to compete in buying slaves in Africa.[45] The

[43] The massacre of Old Calabar in 1767, in which a group of British traders conspired with one faction in Old Calabar to destroy and enslave another faction, provides a particularly clear example of how internal local discord and tension could offer European traders opportunities for short-term gain while sowing distrust and damaging long-term trade relations with the community as a whole. Aftershocks of the massacre were felt for some years after 1767, and provided the context for the alleged poisoning of two Liverpool shipmasters in the 1770s by the damaged party (Sparks, *Two Princes*; Lovejoy and Richardson, 'Trust'; *idem* and *idem*, 'Anglo-Efik Relations').

[44] On the gun trade, see Ray A. Kea, 'Trade, State Formation and Warfare on the Gold Coast, 1600–1826' (Ph.D., University of London, 1973); Joseph E. Inikori, 'The Import of Firearms into West Africa 1750–1807', *Journal of African History*, 18 (1977), 339–68; W. A. Richards, 'The Import of Firearms into West Africa in the Eighteenth Century', *Journal of African History*, 21 (1980), 43–59. Much of the discussion of the exchange of firearms for slaves centres on the guns–slave cycle, in which imported firearms were seen to provoke warfare and thus the supply of captives for export. There are also suggestions, however, that the firearms dispatched to Africa were of inferior quality and highly unreliable (Miller, *Way of Death*, 88–9; Elizabeth A. Isechei, *A History of African Societies to 1870* (Cambridge, 1997), 337). According to Miller, an official check of the gun stock at Luanda revealed that only 5 per cent of the stock met 'the government's standards of military reliability'.

[45] On variations in the 'bundles' of goods exchanged at different African trading venues, see my 'West African Consumption Patterns and their Influence on the Eighteenth-Century English Slave Trade', in *The Uncommon Market: Essays in the Economic History of the Atlantic Slave*

evidence suggests, too, that trade at the African coast was not a trade between unequal parties. On the contrary, it was one in which Europeans had constantly to be aware of changing consumer preferences in African markets, to make appropriate adjustments to the mix of goods shipped to the coast, and to accept that exchange values of different goods against slaves might vary across time and in some cases prove to be extremely poor. Changes in European industry, notably textiles, may have allowed buyers of captives to introduce new items into the bundles of goods exchanged for slaves, but such innovations did not apply uniformly across Atlantic Africa. They were always subject to acceptance by African traders. In short, each series of transactions relating to slaves involved local negotiation over the composition and exchange rate of goods against slaves and in such negotiation a primary, if not dominant, factor was always local African consumer preferences. Thus, for example, in the second half of the eighteenth century, at Cabinda, Luanda and Benguela, East Indian textiles commonly constituted up to two-thirds of the goods exchanged for slaves, whereas at Ouidah, cowrie shells constituted the largest single item bartered for slaves.[46] Similar variations in patterns of demand for trade goods were evident at other leading ports. The explanations for such variations lie within Africa and were largely driven by local African political and social conditions. Together with developments in European industry, such conditions largely shaped the ongoing dialogue or bartering between buyer and seller of slaves at the African coast over the price of slaves and how it should be paid.

Some exchanges of goods for slaves in Africa were based on pure barter between buyer and seller, but such were the complexities of trade negotiations and the varieties of commodities included in the bundles of goods exchanged for slaves that currencies of trade evolved in time.[47] Ultimately, the vast majority of transactions came to be negotiated in coastal currencies. Prices of slaves were commonly recorded in them as were the values of commodities bartered in exchange. Many Europeans even recorded their own coastal accounts in the local currency alongside those of their homeland. Local units of account became, therefore, a third

---

Trade, ed. Henry A. Gemery and Jan S. Hogendorn (New York, 1979), 303–30, esp. 311–15. See also Curto, *Enslaving Spirits*, who emphasises the role of local consumer preferences to explain the displacement of Portuguese fortified wines by Brazilian *cachaça* in trade at Luanda from the late seventeenth century.

[46] Richardson, 'West Africa Consumption Patterns'; Jan S. Hogendorn and Marion Johnson, *The Shell Money of the Slave Trade* (Cambridge, 1986); David Eltis, 'Trade between Western Africa and the Atlantic World before 1870: Estimates of Trends in Values, Composition and Direction', *Research in Economic History*, 12 (1989), 197–239.

[47] Barter remained an important part of trade along the Windward Coast and nearby areas well into the eighteenth century (*The Journal of a Slave Trader (John Newton), 1750–1754*, ed. Bernard Martin and Mark Spurrell (1962), *passim*).

central element in the 'rules' or mentalities of Afro-European exchange. Moreover, just as the demand of goods exchanged for slaves varied from place to place, so, too, did the currencies in which trade was conducted. At Gambia, the Windward Coast and Bonny, the unit of account was the 'bar'; its exchange rate against European currencies differed from one place to the other. At the Gold Coast and at Ouidah, transactions were conducted in 'trade ounces'; at Old Calabar, in 'coppers'; and at Angola, in 'pieces' or 'cloths'.[48] The provenance of such units of value is sometimes obscure but in most cases was clearly linked to items of trade such as bar iron, gold, copperwares or textiles which were or had been important at the locality in question. Whatever their source, local units of account became interwoven into trade negotiation at the African coast, accepted by Europeans and Africans alike. Put another way, like the pidgin languages through which the terms of trade were negotiated, they became central components of the culture of coastal commercial exchange. Enabling profit and loss on exchanges to be calculated, however crudely, they, in turn, enabled such exchange to function more efficiently and thus to grow.

Central, too, of course, to the growth of the transatlantic slave trade was the expansion in demand for African captive labour in the Americas. That labour was largely deployed to expand production of precious metals, notably in Spanish America and after 1700 in Brazil and even more importantly through time in the cultivation of agricultural crops for sale in Europe. Among the crops most dependent on slave labour was sugar, first grown in Brazil from the 1530s and spreading just over a century later to Barbados and in the succeeding two centuries to the whole Caribbean.[49] Other crops also became identified in time with slave labour, notably tobacco, rice, cotton and coffee, but the production of sugar and its derivatives remained critical, accounting perhaps for up to four-fifths of all enslaved Africans taken to the Americas.[50] As sugar cultivation wore

[48] Richardson, 'West Africa Consumption Patterns', 318, 323; Marion Johnson, 'The Ounce in Eighteenth-Century West African Trade', *Journal of African History*, 7 (1966), 197–214; Philip D. Curtin, *Economic Change in Pre-Colonial Africa: Senegambia in the Era of the Slave Trade* (Madison, 1975), ch. 6.

[49] Richard S. Dunn, *Sugar and Slaves: the Rise of the Planter Class in the English West Indies, 1624–1713* (Chapel Hill, 1972); Philip D Curtin, *The Rise and Fall of the Plantation Complex: Essays in Atlantic History* (Cambridge, 1990); Stuart Schwartz, *Sugar Plantations in the Formation of Brazilian Society* (Cambridge, 1984); Barry W. Higman, 'The Sugar Revolution', *Economic History Review*, 53 (2000), 213–36.

[50] On the dominating influence of sugar and sugar-related commodities over slave shipments across the Atlantic, see David Eltis, 'The Slave Economies of the Caribbean: Structure, Performance, Evolution and Significance', in *General History of the Caribbean*, III: *The Slave Societies of the Caribbean*, ed. Franklin W. Knight (Kingston, 1997), 109–19. I recognise that the US came to have the biggest slave population in the Americas in history by 1860 and that cotton production dominated the US antebellum South, but no more than about

out labour, the high concentration of newly arriving captives at sugar colonies also helps to explain the extraordinary 'consumption' of enslaved Africans in production processes in the Americas.[51] That, in turn, dictated that in addition to the growing need for captives to increase output of commodities for European markets, a replacement demand for enslaved labour increasingly reinforced the flow of captives across the Atlantic. At the height of the Atlantic slave trade in the late eighteenth century, that demand accounted for a substantial proportion of all the African captives bound for the Americas.

Whether captives were intended to expand production or replace those dying prematurely, the process mediating between American demand for slaves and African supply was the price mechanism. Unfortunately, evidence relating to prices of slaves on both sides of the Atlantic is thin and uneven before 1650, but from the limited data that are available the trend in prices through much of the sixteenth and seventeenth centuries appears to have been relatively flat.[52] This is perhaps to be expected given the modest scale of the Atlantic slave trade before 1650 and, according to Manning, Africans' 'positive supply response to the higher demand for slaves'.[53] Thereafter, the picture changed as the scale of the trade grew. Firmer price evidence from the late seventeenth century onwards shows that in the century or so through 1807 coastal prices of slaves tended to rise in nominal as well as in real terms.[54] The latter is measured by the quantity of trade goods bartered per slave. This upward trend in coastal prices of

5 per cent of the African captives taken across the Atlantic during the era of the Atlantic slave trade disembarked in what became the United States (www.slavevoyages.com, last accessed 10 Jan. 2009).

[51] On the failure of enslaved Africans to reproduce in areas where sugar cultivation was dominant, see Barry W. Higman, *Slave Population of the British Caribbean, 1807–1834* (Baltimore, 1984); *idem*, 'The Economic and Social Development of the British West Indies, from Settlement to ca. 1850', in *The Cambridge Economic History of the United States: The Colonial Era*, ed. Stanley L. Engerman and Robert E. Gallman (Cambridge, 1996), 307–9; David Eltis and Paul Lachance, 'The Demographic Decline of Caribbean Slave Populations: New Evidence from the Transatlantic and Intra-American Slave Trades', in *Extending the Frontiers: Essays on the New Transatlantic Slave Trade Database*, ed. David Eltis and David Richardson (New Haven, 2008), 335–63.

[52] Richard N. Bean, *The British Trans-Atlantic Slave Trade, 1650–1775* (New York, 1975); Joseph C. Miller, 'Slave Prices in the Portuguese Southern Atlantic, 1600–1830', in *Africans in Bondage: Studies in Slavery and the Slave Trade*, ed. Paul E. Lovejoy (Madison, 1986), 43–79; Manning, *Slavery and African Life*, 93–4.

[53] Manning, *Slavery and African Life*, 94.

[54] Henry A. Gemery and Jan S. Hogendorn, 'Elasticity of Slave Labor Supply and the Development of the Slave Economies in the British Caribbean: The Seventeenth Century Experience', in *Comparative Perspectives on Slavery in New World Plantation Societies*, ed. Vera Ruben and Arthur Tudin, *Annals of the New York Academy of Sciences*, 292 (1977), 72–84; Manning, *Slavery and African Life*, 93–4; Miller, 'Slave Prices'; David Richardson, 'Slave Prices in West and West-Central Africa, 1699–1807: Toward an Annual Series', *Bulletin of Economic Research*, 43 (1990), 21–56; Paul E. Lovejoy and David Richardson, 'British Abolition and its Impact on

captives was more marked after 1750 than earlier in the century, and as such tended to mirror the index of real prices of newly arrived enslaved Africans in the Americas.[55] The transatlantic shadowing of American slave prices by African ones was not to be unexpected given the rising tide of captives crossing the Atlantic before 1807 and improvements in flows of market information within the Atlantic world. Increased volumes of activity encouraged greater integration of markets.

There are also signs, however, that rising demand for captives to unprecedented heights in the middle years of the eighteenth century placed strains on existing African capacity to supply captives for export. The mean time taken by ships to complete their purchases of captives in Atlantic Africa doubled between 1730 and 1775 from three to six months, extending the overall length of slaving voyages from Europe.[56] In the same years, the real price of captives at the coast moved upwards, while European traders earnestly began more intensive exploitation of previously largely neglected potential sources of captives at Sierra Leone, the Windward Coast and the Bight of Biafra.[57] Although the evidence is not conclusive, it seems likely that in this period, too, Europeans were tempted to expand supplies of credit to their African counterparts, with a view perhaps to improving the flow of slaves from inland sources to coastal trading venues and thereby accelerating turnaround times of ships at the African coast. If this was the case, the strategy evidently had some success, for the indications are the loading times of ships in African ports fell back from the 1770s onward.[58] In all these respects, market forces, largely operating through the price mechanism but underscored by Afro-European social capital building that supported innovation in credit arrangements, appear to have determined changes in the intensity and geographical distribution of slaving activity in Africa as American

Slave Prices along the Atlantic Coast of Africa, 1783–1850', *Journal of Economic History*, 55 (1995), 98–120.

[55] On Brazilian prices, see Miller, 'Slave Prices'; on Caribbean prices, see David Eltis and David Richardson, 'Prices of African Slaves Newly Arrived in the Americas, 1673–1865: New Evidence on Long-Run Trends and Regional Differentials', in *Slavery in the Development of the Americas: Essays in Honor of Stanley L. Engerman*, ed. David Eltis, Frank D. Lewis and Kenneth L. Sokoloff (Cambridge, 2004), 181–218; on South Carolina prices, see David Eltis, Frank D. Lewis and David Richardson, 'Slave Prices, the African Slave Trade, and Productivity in Eighteenth-Century South Carolina: A Reassessment', *Journal of Economic History*, 66 (2006), 1054–65.

[56] David Eltis and David Richardson, 'Productivity in the Transatlantic Slave Trade', *Explorations in Economic History*, 32 (1995), 465–84.

[57] On terms of trade, see Henry A. Gemery, Jan S. Hogendorn and Marion Johnson, 'Evidence of English/African Terms of Trade in the Eighteenth Century', *Explorations in Economic History*, 27 (1990), 157–77; on shifting patterns of trade, see David Eltis and David Richardson, 'A New Assessment of the Transatlantic Slave Trade', in *Extending the Frontiers*, ed. Eltis and Richardson, 46–7.

[58] Eltis and Richardson, 'Productivity'.

demand for captives reached new heights in the half century before 1807. In doing so, they also extended the geographical reach of the Afro-European commercial dialogue both coastwise and inland.

Vital though they are in shedding light on shifts in both the geography and balance of power of commercial exchange, time-trends in mean coastal prices of slaves tell only one part of the story of patterns of cross-cultural trade in Atlantic Africa. If we switch focus from time trends of prices to patterns of prices by categories of captives, other cultural adjustments that facilitated growth in commercial exchange are revealed. At the heart of the issue here were American buyers' preferences for slaves and African slave dealers' responses to them. Particularly important was the fact that for cultural as much as other reasons American preferences for enslaved Africans varied in important respects from those of long-established buyers in Africa and other parts of the world. Satisfying Americans' preferences for captive Africans involved, therefore, shifts in African slave dealers' commercial perceptions and, as we shall see, adjustments in cultural practices within Africa from the sixteenth century onwards.

From an early stage in the history of the Atlantic slave trade, relatively clear age and gender preferences among American buyers of African captives were apparent. During the sixteenth century and early seventeenth century, the prime slave or 'pieza de Indias', as it was defined for tax purposes in Spanish America, was considered as a young, healthy, adult aged fifteen to thirty or as a person having a height of least seven *palmos*. Throughout Spanish America, this became the standard against which all other categories of enslaved Africans – superannuated, juvenile, very young or simply of shorter stature – tended to be evaluated.[59] It became in time increasingly refined, focusing more on adult males than males and females and as slave use in other places expanded spread more or less uniformly across every European political jurisdiction in the Americas. At times, too, and especially when the geographical sourcing of captives became wider, gender- and age-based preferences for slaves were underscored by ones based on ethnicity, real or imputed. Indeed, ethnically based stereotypes of captives emerged in time, with some groups being viewed by potential buyers more favourably than others.[60] In this

[59] David H. Chandler, *Health and Slavery: A Study of Health Conditions among Negro Slaves in the Viceroyalty of New Granada and its Associated Slave Trade, 1600–1810* (Tulane, 1972), 83–6; Frederick P. Bowser, *The African Slave in Colonial Peru, 1524–1650* (Stanford, 1974), 39; Colin A. Palmer, *Slaves of the White God: Blacks in Mexico, 1570–1660* (Cambridge, MA, 1976), 12–14; idem, *Human Cargoes: The British Slave Trade to Spanish America, 1700–1739* (Urbana, 1981), 183; Linda A. Newsom and Susie Minchin, *From Capture to Sale: The Portuguese Slave Trade in Spanish South America in the Early Seventeenth Century* (Leiden, 2007), 261.

[60] Darrold D. Wax, 'Preferences for Slaves in Colonial America', *Journal of Negro History*, 58 (1973), 371–401.

respect, Igbo slaves from the Bight of Biafra were commonly viewed with less favour among American buyers than others.

Explaining American preferences for some categories of enslaved Africans over others is complex. As one might anticipate, however, preferences seem to have been heavily influenced by the perceived labour qualities of the enslaved. Some ethnic groups acquired a reputation for hard work, durability and the possession of particular skills, whereas others came to be seen variously as rebellious, lazy or even suicidal. Such stereotypes were attributed to a range of factors, including acquired or inherited African skills or, in some cases, to perceptions of the natural abundance or harshness of the environment from which captives were taken.[61] In terms of age, American buyers obviously sought captives who could immediately be put to work, avoiding the costs of child-rearing, while in the case of gender they obviously seem to have had relatively little regard for the reproductive value of females, even though in most colonial regimes children born to females assumed the legal condition of their mother. Females entering the Atlantic slave trade were destined, in fact, primarily to live and die producing sugar and other crops rather than children. In this respect, like males, they were classified essentially as field or other labourers, with the males commanding a price premium presumably because they were perceived as being better suited physically to withstand the rigours of plantation and mining work.[62]

There is little evidence that stereotypes of captives based on ethnicity translated regularly or consistently into price differentials within American slave markets. When they did, this seems to have been attributable as much to differentials in the purchase cost in Africa of captives and their transport to America as to actual buyer preferences in the Americas.[63] By contrast, when allowance is made for such factors, age- and gender-based preferences were more or less consistently reflected in

---

[61] In terms of acquired or inherited skills, some of the strongest claims have linked the rise of rice cultivation in South Carolina and elsewhere to the skills of imported Africans (Carney, *Black Rice*); cf. Eltis, Morgan and Richardson, 'Agency and Diaspora'). For an identification of the Akan from the Gold Coast with rebelliousness, see Monica Schuler, 'Akan Slave Rebellions in the British Caribbean', *Savacou*, 1 (1970), 8–31.

[62] On female work in sugar and low reproduction see Richard S. Dunn, 'Sugar Production and Slave Women in Jamaica', in *Cultivation and Culture: Labor and the Shaping of Slave Life in the Americas*, ed. Ira Berlin and Philip D. Morgan (Charlottesville, 1993), 49–73. In the case of rice cultivation and associated drainage, ditching and maintenance work, planters regarded men and boys as best equipped to discharge the work. They allocated spades and axes almost entirely to men. Joyce E. Chaplin, *An Anxious Pursuit: Agricultural Innovation and Modernity in the Lower South, 1730–1815* (Chapel Hill, 1993), 227–76; Philip D. Morgan, *Slave Counterpoint: Black Culture in the Eighteenth-Century Chesapeake and Lowcountry* (Chapel Hill, 1998), 155–9

[63] Eltis and Richardson, 'Prices of African Slaves', 197. For price data grouped by ethnicity, see *The Cuban Slave Market, 1790–1880*, ed. Laird W. Bergad, Fe Iglesias Garcia and Maria del Carmen Barcia (Cambridge, 1995), 73–4.

patterns of slave prices in America.[64] Young and healthy adult males were normally among the first captives sold at auction from recently arrived ships from Africa. Males typically fetched premiums of up to 15 per cent or more over those for females, with young adult males achieving premiums of 20 per cent or more over the mean price for whole shiploads of captives. Equally, children under the age of fifteen years usually fetched lower prices than adults, whether male or female, though where sellers distinguished 'men-boys' from other males the differential between women and men-boys might be very small or even non-existent. Overall, nonetheless, price patterns for newly arrived enslaved Africans reflected buyer preferences: adults typically sold for markedly higher prices than children and men for more than women. This was the case regardless of political jurisdiction in the Americas.

Because of oceanic transport costs, prices of slaves at the African coast were naturally lower than those in the Americas.[65] They were commonly recorded, as we have seen, in local units of account, the exchange rate of which with European currencies varied. In whatever currency prices were reported, prices of slaves at the African coast evidently varied by age and gender. Such variations were, moreover, fairly robust and consistent through time and across regional markets. In their general direction, too, they tended to mirror those found at American slave markets. Insofar as one can establish coastal prices, mark ups on adult males were typically 20 per cent and sometimes as high as 40 per cent above the norm for whole purchases of shiploads of slaves.[66] Adults in general usually cost significantly more than children. Such patterns clearly reflect the market power of American buyers of slaves at the African coast. Other things being equal, they also provided strong price signals to African traders regarding the composition of captives to supply. Their responses did

[64] David Galenson, *Traders, Planters and Slaves: Market Behavior in Early English America* (Cambridge, 1986), 63, which shows prices of females were 84 per cent of those of males at Barbados in 1680–1723. Similar ratios are evident in Cuba in the nineteenth century, when, as in Barbados, the dominant crop was sugar but also in the southern US when the crop was cotton and slave numbers largely increased through natural reproduction rather than imports from Africa. For Cuba, see Manuel Moreno Fraginals, Herbert S. Klein and Stanley L. Engerman, 'The Level and Structure of Slave Prices on Cuban Plantations in the Mid-Nineteenth Century: Some Comparative Perspectives', *American Historical Review*, 88 (1983), 1201–18; for the US, see Robert W. Fogel and Stanley L. Engerman, *Time on the Cross: The Economics of American Negro Slavery* (2 vols., Boston, MA, 1974), I, 75–7. For evidence on slave prices in the Caribbean between 1674 and 1807 see Eltis and Richardson, 'Prices of African Slaves'; David Eltis, Frank. D. Lewis and David Richardson, 'Slave Prices, the African Slave Trade and Productivity in the Caribbean, 1674–1807', *Economic History Review*, 58 (2005), 673–700.

[65] On the transport cost 'wedge' between Africa and America, see David Eltis, 'The Relative Importance of Slaves and Commodities in the Atlantic Trade of Seventeenth-Century Africa', *Journal of African History*, 35 (1994), 237–49.

[66] Bean, *British Slave Trade*; Johnson, 'Ounce'.

not always accord with the declared preferences of American buyers, perhaps because at times slave procurement and other cost factors in Africa offset some of the gains from supplying captives with a coast price premium. Whatever the cause, we know that the proportion of females entering the slave trade before 1700 and of juveniles entering the slave trade after 1800 was, in each case, higher than the long-run norm.[67] So, too, was the proportion of females dispatched from the Bight of Biafra relative to other regions. Such variations indicate that the coastal dialogue between buyer and seller of captives could be subject to factors outside their own immediate control. Nevertheless, it remains the case that across all the major African slave embarkation venues and throughout most years of the Atlantic slave trade, male slaves entering the trade typically outnumbered females by significant proportions. In most cases, males outnumbered females by two to one; in some cases the ratio was even higher. Furthermore, even in the Bight of Biafra, where the ratio of males to females was usually lowest, males commonly comprised around six out of ten of captives embarking ship for the Americas. In most cases, too, adults considerably outnumbered children across all supply regions, at least before the nineteenth century. In short, despite some temporal and regional variations, the gender and age composition of slaves supplied by African dealers was consistent with the preferences for slaves expressed by American purchasers.

At one level, such patterns of slave exports from Africa to the Americas may be seen as an understandable and predictable market response by African slave suppliers to overseas demand stimuli. At another level, however, patterns of slave supply embodied a significant cultural adjustment on the part of African traders to an emerging and growing export market opportunity that, in terms of its demand for captives, differed in major ways from other markets with which they may have been familiar. Price data relating to other African-based slave trades are thinner than for the Atlantic slave trade, but they still paint a very different picture of patterns of demand for captives in those markets. In the far older trans-Saharan slave trade, for instance, it was not males but females, especially pre-pubescent ones, who typically commanded the highest prices.[68] Among older age groups, prices were broadly similar for males and females of the same age. The only exception was eunuchs,

[67] David Eltis and Stanley L. Engerman, 'Fluctuations in Age and Sex Ratios in the Transatlantic Slave Trade, 1663–1864', *Economic History Review*, 46 (1993), 308–23.

[68] On the magnitude and price of enslaved Africans entering the trans-Saharan traffic, see Ralph A. Austen, 'The Trans-Saharan Slave Trade: A Tentative Census', in *Uncommon Market*, ed. Gemery and Hogendorn, 23–77; *idem*, 'The Mediterranean Islamic Slave Trade out of Africa: A Tentative Census', in *The Human Commodity: Perspectives on the Trans-Saharan Slave Trade*, ed. Elizabeth Savage (1992), 214–49; Ehud R. Toledano, *The Ottoman Slave Trade and its Suppression 1840–1890* (Princeton, 1982), 10.

who commanded exceptionally high prices. Premiums for young girls and eunuchs in trans-Saharan markets largely reflected the fact that most would end up in the harems and other institutions identified with rich and powerful Muslim households. Elsewhere, in the African internal slave markets, a price premium on females was also commonly found.[69] In this case, it applied to females in their prime working and reproductive years, but in African areas under Islamic influence, pre-pubescent girls again brought a premium price. On this evidence, then, the demand for enslaved females within Africa typically matched or even outpaced that for males. This suggests that enslaved females within Africa may have been valued for both their productive *and* reproductive capacities, with perhaps high proportions being absorbed into the household and kinship groups of their captors.[70]

Enslaved Africans sold in internal markets or into the trans-Saharan trade were typically victims of wars, raids or kidnappings by other ethnic groups or 'nations'. A variety of factors may have been instrumental in triggering violence between communities or states in Africa, but the internal slave price data suggest that an important motivation behind wars and raids was the expected 'crop' of female and juvenile captives that such wars might be expected to yield. Such captives might be retained by their captors or sold on. Wars did not only yield female or juvenile victims, however. They also produced a wide range of captives, prominent among them being adult males. Some would be defeated warriors. Vanquished and doubtless dishonoured and humiliated, such men could easily pose, as long as they lived and remained in captivity locally, a continuing threat to their former enemy. In the absence of alternative outlets for their profitable removal to or disposal at some distance from their homeland or place of capture, the safest option for their captors was to slaughter

[69] Paul E. Lovejoy and David Richardson, 'Competing Markets for Male and Female Slaves: Slave Prices in the Interior of West Africa, 1780–1850', *International Journal of African Historical Studies*, 28 (1995), 261–93.

[70] There is a massive literature on slavery in Africa, much of it concerned with the extent to which enslaved people were assimilated into kinship structures (e.g. *Slavery in Africa: Historical and Anthropological Perspectives*, ed. Suzanne Miers and Igor Kopytoff (Madison, 1977), 7–66) and the degree to which slavery was transformed by commercial forces and predatory state activities (Lovejoy, *Transformations*; Claude Meillassoux, *The Anthropology of Slavery: The Womb of Iron and Gold* (Chicago, 1991)). There seems little doubt, however, that, among the newly enslaved in Africa at least, females often outnumbered males and that this was linked to the reproductive and productive roles of women. Summarising the literature, Frank McGlynn suggested that women 'predominated in the internal market and exchange transactions of African kinship slavery, valued for their reproduction of dependents and production of domestic, craft and agricultural factors' (Frank McGlynn, 'African Slavery', in *Encyclopedia of Social History*, ed. Peter N. Stearns (New York, 1994), 20–1).

them on the battlefield.[71] When placed together with the retention and absorption of female captives, such action might be interpreted as an example of socio-biology in which '[i]n human raids and wars . . . another man is a rival to be killed, but a woman can represent a valuable opportunity to transmit the victor's genes'.[72] Whatever the underlying explanation, the execution of defeated adult males and enslavement of their female brethren probably emerged as important traditional 'rules' of war in much of Africa. In all likelihood, this remained the case in many parts of the continent long after Europeans arrived at the Atlantic littoral of Africa.[73] American demand for African captives, however, with its specific – and by traditional African standards, unusual – preference for adult males arguably radically changed this scenario, placing, in regions accessible to the Atlantic seaboard at least, potentially significant value or 'rents' on groups of wartime captives previously considered as much a threat as an asset to their captors.

Warfare and other forms of violence were just as important in Africa for recruiting captives for American slave markets as they were for domestic African and other export slave markets. As the Atlantic trade grew in importance, it arguably accentuated existing levels of violence in the interior of West and West-Central Africa, increasing the potential pool of all captives available for internal as well as the transatlantic traffic. Some – possibly even a majority – of the females were likely retained within domestic slavery in Africa but, as the total levels of enslavement activities increased, this would still allow some females, including girls, to enter the Atlantic trade. Arguably, such females might have been considered superfluous to domestic demand in Africa. Joining the females destined for transatlantic markets, however, was an evidently even larger tide of males. Some were probably victims of wars and violence linked directly to the Atlantic slave trade.[74] Motivated primarily perhaps to secure captives, especially males, to sell into export markets, such conflicts

[71] On the massacring of prisoners, see Meillassoux, *Anthropology of Slavery*; Robin Law, *The Slave Coast of West Africa, 1550–1750* (Oxford, 1991), 97; Ludwig Ferdinand Romer, *A Reliable Account of the Coast of Guinea* (1760), ed. Selena. A. Winsnes (Oxford, 2000), 128.

[72] Malcolm Potts and Thomas Hayden, *Sex and War: How Biology Explains Warfare and Terrorism and Offers a Path to a Safer World* (Dallas, 2008), 192.

[73] As an example of the conservatism of traditions, a German traveller, Isert, observed in 1785 that the sacrifice of fifty people each year to the king of Dahomey was a 'dreadful custom' and 'financial loss', but that for political reasons the king could not 'terminate a custom that is as old as the kingdom itself' (P. E. Isert, *Letters on West Africa and the Slave Trade* (1785), trans. Selena A. Winsnes (Oxford, 1992), 111).

[74] The motivation of warfare in Africa has been a source of much debate, with claims that wars were often primarily motivated by political, not economic, considerations and would have occurred in any case in the absence of the export slave trade, being challenged by arguments that the possibility of exporting captives helped create a new type of 'predatory' state, transforming its victims into commodities for export. For statements of this argument,

might be considered a direct adjustment in military culture in Africa to the presence of European slave ships at the African coast. Other male captives were probably victims of conflicts arising for other reasons. Historically, many would not have escaped the battlefield alive, but from the sixteenth century onwards the possibility emerged of deporting them profitably through trade networks to remote locations across the Atlantic Ocean. This is not to argue that such captives benefited from the rise of the Atlantic slave trade; on the contrary, sale to Europeans may have heaped added dishonour on them to that arising from military defeat. But whether wars were prompted by the slave trade or by other factors, the ensuing outflow of captives to the Americas seems to have rested on adjustments in the culture or rules – or even the political economy – of warfare in Africa in the face of new slave export opportunities by sea. In tandem with cross-cultural processes of dialogue and institutional change at the Atlantic seaboard, such adjustments were instrumental in allowing African slave suppliers to respond positively to growing demand for enslaved people in the Americas between the sixteenth and eighteenth centuries.

III

The Atlantic slave trade was the largest oceanic coerced movement of people in history. Lasting over three centuries, it had an enduring, even defining, impact on the modern world. It helped to nurture the growth of the post-Columbian Atlantic economy. It fostered racial division and inequality. It ushered in the global remixing of peoples through migration that has become such an important element of modernity. These effects of transatlantic slavery were only possible, however, because the traffic in captives from Africa to the Americas became as large it did. Understanding how that happened sheds light on what Douglass North has defined as a critical turning point in economic change historically, namely, 'the transition from a belief system built to deal with the uncertainties of the physical environment to one confronting the opportunities of the human environment'.[75] The Atlantic slave trade, with its uncertainties as well as its global reach, offers exceptional opportunities to explore how the transition that North describes took place.

The slave trade was often depicted by contemporaries as being unusually hazardous. It is a theme continued by historians. There is little doubt that the physical or 'natural' environment within which the activity occurred contributed to that image. Atlantic Ocean currents and wind systems largely dictated voyage patterns.[76] Harvest seasons in

see Boubacar Barry, *Senegambia and the Atlantic Slave Trade* (1988; Cambridge, 1998 edn), 81–93; Martin A. Klein, *Slavery and Colonial Rule in French West Africa* (Cambridge, 1998), 37–58.

[75] North, *Understanding the Process*, 63.

[76] *Atlas of Slavery*, ed. Eltis and Richardson.

Africa commonly determined the timing of voyages as captives needed to be fed.[77] Viruses and germs were central determinants of shipboard mortality of captives.[78] Hurricanes and drought affected harvests of slave-grown crops, especially in the Caribbean, thereby causing fluctuations in demand for labour. These and other factors made slaving voyages risky enterprises. Developments in the human environment, nonetheless, allowed slave traffickers to counter or at least moderate some of these risks and to respond positively to the commercial opportunities created by European colonisation of the Americas. Historians have identified a number of risk-mitigating technical and financial innovations in the slave trade.[79] Some related to shipboard health and may have contributed to a long-run decline in percentage losses of captives in transit.[80] Others concerned credit and remittance issues, and facilitated the circulation of finance capital.[81] Yet others were rooted in iterative exchange, social capital and knowledge accumulation and transfer.[82] One element in the last was the evolution of the cultures of exchange in Atlantic Africa which have been the focus of this paper and which played a vital factor in shaping African supply responsiveness to external demand for captives. This paper provides an incomplete investigation of that responsiveness. We still have much to learn, for example, not just about how but also why African slave dealers responded in the way they did to American demand for labour. Explanations of such issues are likely to be found in the cosmology or belief systems of African societies, as Harms has reminded us,[83] and in the local structures of power within which African

---

[77] Stephen D. Behrendt, 'Markets, Transaction Cycles and Profits: Merchant Decision-Making in the British Slave Trade', *William and Mary Quarterly*, third series, 58 (2001), 171–204; *idem*, 'Seasonality, African Trade and Atlantic History' (unpublished paper delivered to the International Seminar on the History of the Atlantic World, Harvard University, 21 June 2007).

[78] Simon J. Hogerzeil and David Richardson, 'Slave Purchasing Strategies and Shipboard Mortality: Day to Day Evidence from the Dutch African Trade, 1751–1797', *Journal of Economic History*, 67 (2007), 160–90.

[79] For a general statement see Henry A. Gemery and Jan S. Hogendorn, 'Technological Change, Slavery and the Slave Trade', in *Imperial Impact: Studies in the Economic History of Africa and India*, ed. Clive Dewey and Anthony G. Hopkins (1978), 243–58.

[80] Robin Haines and Ralph Shlomowitz, 'Explaining the Decline in Mortality in the Eighteenth Century British Slave Trade', *Economic History Review*, 53 (2000), 262–83.

[81] Richard B. Sheridan, 'The Commercial and Financial Organisation of the British Slave Trade, 1750–1807', *Economic History Review*, 11 (1958–9), 249–63; Jacob M. Price, 'Credit in the Slave Trade and Plantation Economies', in *Slavery and the Rise of the Atlantic System*, ed. Barbara L. Solow (Cambridge, 1991), 293–339; Robin Pearson and David Richardson, 'Social Capital, Institutional Innovation, and Atlantic Trade before 1800', *Business History*, 50 (2008), 765–80.

[82] Peter Mathias, 'Risk, Credit and Kinship in Early Modern Enterprise', in *The Early Modern Atlantic Economy*, ed. Kenneth Morgan and John J. McCusker (Cambridge, 2000), 15–36.

[83] Harms, *River of Wealth*, 197–215.

traders operated. Equally, there is still much room for debate over the distribution within as well as outside Africa of the costs and benefits arising from transatlantic slavery and their long-term legacies. But the fact that some 12.5 million captives entered the Atlantic slave trade in the three centuries or so before 1850 is tragic testament both to the chronic hunger for captives in the Americas and to the organisational skills and incentive regimes that European traders developed in partnership with their African allies in order to satisfy that hunger. The Atlantic slave trade provided more than a bitter legacy for the modern world. It also provided a telling, if tragic, example of how through adjustments in the balance between the physical and human environment – or through 'the structural change that humans impose on human interaction'[84] – the modern world may actually have been created.

---

[84] North, *Understanding the Process*, 78.

Transactions of the RHS 19 (2009), pp. 181–203 © Royal Historical Society 2009
doi:10.1017/S0080440109990090

SLAVES OUT OF CONTEXT: DOMESTIC SLAVERY AND THE ANGLO-INDIAN FAMILY, *c.* 1780–1830*

By Margot Finn

READ 17 OCTOBER 2008 AT THE UNIVERSITY OF DUNDEE

ABSTRACT. This paper explores the place of domestic slaves in British families resident in India, *c.* 1780–1830, and the ways in which the presence of slaves within these Anglo-Indian households challenged British understandings of slavery as a practice. Drawing upon probate data, private correspondence and the Parliamentary Papers, it suggests that the history of slavery in the British empire must be situated within wider histories of family, household and kin. Located within the family and often conflated with servants, domestic slaves in Anglo-India came to be seen as dependent female subordinates whose gender and status placed them outside the emerging politics of emancipation.

In 1782, Alexander Craufurd of the British East India Company composed a letter to his brother, which he hoped would serve in lieu of an official will. 'As my Disorder Continues obstinate', Craufurd reflected from his deathbed in Chittigong, it was now timely to dispose of his worldly goods, and to secure the future welfare of his household in Bengal.[1] Many of the bequests made in Craufurd's impromptu will reflect the prevailing testamentary practices of propertied men and women in eighteenth-century Britain. Like many of his compatriots at home, he chose a family member to administer his estate, appointing his brother as executor and bequeathing to him a horse and a gold watch as tokens of gratitude and fond remembrance.[2] Several other bequests likewise commemorated

* Research for this paper was funded by an Economic and Social Research Council award for 'Colonial Possessions: Personal Property and Social Identity in British India'. The author thanks Dr Matt Adams for research conducted on this project and Professors Trevor Burnard, Gad Heuman and Carolyn Steedman for their helpful comments on the paper itself.

[1] Will of A. Craufurd, 6 Jan. 1782, in Oriental and India Office Collections, British Library (henceforth OIOC), L/AG/34/29/4.

[2] For the legal norms and conventions of will-making in this period, see *When Death Do Us Part: Understanding and Interpreting the Probate Records of Early Modern England*, ed. Tom Arkell, Nesta Evans and Nigel Goose (Oxford, 2000); and R. J. Morris, *Men, Women and Property in England, 1780–1870: A Social and Economic History of Family Strategies amongst the Leeds Middle Classes* (Cambridge, 2005), esp. pp. 79–141.

his affective ties through the disposition of personal possessions that marked his location within the governing classes and his participation in a wider Georgian consumer society. Craufurd's friend George Hatch thus received a gold ring and breast-pin, fashionable trinkets that signified both luxury and pleasure to eighteenth-century English consumers. His 'very Particular and Sincere friend' Thomas was willed a horse and a bayonet, while Ralph Lecke, described as 'another Sincere and particular friend of mine' was to receive a horse and Craufurd's sporting dogs in Dacca.[3] If these bequests mirrored the testamentary decisions of his affluent contemporaries in England, however, other provisions in his will marked Craufurd emphatically as an Anglo Indian.[4] To the indigenous concubine who had borne his offspring but was named in his will only as his 'Girl', Craufurd left 2,000 rupees, instructing his brother that this sum was 'for her care of my children provided that she places them . . . under your charge without any further trouble'.[5] Then, in an unnerving afterthought, Craufurd recalled that his household also included an Indian slave. 'I had almost forgot a poor Slave Boy (I never have look'd on him as such) who is a good Servant and must have his freedom [plus] 100 Rs as a provision for him', he hastily ordered in a postscript.

Together, Craufurd's belated recognition that he was a slave owner, his assertion that he had 'never . . . look'd on' his slave *as* a slave, his recognition that this seeming non-slave nonetheless required manumission, and his description of his slave-boy as a servant point to the peculiar problems – both for Anglo Indians themselves and for subsequent historians – posed by domestic slavery in British India. Like conceptions of slavery current in the Georgian era, historiographical approaches to British slavery have been dominated by an Atlantic world perspective. The Atlantic world model of slavery takes the plantation system as its

---

[3] Comparable testamentary practices in England are detailed in, for example, *Urban Fortunes: Property and Inheritance in the Town, 1700–1900*, ed. Jon Stobart and Alastair Owens (Aldershot, 2000); and Marcia Pointon, *Strategies for Showing: Women, Possession, and Representation in English Visual Culture 1665–1800* (Oxford, 1997), esp. 307–400. For the fashionable trade in metal trinkets, see Maxine Berg, *Luxury and Pleasure in Eighteenth-Century Britain* (Oxford, 2005), 154–92. The circulation of such goods as memorial objects among Anglo-Indian kin networks is discussed in Margot Finn, 'Colonial Gifts: Family Politics and the Exchange of Goods in British India, c. 1780–1820', *Modern Asian Studies*, 40 (2006), 203–31.

[4] Throughout this paper, the term 'Anglo Indian' is used in its eighteenth- and nineteenth-century sense, to describe persons of British origin in India, rather than in its more modern sense of 'mixed-race' or 'Eurasian'.

[5] Provisions for Indian concubines in Anglo-Indian wills are discussed in Indrani Chatterjee, 'Colouring Subalternity: Slaves, Concubines and Social Orphans in Early Colonial India', *Subaltern Studies*, 10 (Delhi, 1999), 49–97; Durba Ghosh, *Sex and the Family in Colonial India* (Cambridge, 2006), esp. 107–32; and C. J. Hawes, *Poor Relations: The Making of a Eurasian Community in British India, 1773–1833* (1996).

norm, defines slavery as an absence of 'freedom', emphasises the role of slaves as chattel traded within commercial markets, underlines the use of violence as a mechanism for extracting slave labour and highlights the status of slaves as racial 'outsiders'.[6] Viewed against this received Atlantic backdrop, slavery on the Indian subcontinent appears to be an institution out of place, not only in a geographic sense, but in terms of its content, purpose and meaning.[7] Craufurd's eleventh-hour bequest of freedom to an Indian domestic slave whom (he simultaneously insisted) was – conceptually, socially and affectively – not in fact a slave, alerts us to the striking differences that marked British experiences of slavery and emancipation in the Atlantic and the Indian Ocean worlds.

In this paper, I seek to reexamine British understandings of slavery in the later eighteenth and early nineteenth centuries by focusing on the practice of domestic slavery on the subcontinent under East India Company rule. Using probate records (such as Anglo-Indian wills and inventories) alongside private family letters and public documents contained in the Parliamentary Papers, I wish to suggest the centrality of conceptions of family, household and kin for British attitudes to slavery not only on the subcontinent but within the wider British empire. My conception of the family is inspired by a paper delivered to this Society at the University of Greenwich in 2003, in which Professor Leonore Davidoff wisely observed that 'The large bourgeois family, in horizontal or lateral as well as vertical relationships, in extensive kin networks, played a central role in people's lives far beyond our late twentieth-century imagination.'[8] Locating Indian slavery within the history of the family (rather than associating it principally with racial identity or market economics) goes against the grain of Atlantic world interpretations of the history of human bondage, but opens up alternative analytical pathways, and connects Indian slaves as historical actors to wider histories of domesticity as well as of servitude. By examining domestic slavery on the subcontinent at once as an abstract category of Enlightenment social scientific inquiry and as a social practice in which colonial Anglo Indians were fully

[6] See for example Robin Blackburn, *The Making of New World Slavery: From the Baroque to the Modern 1492–1800* (1997); and David Brion Davis, *Inhuman Bondage: The Rise and Fall of Slavery in the New World* (Oxford, 2006).

[7] For useful discussions of the historiographical problems posed by reliance on Atlantic world models of slavery for analysis of Indian Ocean servitude, see Gwyn Campbell, 'Introduction: Slavery and Other Forms of Unfree Labour in the Indian Ocean World', in *The Structure of Slavery in Indian Ocean Africa and Asia*, ed. Gwyn Campbell (2004), vii–xxxii; and Richard M. Eaton, 'Introduction', in *Slavery and South Asian History*, ed. Indrani Chatterjee and Richard M. Eaton (Bloomington, 2006), 1–16.

[8] Leonore Davidoff, 'The Legacy of the Nineteenth-Century Bourgeois Family and the Wool Merchant's Son', *Transactions of the Royal Historical Society*, sixth series, 14 (2004), 27. See also Naomi Tadmor, *Family and Friends in Eighteenth-Century England: Household, Kinship and Patronage* (Cambridge, 2001).

and self-consciously implicated, I seek to shed new light as well on the sharp divergence that had emerged by the 1830s between parliament's normative abolitionism when contemplating West Indian slavery, and its overarching tolerance when considering instead slavery in Britain's Indian empire.

Although statistical profiles of slavery and the slave trade in the Indian Ocean world lack the rigour of corresponding data for New World slavery, they nonetheless establish the wide prevalence of human bondage in both pre-colonial and colonial South Asian polities. A multi-directional slave trade dating from before the Common Era circulated enslaved persons among and between East Africa, Arabia, the Persian Gulf, India, Indonesia, Mauritius and the Cape. Peaking only in the nineteenth century, this intercontinental export industry differed from the Atlantic slave trade not only in its racial diversity but also in its sexual composition and its age profile. Whereas male African slaves were more numerous and typically more costly than female slaves in Atlantic markets, women substantially outnumbered men in the Indian Ocean slave trade, and normally fetched higher prices upon sale.[9] Children, moreover, figured far more prominently in Indian Ocean than in Atlantic slavery. More readily controlled than adult males, children were often seized rather than killed by the victors of military campaigns; upon adulthood, some would gain their freedom, while others continued in servitude to their captors.[10] Reliable estimates of slave numbers in the Indian Ocean world in the eighteenth and nineteenth century are lacking, but perhaps 8 to 9 million Indian slaves lived in bondage in territories under East India Company rule alone as late as the 1840s, a decade after parliament's much-touted emancipation of slaves in the British Atlantic colonies.[11]

On the subcontinent, slave populations were maintained not only by the importation of unfree persons from far-flung Indian Ocean markets but also by a diverse range of Hindu and Muslim practices that created and circulated bonded populations. Two main taproots fed slavery in India prior to and during the early years of East India Company rule: the enslavement of male and female war-captives during military campaigns, and the self-sale of impoverished adults – and of children by family members – in times of dearth. Both the decline of the Mughal empire and the rise of the Company's territorial ambitions created conditions conducive to increased levels of both military and economic enslavement.

<hr/>

[9] Campbell, 'Introduction', esp. ix–x, xxv.
[10] *Ibid.*, xiii.
[11] William Gervase Clarence-Smith, *Islam and the Abolition of Slavery* (2006), 14. For the analytical problems posed for comparative history by the relative lack of statistical evidence for Indian Ocean slavery, see Indrani Chatterjee, 'Renewed and Connected Histories: Slavery and the Historiography of South Asia', in *Slavery and South Asian History*, ed. Chatterjee and Eaton, 20.

Eighteenth-century British and East India Company army campaigns displaced indigenous populations and created thousands of Indian captives vulnerable to enslavement; famine conditions, exacerbated by the rigidity of the Company's administration of the Indian revenue system, likewise fostered the sale of impoverished children, women and families into slavery under British rule. Such slaves circulated within local and long-distance markets, through mechanisms that included cash transactions, tributary payments and gifting.[12] Contemporary British observers distinguished between two main forms of Indian slave labour in the later eighteenth and early nineteenth centuries. Agrestic slaves were tied to specific plots of land and employed in agricultural production. Domestic slaves, ubiquitous in both Hindu and Muslim households, performed tasks that included sweeping, cleaning, cooking and child-care; in more affluent households, domestic slaves were key symbols of their masters' power and status but also performed roles such as concubinage, accountancy and trade.[13] Incorporated into their owners' household units, these domestic slaves were positioned not outside society and the family but rather at the kinship end of what Suzanne Miers and Igor Kopytoff have aptly described as the 'slavery to kinship continuum'.[14]

Despite their conspicuous presence in India, domestic slaves have been curiously absent from British histories of Company rule. 'Unlike scholars of the Dutch in Southeast Asia and the Indian Ocean', Indrani Chatterjee has observed, 'scholars of early British and French empires in South Asia remain indifferent to complicating their "nationalist" pasts with Asian slaves'. Chatterjee proposes that this selective historiographical amnesia derives to a substantial extent from historians' reliance on the copious printed collections of primary sources detailing Company and government policy on the subcontinent, which were first published in the multi-volume Parliamentary Papers on Slavery in India from 1828 to 1841. In this interpretation, by stripping South Asian slavery of its distinctive – and distinctively domestic – markings, the Parliamentary Papers worked to naturalise the Atlantic world model of slavery, positioning 'their [British] readers in an apparently universal mode of slave labor, whose contours were supposed to be the same everywhere'.[15]

In what follows, I read the evidence published in the Parliamentary Papers alongside and against manuscript sources that document slavery in British India to suggest an alternative genealogy for British historical

[12] Eaton, 'Introduction', 5.

[13] D. Banaji, *Slavery in British India* (Bombay, 1933); Amal Chattopadhyaya, *Slavery in Bengal Presidency 1772–1843* (1977).

[14] Suzanne Miers and Igor Kopytoff, 'African "Slavery" as an Institution of Marginality', in *Slavery in Africa: Historical and Anthropological Perspectives*, ed. Suzanne Miers and Igor Kopytoff (Madison, 1977), 3–81.

[15] Chatterjee, 'Renewed and Connected Histories', 21, 31–2.

amnesia toward slavery on the subcontinent. Focusing on domestic slavery, I identify slaves as vital members of Anglo-Indian households, persons whose conspicuous presence in social life was however undercut by their problematic position in social theory. Like servants – with whom they were repeatedly compared – domestic slaves were a problem in Anglo-Indian social and political thought because they inhabited a subject position that lay at the very intersection between the family and the market.[16] Only by resituating slavery within the lived social and economic life of the household, I argue here, can we understand the intellectual and political processes by which nationalist histories of British abolitionism came to exclude Indian slavery from their ambit.

Inventories and wills, traditional tools in the armoury of historians of Atlantic world plantations, have been under-exploited in analyses of Indian domestic slavery under British rule.[17] In sharp contrast to the limited survival of British probate material for this period, detailed probate documentation is – thanks to the Company's obsessive archival zeal – abundantly available for Anglo Indians who died on the subcontinent.[18] Thousands of inventories and wills written by Anglo Indians remain in the British Library's archives; hundreds document the existence of domestic slaves in British households. These records provide rich information about British social life and consumer tastes in India, itemising the possession of (for example) thousands of ruffled shirts, silver teapots, hunting prints, watches, telescopes, shower-baths and dictionaries, and enumerating tens of thousands of printed volumes of poetry, fiction, history, law and political economy owned by Anglo Indians.[19] References to the sale of domestic slaves, although not common, are interspersed at intervals among these items in a wide variety of eighteenth-century inventories in the Company's archives. When Captain John Hunter's estate was settled in Bengal in 1782, for example, the sale of his three slaves raised over half of the inventory's total value.[20] Testifying to the substantial sums that Anglo Indians could invest in human property, such entries provide a forceful reminder that the British participated actively as buyers and sellers in Indian Ocean slave markets.

[16] For the wider history of this problem in Britain at this time, see Carolyn Steedman, *Labours Lost: Domestic Service and the Making of Modern England* (Cambridge, forthcoming), chs. 1–2.

[17] The chief exception is Chatterjee, 'Colouring Subalternity'.

[18] For the wider role of record-keeping in the Company's history and identity, see Miles Ogborn, *Indian Ink: Script and Print in the Making of the English East India Company* (Chicago, 2007).

[19] See for example the evidence in the 'Colonial Possession: Personal Property and Social Identity in British India, 1780–1848' dataset, UK Data Archive SN 5254, www.data-archive.ac.uk/findingData/snDescription.asp?sn=5254.

[20] Inventory of Captain John Hunter, OIOC, L/AG/34/27/3.

Laconic and indeed often gnomic, the entries in probate inventories nonetheless provide an excellent starting point for assessing the place of domestic slaves in British households in India. At one extreme are inventories that conflate Anglo Indians' domestic slaves with their household goods. Suggesting by the use (or the absence) of individual slave names and through the positioning of slave entries that these persons were mere possessions, these records mimic the stylistic conventions used in Atlantic world record systems to mark slaves emphatically as chattel.[21] The generic designation of 'Slave Boy' and 'Slave Girl' similarly speaks to forms of social erasure that situate these domestic slaves outside networks of family and kin.[22] Likewise commodified were the domestic slaves whose purchase was noted directly alongside probate sales of household goods. When Thomas Jones's executors settled his estate in Calcutta in 1776, his unnamed 'Slave Girl', who fetched 91 rupees, was listed in his probate inventory between a book and a horse.[23] Joseph Cooper's inventory, recorded in Bengal in 1781, allowed his slaves a degree of personality by distinguishing them by name. Sold for a total sum of 260 rupees, Cooper's 'Slave Girl named Rhitta' and his 'Slave Boy named Tom' were however listed in his inventory between '3 Tubs' and '2 Peacocks'.[24] Even when record-keepers accorded slaves individual Anglicised forenames, their place at only the cusp of humanity could thus be signalled by their location in an inventory's list of household goods.

Domestic slaves reduced to itemised objects and sold for precise sums on open markets however represent only one, extreme end of the spectrum of property relations recorded in Anglo-Indian probate documents. The stylistic conventions and content of most slave sales in these inventories, indeed, suggest that while British masters *could* conceptualise their Indian domestic slaves as mere marketable chattel, most chose not to do so. Far more typical than records in which domestic slave sales were recorded indiscriminately alongside the disposal of goods were documents that listed them separately at the end of the inventory, together with property such as real estate that was reserved from public auction. This usage indicates that these exchanges were set apart from the sale of household effects. When William Spencer's estate was settled in 1782, 'Mrs Spencer' purchased his unnamed 'Slave Girl' and 'Slave Boy' for 1 rupee each, a price so far below the market value for domestic slaves in Bengal at this

---

[21] See esp. Walter Johnson, *Soul by Soul: Life inside the Antebellum Slave Market* (Cambridge, MA, 1999), 45–77.

[22] Durba Ghosh, 'Decoding the Nameless: Gender, Subjectivity, and Historical Methodologies in Reading the Archives of Colonial India', in *A New Imperial History: Culture, Identity and Modernity in Britain and the Empire 1660–1840*, ed. Kathleen Wilson (Cambridge, 2004), 297–316.

[23] Inventory of Thomas Jones, OIOC, L/AG/34/27/3.

[24] Inventory of Joseph Cooper, OIOC, L/AG/34/27/2.

time as to suggest that this was a nominal transfer between kin designed to retain the slaves within the domestic household, rather than a commercial transaction calculated to dispose of Spencer's property for profit on the open market.[25] The language and content of Mrs Spencer's subsequent will lends further credence to this interpretation. Written in 1795 when she was 'weak of Body but of sound and disposing mind', her will bequeathed diamond rings and strings of pearls to a son, grandson and granddaughter in India. It also remembered and rewarded her erstwhile Indian domestic slave.

> I give and Bequeath unto Lozia a Girl who has been brought up in my House the Sum of Sixteen Rupees after my Decease and a Gold Hair Pin . . . also my wearing apparrels such as Petticoats and Linnen [sic], not Shawls or other valuable Dress, and direct that one hundred Rupees be payed and payable to her on the day of her Marriage

she instructed.[26] Like domestic slaves in Indian households at this time, Lozia was understood by her mistress to be entitled to a settlement upon her marriage.[27] Like domestic servants in Britain, she was not of sufficient status to inherit 'Shawls or other valuable Dress', but nonetheless received the lesser gift of her mistress's petticoats and linen.[28] Occupying the uneasy middle ground shared in Anglo-Indian households by slaves, servants and lesser relations, and described merely as 'a Girl who has been brought up in my House', Mrs Spencer's Lozia inhabited the unstable juridical terrain that divided persons from possessions in eighteenth-century English law.[29]

Evidence from wills complements and substantially elaborates upon the limited perspectives on domestic slavery afforded by the lists of property sales in Anglo-Indian inventories. Ranging from complex and highly formulaic legal documents composed by attorneys, to hasty deathbed missives penned in epistolary style, these wills reinforce the conceptual confusion that marked references to domestic slaves in inventories. To be sure, slaves figured as mere chattel less often in wills than they did in inventories. In a sample of forty-three wills proved in the period 1780 to

---

[25] Inventory of William Spencer, OIOC, L/AG/34/27/3.

[26] Will of Mrs Spencer, 1 Dec. 1795, OIOC, L/AG/34/29/6.

[27] *Slavery in India: Report of the Law Commissioners* (henceforth *Report of the Law Commissioners* (1841)), Parliamentary Papers (House of Commons), XXVIII, 262 (1841), 39–40.

[28] For bequests of clothing to English servants, see for example Anne Buck, 'Buying Clothes in Bedfordshire: Customers and Tradesmen, 1700–1800', *Textile History*, 22 (1991), 228; and Margot Finn, *The Character of Credit: Personal Debt in English Culture, 1740–1914* (Cambridge, 2003), 30, 82–4.

[29] Female slaves occupied an especially paradoxical position in eighteenth-century property debates. See for example Teresa Michaels, '"That Sole and Despotic Dominion": Slaves, Wives and Game in Blackstone's *Commentaries*', *Eighteenth-Century Studies*, 27 (1993–4), 195–216; and Carolyn Steedman, 'Lord Mansfield's Women', *Past and Present*, 176 (2002), 105–43.

1848 which referenced slaves owned by Anglo Indians, only one specified that the slaves were to be sold at probate. Far more common were wills that sought to transfer domestic slaves to other households, or that sought to free them altogether by granting manumission. In the forty-three sampled wills, clear instructions were given for the disposal of eighty slaves or groups of slaves. Of these, forty-four (or just over half) were to be manumitted without further conditions, one was manumitted with conditions and thirty-six were left by bequest to specified individuals.[30]

The wording of individual wills reflects the variegated landscape of personhood that shaped Anglo-Indian conceptions of domestic slavery. Some Anglo-Indian testators made no effort to distinguish among individuals when instructing their executors to manumit them. Mary Bowers's Bengal will, dictated on her deathbed in the 1780s, merely commented, 'as to my slave girls it is my desire that they all have their liberty and that they each should have a trifle of money given to them'.[31] Many other testators, however, tailored their slave bequests, carefully distinguishing among the levels of freedom each was intended to enjoy, just as they distinguished carefully among the different bequests made to each of the other individuals named in their wills. Mary Barclay's testament illustrates the fine distinctions (among both persons and possessions) that could emerge in this context. She gifted her slave Sophia to Mrs Jan Robinson together with linen, wearing apparel and 2,000 rupees; gave her slave Leccy to Mrs Henrietta Gould with 500 rupees; manumitted her slave boy Samuel without further conditions or bequests; and emancipated her slaves Flora, Maria, Phillis and their two slave children, giving each of these five slaves 200 rupees with their freedom.[32]

The wording of testamentary transactions in Anglo-Indian wills, indeed, repeatedly distances domestic slaves from purely chattel status, endowing them with human attributes that included property rights, personal freedom, volition and individual life-stories, without however contesting the validity of domestic slavery as an institution. Anne Cauty gave each of her twelve domestic slaves a bequest (ranging from 15 to 50 rupees), sums considerably in excess of the single rupee she left to her relative Elizabeth Cauty – 'she gone a bad Away [*sic*]', as Cauty commented darkly of Elizabeth in her will. Significantly, two of her female domestic slaves were offered the freedom to accept or reject Cauty's disposal of their persons. One was instructed to live for eight years with Cauty's in-law Nancy Curtin, 'then [to do as] her Please' as Cauty put it;

---

[30] These statistics have been extracted from the 'Colonial Possession' dataset, cited in n. 19 above.
[31] OIOC, L/AG/34/29/4.
[32] OIOC, L/AG/34/29/4.

the other slave, Susana, was likewise to live with Nancy Curtin, but only 'if her Chuse' to do so, Cauty decreed.[33]

For a small but significant minority of domestic slaves in Anglo-Indian households, legacies in wills extended from bequests of cash and clothing to bequests of other enslaved persons, and instructions to executors to give slaves choices as to the households in which they were to serve stretched to encompass the gift of substantial homes to slaves themselves. Most slaves who received such extensive legacies appear to have been the concubines of Anglo-Indian men. Among the testators of Bengal wills proved in the 1780s, for example, John Hollingberry gave two slaves to his Indian concubine, observing that 'two Slave Girls are her[s] Properly'.[34] Thomas Wilmot left a slave named Warwick to one of his executors, but manumitted many others, including Betsy – evidently his slave concubine – who was bequeathed a compound with two houses, furniture, cash and the interest on an investment of 1,000 rupees. To ensure the comfort of this new household, Wilmot also bequeathed Betsy the choice of two of his other domestic slaves, prohibiting her however from selling them on, and instructing that they were in turn to be manumitted upon her death.[35]

Wilmot's will affords brief flashes of access into the domestic lives of Anglo-Indian households, but other documents, exceptionally, expatiate at some length upon these relations. First composed in 1777 and proved in the probate courts in 1780, the will of Robert Grant, a lieutenant in the Company army, was initially framed as a conventional testament but subsequently transmogrified (through the addition of no fewer than six codicils) into an extended, wrenching apologia for the treatment of Grant's slave concubine Zeenut. Not mentioned in Grant's original will, Zeenut first appears a year later, in his first codicil, big with his child and now meriting a legacy of 7,000 rupees from his estate to secure her maintenance. A second codicil further buttressed Zeenut's position and comfort within Grant's household by conferring on her two of his

---

33 OIOC, L/AG/34/29/4.

34 OIOC, L/AG/34/29/4. For similar practices of concubine emancipation and inheritance in the British Caribbean, see Christer Petley, '"Legitimacy" and Social Boundaries: Free People of Colour and the Social Order in Jamaican Slave Society', *Social History*, 30 (2005), 481–98.

35 OIOC, L/AG/34/29/4. The telling of precise and strategic life stories was an integral part of the process of extracting maintenance from the English poor law authorities in this period; Grant's codicils suggest that Anglo Indians may have transferred these narrative strategies to the subcontinent when seeking to dispose of their domestic slaves – many of whom had entered servitude through poverty – through the Company's probate processes. For English narrative strategies, see Carolyn Steedman, 'Enforced Narratives: Stories of Another Self', in *Feminism and Autobiography: Texts, Theories, Methods*, ed. Tess Cosslet, Celia Lury and Penny Summerfield (2000).

other domestic slaves. The wording of this codicil is shot through with ambivalence toward both slavery and slave volition.

> I do further Will & desire that the two young Girls now in my House be given to my said Girl Zeenut if they chuse to go + she chuse to take them, that being in my opinion better for them than being left Children as they are in the wide World.

Grant instructed, 'if either of the parties do not agree to this then the two girls [are] to be disposed of at [the] discretion of my Executors, who will no doubt make for them the most humane provision applicable to their Condition'. Although Zeenut miscarried their child, Grant's conflicted conscience prompted him in subsequent codicils to reiterate not only his commitment to maintain her economically, but also his moral duty to provide her with a life-story that would ensure her continued support by his own blood-kin after his death. 'This Woman I bought at Tyrabad', Grant wrote in his fourth codicil. 'I set [out] her history in a particular paper which my Brother may take the trouble to read. I owe her in justice a maintenance.'[36]

Concubines such as this are among the few South Asian slaves living in Anglo-Indian households to have attracted sustained historical attention, and to have prompted historians to seek to situate Anglo Indians' active engagement with domestic slavery as an institution within wider systems of kinship current in Britain and on the subcontinent. More likely than lesser household members to be mentioned individually in their masters' wills or captured for posterity in portraits, concubines offer historians detailed – if unrepresentative – images of domestic slavery in India. Robert Grant's slave Zeenut thus features in Durba Ghosh's fine monograph, *Sex and the Family in Colonial India*, providing a key example of the conflicted affections that Anglo-Indian men developed for their domestic slave concubines amid their growing commitment to a conception of pure bloodline that increasingly fuelled racial anxieties in this period.[37] However, Ghosh's retelling of Zeenut's tale ignores her role as the intended recipient of bequeathed slaves herself, through Lieutenant Grant's will.[38] Focusing on sexual relations and the master–slave conjugal unit, this interpretation captures the ambiguities borne of slave concubines' unequal status relative to their Anglo-Indian masters and those masters' British blood-kin, but it misses slave concubines' superior location relative to servants and other bonded household members in the distribution of household wealth through processes of

---

[36] OIOC, L/AG/34/29/4. For the challenges of writing Indian life stories in the colonial era, see esp. *Telling Lives in India: Biography, Autobiography and Life History*, ed. David Arnold and Stuart Blackburn (Bloomington, 2004).

[37] Ghosh, *Sex and the Family*, 112. Visual images of Anglo Indians' Indian concubines are documented in Mildred Archer, *India and British Portraiture 1770–1825* (1979).

[38] Ghosh, *Sex and the Family*, 113–16.

inheritance. Slave concubines in Anglo-Indian households were clearly and emphatically viewed as less deserving of property than testators' legitimate wives and white relations. But they were also clearly viewed by their owners as persons who could hold not only property, but property in persons. In this, their perceived rights exceeded those of servants in Anglo-Indian wills, most of whom received bequests of cash, textiles or memorial objects but none of whom were bequeathed domestic slaves by their mistresses or masters.[39] Michael Fennell's will, filed in Madras, nicely encapsulates slave concubines' unstable perch at once within and without the Anglo-Indian family and its inheritance systems. Fennell left his estate in its entirety to his wife Anna in the first instance, but ordered that if she were to predecease him it was to go instead to 'my Slave Girl Catherina'. Neither the enslaved Catherina nor her daughter, the slave Aurellia – who was designated third in the line of succession in Fennell's will – was however manumitted in this document. Although Fennell protested that 'it never was my intention to sell any of them', his failure to emancipate his slaves in his will meant that they featured in this document successively as potential chattel for sale at auction by his heirs and principal legatees of his substantial fortune.[40]

Slippage in these wills between descriptions of slaves as slaves, on the one hand, and of slaves as servants, on the other, further underlines Anglo Indians' inability to fix domestic slavery precisely within the world of labour as they understood it. When Mary Powney, the indomitable matriarch of an extensive Anglo-Indian clan based in Calcutta, died at the age of a hundred in 1780, she left an extensive will that alternated uneasily between designating her domestics as slaves and as servants. Described explicitly as 'my Slave Fellice' and 'my Slave Susanna', two such household members were also named as 'my Two Old Woman Servants Fellice and Susana' in the will in which Powney manumitted both 'my Slave Girl Mantanea' and 'my Servant Joseph'.[41] Confusion as to whether domestic slaves were really slaves or perhaps instead a species of servant persisted for decades in Anglo-Indian households, as the wording of Elizabeth Clayton's Bengal will of 1824 clearly demonstrates.

> To my Female Servant Sambarrow I give and bequeath Freedom Liberty and one hundred Sicca Rupees . . . one set of Gold . . . Buttons and one half of my Malay Clothes. To Mauis my other Malay Servant I also give and bequeath Liberty and Freedom besides twenty Sicca Rupees . . . and the remaining half of my Malay Clothes. To Sarrong Saree the Daughter of Mauis I bequeath liberty from Slavery besides Fifty Sicca Rupees . . . To

---

[39] See 'Colonial Possession' dataset.

[40] OIOC, L/AG/34/29/185. Chatterjee, 'Colouring Subalternity', 78–84, analyses such testamentary gifts as integral mechanisms by which even deceased Anglo Indians exercised 'disciplinary regimes of rewards and punishments' over their slaves (citation 79).

[41] OIOC, L/AG/34/29/185.

Harry my Male Servant I give and bequeath his liberty forever besides twenty Sicca Rupees . . . with all my Cooking Utensils for his Familys [*sic*] use.[42]

Named persons whose loyal service merited individual gifts of clothing, fashionable trinkets, cash and cookware, Elizabeth Clayton's domestic servants were also unambiguously slaves: as late as the 1820s, they were understood to lack 'Liberty and Freedom' and to exist in a state of personal bondage to their mistress, until formally emancipated by her.

Wills and inventories allow us to glimpse Anglo Indians struggling to position South Asian domestic slaves within a wider universe of servitude that included not only the chattel slavery of Atlantic plantations but also the contractual labour regimes of domestic service at home in Britain. These probate documents also reveal Anglo Indians' efforts to accommodate domestic slaves within their own residential households, families that typically comprised only a smattering of nuclear kin but embraced a rich assortment of siblings, in-laws, illegitimate progeny, cousins, retainers, concubines and servants. Such extended household families defy conventional models of the bourgeois conjugal unit.[43] Social life in these baggy, dynamic household families provided a constant, visible and intimate source of material for Anglo-Indian reflections on domestic slavery as an institution. Possession of slaves in turn encouraged Company and government officials to use their own domestic lives as a means for scrutinising the nexus of fundamental categories that lay at the heart of Enlightenment social science – labour, property, person and individual – and for rethinking these categories within the context of quotidian household and family relations.[44]

The copious private correspondence sent between Anglo Indians and their family members in Britain ensured that domestic slaves' contribution to this emerging sociology of colonial knowledge extended far beyond the static endpoints of social life marked by probate documents such as wills and inventories. Known as 'familiar letters', such correspondence survives in great quantities for this period, allowing the historian to eavesdrop on Anglo-Indian efforts to situate domestic slaves within a comprehensible and ordered social universe. The reflections on slavery in the private correspondence of the First Earl Minto provide a case in point.[45] Governor general of India from 1807 to 1813, Minto left his wife,

---

[42] OIOC, L/AG/34/29/36.

[43] Albeit, as Davidoff has abundantly demonstrated in 'The Legacy of the Nineteenth-Century Bourgeois Family', Western families themselves were far more baggy than conventional models would suggest.

[44] Steedman, *Labours Lost*, details the English context of these debates.

[45] For Minto, see Michael Duffy, 'Kynynmound, Gilbert Elliot Murray, first earl of Minto (1751–1814)', *Oxford Dictionary of National Biography* (Oxford, 2004); online edn, January 2008 www.oxforddnb.com/view/article/8661, accessed 23 Jan. 2009.

daughters and heir safely at home in the Scottish Borders when he took up office in Calcutta, surrounding himself at Government House with a shifting constellation of alternative household, family and kin members. Three legitimate younger sons resided with him here at intervals, as did a bastard son born in England to Minto's long-standing mistress, Mrs Barry. Two daughters-in-law, two grandchildren, several aides-de-camp, a Scottish steward, a horde of impecunious lesser relations and innumerable Indian servants shared this capacious home with him. In 1811, eight Malay slaves were gifted to Minto at the close of a military campaign in Java. Returning with the earl to Calcutta in 1812, the slaves were emancipated by him, baptised and given Christian names, joining the ranks of Minto's extended household family at Government House.[46]

A Whig in politics educated at Edinburgh by luminaries that included David Hume,[47] Minto grappled to reconcile his Malay slaves with the competing conceptual claims of racial difference, human equality, Christian piety and familial inclusion. Now freed from their slave status, they no longer offended his Whig sensibilities, but they posed a constant puzzle to their new master, prompting extended musings in his letters home to his wife in which they occupied the full range of subject positions on the great chain of being. In one letter, Minto compared his newly emancipated slaves explicitly to apes, describing an orangutan given to him by the sultan of Pontania as 'one slave more that was given to me' and commenting that this beast was 'really too like a man – that is to say, a Malay man'. Having thus drawn attention to the supposedly simian features of Malay men, however, Minto proceeded to analogise between apes, savages and cultivated Europeans. 'He is much too civilised to deserve the name of wild', he wrote to Lady Minto of the orangutan. 'I saw him yesterday sitting on a stool, and eating his rice on a table like a Christian gentleman.'[48] Minto was clearly vexed by his own inability to distinguish sharply between man and beast in the context of an Indian Ocean gift economy that circulated objects, animals and unfree persons alike as tokens of power, curiosity and submission. Reporting to his family in Scotland on his slaves' collective christening and manumission in Calcutta, he observed that he had dignified two of the emancipated slave boys with the names 'Man' and 'Friend'. 'I gave them the <u>truly</u>

[46] *Lord Minto in India: Life and Letters of Gilbert Elliot, First Earl of Minto from 1807 to 1814 while Governor General of India*, ed. Countess of Minto (1880), 266–7, 334–5.

[47] For Minto's intellectual formation, see Jane Rendall, 'Scottish Orientalism: From Robertson to James Mill', *Historical Journal*, 25 (1982), 43–69, esp. 45, 48, 50–1.

[48] *Lord Minto in India*, 268–9. Nicholas Hudson has noted that such comparisons to animals were, in this period, intended as commentary on perceived levels of cultural and historical attainment, rather than as assertions of fixed biological difference. Hudson, 'From "Nation" to "Race": The Origins of Racial Classification in Eighteenth-Century Thought', *Eighteenth-Century Studies*, 29 (1996), 250.

Christian names of Homo and Amicus that I may always be put in mind to treat my humble property like men and friends instead of cattle', he explained. 'Indeed they deserve it, for better, gentler boys were never born in Christendom.'[49]

These philosophical musings in his familiar letters were no doubt highly satisfying to an erstwhile student of Hume, but the presence of his ex-slaves in Minto's household clearly and emphatically demanded that his treatment of them extend beyond abstract theorisation to the concrete business of social life. For, having been stripped of their slave status and granted English names, the Malays became necessary objects of social incorporation. The boys were distributed between service on a ship captained by Minto's son George and relegation to the family's estate in Scotland, where their arrival again prompted successive efforts by family and household members to assign them a stable position on the slavery to kinship continuum. Writing to her husband in 1814 to announce the arrival of Man and Friend, Lady Minto captured not only their simultaneous location within and outside the category of chattel property, but also their placement at one and the same time within and outside the embrace of Minto's family circle. 'Mr Panton sent me the receipt of them, like a Bail of goods', she reported with disapproval, underscoring 'receipt' to highlight the conceptual error of conflating persons and things. 'Poor things, I have desired [the housekeeper] to give them plenty of Blankets on their Beds', Lady Minto continued. 'She is sure of being very kind to them, she says "Ah poor things they have no father but my Lord [Minto] & a good one he will be."'[50] At once persons and parcels, subjects and objects, kin and 'things', Minto's emancipated slaves repeatedly traversed the porous legal and philosophical boundaries that divided property from humanity in British Enlightenment thought.

Incorporated imaginatively into the family circle as putative sons by Minto's housekeeper before their arrival, Man and Friend continued to provoke worried commentary on their status in and relationship to the family in the following days and weeks. Their residence at the estate caused particular consternation for Minto's infant grandson Gilly, prompting anxious questions as to their potential kinship to (or their fundamental alterity from) him. Possessing little familiarity with the menfolk of his paternal line – most of whom had been absent in India since his birth – Gilly was troubled by the seeming closeness of the ex-slaves'

---

[49] *Lord Minto in India*, 334–5. Chatterjee adduces Minto's renaming of his manumitted slaves to illustrate the politics of dispossession inherent in British emancipation, but their subsequent incorporation into his household suggests the need to expand the parameters of this interpretation. Chatterjee, 'Colouring Subalternity', 69–70, 72.

[50] Countess Minto to First Earl Minto, 4 Mar. 1814, National Library of Scotland (henceforth NLS), MS 11083, fo. 250r–v.

kin relation to him. 'Friend and Man arrived last night and Gilly asked his mother whether they were his Cousins, & on her saying no, he said "Well I am glad of that, for I don't think I should like to have black cousins"', Lady Minto reported to the earl. Her reaction to the Malay ex-slaves revealed her own ambivalence as to whether the boys' similarity or their difference posed a greater threat to their incorporation within the Minto household – and to her self-identity. 'Although I am not in general favorable to Black skins, I do not feel the horror of them I had [expected]', she informed her husband. 'But I am glad the females did not come too, for Black women are much more disgusting to me, you know it is said nobody is pleased with what is like themselves.'[51]

Lady Minto's recognition of the worrying familiarity of her husband's female ex-slaves was muted by her great distance from them, but her sons in Calcutta lacked this layer of insulation, for Minto's former slaves (like countless of his Scottish servants and retainers) were not mere philosophical abstractions but rather social beings who populated actual Anglo-Indian households. Upon their manumission, the female slaves had been settled in a Calcutta school established for the Eurasian progeny of British fathers, a fitting gesture to their identity as fictive daughters in Minto's extended household family.[52] They were kept in school until of an age to enter into domestic service within the family's remaining colonial household in India, a transition that proved to be less than successful. '[My wife] has taken one of the Malay girls into the nursery in order to teach her to be a maid', Minto's youngest son wrote plaintively to his brother in 1820. 'The other is a perfect devil & I fear will never come to any good unless it be the gallows.'[53]

The conspicuous presence of domestic slaves in Anglo-Indian households emerges clearly from an array of late eighteenth- and early nineteenth-century manuscript sources. Physically visible, economically vital and philosophically perplexing, domestic slaves animate the archive of inventories, wills and private letters that documents social life in India under Company rule. The dynamic, conflicted representations of domestic slaves that pervade these documents contrast sharply with depictions of domestic slavery in the successive volumes of Parliamentary Papers published from 1828 to 1841 as the British government, inspired by popular agitation against slavery in the Americas, turned its attention belatedly to bondage in the Indian Ocean world. Constructing domestic slavery as fundamentally foreign to British national identities, the narrative framework elaborated in the Parliamentary Papers worked to

[51] Countess Minto to First Earl Minto, 5 June 1814, NLS, MS 11083, fo. 252r–v.

[52] For the education of Eurasian children at the Calcutta orphanages, see Hawes, *Poor Relations*, 23–32.

[53] John Elliot to Second Earl Minto, 5 Mar. 1820, NLS, MS 11753, fo. 125v.

erase Britons' active participation in Indian Ocean slave markets from the abolitionist conscience and historical memory more broadly.

Between the 1780s and the 1830s, while abolitionist fervour captured the popular imagination in England, guarded, ambiguous and contradictory admissions of Anglo-Indian slave ownership in the 1780s came to be supplanted in the Parliamentary Papers by evidence designed to prove that Britons in India simply did not own slaves. The celebrated jurist and Orientalist scholar Sir William Jones's address to the Supreme Court in Calcutta in 1785 is among the earliest documents adduced by the editors of the Parliamentary Papers in their campaign to construct domestic slavery as foreign alike to British social practice and English national identity. Jones began by stating categorically 'that absolute unconditional slavery, by which one human creature becomes the property of another, like a horse or an ox, is happily unknown to the laws of England'. He then promptly acknowledged owning several Indian child-slaves himself – 'whom I rescued', he explained, 'from death or misery, but consider them as other servants, and shall certainly tell them so, when they are old enough to comprehend the difference of the terms'. Alternately acknowledging and denying, condemning and rationalising British slave ownership in India, Jones sought to distance domestic slavery from Englishness even as he admitted the presence of Indian child slaves within his own domestic circle. Like Anglo-Indian testators, Jones explained away his slaves by designating them servants, a rhetorical sleight of hand that situated them within the established, English norms of domestic service. Continuing by describing 'the condition of slaves within our jurisdiction' as 'beyond imagination deplorable', he exempted Anglo Indians from his strictures against Indian and European slave holding in Calcutta. 'If I except the English from this censure', he observed to the Grand Jury, 'it is not through partial affection to my countrymen, but because my information relates chiefly to people of other nations, who likewise call themselves Christians.'[54]

Jones's critique of slave-owning 'people of other nations, who likewise call themselves christians' was a thinly veiled reference to the substantial Portuguese community in Bengal. By the late 1780s, public pronouncements by British officials that slavery on the subcontinent was a Portuguese and continental European institution had begun to position Anglo Indians rhetorically outside slave holding, incorporating them – in the face of conspicuous evidence to the contrary in their very households – into an emerging public narrative in which Britain featured as a unique and pioneering abolitionist nation. In 1789, Governor General

---

[54] Sir William Jones, charge to the Grand Jury, June 1785, in *Slavery in India: Correspondence and Abstract of Regulations from 1772*, Parliamentary Papers (House of Commons), IV, 125 (1826), 9–10. Jones, of course, was Welsh.

Cornwallis wrote to the Court of Directors to decry the prevalence of slavery 'so shocking to humanity, and so pernicious to your interests' in India. He was careful to implicate European 'others' in this profoundly un-English traffic in persons. The slave trade, he expostulated, had 'long been carried on in this country by the low Portuguese, and even by several foreign European seafaring people and traders, in purchasing and collecting native children in a clandestine manner, and exporting them for sale to the French islands'.[55] 'Low', 'foreign', 'clandestine', 'French' and 'Portuguese', the slave trade depicted in the Parliamentary Papers slotted easily into dominant nationalist stereotypes that contrasted freedom-loving British Protestants to oppressive, Catholic continental Europeans.[56]

Strategically placed anecdotes in the Parliamentary Papers that depicted Britons entering Indian slave markets in the guise of humanitarian abolitionists lent further force to this emerging nationalist stereotype, working to displace Anglo-Indian slave holding from wider British scrutiny of slavery as an institution. Thomas Baber, who had served the Company in a variety of judicial capacities in the first three decades of the nineteenth century, testified in 1832 that decades earlier, in 1803, he had purchased two Indian slaves 'for the sake of emancipating them', and was pleased to report that this manumitted 'boy and girl' had thereby risen 'one to be a gentleman's butler and the other a lady's aya [maid]'.[57] Similarly William Banquière, testifying before the Law Commissioners in 1840, reported having used his appointment as a local justice of the peace as long ago as 1800 to combat the evils of domestic slavery in Calcutta. In this interpretation, abolitionism – not ownership – was normative in Anglo Indians' relations with domestic slaves on the subcontinent. 'It has always been my practice to interfere, when I have heard that children or women have been kidnapped . . . and brought into Calcutta for sale', he testified. 'The number of those whom, after inquiry, I have thought fit to release and restore to their parents, or place with respectable housekeepers, I should think must amount to six or seven hundred.'[58]

[55] Cornwallis to the Court of Directors, 2 Aug. 1789, in *ibid.*, 13.

[56] Linda Colley, *Britons: Forging a Nation 1707–1837* (1996), details the operation of this stereotype within Britain itself. Nationalist tensions with both the French and the Americans were played out globally through abolitionist debates and policies in this period. See esp. Matthew Mason, 'The Battle of the Slaveholding Liberators: Great Britain, the United States, and Slavery in the Early Nineteenth Century', *William and Mary Quarterly*, 59 (2002), 665–96; and Richard B. Allen, 'Licentious and Unbridled Proceedings: The Illegal Slave Trade to Mauritius and the Seychelles during the Early Nineteenth Century', *Journal of African History*, 42 (2001), 91–116.

[57] *Slavery in India: Papers Relative to Slavery in India* (henceforth cited as *Papers Relative to Slavery in India* (1834)), Parliamentary Papers (House of Commons), 128 (1834), 22.

[58] *Report of the Law Commissioners* (1841), 241.

By ignoring Company records that documented domestic slavery as an integral, intimate aspect of domestic relations and private life in British households, the Parliamentary Papers effectively distanced Anglo Indians from their personal knowledge of slave ownership in India. Once it had been re-presented as a institution that operated only outside the Anglo-Indian community, domestic slavery could safely be acknowledged as central to indigenous – but not colonial – family life on the subcontinent. Again and again in the Parliamentary Papers British observers now declared that domestic slavery in India, as practised by Indians themselves, was not really slavery, but rather an indigenous way of managing normative family relationships and household labour. Slavery in the Deccan, a House of Lords Committee was told in 1830, existed only as 'A modified degree of slavery . . . principally confined to females.' This was 'a domestic and mitigated form of slavery' the committee concluded; 'it is the mildest species of servitude', the Lords were informed.[59] Far from consigning slaves to marginal social status, slavery in Assam, the Indian Law Commissioners were told, integrated slaves into families through social processes of incorporation. 'In the poor and middling families, the slaves and bondsmen are treated like the other inmates, the same mess serving for the whole household, and both mistress and maid being entirely clothed in homespun manufactures', commissioner Scott reported. Slave concubines, he continued, 'are in fact regarded as adopted children, and the universal designation for a female slave in Assam is . . . daughter'.[60] Figured as household members who were incorporated into the very fabric of the family through shared engagement in consumption and material culture, domestic slaves were happy slaves in this interpretation. The 1826 Parliamentary Papers made this point emphatically by contrasting domestic slavery in India to plantation slavery in the Atlantic world.

> The ideas of slavery, borrowed from our American colonies, will make every modification of it appear, in the eyes of our own countrymen in England, a horrible evil; but it is far otherwise in this country; here slaves are treated as the children of families to which they belong, and often acquire a much happier state by their slavery than they could have hoped for by the enjoyment of liberty

the report concluded.[61]

---

[59] *Papers Relative to Slavery in India* (1836), 41.

[60] *Report of the Indian Law Commissioners* (1841), 98. The role of gender stereotypes in emancipist rhetoric in India thus presents a radical contrast to the dominant Atlantic world paradigm, in which opponents of slavery underlined its fundamental incompatibility with appropriate gender relations and the privacy of the domestic sphere. See esp. Diane Paton and Pamela Scully, 'Introduction', in *Gender and Slave Emancipation in the Atlantic World*, ed. Diane Paton and Pamela Scully (Durham, 2005), 12; and Catherine Hall, *Civilising Subjects: Metropole and Colony in the English Imagination 1830–1867* (Oxford, 2002), 134–5.

[61] *Slavery in India: Return to an Address of the Honourable House of Common, Dated 13th April 1826*, Parliamentary Papers (House of Commons), 125 (1826), 2.

Conflating slave status with infancy and with female domestic service, the evidence compiled in the Parliamentary Papers was calculated to obviate the need for abolitionist campaigns in British territories on the subcontinent. One former Company official testifying to parliament in 1832 admitted that famine conditions compelled Indian parents in the Madras presidency to sell their children into servitude. This Indian slavery was however, he asserted, slavery only in name.

> A Hindoo . . . who buys a child on such an occasion, treats it as a Briton would; not as a slave, but rather as a servant to whom food and raiment are due, and whose wages have been advanced to maintain the existence of the authors of its being, authorized by nature to contract for its service until it is old enough to confirm or cancel such compact

he explained.[62] Couched in the Lockian language of social compact and legitimate contracts, this line of analysis rendered the abolition of slavery moot: Indian domestic slaves did not require manumission by the British government, for they could emancipate themselves if they simply chose to exercise their individual self-interest upon reaching adulthood. 'Slaves who have been liberated, or left to seek their own livelihood . . . have been frequently known to support their former masters or mistresses from earnings of their industry, or by begging for them', the Law Commissioners thus asserted.[63] Lord Auckland, the governor general of India, concluded from his reading of the evidence in the 1841 Parliamentary Papers that domestic slavery in India had little in common with 'the former oppressive and compulsory slavery of our West Indian settlements', and thus should be removed from parliament's abolitionist agenda. 'In effect, that which constitutes the essence of slavery may be said to have been already abolished nearly everywhere throughout India', he claimed, for the status of 'honour and distinction' within the family enjoyed by Indian domestic slaves ensured that 'the tie of general good treatment, and a supposed self-interest, will prevent a slave from leaving his master and living in freedom'.[64]

Needing no legislation by parliament to emancipate them from servitude, Indian domestic slaves emerged from the Parliamentary Papers as fit objects instead for control by extant Master and Servant legislation. When the Law Commissioners took evidence in 1827 from a judge in the Puna jurisdiction, he testified that he considered 'the law of master and apprentice the most applicable to the present relations of master and slave, slavery being mild and entirely domestic' in India.[65] Executing a neat conceptual pirouette from domestic slavery to domestic

[62] *Papers Relative to Slavery in India* (1834), 30–1.
[63] *Report of the Law Commissioners* (1841), 30.
[64] *Slavery (East Indies). A Copy of the Letter from the Governor-General of India in Council*, Parliamentary Papers (House of Commons), 54, session 2 (1841), 2.
[65] *Report of the Law Commissioners* (1841), 166.

service, legal authorities adroitly shifted the problem of slavery from the abolitionist camp to the magistrate's court. Secured within the Indian domestic sphere, Indian slavery ceased to be a British political imperative. The great burden of the evidence they had collected, the Law Commissioners concluded in 1841, demonstrated 'That the relations now subsisting between master and slave [in India] may be considered as closely approaching that of master and apprentice or servant, or even that of parent and child in respect of power and coercion.'[66]

By aligning the regulation of domestic slavery in India with Master and Servant legislation, the compilers of the Parliamentary Papers endorsed slaves' subjection to an alternative mechanism for coercing labour, one that long outlasted chattel slavery and was to prove especially effective in nineteenth- and twentieth-century colonial contexts.[67] English Master and Servant law defined service (including domestic service) as a contractual relationship between formally unequal parties with asymmetrical responsibilities and rights. Throughout the British empire, Master and Servant disputes criminalised labourers' breaches of contract – subjecting those found guilty of such crimes to forced labour, corporal punishment or imprisonment – but punished masters who failed to fulfil their own obligations only by damages assessed through civil process. Although abolished in England itself in 1875, the Master and Servant framework proved to be a vital mechanism for extracting labour from colonial and indigenous populations. Its genius lay in its ability to coerce labour through contracts and legal processes, generating 'unfree' labour from 'free' servants hired outside systems of slavery, in the open market. As Ravi Ahuja has argued, it was

> precisely in its capacity to provide concrete bridges over the abstract gap between (formal) freedom and servitude . . . in the construction and legitimation of an uninterrupted continuum of legally regulated employment relations between slavery and 'free wage labour', that the . . . remarkable longevity of 'master and servant law' lay.[68]

By arguing that domestic slaves were best considered servants amenable to Master and Servant regulation, the authors of the Parliamentary Papers subjected these labourers to a system of coercion which – in the colonies but not in England itself – was enforced by punishments that included the lash.[69] Indian domestic slaves' designation in the Parliamentary Papers

[66] *Report of the Law Commissioners* (1841), 171.

[67] See especially *Masters, Servants and Magistrates in Britain and the Empire, 1562–1955*, ed. Douglas Hay and Paul Craven (Chapel Hill, 2004); and Peter Karsten, *Between Law and Custom: 'High' and 'Low' Legal Cultures in the Lands of the British Diaspora – the United States, Canada, Australia, and New Zealand, 1600–1900* (Cambridge, 2002).

[68] Ravi Ahuja, 'Making the Empire a Thinkable Whole: Master and Servant Law in Transterritorial Perspective', *International Review of Social History*, 52 (2007), 288.

[69] Ravi Ahuja, 'The Origins of Colonial Labour Policy in Late Eighteenth-Century Madras', *International Review of Social History*, 44 (1999), 186–7.

as servants was thus doubly disabling. As domestic servants, they were supposedly safely ensconced within the family circle, and thus did not merit abolitionist legislation; as domestic servants too, however, they were subsumed as freely contracting agents within the Master and Servant framework, and thereby (like slaves) were subject to corporal punishment to coerce their labour.

In seeking to explain the rise of British anti-slavery sentiment from the 1780s and parliament's enactment of anti-slavery legislation from 1807 onward, historians guided by the Atlantic world model have focused attention on large-scale, popular abolitionist campaigns in Britain and on the ways in which emergent social science informed the abolitionists debate through discourses such as race, Malthusianism and political economy.[70] Framing British slavery and abolitionism within these narrow political and intellectual boundaries produces a satisfying narrative that progresses through successive legislative acts and culminates with the triumph of emancipation in 1837. This history of slavery, however, excludes the East Indian territories from its ambit: successful in tracing formal transitions from bondage to freedom in the British Caribbean, it is incapable of tracking transitions between competing systems of unfree labour in the Indian Ocean world.[71] The processes by which this partial, partisan history of slavery came to be written can be understood only if the evidence adduced in the Parliamentary Papers is resituated to the social sphere and reintegrated with the wider history of the family. Sharing their households with domestic slaves, later eighteenth- and early nineteenth-century Anglo Indians had struggled to assign Indian slavery a fixed position within either the domestic circle or the world of labour. Alexander Craufurd of Chittigong, with whose hastily composed will I began this paper, spoke eloquently to this dilemma – borne of the lived experiences of family and social life – in 1782. 'I had almost forgot a poor Slave Boy (I never have look'd on him as such) who is a good Servant and must have his freedom', Craufurd wrote to his brother on his deathbed. By the later 1820s, Craufurd's belated recognition of his slave boy's slavery and his determination to secure this slave's emancipation had been supplanted within the wider Anglo-Indian community by a shared forgetting of British slave ownership on the subcontinent and a collective consensus that domestic slavery in Indian households was a benign

---

[70] For a brief survey, see Seymour Drescher, *The Mighty Experiment: Free Labour versus Slavery in British Emancipation* (Oxford, 2002), esp. pp. 6–7.

[71] The legislative history of attempts to abolish slavery in India is told in Howard Tempeley, 'The Delegalization of Slavery in British India', *Slavery and Abolition*, 21 (2000), 169–87. Peter Marshall offers an alternative explanation for British abolitionists' blindness to Indian slavery, grounded in imperial politics, in 'The Moral Swing to the East: British Humanitarianism, India and the West Indies', in P. J. Marshall, *'A Free though Conquering People': Eighteenth-Century Britain and Its Empire* (Aldershot, 2003), 69–95.

form of domestic service rather than a species of coerced, illegal bondage. Having made this conceptual leap, the officials who governed in India and the editors who compiled the Parliamentary Papers distanced the institution of slavery in India from the long shadow cast by Atlantic world plantations and succeeded in identifying it instead (through the established norms of Master and Servant legislation) with the acceptable face of unfree labour in Britain and its empire.

ROYAL HISTORICAL SOCIETY
REPORT OF COUNCIL
SESSION 2008–2009

Officers and Council

- At the Anniversary Meeting on 28 November 2008 the Officers of the Society were re-elected.
- Professor M J Daunton retired under By-law XVI and Professor C D H Jones replaced him in the office of President.
- Dr J M Lawrence retired under By-law XV and Professor R A Burns, MA, DPhil was elected to the office of Literary Director.
- The Vice-Presidents retiring under By-law XVII were Professor R J A R Rathbone and Professor P Thane. Professor G W Bernard, MA, DPhil and Miss J M Innes, MA were elected to replace them.
- The Members of Council retiring under By-law XX were Professor G W Bernard, Dr C A Holmes and Professor R I Frost. Professor S F Barton MA, DPhil, Professor J M Cornwall BA, PhD, and Professor C A Whatley BA, PhD were elected in their place.
- Professor S Smith retired early under By-law XXII and Professor N A Miller, MA, MPhil, DPhil was co-opted in his place for the current year.
- The Society's administrative staff consists of Sue Carr, Executive Secretary and Melanie Ransom, Administrative Secretary.
- Kingston Smith were re-appointed auditors for the year 2008–2009 under By-law XXXIX.
- Brewin Dolphin Securities were re-appointed to manage the Society's investment funds.

Activities of the Society during the year

The Annual Report contains individual reports of the activities of the seven Committees which support the work of Council – Research Policy, Teaching Policy, General Purposes, Publications, Finance, Membership and Research Support – and the remarks which now follow are a preface to these more detailed reports.

Throughout the year the Society has maintained its prominent role in defending and advancing the interests of the discipline and the profession.

Council's two main concerns through the year have been the future of the Society's Bibliography, AHRC funding for which ends in 2009, and the results and funding implications of the 2008 RAE. The negotiations over the Bibliography are fully reported under Publications Committee, and the successful outcome of these negotiations – the agreement with the Institute of Historical Research and Brepols to launch the online Bibliography of British History (BBIH) from January 2010 – has been announced in a special issue of the Newsletter. Council wishes to thank Dr Archer for his hard work to secure this outcome and the future of the bibliography as an essential tool for historians.

The results of the 2008 Research Assessment Exercise were announced in December 2008. With a new scoring strategy, immediate analysis and comparison of results by department or institution was difficult, but the History Panel noted the high quality of outputs, continuing recruitment of new researchers, and a significant increase in research funding. Of equal significance for historical research but a much less welcome effect, however, is the impact of the government's research funding strategy, announced in April 2009, which protects science funding; some high-scoring History Departments and their institutions have suffered either static funding or actual cuts. For the future, the Society continues to seek information about and make some input into the strategy for the next assessment, REF (Research Excellence Framework). The President and Honorary Secretary met with Professor Pauline Stafford, chair of the 2008 History Panel and a member of the expert advisory group for REF, and representatives of History UK and the Historical Association for informal discussion in April. Opposition to bibliometrics as a significant component of REF appears to have been successful, but 'impact' now looks set to be a key criterion. The number of subject panels, and the number of submissions per person, will also be significant. The President and Honorary Secretary attended a meeting of representatives of History Departments co-organized by the Society and the Institute of Historical Research, to discuss 'Impact' and its impact, on 1 July. The Society has also joined with other Humanities subject representatives in an informal group known as AHUG (Arts and Humanities User Group, launched in September 2008), to exchange information and concerns and to co-ordinate effective responses especially in relation to AHRC, REF, and initiatives such ERIH (European Reference Index for the Humanities).

The Presidents (outgoing and incoming) and Honorary Secretary have maintained contact with AHRC, and the Society will monitor the operation of the new institutional block grant scheme for postgraduate research grants, implemented in 2009. The Honorary Secretary reported to Council in September 2008 on the questionnaire on research leave funding circulated to History Departments earlier in the year. AHRC's new research leave scheme meets some of the concerns expressed by respondents, but in practice sums available and success rates will determine the value of the scheme. The Honorary Secretary also attended an informal meeting, organised by the Economic History Society, with representatives of ESRC and AHRC (Professor Shearer West, Director of Research at AHRC), along with representatives of economic, social and business history.

The Society continues to work closely with IHR and its new Director, Professor Miles Taylor, on a number of issues, most notably the Bibliography. Professor Taylor has attended by invitation a number of Council meetings during the year. Termly meetings of representatives of the Society, IHR, the HA, and History UK have been held at IHR. The Honorary Secretary participated in the interviews for Postgraduate Fellowships at IHR in June, including the Society's Centenary and Marshall Fellowships. A joint reception was held following the Prothero Lecture on 1 July.

Officers and members of Council made two very successful visits outside London on behalf of the Society. The first, to the Department of History at the University of Dundee on 17 October 2008, offered a valuable opportunity to get to know the department and to hear more about issues of concern, both particular and general. Discussions with the department were followed by a paper reading by Professor Margot Finn of the University of Warwick, and by a reception and dinner hosted by the Principal of the University. The second visit came under the heading of 'regional symposia': the Society sponsored a session at the conference on Poverty and Welfare in Ireland c.1833–1948, hosted by Queen's University Belfast and Oxford Brookes University and held at the Institute of Irish Studies, Queen's University Belfast, on Friday 26 – Saturday 27 June 2009. The President, Honorary Secretary, and Administrative Secretary met the Head and other members of the School of History and Anthropology, QUB.

Collaboration with The National Archives continues, in the form of the Gerald Aylmer seminar and the visit to TNA organised for candidates for the Royal Historical Society/History Today prize for the best undergraduate dissertation. On 1 July, the President and Honorary Secretary attended an announcement at IHR of proposed changes to services at The National Archives, and later the same day Dr Thomas outlined those changes to Council.

Council and the Officers record their gratitude to the Society's administrative staff: the Executive Secretary Sue Carr and the Administrative Secretary, Melanie Ransom. We thank them for their expert and dedicated work on the Society's many activities.

RESEARCH POLICY COMMITTEE, 2008–9

The 2008 G E Aylmer Seminar, co-organized by the committee, on behalf of the Society, together with The National Archives, was held this year in the Weston Room, King's College London (part of the former Public Record Office). This year's topic was '*The Wisdom of the Experts and the Wisdom of the Crowds*'. Presenters reported and reflected on various developments in increasing public input into the creation of historical resources, some making use of opportunities afforded by new technology (wikis etc), others simply on opening up opportunities at the level of local communities. A full report can be accessed via the Society's website.

The committee considered the European Science Foundation's attempt to rank scholarly journals, which had been criticised from a number of quarters both as distorting of the mission of scholarly journals and inappropriate as an approach to determining the quality of academic work. It now appears that the ESF is moving away from this approach.

The committee monitors the activities of AHRC informed by comments from Fellows and Council and the Society's representatives on its panels and committees. Aspects of AHRC activity in which it has taken a close interest include: 1) responses to and proposed changes in the AHRC's research leave scheme. The Society surveyed views of UK History departments on this. Details of the new scheme which have now been released suggest that comments have been taken into effect; 2) the AHRC's interpretation of the 'impact' criterion. The President of the Society organised a meeting at the IHR at which a representative of the AHRC explained the research council's approach to this. In general the research council's strategy is to press government to accept definitions of impact which recognise non-commercial values, and to work with members of the academic community to develop appropriate models of good practice in relation to particular research projects. There remains scope for concern about possible distortions in funding towards issues of possibly ephemeral interest, and away from other strands of high quality research.

The committee has considered the operation and outcomes of the last RAE, and monitors planning for the new Research Excellence Framework (REF). The issue attracting most attention in the past year has been the meaning of the new 'impact' criterion in this context. It is clear that there are concerns about the meaning and implication of this across all academic disciplines. Work is going on at many levels to try to ensure that this notion is interpreted and applied in ways that do not undermine quality in academic work or the effective use of academic time. Significant issues still to be settled include the composition of expert panels: it is hoped that there will continue to be a specific History panel, but there is pressure to define panels more broadly. Another area of concern is the number of pieces of academic work to be submitted; it has been suggested that these might be reduced, to alleviate pressure on panels. Criticism of the value of metrics appears to have had the desired effect of limiting the role they may play. No discussion in train suggests that convincing ways have been found of reducing administrative burdens imposed on universities by the exercise.

Developments in research support in Wales, Scotland and Northern Ireland are also closely watched and helpfully reported upon by members of the committee.

The committee continued to monitor the issue of preservation and management of modern records in the IT age. At the meeting on 'impact' co-organised by the President of the Society at the IHR, representatives of the National Archives also presented their proposals for operating within a constant (rather than the anticipated increased) budget, in the larger context of public spending cuts. There has been concern within the wider historical community about the strategic vision of the National Archives and it is clear that this is a subject to which the committee will need to devote more time and thought.

The committee has considered and commented on the effects of the British Library's and Guildhall Library's increasing orientation towards a wider public on the services they provide to the scholarly community.

The Society on the advice of the committee made representations about the effects of changes in immigration policy on the intake of foreign students.

The President continues to meet regularly with representatives of the Historical Association, the Institute of Historical Research and History UK. The new Director of the Institute of Historical Research, Miles Taylor, has attended a meeting of the committee to outline his plans for the IHR.

TEACHING POLICY COMMITTEE, 2008–9

The Teaching Policy Committee has always adopted a broad interpretation of its remit, to which end it has sought to advise Council on developments ranging from the teaching of History in primary schools to the creation of new History degrees. Hence the year started with consideration of the implications of the Rose Report, continued with involvement in consultations surrounding the proposed new Diploma in Humanities, and embraced with great interest discussion of two new degrees proposed by colleagues at Loughborough and the combined universities of Cornwall.

All the work of this committee benefits from close collaboration with colleagues in the Historical Association, History UK(HE), the Institute of Historical Research and the History Subject Centre. Various events have been jointly sponsored, including the successful conference on 'History in Schools' held at the IHR in the spring of 2009. The History Subject Centre hosted its annual conference in Oxford at Easter, at which Professors Geoff Timmins, Dave Nicholls and Roger Lloyd-Jones reported on the early results of their project on 'History and Numeracy', which the RHS has warmly supported. An interim report on that project has been given to the committee and will be available shortly on the website. The Chair of TPC has continued to represent the RHS as a member of the advisory panel of the subject centre which may shortly emerge as a single subject centre under the leadership of Dr Sarah Richardson.

The committee continues to be represented at meetings of bodies like QAA and QCA and with the encouragement of the latter has convened another meeting of representatives of examination boards to discuss the full implementation of the new A levels, in the design of which members played some part. In alliance with History UK(HE), useful discussions have been held regarding the results of the RAE, consideration of the new REF, and forays into what might be entailed by proposed 'impact measures'.

The Teaching Policy Committee continues to register concern about the steady decline in the number of places made available for the training of secondary History teachers, and supports the valuable work of the HA in drawing attention to the plight of History teaching in schools and the need for specialist CPD courses. These concerns have once again been registered with ministers and civil servants thanks to the restoration of these valuable meetings with politicians. At the last such meeting, the opportunity was taken to register concern about the plight of adult education in the UK, which has seen a dramatic loss in the number of dedicated university departments over the past twenty years – from over fifty to fewer than ten.

The chair of TPC has been greatly impressed and influenced by the work of the Research Information Network over the past two years. He attended one conference on the creation of new 'institutional repositories' and latterly, one actually aimed at the work of learned societies. This has led to a survey of fellows regarding what they feel about the impact of the digital revolution on university libraries, from which limited responses to date it is clear that while historians welcome greater use of materials on line, value their special collections and remain cautiously optimistic, they also appreciate that costs of e-journals and databases are rising to a degree that is threatening take-up in some places.

GENERAL PURPOSES COMMITTEE, 2008–9

The remit of this committee ranges widely across the activities of the Society. It receives suggestions from Fellows and Council for paper-givers and makes recommendations to Council on the card of session, taking into account the need for a balanced programme in terms of chronological and geographical spread. In addition to the regular sessions held at UCL, it is also responsible for the Prothero Lecture, the Colin Matthew Lecture and the Gerald Aylmer Seminar.

The aim of the committee this year has been to broaden the pool from which speakers are drawn and to consider ways in which audience sizes might be increased. It has continued to encourage institutions to put forward proposals for symposia. Glasgow Caledonian University proposed an event for 2010 on 'Science and the Human Subject in History'. Future regional visits were also discussed, as well as collaboration with the Dulwich Picture Gallery supported by the Robinson Fund, and the East London Mosque relating to its centenary and the projected publication of its minute books by the Society.

The Committee is also responsible for the appointment of assessors for the Society's prizes, and receives their reports and proposals for award winners. It also reviews regularly the terms and conditions of the awards. This year it enhanced the advertising of the Whitfield and Gladstone prize competitions, and also revised the criteria for the David Berry essay prize as well as establishing a David Berry book prize to be awarded when an eligible book is runner-up for either the Gladstone or Whitfield Prize. It is grateful to members of Council for their hard work in reading and selecting the prize winners. Attracting entries for the Alexander Prize and the Rees Davies Prize continues to be problematic.

This year the committee has also considered broader administrative and developmental issues aimed at raising the Society's profile within the academic community. The Honorary Secretary produced a document which outlined the Society's modus operandi, with the intention that this should be placed on the website. Plans were also laid for a new archival database of the Society's membership since its inception to the present. The format of Council business has also been reviewed, as also the representation of the Society on external bodies.

Meetings of the Society

Five papers were given in London this year and another was read at a location outside London. A welcome invitation was extended to the Society to visit the History Department at the University of Dundee.

At the ordinary meetings of the Society the following papers were read:

'Communicating Empire: the Habsburgs and their Critics, 1700–1919' Professor Robert Evans (2 July 2008: Prothero Lecture)

'The Slave Trade, Abolition and Public Memory' Professor James Walvin (26 September 2008)
'Slaves out of Context: Domestic Slavery and the Anglo-Indian Family, c. 1780–1820' Professor Margot Finn (17 October 2008 at the University of Dundee)
'Refashioning Puritan New England: the Church of England in British North America, c. 1680–1770' Dr Jeremy Gregory (6 February 2009)
'Oliver Cromwell and the Protectorate' Professor Blair Worden (8 May 2009)

At the Anniversary Meeting on 28 November 2008, the President, Professor Martin Daunton delivered his fourth and final address on 'Britain and Globalization since 1850: IV. Creating the Washington Consensus, 1974–2008'.

The Colin Matthew Memorial Lecture for the Public Understanding of History was given on Wednesday 12 November by Dr Allan Chapman on 'History, Science and Religion. Capturing the Public Imagination'. These lectures continue to be given in memory of the late Professor Colin Matthew, a former Literary Director and Vice-President of the Society.

Prizes

The Society's annual prizes were awarded as follows:

The Alexander Prize was not awarded in 2009.

The David Berry Prize for an article on Scottish history for 2008 attracted 8 entries and was awarded to Gordon Pentland for his article "Betrayed by Infamous Spies"? The Commemoration of Scotland's "Radical War" or 1820', in *Past and Present* 2009.

The judges citation read:

Gordon Pentland's article examines the commemoration of the 1820 Radicals from the nineteenth century to the present day. The study sets up a powerful analysis of the way in which historical events can be used in differing and sometimes conflicting ways to fit current fashion and ideology. Memorialisation has attracted relatively little attention in Scottish historical studies, and the essay provides an important model for future work. Dr Pentland's essay demonstrates considerable skill and discernment in the handling of a large and inchoate body of evidence, presents an articulate, persuasive and accomplished analysis, and makes a substantive contribution to the history and historiography of modern Scotland.

The Whitfield Book Prize for a first book on British history attracted 26 entries.

The prize for 2008 was jointly awarded to:

Stephen Lee, *George Canning and Liberal Toryism, 1801–1827* (Boydell & Brewer/Royal Historical Society, 2008)

The judges citation read:

George Canning, twice Foreign Secretary, and briefly Prime Minister just before his death, was a towering and divisive figure in British politics, but he has been the subject of no serious biography for over thirty years, and much of what has been written about him concentrates on his foreign policy. Stephen Lee has taken a different and refreshing approach, focussing on his career in domestic politics from 1801, when he emerged from the shadow of Pitt, until his central role in the emergence of a new style of Toryism in the 1820s. With abundant documentation, impressively marshalled, Dr Lee demonstrates that Canning's achievements were domestic as much as foreign, and that the Liberal Toryism he espoused was a key part of a new party system, especially with the collapse of the old party structure in 1824–7. His book is learned, lucid, penetrating, and beautifully written; his thesis is provocative but convincing; and he makes a major contribution both on Canning himself (though it is not a biography) and on the nature of party politics in a crucial period of transition.

and

Frank Trentmann, *Free Trade Nation: Commerce, Consumption and Civil Society in Modern Britain* (Oxford University Press, 2008)

The judges' citation read:

Frank Trentmann's brilliant achievement speaks for itself, needing little praise or analysis from us. He identifies Free Trade as 'uniquely central to (British) democratic culture and national identity' between the 1870s and the 1930s. He rightly finds it odd, therefore, that both its dominant role in Edwardian Britain, and its erosion during and after the First World War, have received almost no serious attention – let alone explanation – from historians or social scientists. After all, all western societies generated protectionist pressures after 1900, but what needs explanation is why they were so successfully resisted in Britain by 'a popular Free Trade army'. Professor Trentmann explains with admirable clarity and conviction both that resistance and its later erosion; but his massive study does much more than that. He looks back to the origins of the Free Trade movement in and before the 1840s, and forward to the present, to globalisation and to the rising demands today for Fair Trade rather than Free Trade. It is indeed, as Peter Clarke rightly says, '"a human history of Free Trade" that is at once a delight to read and a cause of profound intellectual stimulation'.

The Gladstone Book Prize for a first book on non-British history attracted 15 entries.

The Prize for 2008 was awarded to:

Caroline Dodds Pennock, *Bonds of Blood: Gender, Lifecycle and Sacrifice in Aztec Culture* (Palgrave Macmillan, 2008)

The judges' citation read:

Few fields of study can present the historian with such a challenge as the world of the pre-conquest Aztecs. It was a sophisticated and highly ordered society whose capital,

Tenochtitlan, was both larger and better planned than any European counterpart. Yet it was also the centre of a cult of human sacrifice whose excesses shocked even the most hardened conquistadores. The inner world of this society, moreover, remains accessible only indirectly, through materials assembled from native sources but filtered through the institutions of post-conquest society. This is the challenge that Caroline Dodds Pennock has taken up, and that she meets so triumphantly. Her study places the blood drenched rituals of Aztec religion in context through a wide ranging study of religious beliefs, life cycle, and family structures. Her analysis of the rich but problematic evidence is unfailingly rigorous, supplemented by insights drawn from modern anthropological and sociological studies, and from gender theory. Both theoretical and methodological sophistication, however, are worn lightly. What emerges is a vivid and convincing reconstruction of a society whose harsh view of life and death was tempered by the experience of warmth, and even joy, achieved through human relationships and the routines of everyday life.

The Society's Rees Davies Essay Prize was not awarded in 2009.

In order to recognise the high quality of work now being produced at undergraduate level in the form of third-year dissertations, the Society continued, in association with *History Today* magazine, to award an annual prize for the best undergraduate dissertation. Departments are asked to nominate annually their best dissertation and a joint committee of the Society and *History Today* select in the autumn the national prizewinner from among these nominations. The prize also recognizes the Society's close relations with *History Today* and the important role the magazine has played in disseminating scholarly research to a wider audience. 35 submissions were made.

The Prize for 2008 was awarded to:

Catherine Martin for her dissertation 'The People's Demobilization: a case study in politics, propaganda and popular will in 1945'.

The article by the prize-winner presenting his/her research will appear in *History Today* in 2009. Twelve prize entrants and five of their respective tutors accepted the invitation to visit the National Archives on 9 January 2008, where they were welcomed by Dr David Thomas (Director of Government and Archive Services), and given a guided tour of the Archives facilities.

The German History Society, in association with the Society, agreed to award a prize to the winner of an essay competition. The essay, on any aspect of German history, including the history of German-speaking people both within and beyond Europe, was open to any postgraduate registered for a degree in a university in either the United Kingdom or the Republic of Ireland.

The prize for the winning essay in 2008 was awarded to Meryn McLaren (University of Sheffield) for her essay on 'Community Building in West German Refugee Camps'.

The Frampton and Beazley Prizes for A-level performances in 2008 were awarded to the following nominations from the examining bodies:

Frampton Prize:

Edexcel: Isabel Richards (Kings Edward IV Handsworth School for Girls)
WJEC: Rhian Jones (Ysgol Gyfun Bro Myrddin School)

Beazley Prize:

CCAE: Katherine O'Donoghue (Sullivan Upper School, Belfast)
SQA: Charlotte Gorman (Lenzie Academy, Glasgow)

The Director of the Institute of Historical Research announced the winner and runners-up of the Pollard Prize, at the Annual Reception on 1 July 2009. The prize is awarded annually to the best postgraduate student paper presented in a seminar at the IHR.

The Pollard Prize for 2009 was awarded to Sebastian Prange for his paper '"Measuring by the Bushell": reweighing the Indian Ocean pepper trade' given to the Economic and Social History of the Premodern World, 1500 – 1800 seminar.

Publications

PUBLICATIONS COMMITTEE, 2008–9

The most important issue for the Publications Committee in the past twelve months has been the future of the Bibliography. A working group was set up in 2008 to consider various options. As we have made clear in previous reports, the research councils and charitable bodies take the view that while they will give seed corn money, they expect resources to become self-sustaining. As the beneficiary of a variety of such support for twenty years, the Bibliography has reached the point at which it must support itself. We did explore the possibility of partnerships with North American institutions but neither the appropriate frameworks nor the necessary resources are available at present. Another idea discussed was the possibility of using wiki technology and allowing the community to generate its own bibliographic resource, but we were sceptical about how we would maintain coverage and consistency of indexing, and about how the funding for the residual staff needed even on such a model would be secured. In the event, we felt that a partnership with a commercial publisher was the best way of securing the future of a high quality resource. We chose Brepols, the Belgian based international publishing house because of its experience with the International Medieval Bibliography, and we are delighted that 100 years after the Society agreed to sponsor historical bibliographies, we are now able to announce its reincarnation.

But the 'new deal' would have been impossible without the commitment of the Institute of Historical Research, for Professor Miles Taylor made it clear immediately upon taking up the post of Director, that he regarded the Bibliography as a core activity and one deserving of support. This was crucial in leveraging the three-way partnership between the RHS, Brepols, and the IHR that lies at the heart of the new arrangement. The complex negotiations, involving not only the principals but also the AHRC, JISC, Oxford University Press, the British Library, and Irish History On-Line, benefited throughout from the very close involvement of the President and the Honorary Treasurer.

We will be rebranded as the Bibliography of British and Irish History (BBIH) with a new logo, but there will be a great deal of continuity: the project structure remains unchanged with Ian Archer as Academic Editor, Jane Winters (Head of Publications at the IHR) as Technical/Publishing Editor, and Simon Baker and Peter Salt as Editors; our unsung heroes, the academic advisors (the section editors) will also carry on. We will retain the existing indexing schemes (by subject, persons, and place), and the ability to search by period covered, as well as the various forms of interoperability we have developed, such as links to full text and library catalogues, using open-url technology. But BBIH will also offer a number of new features, such as an auto-complete function, an auto record count per search field, a multilingual interface and extended export possibilities. Users will be able to choose between a simple or an advanced search, both offering significantly faster returns of results.

As we go to press BBIH will be under trial with librarians, prior to the launch of the subscription only resource from January 2010. We appreciate that this will be a difficult decision for many institutions, particularly at present. The move to a subscription model will be painful, though it is worth remarking that free access has been a by-product of a healthy funding climate since 2000 (the 1998 CD-ROM had to be paid for, as indeed did the underlying Annual volumes published by Oxford University Press). Understandably a few brickbats flew around the 'blogosphere' when we made the initial announcement in July. But it was not a decision lightly made, and it is one which we think ensures the continuity of a high quality internationally recognized resource. We will of course be reviewing issues of take-up and access, as it remains our objective to ensure that this tool is as widely available as possible, and we welcome observations from Fellows about their experience.

More prosaically, the RHS Bibliography (old style) added another 16,700 records in its updates in December 2008 and May 2009; another update will have occurred as this report goes to press. The database now stands at 460,000 records, an increase of over 50% since the launch of the on-line version in 2002. We have also continued to develop interoperability, with the implementation of links to Google books at the end of 2008, and to the publications included on the library of the Archaeology Data Service.

The Bibliography is only part of the Society's on-line presence; the whole back list of *Transactions* from 1872 is now available not only through JSTOR but also through the Digital Archive at Cambridge Journals On-Line (1,728 articles and 36,920 pages). And one of our long cherished ambitions will shortly come to fruition, as Cambridge University Press have agreed to digitise the entire back list of the Camden volumes also to enter the Digital Archive; all volumes in the Fifth Series are already available.

The Publications Committee remains responsible for the ongoing programme. In November 2008 Jon Lawrence stood down as Literary Director and was succeeded by Professor Arthur Burns of King's College, London. London. Professor Burns represents the Society's interests on the Studies in History Editorial Board, Dr Archer edits *Transactions*, and they share responsibility for Camden volumes.

Transactions, Sixth Series, Volume 18 was published during the session, and *Transactions*, Sixth Series, Volume 19 went to press, to be published in November 2009.

In the Camden, Fifth Series, *Marital Litigation in the Court of Requests, 1542–1642*, ed. Tim Stretton (vol. 32) and *Dublin Castle and the First Home Rule Crisis: The Political Journal of Sir George Fotrell, 1884–1887*, ed. Stephen Ball (vol. 33) were published during the session and *Stuart Dynastic Policy and Religious Politics, 1621–1625*, ed. Michael Questier (vol. 34) and *The Political Diaries of the Fourth Earl of Carnarvon, 1857–1890: Colonial Secretary and Lord Lieutenant of Ireland*, ed. Peter Gordon (vol. 35) went to press for publication in 2009–10.

The *Studies in History* Editorial Board continued to meet throughout the year. The second series continued to produce exciting volumes. Dr Stephen Church retired from the Editorial Board. The following volumes were published, or went to press, during the session:

- *Benjamin Worsley (1618–1677): Trade Interest and the Spirit in Revolutionary England*, Thomas Leng
- *Anglo-Australian Relations and the Turn to Europe (1961–1972)*, Andrea Benvenuti
- *Ideology and Politics in the Development of a Labour Party Foreign Policy, 1900–1924*, Paul Bridgen
- *Women and Religion in Medieval Norfolk*, Carole Hill
- *Harold Wilson's Cold War: the Labour Government and East-West Relations, 1964–1970*, Geraint Hughes

○ *Cardinal Bendinello Sauli and church patronage in sixteenth-century Italy*, Helen Hyde
○ *The Dying and the Doctors: The Medical Revolution in Seventeenth-Century England*, Ian Mortimer
○ *Land and Nation in England: Patriotism, National Identity, and the Politics of Land, 1880–1914*, Paul Readman

As in previous subscription years, volumes in *Studies in History* series were offered to the membership at a favourably discounted price. Many Fellows, Associates and Members accepted the offer for volumes published during the year, and the advance orders for further copies of the volumes to be published in the year 2009–2010 were encouraging.

The Society acknowledges its gratitude for the continuing subventions from the Economic History Society and the Past and Present Society to the *Studies in History* series.

Finance

FINANCE COMMITTEE 2008–9

The Finance Committee approves the Society's accounts each financial year and its estimates for the following year. This year, as before, the accounts were very professionally audited by Kingston Smith. They are presented elsewhere in *Transactions*, together with the Trustees' Annual Report. Since that Report discusses the main financial developments of the year, there is very little more to say here.

This dramatic financial year has seen a further fall in the value of the Society's investments, from £2.36m in June 2008 to £1.97m, a decline of 17.5%. This reduces to 13% when withdrawn dividend income is taken into account. Dividends have been resilient and amounted to £95,000. Most of this income looks relatively safe. Fortunately the Society was underweight in the financial sector, where capital values and dividends have been particularly hard-hit. The portfolio continues to be managed by Brewin Dolphin for the longer term. In early 2009, the manager made some significant investments in corporate bonds and bond funds in order to lock in high yields. This strategy also reflected the decline in yields on cash as interest rates fell. Towards the end of the financial year he started modest selective buying of equities as well. The fund is now practically fully invested.

Income and expenditure have been in line with our estimates at the beginning of the year, and there were no major surprises on either side. The Society needed to resume its traditional policy of drawing down most of its dividend income in order to ensure that its books balanced this year. It has also opened a higher-yielding investment account for any cash surpluses that accrue through the year, and this provides a cushion in case of emergencies. One advantage of this new account is that it allows us to save money that will be required to meet the expenses of the Bibliography of British and Irish History in future years. We will need for budget to spend between £20,000 and £30,000 a year on the Bibliography for the six years of the new contract.

After many years of active and committed service, Professor Peter Mathias resigned as an external member of the Finance Committee in May. His advice on the management of the portfolio over the years has been especially useful.

- Council records with gratitude the benefactions made to the Society by:
  - Professor S Akita
  - Mr L C Alexander
  - Professor F Anderson
  - Ms S E Brown
  - Professor Andrew Browning
  - Dr G F Burgess
  - Professor C R Cole
  - Mr R de Giorgio
  - Professor Sir Geoffrey Elton
  - Mr P J C Firth
  - Professor Dr A Gestrich
  - Professor P Gordon
  - Reverend Canon J N Greaves
  - Mr S L Hancock
  - Miss B F Harvey
  - Mr A J Heesom
  - Dr A J Heywood
  - Professor M R Hunt
  - Professor S M Jack
  - Professor A Kadish
  - Professor C E Lindgren
  - Professor W C Lubenow
  - Dr Martin Lynn
  - Dr E C MacKnight
  - Professor P J Marshall
  - Dr W Marx
  - Dr M E Moody
  - Professor S N Mukherjee
  - Professor H Ono
  - Professor D J Power
  - Sir George Prothero
  - Dr L Rausing

- Miss E M Robinson
- Dr K W Schweizer
- Estate of Professor Emeritus Brian Semmell
- Professor D P Smyth
- Mr H M Stuchfield
- Mr A T P Suchcitz
- Dr A F Sutton
- Professor J C B Thiolier
- Dr E G Thomas
- Sir Keith Thomas
- Reverend Dr J A Thompson
- Mr T V Ward
- Dr E B Weaver
- Professor L L Witherell
- Captain R M Woodman

Membership

MEMBERSHIP COMMITTEE, 2008–9

The Committee's main task continues to be reviewing applications for Fellowship and membership of the Society, and making confidential recommendations to Council, which takes the final decisions. We have also been active this year in advising the President and Council on the qualifications for both categories, as the Society is currently revising its criteria; we suggest that applicants meanwhile view the Society's website for the latest position. In the case of the Fellowship, the aim is partly to clarify the criteria for eligibility, which some applicants have found ambiguous; but our main purpose is to encourage more applications for both categories.

The following were elected to the Fellowship:

Dominic Alessio, BA, MA, PhD
Laura Ashe, BA, MPhil, PhD
Sarah L Bastow, BA, PGCE, PhD
James M Beeby, BA, MA, PhD
Adrian Bell, BA, MA, PhD
Duncan S A Bell, BA, MPhil, PhD
Michael Berkowitz, BA, MA, PhD
Adrian Bingham, BA, DPhil
Barbara Bombi, BA, PhD
Jeremy P Boulton, MA, PhD
Gregory F Burgess, MA, PhD
Mark I Choate, BA, MA, MPhil, PhD

Alistair Cole, BSc, DPhil
Hera Cook, BA, PhD
John Cooper, BA, MA
Marios J Costambeys, BA, PhD
Faramerz N Dabhoiwala, BA, MA, DPhil
Hannah Dawson, MA, MPhil, PhD
Robert Dewey, Jr., BA, MPhil, DPhil
Peter H Doyle, MA, PhD
Peter W Fleming, BA, PhD
Douglas Ford, BA, MA, PhD
Elaine K Fulton, MA, MLitt, PhD
Andreas Gestrich, PhD
Matthew R Glozier, BA, MPhil, PhD
Stefan Goebel, MPhil, PhD
Julie Gottlieb, BA, MPhil, PhD
James R T E Gregory, BA, MPhil, PhD
Robert M Guyver, BA, MEd, PhD
Simon L Hancock, BA
Sasha Handley, BA, MA, PhD
Susan M Hardman Moore, BA, MA, PhD
Karen L Harvey, BA, MA, PhD
Robin P W Havers, BA, MA, PhD
William A Hay, BA, MA, PhD
Ariel Hessayon, BA, PhD
Anthony J Heywood, BA, MA, PhD
Andrew J Hopper, BA, MA, DPhil
Mark Horowitz, BA, MA, PhD
Robert G Hughes, BA, MSc, PhD
John Hussey, MA
Helen Jones, BA, MA, PhD
Sandro Jung, MPhil, PhD
Lauren Kassell, BA, MSc, DPhil
Matthew Kelly, BA, MSt, DPhil
Hannes Kleineke, MA, PhD
Peter Kurrild-Klitgaard, BA, MSc, MA, PhD
Tom Lawson, BA, MA, PhD
Stephen M Lee, MA, PhD
Robert E Liddiard, BA, MA, PhD
Malcolm Llewellyn-Jones, MBE, BA, MA, PhD
Robert M Lyman, BA, MS, MA, MA
Brian Mac Cuarta, MA, PhD
Elizabeth C MacKnight, BA, PhD, DEA
Deborah Madden, BA, MA, DPhil
John P Maddrell, MA, LLM, MPhil, PhD

Christopher Maginn, MA, PhD
Antti S Matikkala, MA, PhD
Elaine W McFarland, MA, PhD
Josie McLellan, BA, MSt, DPhil
Barbara J Messamore, BA, MA, PhD
Charlotte M Methuen, BA, MA, BD, PhD
Jan-Werner Muller, BSc, MPhil, MA, DPhil
Holger Nehring, MA, DPhil
Andrew Newby, MA, PhD
James A Onley, BA, DPhil
Christopher L W Page, MA
Jonathan B Parkin, BA, PhD
Hugh Pemberton, BA, MA, PhD
Gordon N Pentland, MA, MSc, PhD
Meir Persoff, MA
Derek Peterson, BA, PhD
Jonathan G Petropoulos, BA, AM, PhD
Simon D Phillips, BA, MA, PhD
Andrew J Priest, BA, PhD
Christopher J Pugsley, DPhil
Michael L R S Rainsborough, BscEcon, MA, PhD
Sarah R Rees Jones, BA, DPhil
Kirsty Reid, MA, PhD
Alice Rio, BA, MA, PhD
Lee Sartain, BA, MA, PhD
John A Schofield, PhD
Alexander H Schulenburg, MA, MPhil, PhD
James A Secord, BA, PhD
Timothy O Smith, BA, MA, PhD
Francois Soyer, MA, MPhil, PhD
Roy S Spurlock, BA, MTh, MSc, PhD
Christopher R Starr, PhD
Michael Staunton, BA, MA, PhD
Laura Stewart, MA, MSc, PhD
John R Strachan, BA, MPhil, DPhil
Timothy Stretton, BA, LLB, PhD
Howard M Stuchfield
Nick Thomas, BA, PhD
Stephen R Twigge, BSc, MSc, PhD
Martine J Van Ittersum, *Doctorandus*, AM, PhD
Hans-Joachim Voth, MSc, DPhil
Dror Wahrman, MA, PhD
Graham S Walker, MA, MA, PhD
Carl P Watts, BA, Master of International Studies, PhD

Ian P Wei, BA
Martin Wellings, MA, MA, DPhil
Jeremy R White, Hon.D.Litt
William H Whyte, BA, MSt, DPhil
Timothy V Wilks, MA, DPhil
Richard J Woolley

The following were announced in the Queen's Honours' Lists during the year:

Professor David Cannadine – Fellow – Knighthood for services to Scholarship
Professor Linda Colley – Fellow – C.B.E. for services to Historical Studies
Professor Carole Hillenbrand – Fellow – O.B.E. for services to Higher Education
Professor Deian Rhys Hopkins – Fellow – Knighthood for services to Higher Education and to Skills

Council was advised of and recorded with regret the deaths of 15 Fellows, 17 Retired Fellows, 1 Associate and 1 Member.

These included:

Professor C J Bartlett – Retired Fellow
Dr B S Benedicz – Fellow
Mr K W Bennett – Associate
Professor N R Cohn – Retired Fellow
Professor A M Everitt – Retired Fellow
Mr A J Farrington – Fellow
Professor V I J Flint – Fellow
Professor N Gash – Fellow
Mr J M Golby – Fellow
Mr M F Hendy – Fellow
Professor G A Holmes – Retired Fellow
Professor L A J Hughes – Fellow
Professor E M Johnson-Liik – Retired Fellow
Professor J P Larner – Retired Fellow
Colonel O J M Lindsay – Retired Fellow
Mr A W Mabbs – Fellow
Professor M E Mallett – Retired Fellow
Mr J S Matthews – Retired Fellow
Professor R J Moore – Retired Fellow
Mr A E B Owen – Fellow
Dr M S Partridge – Fellow
Dr F A Peake – Retired Fellow

Mr W R Powell – Retired Fellow
Mr A D Saunders – Retired Fellow
Professor J Saville – Fellow
Professor B Semmel – Retired Fellow
Miss R Spalding – Fellow
Professor D J Sturdy – Retired Fellow
Dr B Taft – Fellow
Professor C M Turnbull – Retired Fellow
Dr C S White – Fellow
Professor D F Wright – Retired Fellow
Mr I Wynne Jones – Member
Professor P R Ziegler – Fellow

Over the year ending on 30 June 2009, 106 Fellows and 23 Members were elected, and the total membership of the Society on that date was 2,922 (including 1,921 Fellows, 633 Retired Fellows, 15 Honorary Vice-Presidents, 86 Corresponding and Honorary Fellows, 58 Associates and 201 Members).

The Society exchanged publications with 15 societies, British and Foreign.

Representatives of the Society

• The representation of the Society upon other various bodies was as follows:
  ○ Dr Julia Crick on the Joint Committee of the Society and the British Academy established to prepare an edition of Anglo-Saxon charters;
  ○ Professor Nicholas Brooks on a committee to promote the publication of photographic records of the more significant collections of British coins;
  ○ Dr Christopher Kitching on the Council of the British Records Association;
  ○ Mr Phillip Bell on the Editorial Advisory Board of the *Annual Register*;
  ○ Professor Claire Cross on the Council of the British Association for Local History; and on the British Sub-Commission of the Commission Internationale d' Histoire Ecclesiastique Comparée;
  ○ Professor Rosamund McKitterick on a committee to regulate British co-operation in the preparation of a new repertory of medieval sources to replace Potthast's *Bibliotheca Historica Medii Aevi*;
  ○ Professor Richard Rathbone on the Court of Governors of the University of Wales, Swansea;
  ○ Dr Christopher Kitching on the National Council on Archives;
  ○ Professor John Breuilly on the Steering Committee of the British Centre for Historical Research in Germany.

• Council received reports from its representatives.

Grants

RESEARCH SUPPORT COMMITTEE, 2008–9

The committee met five times in the course of the year. It has made grants to young scholars (most commonly graduate students, though doctorands not yet in full-time employment and in the two years after the award of their doctorate are now also eligible) under four headings: (i) towards the cost of attending conferences at which they are giving papers; (ii) towards the costs of research in archives and libraries in the UK; (iii) towards the costs of research in archives and libraries overseas; and (iv) via organisers of conferences, towards the costs of subsiding the attendance of graduate students. In the course of the year the committee agreed that limited contributions could now be made towards applicants' accommodation costs, when a strong case was made, and not just to the costs of travel. The committee has been impressed by the high quality of applications. Awards in the past year were made to applicants from over fifty universities in the UK, indicating that awareness of the Society's grants is now widespread. The committee is pleased that the funds allocated by the Society have proved sufficient to make awards according to its assessment of the academic merits of the applications. In the reports which they are required to submit, one award-holder wrote that 'the grant by the RHS enabled me to meet most of the costs that I incurred during my research trip to London without getting into debt . . . [and] has also made it easier for me to afford a further research trip to The National Archives'; another that 'not only did it facilitate my access to specific documents, it also inspired new thinking on wider issues'. A young scholar awarded a grant to attend a conference reported that 'I benefited greatly from the feedback after my presentation'; another wrote that "I am extremely grateful because I have made a number of important academic contacts in my field'. The committee is in no doubt that the Society's grants make a disproportionately valuable contribution to the studies of the graduates who are made an award.

The Royal Historical Society Centenary Fellowship was awarded jointly in the academic year 2008–2009 to Katie Clark (Corpus Christi College, University of Oxford) for work on 'Sacred Space in XIVc. Avignon' and Giora Sternberg (New College, University of Oxford) for work on 'The Culture of Orders: Status Interactions during the Reign of Louis XIV'.

The Society's P.J. Marshall Fellowship was awarded in the academic year 2008–2009 to Frances Flanagan (University of Oxford) for work on 'The Memory of the Irish Revolution and Intellectual Dissent in Ireland, 1922–1948'.

- Grants during the year were made to the following:

Travel to Conferences (Training Bursaries):

o Roham Alvandi, University of Oxford
  2009 Conference of the Society for Historians of American Foreign Relations
  Falls Church, Virginia, USA, 25th–27th June 2009.
o Carlos Brando, London School of Economics, University of London
  2008 Graduate School on Economic Development, Governance and Economic Policy, Turku, Finland, 17th September 2008.
o Michael Carr, Royal Holloway, University of London
  University of Leeds International Medieval Congress, University of Leeds, 13th–16th July 2009.
o Graham Chernoff, University of Edinburgh
  Sixteenth Century Society Conference, Geneva, Switzerland, 28th–30th May 2009.
o Dr Sarah Cockram, University of Edinburgh
  The Fifty-Fifth Annual Meeting of the Renaissance Society of America
  Los Angeles, 19th–21st March 2009.
o Mark Crowley, Institute of Historical Research, University of London
  2008 Western Conference on British Studies, San Antonio, Texas, USA, 18th–20th September 2008.
o Dr Katherine Davies, University of Manchester
  Translatio Studiorum: Ancient, Medieval and Modern Bearers of Intellectual History, University of Verona, 25th–27th May 2009.
o Dr Delphine Doucet, Royal Holloway, University of London
  The Fifty-Fifth Annual Meeting of the Renaissance Society of America
  Los Angeles, 19th–21st March 2009.
o Jennifer Evans, University of Exeter
  Annual Meeting of the Renaissance Society of America, UCLA and the Getty Museum, Malibu, 19th–21st March 2009.
o Barbara Gribling, University of York
  23rd Annual Conference on Medievalism: Regional Medievalisms, Macon, USA, 9th–11th October 2008.
o Dina Gusejnova, University of Cambridge
  Social Change, UC Berkeley, USA, 8th–11th July 2008.
o Brian Hall, University of Salford
  1918 – The Genesis of Modern Warfare: The Birth of the Royal Air Force and the Hundred Days Campaign, Midland Institute, Birmingham, 2nd–3rd September 2008.
o Katherine Hill, University of Oxford
  Sixteenth Century Society and Conference, St. Louis, Missouri, USA, 23rd–26th October 2008.

- Mark Honigsbaum, University College London
  American Association for the History of Medicine, Annual Meeting, Cleveland, Ohio, 23rd–26th April 2009.
- Ying Ling Huang, University of St Andrews
  The Sixth International Convention of Asia Scholars, Daejeon, Korea, 6th–9th August 2009.
- Mark Hutchinson, Canterbury Christ Church University
  Sixteenth Century Society and Conference, Geneva, 28th–30th May 2009.
- Graciela Iglesias Rogers, University of Oxford
  2009 Consortium on the Revolutionary Era, 1750–1850, Georgia, USA, 18th–22nd February 2009.
- Susan Jones, Leeds Metropolitan University
  Political Women 1500–1900, Umea University, Sweden, 12th–14th November 2008.
- Sjoerd Levelt, Warburg Institute, University of London
  Fifth International Medieval Chronicle Conference, Belfast, 21st–25th July 2008.
- Toby Lincoln, University of Oxford
  Association for Asian Studies Annual Conference, Chicago, 24th–29th March 2009.
- Yu-Jen Liu, University of Oxford
  Association for Asian Studies Annual Conference, Chicago, 26th–29th March 2009.
- Gary Love, University of Cambridge
  Pacific Coast Conference on British Studies, San Diego, USA, 13th–15th March 2009.
- Emily Manktelow, King's College London
  University of Warwick Social History Conference, University of Warwick, 3rd–5th April 2009.
- John Moon, University of Kent
  Canterbury: A Medieval City, Le Havre University, 12th–13th March 2009.
- Julia Moses, University of Cambridge
  The German Studies Association Conference, Minneapolis, Minnesota, USA, 2nd–5th October 2008.
- Ioannis Moutsis, SOAS, University of London
  42nd Middle Eastern Studies Association annual meeting, Washington DC, USA, 22nd–25th November 2008.
- Mara Oliva, Institute for the Study of the Americas, University of London
  British Association for American Studies Annual Conference, University of Nottingham, 16th–19th April 2009.

o Jason Roche, University of St Andrews
  The Society for the Study of the Crusades and the Latin East
  Conference 2008, Avignon, France, 28th–31st August 2008.
o Alan Ross, University of Oxford
  Sixteenth Century Studies Conference, St Louis, USA, 23rd–26th
  October 2008.
o John Sabapathy, University College London
  Gouverner, c'est enquêter. Les pratiques politiques de l'enquête
  princière, XIIIe-XIVe siècles, Marseille, France, 19th–21st March 2009.
o Shohei Sato, University of Oxford
  2009 Annual Conference of the Society for Historians of American
  Foreign Relations, Falls Church, Virginia, USA, 25th–27th June 2009.
o Stefano Taglia, SOAS, University of London
  Middle East Studies Association Annual Meeting, Washington DC,
  USA, 22nd–25th November 2008.
o Erica Wald, University of Cambridge
  Annual Conference on South Asia, Madison, Wisconsin, USA, 15th–
  19th October 2008.
o (Tracey) Michelle Walker, Bangor University
  2008 North American Association for the Study of Welsh Culture and
  History Conference, 31st July–2nd August 2008.
o Martin Wright, Cardiff University
  North American Association for the Study of Welsh History and
  Culture, Toronto, Canada, 31st July–2nd August 2008.
o Larysa Zariczniak, University of Exeter
  International Conference on Politics and International Affairs, Athens,
  Greece, 22nd–25th June 2009.

Research Expenses Within the United Kingdom:

o Francisco Alvarez Lopez, University of Manchester
  Archives in London, 23rd–27th June 2008.
o Zoe Bagley, King's College London
  Archives in London, March – April 2009.
o Anne Baldwin, University of Huddersfield
  Archives in Durham, Essex, Kent and London, January – March 2009.
o Benjamin Bankhurst, King's College London
  Archives in Belfast, 19th April–4th May 2009.
o Luke Blaxhill, King's College London
  Archives in East Anglia and London, December 2008–July 2009.
o Alison Brown, Open University
  Archives in Edinburgh, November 2008–July 2009.
o Benjamin Coombs, University of Kent
  Archives in London, Cambridge and Oxford, June–July 2009.
o David Gill, University of Aberystwyth
  Archives in Oxford, 19th–22nd May 2009.

o Mark Hailwood, University of Warwick
  Archives in Cheshire, 23rd–27th March 2009.
o George Hay, University of Kent
  Archives in Devon, Dorset, Wiltshire, Staffordshire, Warwickshire, Buckinghamshire, Essex, Yorkshire and Scotland, Summer/Autumn 2009.
o Mark Hutchinson, Canterbury Christ Church University
  Archives in London, 11th August–5th September 2008.
o Mark Jervis, University of York
  Archives in London, Oxford, West Yorkshire and Sussex, Summer 2009.
o Simon Lambe, St Mary's College, University of Surrey
  Archives in Somerset, April 2009.
o Katie McDade, University of Nottingham
  Archives in Bristol, January–May 2009.
o Ethan Sanders, University of Cambridge
  Archives in London, October–December 2009.
o John Toller, University of Dundee
  Archives in Inverness, Dumbarton, Dumfries and Ayr, 30th March–24th April 2009.
o Yasuko Ukioka-Minegishi, Royal Holloway, University of London
  Archives in Edinburgh, 29th October–6th November 2008.
o Tiago Viula de Faria, University of Oxford
  Archives in London, September–November 2008.
o Leonie Wells-Furby, University of Kent
  Archives in London, November 2008–January 2009.

Research Expenses Outside the United Kingdom:

o Jose Antony, University of Leeds
  Archives in India, 15th November 2008–5th January 2009.
o Thomas Beaumont, University of Exeter
  Archives in France, 14th–25th September 2009.
o James Blackstone, University of Cambridge
  Archives in the USA, March–May 2009.
o Anne Byrne, Birkbeck College, University of London
  Archives in France, February–March 2009.
o Anna Campbell, University of Reading
  Archives in France, July and August 2008.
o Matthew Carnell, University of Sheffield
  Archives in India, 8th June–20th July 2009.
o Charlotte Cartwright, University of Liverpool
  Archives in France, 24th–27th March 2009.
o Lara Cook, University of Newcastle
  Archives in Russia, 9th March–3rd April 2009.

- Jessica-Sarah Dionne, SOAS, University of London
  Archives in Switzerland, 1st October–9th November 2009.
- Jonathon Earle, University of Cambridge
  Archives in Uganda, November 2008–September 2009.
- Laura Evans, University of Sheffield
  Archives in South Africa, 20th June–1st August 2009.
- Bronwen Everill, King's College London, University of London
  Archives in Sierra Leone and Liberia, 6th October–5th December 2008.
- Nicholas Grant, University of Leeds
  Archives in USA, 1st–14th April 2009.
- Brian Hall, University of Salford
  Archives in the USA, May or June 2009.
- Christopher Lash, University of Manchester
  Archives in Poland, 1st July–15th August 2009.
- Sarah Lynch, University of Leeds
  Archives in France, 15th September–15th December 2008.
- Alois Madersdpacher, University of Cambridge
  Archives in Cameroon, 26th July–21st September 2008.
- Emily Manktelow, King's College London
  Archives in South Africa, 16th April–16th May 2009.
- David Motadel, University of Cambridge
  Archives in USA, 6th–17th January 2009.
- Rory Pilossof, University of Sheffield
  Archives in South Africa, 5th–29th July 2009.
- Stephen Robinson, University of Southampton
  Archives in the USA, 22nd September–22nd November 2008.
- Tina Schwenk, University of Stirling
  Archives in the USA, 29th September–31st October 2008.
- Marcella Sutcliffe, University of Newcastle upon Tyne
  Archives in The Netherlands, 17th–20th March 2009.
- Faye Taylor, University of Nottingham
  Archives in Italy, 23rd–29th November 2008.
- Thomas Tunstall Allcock, University of Cambridge
  Archives in the USA, 10th April–9th May 2009.
- Theresa Tyers, University of Nottingham
  Archives in Italy, 14th–30th April 2009.

Conference Organisation (Workshop):

- Lucy Allwright
  "'Envisioning Community' Space, Place and Translating Past in C19th and C20th Britain", University of Warwick, 27th February 2010.
- Alexandra Bamji
  "The Venetian Seminar 2009", University of Leeds, 16th May 2009.

- Geoff Belknap
  "2nd Annual History of Science, Technology and Medicine Postgraduate Workshop, 2009", University of Cambridge, 15th–16th June 2009.
- Adrian Bell
  "England's Wars, 1272–1399", University of Reading, 20th–22nd July 2009.
- Lawrence Black
  "Reassessing the 1970s", Institute of Historical Research, 24th–25th September 2009.
- Alison Brown
  "Crime and Policing in Scottish Society", Stirling Management Centre, 26th September 2009.
- Erica Charters
  "Civilians and War in Europe c.1640–1815", University of Liverpool, 18th–20th June 2009.
- Thomas Corns
  "The Bangor Conference on the Restoration: politics, religion and culture in Britain and Ireland in the 1680s", University of Wales, Bangor, 28th–30th July 2009.
- Nicola Cowmeadow
  "Peripheral Visions", University of Glasgow, 22nd–23rd May 2009.
- Amy Culley
  "Lives in Relation: An interdisciplinary conference on life writing", University of Lincoln, 30th October 2009.
- Mary Cunningham
  "Sailing from Byzantium: Themes and Problems in Sylvester Syropoulos' *Memoirs*, Book IV", University of Birmingham, 26th–28th June 2009.
- Elaine Fulton
  "19th Annual Conference of the European Reformation Research Group (ERRG)"
  University of Plymouth, 2nd–4th September 2009.
- Michael Gale
  "Music, Literature and Manuscript Culture in Early Modern England", Chawton House Library, Chawton, Hampshire, 16th–17th February 2010.
- Claudia Gazzini
  "Libya: Legacy of the Past, Prospects for the Future", St. Antony's College, Oxford, 25th–27th September 2009.
- Kathryn Gleadle
  "Women, gender and political spaces: historical perspectives", St Hilda's College, Oxford, 11th–13th September 2009.

- Anna Glomm
  "East & West: Cross-cultural Encounters", University of St Andrews, 11th–12th September 2009.
- Benjamin Heller
  "Social Cohesion in Pre-Modern England, 1500–1800", Lincoln College, University of Oxford, 2nd May 2009.
- Tobias Hochscherf
  "Transnationalism and Visual Culture in Britain: Emigres and Migrants, 1933–1956", Northumbria University, 9th–11th September 2009.
- Mark Honigsbaum
  "Methods in Theory and Practice: A Conference for Research Students in History of Medicine and Allied Sciences", Wellcome Trust Centre for the History of Medicine at UCL, 25th–26th June 2009.
- Joanna Huntingdon
  "Virtue, vice and virility: high status men in the middle ages", Newcastle University, 20th–21st July 2009.
- Peter Jones
  "'Where Genius and the Arts Preside': Matthew Boulton and the Soho Manufactory, 1809–2009", University of Birmingham, 3rd–5th July 2009.
- Jennifer Jordan
  "Conceptualising Men: Collective identities and the 'self' in the history of masculinity", University of Exeter, 27th–28th July 2009.
- Helen McCarthy
  "We the Peoples: Democratising international relations in Britain and Beyond"
  St John's College, Cambridge, 8th–9th January 2010.
- Briony McDonagh
  "Landscape, Enclosure and Rural Society in Post-Medieval Britain and Europe"
  University of Hertfordshire, 25th–26th June 2009.
- Iwan Morgan
  "Historians of the C20th United States: Second Annual Conference", Madingley Hall, Cambridge, 26th–28th June 2009.
- Marcus Morris
  "HISTFEST", Lancaster University, 9th–10th May 2009.
- Anthony Musson
  "The 19th British Legal History Conference", University of Exeter, 8th–11th July 2009.
- Liz Mylod
  "Within Reach: European Peripheries in the Middle Ages", University of Leeds, 25th April 2009.

- o Gabriel Paquette
  "Re-thinking the 1820s: Europe, Ibero-America, and the Persistence of Influence in a Decade of Transformation", Trinity College, University of Cambridge, 29th–30th May 2009.
- o John Price
  "'My Hero!': defining and constructing non-military heroism", King's College London, 24th–25th June 2009.
- o Pierre Ranger
  "Life on the fringe? Ireland and Europe between 1800 and 1922", Queen's University Belfast, 3rd–4th April 2009.
- o Laura Rowe
  "Other Combatants, Other Fronts: Competing histories of the First World War"
  The Imperial War Museum, London, 10th–12th September 2009.
- o Andrew Smith
  "War and Medieval Communities", University of Glasgow, 3rd–5th September 2009.
- o Hannah Smith
  "Women and religion in Britain, 1660–1760", St Hilda's College, Oxford, 25th–27th June 2009.
- o Andrew Spicer
  "The Early Modern Parish Church", Worcester College, Oxford, 6th–8th April 2009.
- o Helen Steele
  "Postgraduate Conference on social and political transformations in Austria and Germany, pre and post 1945", Swansea University, 3rd–5th July 2009.
- o James Thompson
  "Languages of Politics: Mapping Britain's Long Nineteenth Century", University of Durham, 2nd–4th April 2009.
- o John Toller
  "The Scottish Burgh in Context, c.1450–1750", University of Edinburgh, 20th February 2009.
- o Laura Ugolini
  "Retailing and Distribution History", University of Wolverhampton, 9th–10th September 2009.
- o Brodie Waddell
  "Plebeian Cultures in Early Modern England: 35 Years After E.P. Thompson"
  University of Warwick, 21st February 2009.
- o Andrew Wareham
  "Charity and Community", Roehampton University, 13th–15th June 2009.

- Fiona Williamson
  "Women's Voices: the power of words in medieval and early modern England and Wales", University of East Anglia, 17th October 2009.

Martin Lynn Scholarship:

- Hannah Whittaker, School of Oriental and African Studies, University of London
  Archives and interviews in Kenya, September 2008–January 2009.

Royal Historical Society Postgraduate Speakers Series (RHSPSS):

- University of Exeter
- University of Northampton

25 September 2009

FINANCIAL STATEMENTS
FOR THE YEAR ENDED
30 JUNE 2009

THE ROYAL HISTORICAL SOCIETY REFERENCE AND ADMINISTRATIVE INFORMATION

Members of Council:

Professor C D H Jones, BA, DPhil, FBA	President – Officer (from November 2008)
Professor M J Daunton, BA, PhD, FBA	President – Officer (to November 2008)
V A Harding, MA, PhD	Honorary Secretary – Officer
I W Archer, MA, DPhil	Literary Director – Officer
Professor R A Burns, MA, DPhil	Literary Director – Officer (from November 2008)
J E Lawrence, BA, DPhil	Literary Director – Officer (to November 2008)
J P Parry, MA, PhD	Honorary Treasurer – Officer
Professor M F Cragoe, MA, DPhil	Honorary Director of Communications – Officer
Professor G W Bernard, MA, DPhil	Vice President (from November 2008)
Professor A Curry, MA, PhD	Vice-President
R K Fisher, MA	Vice-President
A W Foster, BA, DPhil	Vice-President
J M Innes, MA	Vice President (from November 2008)
Professor D M Palliser, MA, DPhil	Vice-President
Professor R J A R Rathbone, PhD	Vice-President (to November 2008)
Professor P M Thane, MA, PhD	Vice-President (to November 2008)
Professor S F Barton, BA, MA, DPhil	Councillor (from November 2008)
Professor G W Bernard, MA, DPhil	Councillor (to November 2008)
Professor P G Burgess, MA, PhD	Councillor
Professor S Connolly, DPhil	Councillor
Professor J M Cornwall, PhD	Councillor (from November 2008)
Professor S R I Foot, MA, PhD	Councillor
Professor R I Frost, MA, PhD	Councillor (to November 2008)
Professor C Given-Wilson, MA, PhD	Councillor
Professor T Hitchcock, AB, DPhil	Councillor
Professor N A Miller, PhD	Councillor (from November 2008)
C A Holmes, MA, PhD	Councillor (to November 2008)
Professor M Ormrod, BA, DPhil	Councillor
Professor S Smith, MSocSci, PhD	Councillor (to November 2008)
Professor G A Stone, MA, PhD	Councillor
D Thomas, PhD	Councillor
Professor C A Whatley, BA, PhD	Councillor (from November 2008)

Executive Secretary:	S E Carr, MA
Administrative Secretary:	M F M Ransom, BA
Registered Office:	University College London Gower Street London WC1E 6BT
Charity registration number:	206888
Auditors:	Kingston Smith LLP Chartered Accountants Devonshire House 60 Goswell Road London EC1M 7AD
Investment managers:	Brewin Dolphin 12 Smithfield Street London EC1A 9BD
Bankers:	Barclays Bank Plc 27 Soho Square London W1A 4WA

THE ROYAL HISTORICAL SOCIETY
REPORT OF THE COUNCIL (THE TRUSTEES)
FOR THE YEAR ENDED 30 JUNE 2009

The members of Council present their report and audited accounts for the year ended 30 June 2009.

STRUCTURE, GOVERNANCE AND MANAGEMENT

The Society was founded on 23 November 1868 and received its Royal Charter in 1889. It is governed by the document 'The By-Laws of the Royal Historical Society', which was last amended in November 2006. The elected Officers of the Society are the President, six Vice-Presidents, the Treasurer, the Secretary, the Director of Communications and not more than two Literary Directors. These officers, together with twelve Councillors constitute the governing body of the Society, and therefore its trustees. The Society also has two executive officers: an Executive Secretary and an Administrative Secretary.

Appointment of Trustees

The identity of the trustees is indicated above. All Fellows and Members of the Society are able to nominate Councillors; they are elected by a ballot of Fellows. Other trustees are elected by Council.

The President shall be *ex-officio* a member of all Committees appointed by the Council; and the Treasurer, the Secretary, the Director of Communications and the Literary Directors shall, unless the Council otherwise determine, also be *ex-officio* members of all such Committees.

In accordance with By-law XVII, the Vice-Presidents shall hold office normally for a term of three years. Two of them shall retire by rotation, in order of seniority in office, at each Anniversary Meeting and shall not be eligible for re-election before the Anniversary Meeting of the next year. In accordance with By-law XX, the Councillors shall hold office normally for a term of four years. Three of them shall retire by rotation, in order of seniority in office, at each Anniversary Meeting and shall not be eligible for re-election before the Anniversary Meeting of the next year.

At the Anniversary Meeting on 28 November 2008, the Officers of the Society were re-elected, with the exception of Dr J Lawrence retiring as Literary Director. Professor A Burns was elected in his place. The Vice-Presidents retiring under By-law XVII were Professor R Rathbone and Professor P Thane. Ms J Innes and Professor G Bernard were elected to replace them. The Members of Council retiring under By-law XX were Professor R Frost, Dr C Holmes and Professor G Bernard. In accordance with By-law XXI, Professor S Barton, Professor M Cornwall and Professor C Whatley were elected in their place. Professor S Smith resigned a councillor with effect from September 2008, on taking up an appointment abroad. Professor N Miller was co-opted in accordance with By-law XXII to replace him for one year from the Anniversary Meeting in November 2008. Following the meeting, Professor M Daunton retired as President and Processor C Jones took office as President.

Trustee training and induction process

New trustees are welcomed in writing before their initial meeting, and sent details of the coming year's meeting schedule and other information about the Society and their duties. They are advised of Committee structure and receive papers in advance of the appropriate Committee and Council meetings, including minutes of the previous meetings. Trustees are already Fellows of the Society and have received regular information including the annual volume of *Transactions of the Royal Historical Society* which includes the annual report and accounts. They have therefore been kept apprised of any changes in the Society's business. Details of a Review on the restructuring of the Society in 1993 are available to all Members of Council.

<table>
<tr><td>MEMBERSHIP COMMITTEE:</td><td>Professor D Palliser – Chair)
Professor G Burgess (from November 2008)
Professor T Hitchcock (to November 2008)
Dr C Holmes (to November 2008)
Professor G Stone (from November 2008)</td></tr>
<tr><td>RESEARCH SUPPORT COMMITTEE:</td><td>Professor R J A R Rathbone – Chair (to November 2008)
Professor G W Bernard – Chair (from November 2008)
Professor P G Burgess (to November 2008)
Professor S R I Foot (from November 2008)
Professor M Ormrod (from November 2008)
Professor S Smith (to November 2008)
Professor T Hitchcock (from November 2008)</td></tr>
</table>

Risk assessment

The trustees are satisfied that they have considered the major risks to which the charity is exposed, that they have taken action to mitigate or manage those risks and that they have systems in place to monitor any change to those risks.

OBJECTS, OBJECTIVES, ACTIVITIES AND PUBLIC BENEFIT

The Society remains the foremost society in Great Britain promoting and defending the scholarly study of the past. The Society promotes discussion of history by means of a full programme of public lectures and conferences, and disseminates the results of historical research and debate through its many publications. It also speaks for the interests of history and historians for the benefit of the public.

The Society offers grants to support research training, and annual prizes for historical essays and publications. It produces the Bibliography of British and Irish History, a database of over 460,000 records, by far the most complete online bibliographical resource on British and Irish history, including relations with the empire and the Commonwealth. The Bibliography is updated annually, and includes near-comprehensive coverage of works since 1901 and selected earlier works.

The Society's specific new objectives for the year are set out in 'Plans for Future Periods' below.

The Society relies on volunteers from among its Fellows to act as its elected Officers, Councillors and Vice-Presidents. In many of its activities it also relies on the goodwill of Fellows and others interested in the study of the past. It has two salaried staff, and also pays a stipend to the Series Editor of Studies in History and to certain individuals for work on the Society's Bibliography.

The Society has referred to the guidance in the Charity Commission's general guidance on Public Benefit when reviewing its aims and objectives and in planning its future activities. In particular, the trustees consider how planned activities will contribute to the aims and objectives they have set.

ACHIEVEMENTS AND PERFORMANCE

Grants

The Society awards funds to assist advanced historical research, by distributing grants to individuals. A wide range of people are eligible for these research and conference grants, including all postgraduate students registered for a research degree at United Kingdom institutions of higher education (full-time and part-time). The Society also considers applications from individuals who have completed doctoral dissertations within the last two years and are not yet in full-time employment. It operates five separate schemes, for each of which there is an application form. The Society's Research Support Committee considers applications at meetings held regularly throughout the year. In turn the Research Support Committee reports to Council. This year the grants budget was maintained at £30,000, and this was fully allocated, though the accounts show a lower sum expended, as grants are paid after travel has taken place.

The Society was also able to award its Centenary and Marshall Fellowships this year. Those eligible are doctoral students who are engaged in the completion of a PhD in history (broadly defined) and who will have completed at least two years' research on their chosen topic (and not more than four years full-time or six years part-time) at the beginning of the session for which the awards are made. Full details and a list of awards made are provided in the Society's Annual Report.

Lectures and other meetings

During the year the Society holds meetings in London and at universities outside London at which papers are delivered. Lectures are open to the public and are advertised on the website. In 2008–9 it visited Dundee and Belfast. It continues to sponsor the joint lecture for a wider public with Gresham College. It meets with other bodies to consider teaching and research policy issues of national importance. It organised the annual Gerald Aylmer seminar, between historians and archivists, in November. Full details are provided in the Annual Report.

Publications

This year, as in previous years, it has delivered an ambitious programme of publications – a volume of *Transactions*, two volumes of edited texts in the *Camden* Series and six further volumes in the *Studies in History* Series have appeared. It has continued to support the Bibliography of British and Irish History and has been involved in extensive negotiations to ensure its continued existence and widespread availability after its period of AHRC funding ends in December 2009.

Library

The Society decided that it would not be cost-effective to sell the remainder of its library holdings, which will still be held in the Council Room. It also continues to subscribe to a range of record series publications housed in the room immediately across the corridor from the Council room, in the UCL History Library.

Membership services

In accordance with the Society's 'By-laws', the membership is entitled to receive, after payment of subscription, a copy of the Society's *Transactions*, and to buy at a preferential rate copies of volumes published in the *Camden* series, and the *Studies in History* series. Society Newsletters continue to be circulated to the membership twice annually, in an accessible format. The membership benefits from many other activities of the Society including the frequent representations to various official bodies where the interests of historical scholarship are involved.

Investment performance

The Society holds an investment portfolio with a market value of about £1.97 million (2008: £2.36 million). It has adopted a "total return" approach to its investment policy. This means that the funds are invested solely on the basis of seeking to secure the best total level of economic return compatible with the duty to make safe investments, but regardless of the form the return takes.

The Society has adopted this approach to ensure even-handedness between current and future beneficiaries, as the focus of many investments moves away from producing income to maximising capital values. The total return strategy does not make distinctions between income and capital returns. It lumps together all forms of return on investment – dividends, interest, and capital gains etc, to produce a "total return". Some of the total return is then used to meet the needs of present beneficiaries, while the remainder is added to the existing investment portfolios to help meet the needs of future beneficiaries.

During the year Brewin Dolphin plc continued to act as investment managers. They report all transactions to the Honorary Treasurer and provide three-monthly reports on the portfolios, which are considered by the Society's Finance Committee which meets three times a year. In turn the Finance Committee reports to Council. A manager from Brewin attends two Finance Committee meetings a year.

The Society assesses its portfolio against the FTSE APCIMS balanced benchmark. During the year the portfolio generated a negative return, owing to the state of world markets. The total value fell by 13% as against 11.4% for the benchmark and 22% for the FTSE 100 index. The estimated yield on current values is 4.8%. Fees are 0.5% of the value of the portfolio. The Society has a policy of not drawing down more than 4% of the market value of the portfolio (valued over a 3-year rolling period) in any one year, and informally currently prefers a limit of 3.5%. Thus, though the Society operates a total return investment policy, it is not currently using any of its capital.

FINANCIAL REVIEW

Results

The Society generated a surplus this year. Subscription income was maintained, as was investment income. This was because of the defensive nature of its portfolio, and helped to offset the substantial decline in capital value of investments through the year. Royalty income improved, owing to increased profits from the joint publishing agreement with Cambridge University Press in 2008.

From 2010 the Society will have to bear substantially increased costs for the production of the Bibliography of British and Irish History. The cost of keeping the Bibliography live, up-to-date, and widely accessible will be shared with the Institute of Historical Research, the publishers Brepols, and paying subscribers. A six-year contract has been signed with Brepols and the Institute of Historical Research, with a break clause after three years. The cost to the Society is estimated to average £25,000 per year over the next three years. The Society has set up a new cash investment account, partly in order to ensure that it has reserves immediately available to meet this cost.

Fixed assets

Information relating to changes in fixed assets is given in notes 5 and 6 to the accounts.

Risk assessment

The trustees are satisfied that they have considered the major risks to which the charity is exposed, that they have taken action to mitigate or manage those risks and that they have systems in place to monitor any change to those risks.

Reserves policy

Council has reviewed the reserves of the Society. To safeguard the core activities in excess of the members' subscription income, Council has determined to establish unrestricted, general, free reserves to cover three years' operational costs (approximately £650,000). Unrestricted, general, free reserves at 30 June 2009 were £1,876,934 (after adjusting for fixed assets). Council is satisfied with this level.

The Society's restricted funds consist of a number of different funds where the donor has imposed restrictions on the use of the funds which are legally binding. The purposes of these funds are set out in notes 11–13.

PLANS FOR FUTURE PERIODS

Council plans to use its new website, updated during the year, to improve communication and interaction with Fellows and Members. Specifically it plans to make available to all Fellows and Members, via its website, a copy of its library catalogue, so that they will have easier access to the holdings. It also plans to continue its extensive involvement in public discussions about teaching and research issues. It will continue to offer support for wide-ranging seminar/lecture events outside London each year, some to be held at universities, and some run by consortia of local universities and other academic institutions. The Society will maintain the level of its current financial support to postgraduate and other young historians. From 2010, the Bibliography of British and Irish History will be made available to the public on a subscription basis, in order to provide the resources necessary to continue to update it; the Society will increase its own subsidy of the operation. It is to be offered to all universities at institutional rates, and made available free to members consulting it at the Institute of Historical Research.

STATEMENT OF COUNCIL'S RESPONSIBILITIES

The Council members are responsible for preparing the Trustees' Report and the financial statements in accordance with applicable law and United Kingdom Accounting Standards (United Kingdom Generally Accepted Accounting Practice.)

The law applicable to charities in England & Wales requires the Council to prepare financial statements for each financial year which give a true and fair view of the state of the affairs of the charity and of the incoming resources and application of resources of the charity for that period. In preparing these financial statements, the trustees are required to:

- select suitable accounting policies and then apply them consistently;
- observe the methods and principles in the Charities SORP;
- make judgements and estimates that are reasonable and prudent;
- state whether applicable accounting standards have been followed, subject to any material departures disclosed and explained in the financial statements;
- prepare the financial statements on the going concern basis unless it is inappropriate to presume that the charity will continue in business.

The Council is responsible for keeping proper accounting records that disclose with reasonable accuracy at any time the financial position of the charity and enable them to ensure that the financial statements comply with the Charities Act 1993, the Charity (Accounts and Reports) Regulations 2008 and the provisions of the Royal Charter. It is also responsible for safeguarding the assets of the charity and hence for taking reasonable steps for the prevention and detection of fraud and other irregularities.

In determining how amounts are presented within items in the statement of financial activities and balance sheet, the Council has had regard to the substance of the reported transaction or arrangement, in accordance with generally accepted accounting policies or practice.

AUDITORS

Kingston Smith LLP were appointed auditors in the year. They have indicated their willingness to continue in office and a proposal for their re-appointment will be presented at the Anniversary meeting.

By Order of the Board

Honorary Secretary

Dr V Harding

25 September 2009

THE ROYAL HISTORICAL SOCIETY
INDEPENDENT AUDITORS' REPORT TO THE TRUSTEES OF THE ROYAL HISTORICAL SOCIETY

We have audited the financial statements of the Royal Historical Society for the year ended 30 June 2009 which comprise the Statement of Financial Activities, the Balance Sheet and the related notes. These financial statements have been prepared in accordance with the accounting policies set out therein.

This report is made solely to the charity's trustees, as a body, in accordance with section 43 of the Charities Act 1993 and regulations made under section 44 of that Act. Our audit work has been undertaken for no purpose other than to draw to the attention of the charity's trustees those matters which we are required to include in an auditor's report addressed to them. To the fullest extent permitted by law, we do not accept or assume responsibility to any party other than the charity and charity's trustees as a body, for our audit work, for this report, or for the opinion we have formed.

Respective Responsibilities of Trustees and Auditors
The trustees' responsibilities for preparing the Trustees' Annual Report and the financial statements in accordance with applicable law and United Kingdom Accounting Standards (United Kingdom Generally Accepted Accounting Practice) are set out in the Statement of Trustees' Responsibilities.

We have been appointed as auditors under section 43 of the Charities Act 1993 and report in accordance with regulations made under section 44 of that Act. Our responsibility is to audit the financial statements in accordance with relevant legal and regulatory requirements and International Standards on Auditing (UK and Ireland).

We report to you our opinion as to whether the financial statements give a true and fair view and are properly prepared in accordance with the Charities Act 1993. We also report to you if, in our opinion, the information given in the Trustees' Annual Report is not consistent with the financial statements, if the charity has not kept sufficient accounting records, if the charity's financial statements are not in agreement with the accounting records or if we have not received all the information and explanations we require for our audit.

We read the Trustees' Annual Report and consider the implications for our report if we become aware of any apparent misstatements within in.

Basis of audit opinion
We conducted our audit in accordance with International Standards on Auditing (UK and Ireland) issued by the Auditing Practices Board. An audit includes examination, on a test basis, of evidence relevant to the amounts and disclosures in the financial statements. It also includes an assessment of the significant estimates and judgements made by the trustees in the preparation of the financial statements, and of whether the accounting policies are appropriate to the charity's circumstances, consistently applied and adequately disclosed.

We planned and performed our audit so as to obtain all the information and explanations which we considered necessary in order to provide us with sufficient evidence to give reasonable assurance that the financial statements are free from material misstatement, whether caused by fraud or other irregularity or error. In forming our opinion we also evaluated the overall adequacy of the presentation of information in the financial statements.

Opinion
In our opinion the financial statements:

- give a true and fair view, in accordance with the United Kingdom Generally Accepted Accounting Practice, of the state of the charity's affairs as at 30 June 2009 and of its incoming resources and application of resources, including its income and expenditure for the year then ended; and
- have been properly prepared in accordance with the Charities Act 1993.

Devonshire House
60 Goswell Road
London EC1M 7AD

Kingston Smith LLP
Chartered Accountants
and Registered Auditors

THE ROYAL HISTORICAL SOCIETY

STATEMENT OF FINANCIAL ACTIVITIES
FOR THE YEAR ENDED 30 JUNE 2009

	Note	Unrestricted Funds £	Endowment Funds £	Restricted Funds £	Total Funds 2009 £	Total Funds 2008 £
INCOMING RESOURCES						
Incoming resources from generated funds						
Donations, legacies and similar incoming resources	2	18,086	–	–	18,086	6,200
Investment income	6	100,928	–	3,068	103,996	100,713
Incoming resources from charitable activities						
Grants for awards		–	–	11,000	11,000	10,000
Grants for publications		6,000	–	–	6,000	4,000
Subscriptions		102,685	–	–	102,685	102,834
Royalties		39,890	–	–	39,890	34,481
Other incoming resources		2,614	–	–	2,614	21,056
TOTAL INCOMING RESOURCES		270,203	–	14,068	284,271	279,285
RESOURCES EXPENDED						
Cost of generating funds						
Investment manager's fees		10,204	–	315	10,519	14,040
Charitable activities						
Grants for awards	3	48,421	–	14,304	62,725	45,734
Lectures and meetings		13,513	–	–	13,513	9,936
Publications		78,773	–	–	78,773	70,559
Library		4,245	–	–	4,245	4,859
Membership services		45,080	–	–	45,080	48,025
Governance		19,220	–	–	19,220	20,620
TOTAL RESOURCES EXPENDED	4a	219,456	–	14,619	234,076	213,774
NET INCOMING/(OUTGOING) RESOURCES BEFORE TRANSFERS		50,747	–	(551)	50,195	65,511
Gross transfers between funds		(663)	–	663	–	–
NET INCOMING/(OUTGOING) RESOURCES BEFORE GAINS		50,084	–	112	50,195	65,511
Other recognised gains and losses						
Net (loss)/gain on investments	6	(383,586)	(11,864)	–	(395,450)	(354,995)
NET MOVEMENT IN FUNDS		(333,502)	(11,864)	112	(345,255)	(289,484)
Balance at 1 July 2008		2,309,857	68,059	2,800	2,380,716	2,670,200
Balance at 30 June 2009		1,976,355	56,195	2,912	2,035,462	2,380,716

The notes on pages 11 to 17 form part of these financial statements.

THE ROYAL HISTORICAL SOCIETY

BALANCE SHEET AT 30 JUNE 2009

	Note	2009 £	2009 £	2008 £	2008 £
FIXED ASSETS					
Tangible assets	5		907		1,489
Investments	6		1,970,280		2,361,968
COIF Investments			71,097		–
			2,042,284		2,363,457
CURRENT ASSETS					
Debtors	7	2,118		5,484	
Cash at bank and in hand		16,601		35,464	
		18,719		40,948	
LESS: CREDITORS					
Amounts due within one year	8	(25,541)		(23,689)	
NET CURRENT ASSETS			(6,822)		17,259
NET ASSETS			2,035,462		2,380,716
REPRESENTED BY:					
Endowment Funds	10				
A S Whitfield Prize Fund			37,643		45,552
The David Berry Essay Trust			18,552		22,507
Restricted Funds	11				
A S Whitfield Prize Fund			1,762		1,687
P J Marshall Fellowship			–		–
The David Berry Essay Trust			1,150		1,113
The Martin Lynn Bequest			–		–
Unrestricted Funds					
Designated – E M Robinson Bequest	12		98,514		118,098
General Fund	13		1,877,841		2,191,759
			2,035,462		2,380,716

The accounts have been prepared in accordance with the Financial Reporting Standard for Smaller Entities (effective April 2008).

The notes on pages 11 to 17 form part of these financial statements.

The financial statements were approved and authorised for issue by the Council on . . . . and were signed on its behalf by:

. . . .
Professor C Jones – **President**

       . . . .
       Dr J Parry – **Honorary Treasurer**

THE ROYAL HISTORICAL SOCIETY

NOTES TO THE FINANCIAL STATEMENTS FOR THE YEAR ENDED 30 JUNE 2009

1. ACCOUNTING POLICIES

Basis of accounting
The financial statements have been prepared under the historical cost convention, as modified to include the revaluation of fixed assets including investments which are carried at market value, in accordance with the Statement of Recommended Practice (SORP 2005) "Accounting and Reporting by Charities", published in March 2005, with applicable accounting standards and the Financial Reporting Standard for Smaller Entities (effective April 2008).

Depreciation
Depreciation is calculated by reference to the cost of fixed assets using a straight line basis at rates considered appropriate having regard to the expected lives of the fixed assets. The annual rates of depreciation in use are:

Furniture and equipment   10%
Computer equipment   25%

Stock
Stock is valued at the lower of cost and net realisable value.

Library and Archives
The cost of additions to the library and archives is written off in the year of purchase.

Subscription Income
Subscription income is recognised in the year it became receivable with a provision against any subscription not received.

Investments
Investments are stated at market value. Any surplus/deficit arising on revaluation is included in the Statement of Financial Activities. Dividend income is accounted for when the Society becomes entitled to such monies.

Donations and Other Voluntary Income
Donations and other voluntary income are recognised when the Society becomes legally entitled to such monies.

Royalties
Royalties are recoginised on an accruals basis in accordance with the terms of the relevant agreement.

Grants Payable
Grants payable are recognised in the year in which they are approved and notified to recipients.

Funds
Unrestricted: these are funds which can be used in accordance with the charitable objects at the discretion of the trustees.
Designated: these are unrestricted funds which have been set aside by the trustees for specific purposes.
Restricted: these are funds that can only be used for particular restricted purposes defined by the benefactor and within the objects of the charity.
Endowment: permanent endowment funds must be held permanently by the trustees and income arising is separately included in restricted funds for specific use as defined by the donors.
The purpose and use of endowment, restricted and designated funds are disclosed in the notes to the accounts.

Allocations
Wages, salary costs and office expenditure are allocated on the basis of the work done by the Executive Secretary and the Administrative Assistant.

Pensions
Pension costs are charged to the SOFA when payments fall due. The Society contributed 12.5% of gross salary to the personal pension plan of two of the employees.

2. DONATIONS AND LEGACIES	2009 £	2008 £
G R Elton Bequest	424	1,308
Donations via membership	6,134	709
Gladstone Memorial Trust	600	600
Browning Bequest	–	63
Vera London	7,997	–
Sundry income	–	500
Gift Aid reclaimed	2,931	3,021
	18,086	6,200

3. GRANTS FOR AWARDS

	Unrestricted Funds £	Restricted Funds £	Total funds 2009 £	Total funds 2008 £
RHS Centenary Fellowship	10,000	–	10,000	2,500
Research support grants (see below)	24,750	2,391	27,141	19,110
A-Level prizes	400	–	400	200
AS Whitfield prize	–	1,000	1,000	1,000
E M Robinson Bequest				
Grant to Dulwich Picture Library	4,000	–	4,000	4,000
Gladstone history book prize	1,000	–	1,000	1,000
P J Marshall Fellowship	–	10,663	10,663	10,000
David Berry Prize	–	250	250	250
Staff and support costs (Note 4a)	8,271	–	8,271	7,674
	48,421	14,304	62,725	45,734

During the year Society awarded grants to a value of £27,141 (2008 – £19,110) to 123 (2008 – 85) individuals.

GRANTS PAYABLE

	2009 £	2008 £
Commitments at 1 July 2008	–	–
Commitments made in the year	55,754	38,060
Grants paid during the year	(54,454)	(38,060)
Commitments at 30 June 2009	1,300	–

Commitments at 30 June 2009 and 2008 are included in creditors.

4a. TOTAL RESOURCES EXPENDED

	Staff costs £	Support costs £	Direct costs £	Total £
Cost of generating funds				
Investment manager's fee	–	–	10,519	10,519
Charitable activities				
Grants for awards (Note 3)	5,694	2,577	54,454	62,725
Lectures and meetings	5,694	1,289	6,529	13,512
Publications	10,123	5,154	63,496	78,773
Library	2,531	1,289	426	4,245
Membership services	31,633	12,885	561	45,080
Governance	7,592	2,577	9,051	19,220
Total Resources Expended	63,267	25,772	145,036	234,075
	(Note 4b)	(Note 4c)		

4b. STAFF COSTS

	2009 £	2008 £
Wages and salaries	51,687	48,642
Social security costs	5,194	4,705
Other pension costs	6,386	6,097
	63,267	59,444

4c. SUPPORT COSTS

	2009 £	2008 £
Stationery, photocopying and postage	12,788	10,161
Computer support	460	684
Insurance	923	923
Telephone	255	181
Depreciation	583	831
Bad debts	–	4,113
Other	10,763	6,347
	25,772	23,241

The average number of employees in the year was 2 (2008 – 2). There were no employees whose emoluments exceeded £60,000 in the year.

During the year travel expenses were reimbursed to 24 (2008: 20) Councillors attending Council meetings at a cost of £2,201 (2008 – £1,531). No Councillor received any remuneration during the year (2008 – £Nil).

Included in governance is the following:

	2009 £	2008 £
Auditors Remuneration – current year	7,100	8,343
Auditors Remuneration – in respect of prio years	524	–
Auditors Remuneration for non-audit services	1,398	–

5. TANGIBLE FIXED ASSETS

	Computer Equipment £	Furniture and Equipment £	Total £
COST			
At 1 July 2008 and 30 June 2009	33,224	2,307	35,531
DEPRECIATION			
At 1 July 2008	32,755	1,287	34,042
Charge for the year	469	113	582
At 30 June 2009	33,224	1,400	34,624
NET BOOK VALUE			
At 30 June 2009	–	907	907
At 30 June 2008	469	1,020	1,489

All tangible fixed assets are used in the furtherance of the Society's objects.

6. INVESTMENTS

	General Fund £	Designated Robinson Bequest £	Whitfield Prize Fund £	David Berry Essay Trust £	Total £
Market value at 1 July 2008	2,173,011	118,098	47,239	23,620	2,361,968
Additions	169,236	9,198	3,679	1,840	183,953
Disposals	(165,775)	(9,010)	(3,604)	(1,802)	(180,191)
Net loss on investments	(363,814)	(19,772)	(7,909)	(3,955)	(395,450)
Market value at 30 June 2009	1,812,658	98,514	39,405	19,703	1,970,280
Cost at 30 June 2009	1,906,917	103,637	41,455	20,727	2,072,736

	2009 £	2008 £
UK Equities	1,335,916	1,399,452
UK Government Stock and Bonds	283,132	467,151
Overseas Equities	304,545	267,424
Uninvested Cash	46,687	227,941
	1,970,280	2,361,968
Dividends and interest on listed investments	102,281	100,524
Interest on cash deposits	1,715	189
	103,996	100,713

7. DEBTORS

	2009 £	2008 £
Other debtors	650	3,710
Prepayments	1,468	1,774
	2,118	5,484

8. CREDITORS: Amounts due within one year

	2009 £	2008 £
Sundry creditors	6,408	7,608
Taxes and social security	1,444	1,444
Subscriptions received in advance	5,289	3,494
Accruals and deferred income	12,400	11,143
	25,541	23,689

Included within Sundry creditors is an amount of £358 (2008: £358) relating to pension liabilities.

9. LEASE COMMITMENTS

The Society has the following annual commitments under non-cancellable operating leases which expire:

	2009 £	2008 £
Within 2–5 years	9,846	9,846

10. ENDOWMENT FUNDS

	Balance at 1 July 2009 £	Investment Loss £	Balance at 30 June 2009 £
A S Whitfield Prize Fund	45,552	(7,909)	37,643
The David Berry Essay Trust	22,507	(3,955)	18,552
	68,059	(11,864)	56,195

A S Whitfield Prize Fund

The A S Whitfield Prize Fund is an endowment used to provide income for an annual prize for the best first monograph for British history published in the calendar year.

The David Berry Essay Trust

The David Berry Essay Trust is an endowment to provide income for annual prizes for essays on subjects dealing with Scottish history.

11. RESTRICTED FUNDS

	Balance at 1 July 2008 £	Incoming Resources £	Outgoing Resources £	Transfers £	Balance at 30 June 2009 £
A S Whitfield Prize Fund	1,687	2,045	(1,970)	–	1,762
P J Marshall Fellowship	–	10,000	(10,663)	663	–
The David Berry Essay Trust	1,113	1,022	(985)	–	1,150
Martin Lynn Bequest	–	1,000	(1,000)	–	–
	2,800	14,067	(14,619)	663	2,912

A S Whitfield Prize Fund Income

Income from the A S Whitfield Prize Fund is used to provide an annual prize for the best first monograph for British history published in the calendar year.

P J Marshall Fellowship

The P J Marshall Fellowship is used to provide a sum sufficient to cover the stipend for a one-year doctoral research fellowship alongside the existing Royal Historical Society Centenary Fellowship at the Institute of Historical Research.

The David Berry Essay Trust Income

Income from the David Berry Trust is to provide annual prizes for essays on subjects dealing with Scottish history.

The Martin Lynn Bequest

This annual bequest is used by the Society to give financial assistance to postgraduates researching topics in African history.

12. DESIGNATED FUND	Balance at 1 July 2008 £	Incoming Resources £	Outgoing Resources £	Investment Loss £	Transfers £	Balance at 30 June 2009 £
E M Robinson Bequest	118,098	5,114	(4,926)	(19,772)	–	98,514

E M Robinson Bequest

Income from the E M Robinson Bequest is to further the study of history and to date has been used to provide grants to the Dulwich Picture Gallery.

13. GENERAL FUND	Balance at 1 July 2008 £	Incoming Resources £	Outgoing Resources £	Investment Loss £	Transfers £	Balance at 30 June 2009 £
	2,191,759	265,089	(214,530)	(363,814)	(663)	1,877,841

14. ANALYSIS OF NET ASSETS BETWEEN FUNDS

	General Fund £	Designated Fund £	Restricted Funds £	Endowment Funds £	Total £
Fixed assets	907	–	–	–	907
Investments	1,812,659	98,514	2,912	56,195	1,970,280
COIF investments	71,097	–	–	–	71,097
	1,884,663	98,514	2,912	56,195	2,042,284
Current assets	18,719	–	–	–	18,719
Less: Creditors	(25,541)	–	–	–	(25,541)
Net current assets/(liabilities)	(6,822)	–	–	–	(6,822)
Net Assets	1,877,841	98,514	2,912	56,195	2,035,462